Cambridge English

Grammar AND Vocabulary
FOR ADVANCED
with answers

MARTIN HEWINGS
SIMON HAINES

Cambridge University Press
www.cambridge.org/elt

Cambridge Assessment English
www.cambridgeenglish.org

Information on this title: www.cambridge.org/9781107481114

© Cambridge University Press 2015

This publication is in copyright. Subject to statutory exception
and to the provisions of relevant collective licensing agreements,
no reproduction of any part may take place without the written
permission of Cambridge University Press.

First published 2015

20 19 18 17 16 15 14 13 12 11 10 9 8

Printed in Italy by Rotolito S.p.A.

A catalogue record for this publication is available from the British Library

ISBN 978-1-107-48111-4 Book with answers with Audio

Additional resources for this publication at www.cambridge.org/grammarvocabadvanced

The publishers have no responsibility for the persistence or accuracy of URLs
for external or third-party internet websites referred to in this publication, and
do not guarantee that any content on such websites is, or will remain, accurate
or appropriate. Information regarding prices, travel timetables, and other factual
information given in this work is correct at the time of first printing but the
publishers do not guarantee the accuracy of such information thereafter.

Acknowledgements

Simon and Martin would like to thank the following people at Cambridge University Press for all their assistance and encouragement at various stages of the project: Charlotte Adams, Aldona Gawlinski, Sharon McCann, Ann-Marie Murphy, Lorraine Poulter and Chloé Szebrat, as well as the editors Ruth Cox and Nik White.

Martin would also like to thank Ann for her constant support.

The authors and publishers acknowledge the following sources of copyright material and are grateful for the permissions granted. While every effort has been made, it has not always been possible to identify the sources of all the material used, or to trace all copyright holders. If any omissions are brought to our notice, we will be happy to include the appropriate acknowledgements on reprinting.

p. 78: Guardian News and Media Ltd for the adapted extract 'My life as a human speed bump' by George Monbiot, *The Guardian* 23/10/2006. Copyright © Guardian News & Media Ltd 2006; p. 91: Telegraph Media Group Limited for the adapted extract from 'Gadgets to make your home energy efficient' Comment, *The Telegraph* 14/04/2007. © Telegraph Media Group Limited 2007; pp. 132–133: Telegraph Media Group Limited for the extract from 'Alexander McCall Smith: Terrible Orchestra?' by Alexander McCall Smith, The Telegraph 01/11/2007. © Telegraph Media Group Limited 2007; p. 160: Nick Rennison for the extracts from 'Waterstone's Guide to Popular Science Books' edited by Nick Rennison. The extracts from Waterstone's Guide to Popular Science appear with the permission of the editor, Nick Rennison. Published by Waterstone's Booksellers Ltd, Capital Court, Capital Interchange Way, Brentford, Middlesex TW8 0EX (ISBN: 1-902603-20-60); pp. 182–183: Telegraph Media Group Limited for the extract adapted from 'Rome: ancient life in a modern city' by Professor Mary Beard, The Telegraph 20/04/2012. © Telegraph Media Group Limited 2012; p. 186: Ed Victor Ltd Literary Agency for the extract adapted from 'Speaking for Myself' by Joan Bakewell, *The Author*, Winter 2003; p. 190: PlayShakespeare.com for the extract adapted from 'Law Dares to be a great Hamlet' by Denise Battista, *PlayShakespeare.com* October 2009 http://www.playshakespeare.com/ hamlet/theatre-reviews/3881-law-dares-to-be-a-great-hamlet © 2014 PlayShakespeare.com. Used with permission. All rights reserved; p. 192: Peter Stalker for the adapted extract from 'Types of Migrant (Stalkers' Guide to International Migration)' by Peter Stalker. With permission from Peter Stalker; p. 198: Text adapted from 'Five steps to risk assessment' Health and Safety Executive website - www.hse.gov.uk/risk/fivesteps.htm, licensed under the Open Government Licence; pp. 199–200: Telegraph Media Group Limited for the adapted extract from 'Should cyclists be forced to wear helmets?' by Matthew Sparkes, *The Telegraph* 02/08/2013. © Telegraph Media Group Limited 2013; p. 205: Montessori for the adapted extract from 'What is Montessori', www.montessori.org © All Rights Reserved Montessori St Nicholas; p. 207: Professor Mitch Smooke for the adapted extract from 'Mechanical Engineering' by Mitchell D. Smooke, *Yale School of Engineering and Applied Science*. With permission from Professor Mitch Smooke; p. 210: Anup Shah for the adapted extract from 'Millions Die Each Year, Needlessly' by Anup Shah, *Global Issues*. With permission from Anup Shah, Global Issues www.globalissues.org/article/588/global-health-overview, globalissues.org; p. 226: www.indianchild.com for the adapted extract from 'The role of grandparents in children's upbringing' by M. Hemdev *IndianChild.com*. © www.indianchild.com; p. 235: Thomas Baekdal for the adapted extract from 'Where is everyone?' by Thomas Baekdal, www.baekdal.com 27/04/2009. http://www.baekdal.com/media/market-of-information; p. 244: Extract adapted from 'Low holiday spending due to economic worries' by Martha C. White, *www.dailyfinance.com* 05/11/2009; p. 245: newbusiness.co.uk for the adapted extract from 'How to grow your start up' *www.newbusiness.co.uk* 17/08/2010. Copyright © 2000 – 2013 newbusiness.co.uk. All rights reserved; p. 261: Engineering and Technology for the adapted extract 'Batteries are putting the brakes on electric car take-up' *The Guardian* 14/06/2010. © Institution of Engineering and Technology.

The authors and publishers acknowledge the following sources of copyright material and are grateful for the permissions granted. While every effort has been made, it has not always been possible to identify the sources of all the material used, or to trace all copyright holders. If any omissions are brought to our notice, we will be happy to include the appropriate acknowledgements on reprinting.

Key: T = Top, M= Middle, B = Below, L = Left, R = Right, B/G = Background

p. 10 (TL): Getty Images/© DragonImages; p. 10 (TM): Alamy/© DBURKE; p. 10 (TR): Getty Images/© Minerva Studio; p. 25 (L): Alamy/© Greg Balfour Evans; p. 25 (R): Shutterstock/© CBCK; p. 39: Getty Images/© JGI/Jamie Grill; p. 54 (a): Corbis/© Maurizio Rellini/SOPA RF/SOPA; p. 54 (b): Superstock/© Axiom Phtotographic/Design Pics; p. 54 (c): Getty Images/© Amulf Husmo; p. 66: Getty Images/© Fuse; p. 72: Shutterstock/© Gargonia; p. 80 (a): Alamy/© Andrzej Tokarski; p. 80 (b): Sam Hallas; p. 80 (c): Alamy/© ClassicStock; p. 80 (d): Alamy/© The Print Collector; p. 80 (e): Corbis/© DK Limited; p. 100 (a): Alamy/© RIA Novosti; p. 100 (b): FLPA/© Bernd Rohrschneider; p.100 (c): Alamy/© Adrian Sherratt; p. 119: Alamy/© Alvey & Towers Picture Library; p. 154 (L): Rex Features/© KeystoneUSA-ZUMA; p. 154 (R): Alamy/© Hemis; p. 179: Shutterstock/© donsimon; p. 186: Rex Features/© David Hartley; p. 193 (BL): Corbis/© Jose Fuste Raga; p. 193 (BR): Alamy/© Ange; p. 202: Rex Features/© Aflo; p. 214: Getty Images/© Jordan Siemens; p. 231: Getty Images/© Yuri Arcurs; p. 248: Getty Images/© Miroslaw Kijewski; p. 260: Alamy/© motorlife.

Illustrations: Clive Goodyer
Typeset by Blooberry Design Ltd
Text permissions clearance by Sarah Deakin
Picture research by Kevin Brown
Audio produced by Leon Chambers and recorded at dSound, London

3

Contents

Introduction	5
Exam summary	6
Map of the book	8

GRAMMAR SECTION

Unit 1	Tenses	10
Unit 2	The future	17
Unit 3	Modals (1)	25
Unit 4	Modals (2)	32
Unit 5	Nouns, agreement and articles	39
Unit 6	Determiners and quantifiers	47
Unit 7	Adverbs and adjectives	54
Unit 8	Comparison	60
Unit 9	Verb patterns (1)	66
Unit 10	Verb patterns (2)	72
Unit 11	Relative clauses (1)	80
Unit 12	Relative clauses (2)	87
Unit 13	Adverbial clauses	94
Unit 14	Conditionals	100
Unit 15	Participle, to-infinitive and reduced clauses	107
Unit 16	Noun clauses	113
Unit 17	Conjunctions and connectors	119
Unit 18	The passive	126
Unit 19	Reporting	134
Unit 20	Substitution and ellipsis	140
Unit 21	Word order and emphasis	148
Unit 22	Nominalisation	154
Unit 23	*It* and *there*	161
Unit 24	Complex prepositions and prepositions after verbs	168
Unit 25	Prepositions after nouns and adjectives	174

VOCABULARY SECTION

Unit 26	Cities	179
Unit 27	Personal history	184
Unit 28	The arts	188
Unit 29	Migrations	192
Unit 30	Risking it	196
Unit 31	Gender issues	201
Unit 32	Education	205
Unit 33	Health	210
Unit 34	Getting about	214
Unit 35	Moods	218
Unit 36	Fame and fortune	222
Unit 37	Relationships	226
Unit 38	Time off	230
Unit 39	Media	235
Unit 40	The world of work	239
Unit 41	Economics and business	243
Unit 42	The living world	247
Unit 43	Personal contact	251
Unit 44	The environment	255
Unit 45	Science and technology	259
Answer key		263

Introduction

What does the book contain?
This book is updated for the new *Cambridge English: Advanced* examination introduced in 2015 and contains two sections: **Grammar** (Units 1–25) and **Vocabulary** (Units 26–45).

What does the book aim to do?
This book aims to provide complete coverage of the grammar and vocabulary needed for success in the *Cambridge English: Advanced*, also known as the *Certificate in Advanced English (CAE)*. Regular exam practice is provided throughout the book.

Units 1–25 present grammar in context followed by a detailed analysis of the language for advanced learners of English. **Units 26–45** extend vocabulary knowledge – including of collocations and idioms – and introduce ways of studying vocabulary which will help you pass the exam.

Who is the book aimed at?
This book is for anyone preparing for success in the *Cambridge English: Advanced*. It is designed primarily for students working alone who want to revise, extend and practise their knowledge and understanding of grammar and vocabulary, but it can also be used on a *Cambridge English: Advanced* preparation course in the classroom, or can be set as homework by a teacher.

How do I use the book?
You can work through the units in any order, but we advise you to study every unit if you want to prepare thoroughly for the exam. It is best to work through a unit from beginning to end, as exercises may revise grammar or vocabulary from an earlier part of the same unit.

Each of the 25 units in the **Grammar** section is divided into three sections. **Context listening** introduces the grammar of the unit in context to help you understand it more easily. **Grammar** provides detailed explanations of specific grammar points and includes *Start points* which act as a brief reminder of grammar you may already know. **Grammar exercises** provide practice of the grammar of each unit.

Each of the 20 units in the **Vocabulary** section is based on a general topic (e.g. *Cities*) and presents general exercises on vocabulary for two areas within the main unit topic (e.g. *Urban growth* and *Urban living*).

Each unit of the book includes an **Exam practice** section which provides practice of the types of tasks you will face in the *Reading and Use of English*, *Writing* and *Listening* sections of the *Cambridge English: Advanced* examination. Note: Some of the Exam practice tasks test mainly the grammar or vocabulary taught in the same unit, to give extra practice. However, in the real exam each question tests a different grammar/vocabulary point or a different aspect of language.

The **Answer key** contains answers to all the exercises in the book, including alternative answers where more than one correct answer is possible.

What does this symbol mean?
This symbol appears in the *Error warning!* boxes of the **Vocabulary** section and indicates that the errors were found in the *Cambridge Learner Corpus*, a database made up of many thousands of exam scripts written by students taking Cambridge English exams around the world. The exam practice tasks have been informed by the *English Vocabulary Profile*. *The English Vocabulary Profile* is an online resource with detailed and up-to-date information about the words, phrases, phrasal verbs and idioms that learners of English know at each of the six levels of the *Common European Framework* (A1 to C2), which guarantees suitable treatment of words, phrases and phrasal verbs at C1 level.

When should I use a dictionary?
To get the most out of the **Vocabulary** section, you will need a good dictionary. Use the *Cambridge Advanced Learner's Dictionary* or another suitable monolingual dictionary. You should try to do each vocabulary exercise without a dictionary first, then use your dictionary to help you with answers you didn't know. Use the **Answer key** as a final check. When you see the dictionary symbol, you are advised to use a dictionary to complete the exercise.

What material can I find online?
The following material for use with this book can be found online at www.cambridge.org/grammarvocabadvanced:

- **Audio recordings** for all listening exercises and for exam practice Listening tasks
- Complete **Recording scripts** for each audio file
- **Reference notes** which give further information and support on the grammar and vocabulary in this book
- **Wordlists** for key items in the **Vocabulary** section
- **Model answers** to the **Exam practice: Writing tasks** Parts 1 and 2

Exam summary

Reading and Use of English (1 hour 30 minutes)

Part	What are the tasks?	What do I have to do?	How many questions?
1	Multiple-choice cloze	You read a text with eight gaps. For each gap you choose the correct word from one of four possible answers (A, B, C or D).	8
2	Open cloze	You read a text with eight gaps. You must write one word in each gap.	8
3	Word formation	You read a text with eight gaps. For each gap you write the correct form of the word at the end of each line.	8
4	Key word transformation	You are given a complete sentence and a second gapped sentence. You complete the second sentence so that it has the same meaning using a given 'key word'.	6
5	Multiple choice	You read a text and answer six multiple-choice questions. You choose from four possible answers (A, B, C or D).	6
6	Cross-text multiple matching	You read four short texts on the same topic. You have to match each question to the correct text.	4
7	Gapped text	You read a text from which paragraphs have been removed and put in a jumbled order. You have to choose which paragraph fits into which space. There is a paragraph which does not fit into any space.	6
8	Multiple matching	You scan a text or several short texts and decide which part of a text or text each question refers to. Some questions may refer to more than one part of a text or text.	10

Writing (1 hour 30 minutes)

Part	What are the tasks?	What do I have to do?	How many questions?
1	Write an essay	You plan and write an essay on the topic given in the question paper. Your essay must be 220–260 words.	1
2	Write a text of a particular type	You choose, plan and write only one of the following possible text types: a letter, a proposal, a report or a review. Your text must be relevant to the situation described in the question. Your text must be 220–260 words.	1 from a choice of 3

Listening (40 minutes)

Part	What are the tasks?	What do I have to do?	How many questions?
1	Multiple choice	You hear three short extracts and have to answer two multiple-choice questions on each extract. For each question you choose one of three possible answers (A, B or C).	6
2	Sentence completion	You use information you hear to complete sentences with gaps.	8
3	Multiple choice	You hear a recording with six multiple-choice questions. For each question you choose one of four possible answers (A, B, C or D).	6
4	Multiple matching	You hear five short themed monologues with multiple-matching questions. You match a statement or opinion from a list of six options for each speaker.	10

Speaking (15 minutes)

Part	What are the tasks?	What do I have to do?	How long is each part?
1	General conversation	You answer questions about general topics such as your daily life, your interests or your experiences.	2 minutes
2	Individual 'long turn'	You talk about a set of three pictures on your own for around a minute. Then you listen to your partner talk about a different set of pictures before commenting on what they have said.	4 minutes
3	Discussion	You and your partner are given some written instructions for a discussion task.	4 minutes
4	Discussion	You and your partner discuss topics related to the task in Part 3.	5 minutes

Map of the book

GRAMMAR

Unit	Title	Topics	Exam practice
1	Tenses	Simple and continuous tenses; perfect tenses; present perfect continuous and past perfect continuous	Reading and Use of English Part 2
2	The future	*Will, be going to* + infinitive, *shall*; present tenses for the future; future continuous, future perfect and future perfect continuous; *be to* + infinitive; future in the past	Reading and Use of English Part 8
3	Modals (1)	Ability; possibility; conclusions, willingness, habitual events; necessity, deduction; 'not necessary'; obligation	Listening Part 1
4	Modals (2)	Complex modal forms; *dare* and *need*; *had better*; *be allowed to*; *be supposed to*; other verbs with modal meanings	Reading and Use of English Part 4
5	Nouns, agreement and articles	Compound nouns and noun phrases; subject–verb agreement; countable and uncountable nouns; articles	Reading and Use of English Part 2
6	Determiners and quantifiers	*No, none, not a, not any; much, many, a lot of, lots of; all, both, whole; every, each; (a/the) few, little; less, fewer (than); much, many,* etc. + *(of)*	Listening Part 2
7	Adverbs and adjectives	Position of adverbs; *quite, rather, already, yet, still, even, only, really*; position of adjectives; gradable adjectives; patterns after adjectives	Reading and Use of English Part 3
8	Comparison	Comparative and superlative forms of adjectives and adverbs; comparisons with *as …*; comparisons with *so …, too …, enough*	Reading and Use of English Part 3
9	Verb patterns (1)	Verbs with two objects; verb + object + adjective; verb + reflexive pronoun; verb + *each other / one another*	Reading and Use of English Part 4
10	Verb patterns (2)	Verb + *to*-infinitive / *-ing*; verb + (object) + bare infinitive; verb + object + *to*-infinitive / *-ing*; verb + object / possessive + *-ing*; other patterns after verbs	Reading and Use of English Part 5
11	Relative clauses (1)	Defining and non-defining relative clauses; relative pronouns; other words beginning relative clauses; prepositions in relative clauses	Reading and Use of English Part 1
12	Relative clauses (2)	Participle clauses; *to*-infinitive clauses; adjective phrases; prepositional phrases	Reading and Use of English Part 5
13	Adverbial clauses	Adverbial clauses including time clauses, contrast and concession clauses, reason clauses, purpose and result clauses	Reading and Use of English Part 2
14	Conditionals	Real and unreal conditionals; *if … not* and *unless*; *even if* and *even though*; *if only* and *wish*; other conditional expressions	Listening Part 4
15	Participle, *to*-infinitive and reduced clauses	Participle clauses including present participle (*-ing*) clauses, past participle (*-ed*) clauses, participle clauses after conjunctions and prepositions, *to*-infinitive clauses, reduced clauses	Reading and Use of English Part 3
16	Noun clauses	*That*-noun clauses; *wh*-noun clauses; *whether* and *if*	Reading and Use of English Part 1
17	Conjunctions and connectors	*Before, hardly, first(ly), however, even so, on the other hand,* etc.	Reading and Use of English Part 6
18	The passive	Using the passive; active and passive verb forms; passive forms of verbs with two objects; *get* + past participle; *get/have* + object + past participle	Reading and Use of English Part 7
19	Reporting	Structures in the reported clause: *that*-clause, *to*-infinitive and *-ing*; verb tenses in reporting; modal verbs in reporting; reporting questions; *should* in *that*- clauses	Listening Part 4
20	Substitution and ellipsis	*One/ones; so* + auxiliary verb + subject; *neither, nor, not … either; do so*; leaving out words after auxiliary verbs and after *to*	Listening Part 3
21	Word order and emphasis	Fronting; cleft sentences; inversion; inversion in conditional sentences	Reading and Use of English Part 4
22	Nominalisation	Nominalised forms; *do, give, have, make, take* + noun	Reading and Use of English Part 8
23	*It* and *there*	Introductory *it* as subject and object; *there*; common expressions with *it's no …* and *there's no …*	Reading and Use of English Part 4

8

24	Complex prepositions and prepositions after verbs	Complex prepositions; verb + preposition: common patterns; phrasal verbs: word order	Listening Part 1
25	Prepositions after nouns and adjectives	Noun + preposition: related verbs and adjectives; noun + preposition + -ing or noun + preposition + noun; noun + *of* +-*ing* or noun + *to*-infinitive; noun + *in* or noun + *of*; adjective + preposition	Reading and Use of English Part 1

VOCABULARY

Unit	Title	Topics	Exam practice
26	Cities	Urban growth Urban living	Reading and Use of English Part 5
27	Personal history	Ancestry Autobiography	Writing Part 1 An essay
28	The arts	Arts events Reviews	Reading and Use of English Part 1
29	Migrations	Departures Personal stories	Listening Part 2
30	Risking it	Extreme sports Risk-taking	Reading and Use of English Part 7
31	Gender issues	Language Gender in sport	Reading and Use of English Part 4
32	Education	Learning Training	Reading and Use of English Part 6
33	Health	World health Water and health	Writing Part 2 A report
34	Getting about	Private journeys Public transport	Listening Part 1
35	Moods	Attitudes Memory	Reading and Use of English Part 1
36	Fame and fortune	Celebrity culture Reality television	Reading and Use of English Part 2
37	Relationships	Families Friends	Listening Part 3
38	Time off	Holidays Enjoying exercise	Reading and Use of English Part 8
39	Media	News and information Press freedom	Reading and Use of English Part 4
40	The world of work	Employment patterns Economic migration	Reading and Use of English Part 3
41	Economics and business	Economic problems Business tips	Writing Part 1 An essay
42	The living world	Animal life Trees and plants	Listening Part 4
43	Personal contact	Social networking Letter writing	Reading and Use of English Part 2
44	The environment	Issues Protection	Reading and Use of English Part 3
45	Science and technology	Discovery Solutions	Writing Part 2 A letter

1 Tenses

Simple and continuous tenses; perfect tenses; present perfect continuous and past perfect continuous

Context listening

1.1 You are going to hear part of a radio phone-in programme. Before you listen, look at the photos. What do you think the topic of the phone-in is?

1.2 ▶02 Listen and check whether you were right. As you listen, answer the questions.

Which of the callers, Karen, Liam, Sahar or Luka …

1 … lost something on the train one day? _____Sahar_____
2 … travels to work by bus? _____
3 … works at home permanently? _____
4 … may buy a motorbike? _____
5 … has always liked travelling by train? _____
6 … used to catch the train at a quarter past seven in the morning? _____
7 … is working at home temporarily? _____
8 … has never owned a car? _____

1.3 ▶02 Listen again and fill in the gaps.

1 I __commuted__ to London for over ten years.
2 I _____ over an hour when they announced that the train was cancelled.
3 I _____ of buying a motorbike.
4 I _____ at home while our office block is being renovated.
5 I _____ to her only a couple of times before then.
6 I _____ travelling by train ever since I was young.
7 I _____ to phone in to your programme for the last half hour.
8 Yesterday, I _____ all my work by 2.30 pm.

1.4 Identify the tenses you used in 1.3.

1 – past simple

Tenses 1

Grammar

2.1 Simple and continuous tenses

START POINT

Present continuous
I'm **working** at home while our office block is being renovated. (= temporary state)
I'm **phoning** from the train. (= action in progress)
Present simple
Public transport **has** a number of advantages over driving. (= permanent state)
I **catch** the train at 7.05 at the station near my home every morning. (= habit or regular event)
Past continuous
I **was travelling** home when the train broke down. (= action in progress at past point)
Past simple
I **sold** my car last week. (= completed past action)
I **drove** to work for a couple of years. (= past situation that doesn't exist now)
I **caught** the train every morning at 7.15. (= repeated past action)

We usually use simple tenses with verbs that describe an unchanging state rather than an action:
I **love** trains.

We can use continuous tenses with state verbs to suggest that a situation is temporary or untypical:
I'm **appreciating** being able to get up later than usual. (= suggests a temporary arrangement)
Now that I work at home I **appreciate** being able to get up late. (= suggests a more permanent arrangement)

With some verbs that describe mental states (e.g. *consider, understand*) and attitudes (e.g. *hope, regret*), continuous tenses suggest a process going on at the time of speaking, or emphasise that the process continues to develop:
I'm **regretting** selling my car already. (= suggests that I have started to regret it and that this regret may grow)
I **regret** selling my car. (= describes an attitude that is unlikely to change)

Some verbs have different meanings when talking about states and describing actions:
I'm now **thinking** of buying a motorbike. (*think of* (action) = consider)
Do you **think** that's a good idea? (*think* (state) = asking about an opinion)

We usually use the present simple with verbs that describe what we are doing as we speak:
I **admit** that it can be frustrating at times. (= I agree that it is true when I say 'I admit')
I **predict** that increasing numbers of people will start working at home.

We often use the past simple in a narrative (e.g. a report or a story) to talk about a single completed past action, and the past continuous to describe the situation that existed at the time:
I **dropped** my purse while I **was getting** off the train.

When we talk about two or more past completed actions that followed one another, we use the past simple for both:
She **woke** me up and **offered** me a lift.

When we talk about two actions that went on over the same period of past time, we can often use the past continuous or the past simple for both:
I **was listening** to music while I **was driving** here. or I **listened** to music while I **drove** here.

We can use continuous tenses with the adverbs *always, constantly, continually* and *forever* to emphasise that something is typical of a person, group or thing because they do it so often:
I **was forever arriving** late for work.

1 Tenses

We can use either the present continuous or present simple to describe something we regularly do at a certain time:
*At 8 o'clock I'**m** usually **having** a leisurely breakfast.* or *At 8 o'clock I usually **have** …*

We often use the present continuous or past continuous:
- to make an enquiry or a statement less certain because we don't know if we're right:
  *I'**m hoping** we've got Dave Jones on the line.* (= suggests that the speaker is not sure whether Dave Jones is there)
- to make a request or an offer more polite:
  *Karen, **were** you **wanting** to say something?*

2.2 Perfect tenses

> **START POINT**
>
> Present perfect
> *I'**ve lived** in Spain, and the trains are so much more reliable there.* (past situation relevant to the present)
> *I'**ve** just **sold** my car and so now I go to work by bus.* (recent action with consequences for the present)
> *I'**ve enjoyed** travelling by train ever since I was young.* (situation continuing until the present)
> Past perfect
> *This morning I'**d read** a couple of reports before I got off the train.* (past event before another past event)

We use the present perfect to talk about a situation that existed in the past and still exists now, and the past simple when the situation no longer exists:
*I'**ve commuted** to London every weekday for over ten years, and I actually enjoy it.*
*I **commuted** to London every weekday for over ten years before I started working at home.*

We use the present perfect to talk about a repeated action that might happen again:
*I'**ve arrived** late for work twice this week so far.*
and the past simple for a repeated action that won't happen again:
*I **arrived** late for work twice this week.* (= the working week is over; I won't arrive late again this week)

When we give news or information, we often introduce a topic with the present perfect and then give details with other past tenses:
*The new high speed rail link between the north of England and the Channel Tunnel **has opened**.*
*It **took** 15 years to build and **cost** nearly ten billion pounds.*

When we use a time expression (e.g. *after, as soon as, before, when*) to say that one event happened after another, we can use either the past simple or past perfect for the first event:
*I'**d read** a couple of reports **before** I even got to work.* or *I **read** a couple of reports **before** I even got to work.*

2.3 Present perfect continuous and past perfect continuous

We use the present perfect continuous (*have been* + *-ing*) to talk about an action in progress in the past for a period until now, and which is either still in progress or recently finished:
*I'**ve been working** at home for the last five years.* (= action still in progress)
*Sorry I'm late. I'**ve been trying** to find a parking place.* (= action recently finished)

We often prefer the present perfect continuous to say how long an action has been in progress:
*I'**ve been trying** to phone in to your programme **for the last half hour**.*

We use the present perfect to talk about a completed action or series of actions when we are interested in the result:
*I'**ve called** the bus company a number of times to complain.*
*They'**ve bought** new trains and have really improved the service.*

Tenses 1

We use the past perfect continuous (*had been* + *-ing*) to talk about an action in progress over a period up to a particular past point in time:
I'd been waiting over an hour when they announced that the train had been cancelled.

If we are not interested in how long the action went on, we often use the past continuous rather than the past perfect continuous:
I was waiting on the platform when they announced that the train had been cancelled. rather than
I'd been waiting on the platform when … (= there is no mention of how long the person was waiting.)

We use the past perfect when we say how many times something happened in a period up to a particular past time:
I'd spoken to her only a couple of times before then.

We don't usually use the present perfect continuous or the past perfect continuous to describe states:
I'd owned a car ever since I left college. (not *I'd been owning* …)

Grammar exercises

3.1 Choose the correct or more natural answer in this radio news report.

Emergency services were bombarded with phone calls from all over the north of the country last night by people who **(1)** *are reporting / reported* seeing blue objects shoot across the sky. Mrs Sophia Olsen **(2)** *drove / was driving* along the main road at the time.

'I **(3)** *'m usually coming / usually came* along that bit of road at about ten. As I **(4)** *was going / go* past the old barn, I **(5)** *was seeing / saw* a single bright blue light going across the road in front of my car. I **(6)** *stopped / stop* the car and **(7)** *was watching / am watching* it for about fifteen minutes. It **(8)** *was travelling / travels* quite slowly from east to west and then it **(9)** *'s suddenly disappearing / suddenly disappeared*. Until now I **(10)** *wasn't believing / didn't believe* in UFOs, although my son **(11)** *is forever trying / forever tries* to persuade me that they **(12)** *are existing / exist*. But now I **(13)** *thought / 'm thinking* that maybe he **(14)** *was being / was* right.'

Dr Maria Walker, a lecturer in astronomy at Trumpton University, **(15)** *offers / is offering* a simple explanation. 'The reports that **(16)** *were coming / come* in last night **(17)** *are suggesting / suggest* that it **(18)** *was / is* a meteor shower. This **(19)** *is / was* not unusual on a small scale, but last night's shower **(20)** *is seeming / seems* to have been very large. In fact, we **(21)** *were getting / are getting* an increasing number of meteor showers, and my department **(22)** *is currently researching / currently researches* possible reasons for this.'

But many witnesses to the events **(23)** *believe / are believing* that they **(24)** *are observing / were observing* more than a meteor shower, and that last night the Earth was actually visited by beings from outer space.

1 Tenses

3.2 Complete the sentences using the verbs in the box. Use the same verb in each pair of sentences. Use the present simple, present continuous, past simple or past continuous.

attract   expect   imagine   measure   see   ~~think~~

1 a I ___'m thinking___ about taking a gap year before I go to university and going travelling around South America.

   b A: Why's Yusuf having a party?
      B: I ___think___ it's his birthday.

2 a A: How did the cat get up into the tree?
      B: I _____ he was chasing a bird.

   b A: Let me know when the post arrives.
      B: Why, _____ you _____ something important?

3 a A: What happened to your wrist?
      B: I _____ the window for some new curtains and I fell off the ladder.

   b I was given this pedometer for my birthday. You just hook it on your belt and it _____ how far you walk during the day.

4 a This month's special exhibition of South African art _____ over 5,000 visitors a day to the museum, whereas we normally only get about 2,000.

   b As the home of William Shakespeare, Stratford _____ tourists from all over the world.

5 a _____ you _____ that big house over there? It's my uncle's.

   b I split up with Alex when I found out that he _____ someone else.

6 a I _____ Giulia's under a lot of stress at the moment with moving house and starting a new job.

   b The baby's smiling in her sleep. I wonder what things she _____ in her dreams.

3.3 Complete the sentences with an appropriate form of the verb given. Use the past simple, present perfect, past perfect and past perfect continuous tenses. Use each tense only once in each group of four sentences.

1 play

   a We ___have played___ 35 matches so far this season, so we're all feeling pretty tired.

   b After the match, she admitted that she _____ badly.

   c _____ you _____ rugby or football at the school you went to?

   d Ireland _____ really well all year, so it came as a big surprise when they were beaten by Wales last December.

2 make

   a We _____ the right decision in emigrating to Canada in the mid-1990s.

   b Henson never thought about retirement. In fact, he _____ a documentary film about the indigenous people of Chile when he died.

   c A: When did you realise that you _____ a mistake in joining the army?
      B: When I was posted to a boiling hot jungle.

Tenses 1

    d Korean scientists believe that they _____ a breakthrough in the fight against cancer by developing a technique for containing the disease. They reported their findings at the AAL conference in New York this week.

3 *run*

    a Over the last year I _____ workshops on creative writing in twelve colleges and universities.

    b She was breathing hard as if she _____ .

    c She _____ only two marathons before breaking the world record in the Pan-African Games.

    d I was late for work so I _____ most of the way.

3.4 Complete the sentences using either the present perfect or present perfect continuous form of the verb given. Where both are possible, choose the more likely tense.

1 Alice *has competed* (compete) in the Athens Marathon twice before, but hopes to achieve her best time this year.

2 Income from manufacturing exports still provides the largest proportion of the country's export earnings, but the proportion _____ (*drop*) for many years.

3 The house _____ (*belong*) to the Beecham family for over 250 years, but the present owner, Donald Beecham, is selling it.

4 Melnik _____ (*serve*) a life sentence for murder since 1990, but his lawyers are arguing for an early release.

5 **A:** I'd like a career where I can travel and meet people.
    B: _____ (*consider*) becoming a tour guide?

6 **A:** _____ (*swim*)? You look really exhausted.
    B: I am. I did 50 lengths of the pool.

7 **A:** Did you manage to get in touch with Chloe?
    B: No, I _____ (*try*) three times in the last hour, but she's always engaged.

3.5 Choose the correct tense.

A: Good morning, Mr Nilsson. What can I do for you?
B: Well, doctor, (1) *I've been getting* / *I've got* some really bad headaches.
A: Okay. Can you tell me exactly when these headaches (2) *were starting* / *started*?
B: Oh, yes, I (3) *have remembered* / *remember* it vividly – it was on a Friday three weeks ago. I (4) *had been working* / *worked* in front of my computer all week because I (5) *did* / *was doing* a job for an important client – (6) *I was working* / *I've been working* as a website designer for the last few years, you see. I (7) *had just finished* / *had just been finishing* when the pain started, and by the end of that day I (8) *was feeling* / *have felt* really bad.
A: Okay. And how (9) *have you slept* / *have you been sleeping*?
B: Not very well, actually. Usually I'm asleep as soon as my head (10) *hits* / *is hitting* the pillow, but recently (11) *I've been having* / *I'm having* difficulty getting to sleep.
A: I see. Now, (12) *I'm noticing* / *I notice* that you wear glasses. (13) *Have you had* / *Were you having* your eyes tested recently?
B: No, I (14) *haven't had* / *didn't have* them tested for a couple of years, I suppose.
A: Okay, what (15) *I suggest* / *I'm suggesting* is that first you get your eyes tested. Then when you (16) *are working* / *have worked* at your computer, take frequent breaks to rest your eyes. If that (17) *hasn't solved* / *doesn't solve* the problem, come back and see me again.

Exam practice

Reading and Use of English Part 2

For questions **1 – 8**, read the text below and think of the word which best fits each gap. Use only **one** word in each gap. There is an example at the beginning **(0)**.

Planets beyond our solar system

Throughout history we have wondered about the possibility **(0)** ___of___ life beyond the Earth. It is only in recent years, however, that advances in technology **(1)** _____ revealed the existence of extrasolar planets (or 'exoplanets'); **(2)** _____ is to say, planets which orbit not our own Sun, but other stars in the universe. So **(3)** _____, astronomers have identified a few thousand exoplanets, but believe that billions more exist.

Although many astronomers believe that a large number of planets in the universe are capable of supporting **(4)** _____ kind of living organism, whether or not life has developed on any of them **(5)** _____ not yet known. An essential requirement for life is liquid water. **(6)** _____ a planet is to have liquid water on its surface, its temperature must be **(7)** _____ too hot nor too cold. However, **(8)** _____ a planet, other than the Earth, has yet to be discovered.

2 The future

Will, be going to + infinitive, shall; present tenses for the future; future continuous, future perfect and future perfect continuous; be to + infinitive; future in the past

Context listening

1.1 Which of these activities would you like to do on a visit to the USA?

1.2 ▶03 Jessica is doing a course in American Studies at a British university. As part of this programme she will spend her third year studying at a university in Los Angeles in California. Her friend, Kelly, wants to visit her while she is there. Listen to them talking about their plans. Which of the activities shown in 1.1 do they mention?

1.3 ▶03 Listen again and fill in the gaps.

1 I *'m spending* a few days sightseeing in New York.
2 I _____ in Los Angeles on the 20th.
3 I _____ for my own place.
4 It _____ a long time to catch up.
5 I _____ up there if it's not too expensive.
6 _____ you stop over anywhere on the way out?
7 When I come to see you, you _____ in California for nearly six months.
8 You _____ longer, won't you?

1.4 How many different ways of referring to the future did you use in 1.3? _____

2 The future

Grammar

2.1 Will, be going to + infinitive and shall

> **START POINT**
>
> *Will*
> I think I**'ll fly** directly to Los Angeles. (= a decision made without planning)
> I'm sure you**'ll have** a fantastic time. (= a prediction based on opinion or experience)
> I**'ll be** 21 on 2nd January. (= a fact about the future)
> I**'ll meet** you at the airport. (= willingness)
> *Be going to* + infinitive
> First I**'m going to stay** with Daniel and Susanna. (= a decision already made)
> The cloud's building up. It**'s going to rain** this afternoon. (= a prediction based on outside evidence)

We can sometimes use *will* instead of *be going to* to make a prediction based on evidence, but when we do, we usually include an adverb:
The cloud's building up. It**'ll definitely rain** / It**'s definitely going to rain** this afternoon.

We can use *will* or *be going to* in the main clause of an *if*-sentence with little difference in meaning when we say that something is conditional on something else:
If I don't go now, I**'ll be** / I**'m going to be** late for my next lecture.

We use *will*, not *be going to*, when the main clause refers to offers, requests, promises and ability:
If my plans change, I**'ll let** you know, of course. (= promise)
If you bring your tent, we**'ll camp** on the coast for a few days. (= ability; 'we will be able to camp')

In formal contexts, we can use *shall* instead of *will* with *I* or *we*:
- in questions that ask about intentions:

Shall I/we see you before you leave? (= Will I/we have the opportunity to see you?)
- in statements about the future, although *will* is more usual:

When I finish my course I **shall/will have** some time to travel around America.

2.2 Present continuous and present simple for the future

> **START POINT**
>
> Present continuous
> I**'m spending** a few days sightseeing. (= event intended or arranged)
> Present simple
> Lectures **start** on 27th July. (= event as part of an official schedule)

Compare the use of the present continuous for the future and *be going to*:
I**'m flying** on 15th July at ten in the evening. (= already arranged)
I**'m going to fly** up there if it's not too expensive. (= the speaker intends to fly but has not made the arrangements yet)

We tend to avoid *be going to go* and use the present continuous (*be going to*) instead:
Then I**'m going to** San Francisco. rather than Then I**'m going to go** to San Francisco.

We can't use the present continuous for future events which are not controlled by people:
It**'s going to rain** this afternoon. (not ~~It's raining this afternoon.~~)

The future 2

We can use either the present simple or *will* to talk about formal arrangements made by, for example, a university or company:
*The semester **begins** on 7th December.* or *The semester **will begin** on 7th December.*

The present continuous is used in informal arrangements:
*You**'re not staying** with them the whole time, then?* (= informal arrangement) (not *You don't stay with them the whole time, then?*)

We use the present simple, or sometimes other present tenses, to refer to the future in time clauses with a conjunction (e.g. *after, as soon as, before, by the time, when, while, until*); in conditional clauses with *if, in case, provided* and *unless*; and in clauses beginning with *suppose, supposing* and *what if*:
*As soon as I **book** my tickets, I'll let you know.* (not *As soon as I will book* …)
*It'll be good to know I can contact them **in case** I **have** any problems.* (not … *in case I will have* …)
*What **if** I **don't like** it?* (not *What if I won't like it?*)

2.3 Future continuous, future perfect and future perfect continuous

We use the future continuous (*will + be +* present participle) to talk about something predicted to happen at a particular time or over a particular period in the future:
*I**'ll be studying** really hard **during the semesters**.*

We use the future perfect (*will + have +* past participle) to make a prediction about an action we expect to be completed by a particular time in the future:
***By the time you come** I'm sure I**'ll have got** to know the city really well.*

We use the future perfect continuous (*will + have been +* present participle) to emphasise the duration of an activity in progress at a particular point in the future:
***When I come to see you**, you**'ll have been living** in California **for nearly six months**.*

We can also use the future continuous, future perfect and future perfect continuous to say what we believe or imagine to be true:
*Dad **won't be using** his car, so I'm sure it's okay to borrow it.* (= an activity happening now or at a particular point in the future)
*They**'ll have forgotten** what I look like.* (= an event that took place before now or before a particular point in the future)
*My plane's been delayed. Daniel and Susanna **will have been waiting** for me at the airport for hours.* (= an activity continuing to now)

2.4 *Be to* + infinitive

Be to + infinitive is commonly used:
- in news reports:

*Extra lifeguards **are to be posted** at the beach after a shark was seen close to the shore.*
- to talk about formal plans, and rules or instructions:

*Students **are to hand** in project reports at the end of semester two.* (active)
*Project reports **are to be handed** in at the end of semester two.* (passive)

We only use *am/is/are to* + infinitive to talk about future events that people can control:
*The weather **will** still **be** warm even in winter.* (not *The weather is still to be warm.*)

We often use *be to* + infinitive in *if*-clauses when we mean 'in order to':
*If she **is to get** a good grade in her project report, she needs to work on her statistics.* (= in order to get a good grade, she needs to work on her statistics)

19

2 The future

2.5 Future in the past

A number of forms can be used to talk about a past activity or event that was still in the future from the point of view of the speaker:

I **was going to see** an aunt in Seattle a couple of years ago, but I cancelled the trip because she got ill. (= a plan that didn't happen)
I knew I **would be feeling** awful by the end of the flight. (= a prediction made in the past)

Grammar exercises

3.1 Complete the sentences using the verbs in the box. Choose the most appropriate form.

miss / will miss	will have / am having	is going to melt / is melting
persuades / will persuade	will be enjoying / enjoys	~~am starting out / will start out~~
will rise / are to rise	see / are going to see	

1 **A:** Do you want to come out for a meal tonight?
   B: I _'m starting out_ early tomorrow morning – my flight's at six – so I don't think I'll come, thanks.
2 I _____ some friends over for dinner on Saturday. Do you want to join us?
3 They reckon the Greenland ice sheet _____ within a few years.
4 **A:** Yoshi doesn't want to come on holiday with us, then.
   B: He says that now, but I'm sure Hannah _____ him to change his mind.
5 By the middle of the week, temperatures _____ to 30°C.
6 I'm not sure when I'll be home tonight. Expect me when you _____ me.
7 **A:** The coach leaves Kiev at exactly 5.00 from the bus station.
   B: What if I _____ it?
   A: You'll have to take the train.
8 **A:** It's Lucia's first week away at university. I wonder how she's getting on?
   B: I'm sure she _____ herself.

3.2 Choose the correct future form.

1 You'll freeze if you_'ll go / go_ out dressed like that. Put on a warm coat!
2 When I retire next year, I'm _doing / going to do_ a lot of travelling around South America.
3 Look at that stupid cyclist! He's _going to cause / causes_ an accident.
4 **A:** What do you want done with this box?
   B: If you just leave it there, I'll _take / 'm taking_ it upstairs when I go.
5 **A:** What _are you doing / do you do_ this evening?
   B: Oh, I don't know. Maybe I'll _Skype / 'm Skyping_ Lydia.
6 Please note that next week's concert _is commencing / will commence_ at 7.00, not 7.30 as advertised in the programme.

The future 2

7 **A:** Adele *will do / is doing* a concert in Milan next month.

   B: *Will / Shall* I book some tickets?

8 When Stefan *is / will be* 50, Sofia *is to be / will be* 18.

3.3 Complete the sentences using a future form of the verbs given. Use the same future form for all three sentences in each group. Use:

~~present simple~~	future continuous	be to + infinitive	be going to + infinitive
future perfect	present continuous	future perfect continuous	

1 **get   go   terminate**
   a All change, please – this train ___terminates___ here.
   b What time _does our plane get_ (our plane) to Athens?
   c The cat runs away from me as soon as I _____go_____ near it.

2 **buy   have   need**
   a **A:** What are you going to town for?
      B: I _____ some new shoes.
   b **A:** Jane's not looking very well.
      B: No, apparently, she _____ a major operation.
   c **A:** I've made a list of the things you _____ for the field trip to Iceland.
      B: Thanks, that's really helpful.

3 **negotiate   watch   work**
   a On April 1st next year I _____ at the university for 25 years.
   b **A:** It's such a pity that Ella is away and can't watch the match with us. You know how much she loves tennis.
      B: I'm sure she _____ it on TV in her hotel room.
   c The next statement from the trade union leaders is expected at ten o'clock tonight. By that time they _____ with the employers for 36 hours.

4 **come   do   support**
   a Justin's not feeling well, so he _____ tonight after all.
   b Who _____ (you) in the world cup final, France or Brazil?
   c **A:** What do you think Lola _____ at the moment?
      B: Oh, she'll still be in bed.

5 **create   launch   leave**
   a The computer firm Clarken _____ 300 new jobs at its assembly plant just outside Dublin.
   b All mobile phones _____ outside the examination room.
   c The government _____ an enquiry next week into allegations of corruption in the civil service.

21

2 The future

6 analyse   have   move

a The bank predicts that by the end of next year, over 80% of its customers _____ to online banking.

b Natasha _____ her exam results by now. I wonder how she's got on.

c My research is going rather slowly at the moment, but I'm certain by the end of the year all of my data _____ .

7 go   have   make

a She _____ a speech at the conference next week.

b I _____ out there – it's pouring with rain and I haven't got an umbrella.

c We _____ risotto for dinner. Is that okay with you?

Exam practice

The future **2**

Reading and Use of English Part 8

You are going to read a magazine article in which five career consultants give advice on interview technique. For questions **1 – 10**, choose from the consultants **(A – E)**. The consultants may be chosen more than once.

Which consultant makes the following statements?

Interviewers look for applicants with specific skills.	**1**
Try to make a good impression early in the interview.	**2**
Insufficient preparation by applicants is a common weakness.	**3**
Doing prior research helps distinguish you from other applicants.	**4**
Give yourself a moment to think about your answers to interviewers' questions.	**5**
You should be able to support your application with additional information at an interview.	**6**
Find out the opinion of other people who deal with the organisation.	**7**
Consider the match between the job requirements and your experience.	**8**
Getting an interview indicates that the employer believes you can do the job.	**9**
Use a number of sources to discover more about the organisation.	**10**

23

Exam practice

Job interviews: expert advice for graduates
Are you a graduate about to apply for jobs? We asked five career consultants to give some tips on performing well in interviews.

Consultant A

Ask recruiters what disappoints them most about the people they interview and the answer is often the same – lack of knowledge of their organisation. And lack of knowledge suggests lack of interest. You will have learned research skills in your university degree, so apply them to job hunting and don't forget that social networks can also provide a lot of inside information. Find out how the organisation you are applying for has developed in recent years, how its products or services and markets have changed, who its competitors are, what its ethos is. Then use that information intelligently – simply regurgitating facts won't impress the interviewers. Instead, you need to demonstrate an understanding of what it all means for you as a prospective employee, what the challenges would be and the skills and attributes you'll need to make a positive contribution.

Consultant B

Three-quarters of interviews are failed within three minutes of entering the room. Interviewers are put off by weak handshakes, a lack of eye contact, poor body language and poor posture (slumped shoulders suggest a lack of confidence). Many recruiters make early judgements about your trustworthiness, likeability and professionalism and spend the rest of the interview confirming these opinions. You should shake hands firmly and warmly, but wait to be invited to sit down. Strong handshakes communicate sociability and friendliness – normally desirable qualities in candidates – whereas weak handshakes may communicate introversion and shyness. At the start of the interview you should smile at and maintain good eye contact with the interviewer. Take a little time to consider your response to what the interviewers ask before speaking. Then, when you have decided what to say, speak clearly and not too fast.

Consultant C

Inevitably, you will be asked at some stage during the interview why you want to work for the organisation you are applying to. This is a great chance to show your business awareness, but you'll need to prepare. Before the interview, contact one of the organisation's customers – you should be able to identify some through an internet search – and ask them questions such as: 'What's it like to do business with company X?', 'What makes them stand out?', 'What makes them successful (or not)?' And then at interview explain the research that you've done and include their customer's responses in your answers. That way you'll stand out from the crowd; not only will you give evidence of your personal enterprise and your genuine interest in the organisation, but also your understanding of the business world.

Consultant D

Most employers will want you to demonstrate a particular set of abilities which they believe are essential to the job role, for example team work, communication, problem solving and time management. At interview, you are likely to be asked to give specific examples of times when you have demonstrated those abilities. Employers recognise that you might not have lots of directly relevant work experience, so when they ask these questions they will usually be happy for you to provide examples from any aspect of your life, such as your studies, part-time work, volunteering, interests or extra-curricular activities. So before you go to an interview, check the job description for the skills and competencies required, then reflect on your experiences and think about examples that you could use as evidence.

Consultant E

It's natural to be nervous, but if an employer thought you weren't good enough, they simply wouldn't waste their time on getting to know you in an interview. What interviewers aim to do is find out whether what's written in your application is genuine and how well you'll fit in. So the best advice I can give is: just be yourself in the interview. Of course, they'll also be testing your understanding, motivation and ability, most often by asking you to talk them through examples of your practical knowledge that show you have the expertise the job requires. You'll need to expand on what you've written and it's a good idea to have some new examples ready, too.

3 Modals (1)

Ability; possibility; conclusions, willingness, habitual events; necessity, deduction; 'not necessary'; obligation

Context listening

1.1 Look at these newspaper headlines and photos. What do you think the stories are about?

More air travel chaos looms

School evacuation in South Wales

Borland link opened

Sport the answer to obesity crisis

1.2 ▶04 Listen to a radio news summary and check whether you were right.

1.3 ▶04 Listen again and fill in the gaps.

1. Air passengers _could be hit_ badly today.
2. The cabin staff _____ the new working conditions.
3. Up to 200 teachers and pupils _____ evacuated from Northfield Primary School.
4. Firefighters _____ the fire under control fairly quickly.
5. I think it _____ of great benefit to the island.
6. There _____ restrictions on the number of people moving here.
7. They _____ their children whatever encouragement they can.
8. It _____ warm, sunny and dry, with temperatures up to 22°C.

1.4 In which of the extracts do the words you have written refer to:

1. ability?   __4__
2. necessity?   _____
3. obligation?   _____
4. possibility?   _____
5. prediction?   _____

25

3 Modals (1)

Grammar

> **START POINT**
>
> *Can/could*
> We'll get wealthy people from the mainland who **can** afford second homes. (= general ability)
> Before the bridge was built we **could** only get to the island by ferry. (= general ability in the past)
> *May/could/might*
> Up to 100,000 people **may** experience delays. (= it's possible this will happen)
> Air passengers **could** be hit badly today. (= it's possible)
> It **might** be a number of months before the sports centre is back in operation. (= it's possible this is true; less certain than *may* or *could*)
> *Will/would*
> That **will** push up house prices. (= prediction about the future)
> If schools highlighted the importance of physical exercise, this **would** have a major positive impact on children's attitudes to sport. (= prediction about an imaginary situation)
> *Must*
> The cabin staff **must** accept the new working conditions. (= a rule or order)
> This negative attitude to sport **mustn't** be allowed to continue. (= it's not allowed or not a good idea)
> *Don't need to / needn't / don't have to*
> Parents **don't need to / needn't** be very interested in sport themselves. (= it's not necessarily true)
> I'm sure I **don't have to** spell out the chaos being caused in the airline industry. (= it's not necessary)
> *Ought to / should*
> Parents **ought to / should** give their children whatever encouragement they can. (= obligation and recommendation)

2.1 *Can, could, be able to*: ability

We can use *be able to* instead of *can* or *could*, particularly in more formal contexts:
The hotels on the island **are able to** accommodate hundreds of visitors. (more formal) or *The hotels on the island* **can** *accommodate …* (less formal)

We use *be able to* to talk about ability on a specific occasion in the past:
Firefighters **were able to** bring the fire under control fairly quickly. (not *Firefighters could bring* …)
We can use either *could* or *be able to* in negatives in the past:
They **couldn't / weren't able to** prevent the fire damaging the school's sports centre.

We usually prefer *can* or *could* with verbs of sense (e.g. *feel, hear, see, smell, taste*) and verbs of thinking (e.g. *believe, remember, understand*):
I **can't believe** Mr Wade is being so confrontational.
We use *be able to* in perfect tenses, *-ing* forms, infinitives and after modal verbs:
We've now **been able to** contact him.
The film star hates **not being able to** leave her house.
They've **got to be able to** adapt to change.
Parents **might be able to** help.
We prefer *can* and *could* in passives:
The news **can be read** on our website.
To talk about a future ability, we use *will be able to*:
Islanders **won't be able to** buy properties.

26

Modals (1) 3

We use *can* or *be able to* to talk about possible future arrangements and *can* (or more politely *could*) to ask for permission:
*The President **can't** / **is not able to** visit the country until next month.*
***Can/Could** I ask you what you think of the new bridge?*

2.2 *May, might, can, could*: possibility

To talk about a more general possibility of something happening we can use *can* or *may*:
*The temperature in the mountains **can/may fall** below freezing even at this time of year.*

We use *could* to say that something was possible in the past:
*It **could be** a very rough journey, too.*

We don't use *may* to ask questions about the possibility of something happening. Instead we use *could* or the phrase *be likely to*:
***Could** the negotiations **finish** today, do you think?*
*What time **is** the meeting **likely to finish**?*
Might is sometimes used in questions, but is rather formal.

We can use these modals in negative sentences, including those with words like *only* or *hardly*, to say that things are not possible or that it is possible that things are not the case:
*The company **can hardly be described** as a success.* (= it is not possible to describe it as a success)
*I think we should call off the strike, but other people **may/might not agree** with me.* (= it's possible that people don't agree with me)

2.3 *Will, would, used to*: conclusions, willingness, habitual events

We can use *will* to draw conclusions or state assumptions about things we think are true:
*No doubt you **will have heard** the news by now.*

We use *will* (*not*) to talk about (un)willingness or refusal to do something:
*The minister says he **will resign** if no solution is found.*
*We **will not be bullied** by management.*
*The computer **won't let** me print documents.* (We can say that inanimate objects, such as machines, can be unwilling or refuse to do something.)

We use *would* to talk about willingness in the future, in conditionals, and when we say that we are willing but unable to do something:
*Many people **would be** happy to pay higher taxes for better public services.*
*The minister **would be** pleased to accept the invitation if it were not for other commitments.*
We don't use *would* to talk about willingness on a specific occasion in the past:
David Wade agreed to meet the union representatives. (not *David Wade would agree* ...)

We can use *will* (present) and *would* (past) to talk about characteristic behaviour or habits, or about things that are true now or were true in the past:
*Some parents **will** actually **discourage** their children from taking up a sport.*
*Many passengers **would get** seasick during the crossing.*

We can use either *would* or *used to* to talk about things that happened repeatedly in the past:
*The crossing **would/used to** take over an hour at least.*

We don't use *would* to talk about past states:
*We **used to be** terribly **isolated** here because the ferry service was so bad.* (not *We would be terribly isolated* ...)

27

3 Modals (1)

2.4 *Must, have (got) to*: necessity, deduction

We can use either *must* or *have to* to say that it is necessary to do something, although *have to* is less formal and is also preferred in questions:
*The cabin staff **must** / **have to accept** the new working conditions if the airline is to compete.*

When we say that something was necessary in the past we use *had to*, not *must*:
*Up to 200 teachers and pupils **had to be evacuated** from a school in South Wales today.*
To say something is necessary in the future we use *will have to*:
*To stay in business we **will have to cut** our costs.*

We use *must* when we decide that, in our opinion, something is necessary or important:
*I **must give** you my email address.*
Have to suggests that the necessity comes from outside; for example, from a rule or official order:
*The council **has to close** two city centre car parks following a health and safety report.*

We usually use *must*, rather than *have to*, when we conclude that something (has) happened or that something is true.
*The bridge **must have cost** a fortune.*

When we conclude that something is impossible, we use *can't* or *couldn't*:
*That **can't be** right, surely?* (not *That mustn't be right, surely?*)

Sometimes we can use either *have to* or *have got to*, although *have got to* is more informal. We use *have to* with frequency adverbs and with other modal verbs:
*Islanders **normally have to queue** for half an hour to get on the ferry.*
*The airlines **will have to return** to the negotiating table.*
If *have* is contracted (e.g. *I've*), then we must include *got*:
*They**'ve got to** be changed.* (not *They've to be changed.*)
When we use the past simple we prefer *had to* rather than *had got to*:
*The manager seemed to be doing a good job. Why **did** he **have to** go?* (not *Why had he got to go?*)

2.5 *Didn't need to, didn't have to, needn't have*: 'not necessary'

To say it was not necessary to do something in the past, we use *didn't need to* or *didn't have to*:
*He **didn't have to wait** long for a response.* (= he didn't actually wait long)

When we think something that was done in the past was not necessary, we use *need not* (*needn't*) *have*:
*The event organisers expected the bad weather to affect ticket sales. However, they **need not have worried**, as every ticket was sold.* (= they worried but it was not necessary)

2.6 *Should, ought to*: obligation

We can often use either *should* or *ought to* to talk about obligation (in giving advice and recommendations, saying what we think is a good idea and talking about responsibility):
*I think we **ought to** / **should keep** Borland for the islanders!* (= it's a good idea)
*The authorities **ought to** / **should prosecute** companies that cause pollution.* (= talking about responsibility)

We can use either *should* or *ought to* to say that something is likely because we have planned it or expect it to happen:
*They say the road will be ready in five years, but they **should** / **ought to be able to** build it faster.*

We use *shouldn't* rather than *oughtn't to* if something is unlikely:
*If you're in the south of the country, you **shouldn't be troubled** by any rain today.*

Modals (1) 3

Grammar exercises

3.1 Choose the correct verb.

1 Adult ladybirds *may* / *might* be black, red or yellow.
2 We *can* / *'ll be able to* get to the airport in 20 minutes when the new line is finished next year.
3 I left home because I *wasn't able to* / *can't* find a job there.
4 A: I can't find my purse anywhere.
   B: *May* / *Could* you have left it in the restaurant?
5 Not so long ago, more than 20 species of fish *could* / *were able to* be found in this river.
6 A: Apparently, there's been an accident in the High Street.
   B: That *might* / *is able to* explain why the bus is taking so long.
7 A: Lena says she'll definitely pay the money back.
   B: I wish I was *able to* / *could* trust her.
8 This camera is a bit cheaper than the other one, but it *mightn't* / *can't* be as good, of course.

3.2 Amir is talking to Martha just before and after a job interview. Choose the correct verb.

Before the interview
A: What time (1) *have you to* / *have you got to* / *must* you be there by?
M: 10.30.
A: You (2) *must* / *have to* / *have got to* be really nervous.
M: Terrified! But it doesn't matter, I know I won't get the job.
A: You (3) *haven't got to* / *mustn't* / *can't* be sure of that. You've got just the right experience and qualifications.
M: But I feel tense. I'm worried I (4) *can't* / *couldn't* / *mightn't* make a good impression in the interview.
A: I'm sure you'll be okay.

After the interview
M: I got it!
A: Congratulations! What (5) *had you got to* / *must you* / *did you have to* do?
M: Well, mainly I (6) *had got to* / *had to* / *must* tell them why I wanted to work there.
A: And does the job sound good?
M: Fantastic. I'll (7) *have to* / *must* / *have got to* do a lot of travelling.
A: Well that (8) *oughtn't to* / *shouldn't* / *mustn't* be a problem for you.
M: No, and I may (9) *must* / *have to* / *have got to* spend some time in Barcelona.
A: Well, I think we should certainly go out for a meal to celebrate.
M: Great idea.

3.3 Choose the correct sentence ending. Sometimes both are possible.

1 I have to get up early tomorrow, so I …
   a mustn't be too late going to bed tonight.
   b don't need to be too late going to bed tonight.
2 When we got to the station, we found that the train was half an hour late, so we …
   a didn't need to rush after all.
   b needn't have rushed after all.

3 Modals (1)

3 The meeting will be quite informal, so you …
   a don't need to wear a suit.
   b don't have to wear a suit.

4 Fortunately, he wasn't badly hurt in the accident, so he …
   a needn't go to hospital.
   b didn't need to go to hospital.

5 Gwen has lost a lot of weight during her illness, so you …
   a needn't look surprised when you see her again.
   b mustn't look surprised when you see her again.

6 The tennis courts are open to the public, so you …
   a needn't be a member of the club to play here.
   b mustn't be a member of the club to play here.

7 The house was in good condition when I bought it, so I …
   a didn't need to decorate before I moved in.
   b didn't have to decorate before I moved in.

8 As it turned out, the exam was quite easy, so I …
   a didn't have to spend all that time revising.
   b needn't have spent all that time revising.

3.4 Match a sentence beginning with one of the endings. You won't need to use all the endings.

1 I said I'd pay for her ticket but she
2 In just a few years from now people
3 I still remember how they
4 Forecasters are warning that heavy snow
5 Here's some really nice cheese that I don't think you
6 We live in an old house that
7 Writing my geography assignment

a could cause dangerous driving conditions.
b shouldn't take me too long.
c can do 3D printing in their own homes.
d wouldn't accept my offer.
e would play together so well as children.
f would be a school.
g will be able to control their car using an app.
h used to belong to a politician.
i will have tasted before.
j might have tried.

Exam practice

Modals (1) **3**

Listening Part 1

▶ 05 You will hear three different extracts. For questions **1 – 6**, choose the answer (**A**, **B** or **C**) which fits best according to what you hear. There are two questions for each extract.

Extract One

You hear two people on a radio programme discussing music education for children.

1   They agree that young children should
    A   learn an instrument that requires a lot of concentration.
    B   be started on instruction at an early age.
    C   focus largely on music theory.

2   What does the woman say about the piano?
    A   It is not possible to play simple tunes on it.
    B   Playing it can discourage children from learning another instrument.
    C   Most young children are not mature enough to learn it.

Extract Two

You hear part of an interview with a rock climber called Ben.

3   In Ben's view, what is the best way to improve as a climber?
    A   take the advice of other climbers
    B   learn from the mistakes you make
    C   watch more experienced climbers

4   Why does Ben prefer not to climb alone in icy conditions?
    A   He can learn new techniques from other people.
    B   He gets nervous when rocks have ice on them.
    C   He lacks experience of climbing on ice.

Extract Three

You hear part of an interview with a restaurant critic called Amanda Downing.

5   How do most waiters react when they realise who Amanda is?
    A   They give her special attention.
    B   They are overcome with nerves.
    C   They provide her with free food.

6   In what way, according to Amanda, are most restaurant owners completely wrong?
    A   They think customers choose a restaurant only for its quality of service.
    B   They don't understand customers' motivation for eating in restaurants.
    C   They think their priorities are different to those of their customers.

31

4 Modals (2)

Complex modal forms; *dare* and *need*; *had better*; *be allowed to*; *be supposed to*; other verbs with modal meanings

Context listening

1.1 ▶06 Listen to this extract from a radio drama. Two police officers are discussing a major art theft from the fourth floor of a modern art gallery. Which of these pictures (a–f) do the police officers discuss?

1.2 ▶06 Listen again and match the sentence beginnings and endings.

1	Anybody trying to do that would	a	have opened the door from the inside.
2	After that they might	b	be hiding some information from us.
3	So someone else must	c	have been seen from the street below.
4	Do you think he might	d	have finished examining the building by now.
5	But of course, he might	e	have been expecting them and that he was part of the gang?
6	I suppose he could	f	have been lowered by rope from the roof.
7	The driver must	g	have been waiting nearby.
8	The forensic team should	h	be lying.

1.3 Which of the sentences in 1.2 include these grammatical patterns?

1 modal verb + *have been* + past participle   __1c__ , _____ (would have been seen)
2 modal verb + *have* + past participle   _____ , _____
3 modal verb + *have been* + present participle   _____ , _____
4 modal verb + *be* + present participle   _____ , _____

32

Modals (2) 4

Grammar

2.1 May / might / could + be + present participle; may / might / could + have + past participle

START POINT

*But of course, he **might be lying**.* (not ~~But of course, he can be lying.~~) (= in the present: it's possible he's lying)
*They **could have got** in through a window up on the fourth floor.* (= in the past: it's possible they got in)

With a future time reference we can use *may / might / could + be* + present participle and *may / might / could + have* + past participle to say it is possible that something will happen in the future:
*Nik's flight was cancelled, so he **may/might/could be arriving** much later than expected.*
*The thieves **may/might/could have left** the country by the time we get to the airport.*

2.2 May / might / could + have been + present participle

We can use *may/might/could + have been* + present participle to talk about situations or activities that were possibly happening at a particular past time:
*Do you think he **might have been expecting** them?*

2.3 Would / will + have + past participle

We use *would have* + past participle to talk about an imaginary past situation:
*People **would have seen** them from the street below.*

To show that we think a past situation actually happened, we use *will have* + past participle:
*If they smashed a window to get in, people living nearby **will** certainly **have heard** something.*

2.4 Should / ought to + have + past participle

We use *should / ought to + have* + past participle to talk about something that didn't happen in the past, particularly when we want to imply some regret or criticism:
*He must know that he **ought to have called** the police as soon as he found the door open.*
*We **should have been contacted** earlier.* (passive)

We can also use *should / ought to + have* + past participle to talk about an expectation that something happened, has happened, or will happen:
*The forensic team **should have finished** examining the building by now.*

2.5 Must / can't / couldn't + have + past participle

START POINT

*So someone else **must have opened** the door from the inside.* (active)
*It **must have been opened** from the inside.* (passive)
We can use *must have* + past participle to draw a conclusion about something in the past.

To draw a conclusion about a past event, saying that it was not possible, we use *can't have* + past participle or *couldn't have* + past participle:
*One man alone **couldn't have carried** all those paintings.* (not ... ~~mustn't have carried~~ ...)

33

4 Modals (2)

To draw a conclusion about something happening at a particular past time, saying that it was likely or certain, we use *must have been* + present participle:
The driver **must have been waiting** nearby.

2.6 *Must be* + present participle

We can use *must be* + present participle to draw a conclusion about something happening around the time of speaking. We can use *must be* + present participle or *must be going to* to draw a conclusion about something likely to happen in the future:
I'll speak to the curator of the museum later. She **must be feeling** devastated.
They're taking the head cleaner to the police car. They **must be going to arrest** him. or They **must be arresting** him.

2.7 *Dare* and *need*

> **START POINT**
>
> He gets annoyed easily, so I **daren't criticise** him. / A good car **needn't cost** a lot.
> She **dared** me to jump across. / We **need** to talk to them.
> *Dare* and *need* can be used either as modal verbs (+ bare infinitive) or ordinary verbs (+ *to*-infinitive).

As modals, *dare* and *need* are mostly used in negative contexts. We can use either *dare to* or *dare* (without *to*) when it is not followed by *not*:
But no one would have **dared** (**to**) **climb** up the outside of the building.
I **daren't tell** him I've got another job. (not ~~I daren't to tell~~ ...)

We can't include *to* after *needn't*:
We **needn't interview** everyone in the block. (not ~~We needn't to interview~~ ...)

2.8 *Had better*

We can use *had better* instead of *should / ought to*, especially in spoken English, to say that we think it is a good idea (or not) to do something:
We**'d better find out** all we can about that guard as soon as possible.
We**'d better not go** in until the forensic team has finished.

We use *should* or *ought to* when we talk about the past or make general comments:
I **should / ought to have phoned** her earlier.
People **should / ought to support** the police more. (not ~~People had better~~ ...)

2.9 *Be allowed to*

We can use *could* or *was/were allowed to* to say that in the past someone had general permission to do something:
Only the security guard **could** / **was allowed to stay** in the museum after it closed.

To talk about permission on a particular occasion, we use *was/were allowed to* (not *could*):
Although he had no ID, the man **was allowed to enter** the building.

In negative sentences we can use either *could* or *was/were allowed to* when talking about permission in general or on particular occasions:
They let reporters into the crime scene, but they **couldn't** / **weren't allowed to take** photos.

Modals (2) 4

2.10 Be supposed to

We can use *be supposed to* to express a less strong obligation than with *should* or *ought to*. Using *be supposed to* often suggests that events do not happen as expected:

The entry code **is supposed to be known** *only by the security guard.* (= suggests that it was in fact known by others)

We can use *be supposed to* to report what people think is true:

The building **is supposed to be** *one of the most secure in the country.* (= people say it is.) (not ~~The building should / ought to be~~ ...)

2.11 Other verbs with modal meanings

A number of other verbs are used with similar meanings to modal verbs:

No one **is to** *enter the building until the police give permission.* (= obligation – formal)
Everyone present **was required to** *give a statement to the police.* (= obligation)
How did they **manage to** *get in?* (= ability)
We **have succeeded in** *narrowing down the list of suspects.* (= ability)
He might **be prepared to** *tell us more.* (= willingness)
The suspects **have refused to** *co-operate.* (= unwillingness)
From the evidence found, **it follows that** *it was carefully planned.* (= conclusion – formal)
We can **conclude that** *the paintings were stolen by professionals.* (= conclusion)

Grammar exercises

3.1 Choose the correct verbs.

1. You *should* / <u>*must*</u> have been mad to jump off the wall like that. You *might* / *will* have broken a leg.
2. I *didn't dare to admit* / *couldn't be admitting* that I'd dropped his laptop. He *will have been* / *would have been* so angry with me.
3. The weather forecast said it *might be raining* / *can be raining* later, so *we'd better to* / *we'd better* take an umbrella when we go out.
4. The work on repairing the bridge *is supposed to start* / *ought to start* next month, but there have been a lot of complaints about it. It's the height of the tourist season, so they *couldn't* / *mustn't* have chosen a worse time to do it.
5. Jan *must have to know* / *must have known* the brakes on the car weren't working properly. He really *should have warned* / *had better have warned* me when he sold it to me.
6. There have been yet more delays in building our new office block. They *must* / *were supposed to* have finished by now, but I'm starting to think that I *might* / *can* have retired before it's built.

4 Modals (2)

3.2 Complete the sentences using the verbs from the box in one of these forms:

have + past participle   *be* + present participle
have been + past participle   *have been* + present participle

cause   change   find   ~~snow~~   talk   tempt   wait   work

1 **A:** The clouds are getting really dark.
   B: Yes, I think it could ___be snowing___ by morning.

2 **A:** So how did the explosion happen?
   B: They think it may _____ by a gas leak.

3 **A:** You were born in Wooton, weren't you? It's supposed to be a lovely village.
   B: It certainly used to be, but it may _____ since then – I haven't been there for years.

4 **A:** I rang Wei's doorbell twice, but there was no answer.
   B: He must _____ in the garden.

5 **A:** Cutting those roses was so difficult. I've still got thorns in my hands.
   B: You might _____ it easier if you'd been wearing gloves.

6 **A:** I thought we were meeting Anika outside the theatre.
   B: Yes, but I can't see her. I suppose she might _____ for us inside.

7 **A:** Did you apply for that job in Canada I told you about?
   B: Well, if the salary was higher I might _____ but it was even less than I'm earning now.

8 **A:** When Aya said 'He's really lazy', do you think she meant me?
   B: Well, she could _____ about someone else, I suppose.

3.3 A group of geography students are going on a field trip to Iceland. Their teacher is talking about the arrangements. Rewrite the underlined parts using one of the words or phrases from the box. You need to add extra words in each case.

allow   are to   compulsory   managed   possibility of   recommend   ~~refused~~   succeeded

'Unfortunately, the authorities (1) <u>won't</u> allow us to carry out fieldwork on the glacier. Apparently, because of weather conditions it's not safe at the moment. Instead, (2) <u>we've been able</u> to arrange a boat trip to study coastal features, and (3) <u>we may see</u> whales. So I think (4) <u>you should</u> bring a pair of binoculars if you can. You might want to bring a camera, too. In past years, students have (5) <u>been able to take</u> some excellent photographs during our Iceland fieldwork. Let me remind you, however, that no portable stereos with external speakers (6) <u>should be taken</u> on the trip, although (7) <u>you may</u> bring an MP3 player if you want to. And finally, can you remember that (8) <u>everyone must</u> arrange their own private medical insurance for the trip. I'll check next week that everyone has done this …'

1 ___have refused to___   5 _____
2 _____   6 _____
3 _____   7 _____
4 _____   8 _____

Modals (2) 4

3.4 Read these extracts from newspaper and magazine articles. Choose <u>one</u> phrase from each of the pairs in the box to complete the sentences.

could be facing / can be facing	~~could have been prevented~~ / ~~can have been prevented~~
ought to give / ought to have given	would not have been able to grow / will not be able to grow
might be working / might have been working	must get easier / must be getting easier

1 An enquiry into last year's explosion at the Amcon Refinery that killed 25 workers concluded that it ____could have been prevented____ if the refinery had installed a hazard warning system, as safety officers had recommended.

2 There is some evidence to suggest that Jon Ricci _____ as a secret agent during the 1960s, although even after the end of the Cold War this was never confirmed.

3 Mateus Weber, chief executive of the Schools Examination Authority, said: 'The newspapers claim that the improving results show that exams _____ . But we are absolutely certain that standards have remained the same.'

4 Mr Rosi will return to court on 31 January to hear his sentence, having been warned yesterday that he _____ a long period in prison.

5 Mesi _____ them the lead just before half time, but he shot straight at the goalkeeper, who made an easy save.

6 For centuries the flooding of the Nile was very important because, without it, the people _____ crops in the dry desert. But global warming has changed the traditional patterns of agriculture in this part of the world.

Exam practice

Reading and Use of English Part 4

For questions **1 – 6**, complete the second sentence so that it has a similar meaning to the first sentence, using the word given. **Do not change the word given**. You must use between **three** and **six** words, including the word given. Here is an example **(0)**.

---

0 Those working with pre-school age children will probably find the course interesting.
INTEREST
The course is likely _to be of interest to_ those working with pre-school age children.

1 During the winter I prefer watching football to playing it.
SOONER
During the winter I _____ it.

2 Karen says it takes less than an hour to drive there, but I'm sure she has got it wrong.
MUST
Karen says it takes less than an hour to drive there, but she _____ a mistake.

3 Students wishing to enrol on the course should complete all sections of the application form.
REQUIRED
Students wishing to enrol on the course _____ in all sections of the application form.

4 I wish I had considered the question more carefully before answering.
THOUGHT
I should _____ the question more carefully before answering.

5 The factory has been able to reduce its CO_2 emissions by 50% in the last year.
SUCCEEDED
The factory _____ back its CO_2 emissions by 50% in the last year.

6 It's a long walk home, so I advise you not to miss the last train.
BETTER
It's a long walk home, so _____ the last train.

5 Nouns, agreement and articles

Compound nouns and noun phrases; subject–verb agreement; countable and uncountable nouns; articles

Context listening

1.1 Nazim has applied to do a college course in Environmental Science. You are going to listen to part of his interview for a place on the course. What questions do you think the interviewer will ask?

1.2 ▶07 Listen and check whether you were right.

1.3 ▶07 Listen again and write one word in each gap to complete the compound nouns.

1 climate ____change____
2 _____-making
3 rain _____
4 river _____
5 _____-saving
6 lighting _____
7 _____ scheme
8 the arms _____
9 mountain _____

1.4 Which of the following forms do each of the compound nouns from 1.3 take?

noun + noun ____1,____   -ing form + noun _____   noun + -ing form _____

1.5 Ignoring the shaded parts for now, complete these pairs of sentences from the interview with *a*, *the* or – (=no article).

1 a There's been _____ drought there for a number of months, and river levels are low.
  b The main problem has been the effect of _____ drought on food supplies.
2 a And what are your plans for _____ future?
  b It's hard to imagine _____ future without farming in an area like that.
3 a What do you want to do after you've left _____ college?
  b Have you got any questions about the course here at _____ college?

1.6 Can you explain the difference in meaning of the shaded parts of the sentences?

39

5 Nouns, agreement and articles

Grammar

2.1 Compound nouns and noun phrases

START POINT

Common compound noun patterns:

noun + noun	-ing form + noun	noun + -ing form
climate change	recycling scheme	energy-saving

Some compound nouns are usually written as one word (e.g. *rainforest*), some as separate words (e.g. *river levels*), and others with a hyphen (-) (e.g. *decision-making*).

The first noun in a compound usually has a singular form, even if it has a plural meaning:
decision-making (not *decisions-making*)

Instead of a compound noun we can use:
- noun + 's + noun when the first noun is the user of the second noun:
  a **women's** clinic, a **boys'** school
- noun + preposition + noun:
  a **book about energy conservation**, a **book about grammar** (*a grammar book* is also common)

We can sometimes use noun + 's + noun or noun + *of* + noun with a similar meaning:
the **charity's aim** or the **aim of the charity**

We are more likely to use noun + 's + noun:
- when the first noun refers to a particular person or group of people or to talk about time:
  Mike's job, **next year's** field trip

We more often use noun + *of* + noun:
- when the second noun is a non-living thing:
  the **title of the CD**
- when we talk about a process or change over time:
  the **destruction of the rainforest**
- with a long noun phrase:
  Mike is **the brother of someone I went to school with**.

Compounds often combine with other nouns or compounds to form longer combinations:
decision-making process, energy conservation scheme

2.2 Subject–verb agreement

Some nouns with a singular form, referring to a group (e.g. *government, class, department, team*), can be used with either a singular or plural form of the verb, although in formal contexts a singular verb is often preferred:
*The government **has** (or **have**) introduced some really interesting projects.*

We usually use a singular verb:
- when names and titles (e.g. of countries, newspapers, books, films) ending in *-s* refer to a single unit:
  *The **Netherlands has** begun to tackle the problem.*
- with a phrase referring to a measurement, amount or quantity:
  *Only **a few miles separates** the villages.*
- after *percent* (also *per cent* or %) referring to a singular or uncountable noun:
  *... **10%** of the country's **energy comes** from wind power.*

Nouns, agreement and articles 5

But if *percent* refers to a plural noun we use a plural verb:
*… **60%** of **people** there **are** malnourished.*

We usually use a plural verb:
- with nouns that normally have a plural form: *congratulations, outskirts, clothes*. But note that the following nouns ending in *-s* take a singular verb – *news, linguistics, mathematics, physics, politics, statistics* and *economics* when they refer to the academic subject:
 ***Statistics is** included in the course.* (not *Statistics are* …)
- after *a/the majority of, a/the minority of, a number of, a lot of, plenty of, all (of), some of* + a plural noun / pronoun:
 ***The majority of** people there **are** farmers.*
 But note that we use a singular verb with *the number of*:
 ***The number of** people suffering from malnutrition **is** increasing.*

The following verb must agree with the main noun in a sentence with a complex subject:
***Levels** of income from the sale of handicrafts **have** increased.*

When the subject follows the verb, the verb agrees with the subject:
*Among the projects invested in by the government **is the use** of low-energy light bulbs.*

2.3 Countable and uncountable nouns

> **START POINT**
>
> Many nouns in English are uncountable: they are not used with *a/an* or in the plural. For example: *advice, equipment, information*.

Some nouns are used uncountably when we are talking about the general idea, but countably when we are talking about particular examples:
*You'd be able to get by with **a** basic **knowledge** of some statistical techniques.* but *The desire for **knowledge** is a fundamental human instinct.*
*The charity's project has been **a success**.* (= a particular example of success)
*Financial **success** isn't everything.* (= success in general)
Other nouns like this include: *business, education, sound*. Some of these (e.g. *education*) are only used countably in the singular.
Some nouns (e.g. *accommodation, speech, work*) have a different meaning when they are used countably and uncountably. Compare:
*She gave **a speech** about global warming.*
*Children usually develop **speech** in their second year.*

We can use *a good / great deal of* and *amount of* before uncountable nouns:
*There's **a great deal of** interest in recycling in the country.*
*It's saving an enormous **amount of** waste.*
Using these before a plural countable noun is incorrect and you should avoid it in exams. However, they are sometimes used in this way in informal contexts.

We use *a number of* before plural countable nouns:
*There's been a drought there for **a number of months**.*
and *plenty of* and *a quantity of* before either uncountable or plural countable nouns:
*There was **plenty of opportunity** for me to travel around the country.*
*I saw **a** huge **quantity of trees** being cut down.*

41

5 Nouns, agreement and articles

2.4 Articles

We use *the*:
- with singular, plural or uncountable nouns when we expect the listener or reader to be able to identify the thing or person referred to:
  It's a project run by a European charity. **The** *charity's aim …*
- when a following phrase or clause identifies what particular thing we are talking about:
  the *climate* **in this region**, **the** *impact* **of climate change**, **the** *ecology* **of mountain environments*
- when we talk about things that are unique:
  in one part of **the** *world,* **the** *sky,* **the** *future;* **the** *first/next time;* **the** *only/main problem;* **the** *smallest improvement,* **the** *arms trade,* **the** *environment*
  Some 'unique' nouns can be used with *a/an* when we describe a type or aspect of the thing. Compare:
  What are your plans for **the** *future?* and *It's hard to imagine* **a** *future without farming in an area like that.*

We use *a/an*:
- when a singular countable noun is introduced for the first time into a spoken or written text:
  He's the head of **a** *project run by* **a** *European charity.*
- to talk about an unspecified person, thing or event:
  I didn't have **a** *shower for days.*
- to describe someone/something or say what type of thing someone/something is:
  It's **a** *beautiful country.*   *It's* **an** *international organisation.*
- to say what a person's job is:
  You think that as **a** *politician, you'd be able to do this?*
  But note that we use *the* or no article to give a person's title or their unique position:
  He's **the** *head of a project there.* or *He's head of a project there.*
- in number and quantity expressions:
  a *month or so,* **a** *couple of weeks, half* **an** *hour, three times* **a** *year, 50 cents* **a** *litre,* **a** *huge number of,* **a** *bit*

We use no article:
- with uncountable and plural nouns when we talk generally about people or things rather than about specific people or things:
  I've always been fascinated by **plants** *and* **animals***.*   *They haven't had* **rain** *for months.*
- with some singular nouns referring to institutions (e.g. *school, college, hospital, prison, university, work*) when we talk about them generally. Compare: *after you've left college* and *the course here at* **the** *college*
- with most countries: *Brazil, Switzerland, Norway* but **the** *Netherlands,* **the** *USA,* **the** *UK,* **the** *Philippines,* **the** *Gambia*
- with the names of months and days of the week: *in June, on Monday;* special times of the year: *during Ramadan, at Easter;* (or *the*) with seasons: *I like to go skiing in winter* or *… in the winter.* However, we generally use *the* to talk about a particular month, day, etc.: *I'm going to Nepal in* **the** *summer* (= next summer)
- with meals when we talk about the next one: *What's for dinner?*; a recent one: *What did you have for breakfast?*; or a meal in general: *I usually have toast for breakfast.* However, we generally use articles to talk about a particular meal or particular meals: *We had* **an** *early dinner,* **The** *breakfast in the hotel is great.*
- with *by* to talk about means of communication and transport: **by** *post/email/phone;* **by** *car/taxi/bus/plane/air/sea*

5 Nouns, agreement and articles

Grammar exercises

3.1 Choose the correct phrase.

1 I don't like tomatoes, so I left them at *the side of the plate* / *the plate's side*.
2 It was *the decision of Adam* / *Adam's decision* to take out the loan, so he has to take responsibility for repaying it.
3 I saw two great TV programmes last week. The first was *an action film* / *a film about action*, and the second *a documentary about young entrepreneurs* / *a young entrepreneurs documentary*.
4 John is someone *I worked with in Malaysia's brother* / *the brother of someone I worked with in Malaysia*.
5 He apologised without *the hesitation of a moment* / *a moment's hesitation*.
6 My house is by *a children playground* / *a children's playground*, so it can be quite noisy.
7 *The construction of the new library* / *The new library's construction* took so long that building costs were ten times higher than first expected.
8 When I got home I found that an envelope had been pushed through my *letters box* / *letter box*. In it was *a congratulations card* / *a congratulation card* from Aunt Alice.

3.2 Nazim has been accepted on the Environmental Science course (see 1.1). Read this email he sent to a friend during a field trip. Fill in the gaps with a present tense form of the verbs in brackets.

Hi Cathy,

Greetings from Nepal! I'm sending this from an internet café in a small town north of Kathmandu.
The town itself isn't very interesting, but the surroundings **(1)** ___are___ (*be*) beautiful – I can see the Himalayas through the café window!

The lectures here are brilliant. The Politics and Ecology courses are great, but Economics **(2)** _____ (*be*) really difficult – although maths **(3)** _____ (*be*) certainly not my strong point! I'm really learning a lot about the country and its environmental problems. A lot of Nepal's population **(4)** _____ (*live*) in the mountainous parts of the country south of the Himalayas, and the majority of these people **(5)** _____ (*depend*) on growing crops and keeping animals. The standard of living in Kathmandu and the other cities **(6)** _____ (*have*) risen a lot recently, and the number of people likely to move into the cities **(7)** _____ (*be*) expected to increase. It's a real problem here. The Himalayan Times, the local English-language newspaper, **(8)** _____ (*have*) just published a survey showing that most young people would stay in their home villages if jobs were available.

I was planning on coming home at the end of June, but the college **(9)** _____ (*have*) arranged for a few of us to stay during the summer on a WWF conservation project in a region in the north called Helambu – there **(10)** _____ (*be*) just a few kilometres between the village where I'll be working and the border with China. Among the various projects that have been set up **(11)** _____ (*be*) a scheme for producing biogas locally – that's gas produced from plant and animal waste. All my living expenses **(12)** _____ (*be*) being paid for by the WWF.

Hope all is well with you. I'll send more news when I can.

Nazim

43

5 Nouns, agreement and articles

3.3 Choose one word or phrase from each of the pairs in the box to complete the sentences. In some cases, both words or phrases are correct.

advertising / advertisements	advice / tips	explosives / ammunition
fresh fruit / vegetables	jobs / work	~~meetings / foreign travel~~
rubbish / empty bottles	salt / cups of coffee	

1 Her job involves a good deal of _foreign travel_ .
2 Make sure you eat plenty of _____
3 What I don't like about the magazine is the huge number of _____ in it.
4 I think you ought to cut down on the amount of _____ you have. It's not good for you.
5 The Students' Handbook includes a great deal of _____ on study skills.
6 The police found a rifle and a large quantity of _____ in his apartment.
7 I have a huge amount of _____ to do at the weekend.
8 I was shocked by the amount of _____ left behind after the party.

3.4 Fill in the gaps using the words in the box. Use the same word to complete the sentences in each pair. Add *a*/*an* if necessary.

| competition | ~~conversation~~ | importance | iron | knowledge | paper | shampoo | time |

1 a He lists his interests as reading, listening to music and good _conversation_ .
  b It's difficult to hold _a conversation_ with Sarah because she keeps interrupting.
2 a Customers have benefited from lower prices resulting from _____ between the supermarkets.
  b A: I see you've bought a new bike.
    B: Actually, I won it in _____ .
3 a Our council is encouraging everyone to recycle _____ .
  b Professor Tench has recently published _____ on her research.
4 a You can only tell whether you like _____ by washing your hair with it a few times.
  b A: Do we need anything from the chemist's?
    B: Just _____ and a tube of toothpaste.
5 a Don't leave the flower pot outside. It's made of _____ and it'll rust.
  b I burnt a hole in my trousers with _____ .
6 a Has there ever been _____ when you've regretted moving to Australia?
  b Definitions of poverty have changed over _____ .
7 a When parents take an active role in schools, children see their parents placing _____ on their education.
  b The manuscript is of great historical _____ .
8 a Humans are driven by the pursuit of _____ .
  b Living in Dublin gave me _____ of Irish history.

Nouns, agreement and articles 5

3.5 Add *a*, *an* or *the* to these texts where necessary.

1 a   an   the (x 3)

My brother wasn't very good at taking exams and he left school at 16. At first he went to work in **the** construction industry. But he didn't enjoy it, so he took evening course in accounting. Eventually, he started company offering financial advice. He's now managing director, and it seems that company's doing really well.

2 a (x 3)   an   the (x 3)

A: Do you remember summer we went to Sweden? 1995, I think it was.

B: It was wonderful holiday, wasn't it? And so good to see Joakim again. I'll never forget picnic we had with him. There were huge number of mosquitoes.

A: Yes, I remember. And when sun was going down there was amazing red sky.

B: And then his car broke down on the way home, and we had to go back by bus.

A: No, we got taxi, didn't we?

B: Oh yes, that's right.

3 a (x 4)   the (x 5)

Fatimah has busy life as lawyer, but in her free time she really enjoys hiking. Most weekends she drives out into countryside and walks for few hours. She says she likes to forget about work, and she doesn't even take mobile phone with her. In summer she's going hiking in Philippines. She's never been there before, but friend she's going with knows country well.

Exam practice

Reading and Use of English Part 2

For questions **1 – 8**, read the text below and think of the word which best fits each gap. Use only **one** word in each gap. There is an example at the beginning **(0)**.

The origins of chess

A great **(0)** _deal_ has been written about the origins of modern chess, and there **(1)** _____ still considerable debate about the subject. **(2)** _____ theory most widely accepted is that its earliest ancestor was Shaturanga, a game played in India from around AD 600. **(3)** _____ with modern chess, Shaturanga was played on a board with 64 squares. Pieces such as kings, queens and knights were able to move in different ways with **(4)** _____ aim of capturing other pieces and, at the end of the game, the opponent's king. Unlike chess, it was played by four people. In the form in **(5)** _____ it is played today, chess appeared in southern Europe around the end of the fifteenth century. Today, chess has become one of the world's **(6)** _____ popular games. It is played by millions of people both informally and in tournaments, and **(7)** _____ number of people playing online **(8)** _____ increasing with access to the Internet.

6 Determiners and quantifiers

No, none, not a, not any; much, many, a lot of, lots of; all, both, whole; every, each; (a/the) few, little; less, fewer (than); much, many, etc. + (of)

Context listening

1.1 You are going to listen to three people talking about running. Make notes on three benefits and three possible problems of taking up running as a hobby.

_____
_____

1.2 ▶08 Listen to three people giving their views on running. Which of the benefits and possible problems you have listed do the speakers mention?

_____
_____

1.3 ▶08 Listen again and fill in the gaps.

1 a Until then I did a bit of sport at school, but I didn't do ___*much*___ outside school at all. (*Speaker 1*)

   b In fact, I suppose I didn't have _____ interests. (*Speaker 1*)

2 a Now I run a few kilometres _____ day. (*Speaker 2*)

   b You can be sure that _____ one of us will have a really good time. (*Speaker 3*)

3 a Inevitably you get _____ injuries, too – everyone gets aching muscles after a long run. (*Speaker 3*)

   b It's one of _____ sports where no special equipment's needed. (*Speaker 2*)

4 a I certainly go out a lot _____ during the winter. (*Speaker 3*)

   b But surprisingly I seem to have _____ injuries now than when I was younger. (*Speaker 3*)

1.4 In which pair of sentences is each word or phrase possible in both gaps?

_____

6 Determiners and quantifiers

Grammar

2.1 No, none, not a, not any

> **START POINT**
>
> **No** two pairs of running shoes are the same. (= not any)
> **None of** them like the thought of running long distances. (= not any of)

We use *neither of* instead of *none of* when we talk about two people or things:
Neither of us did any exercise.

We don't usually use *not a* / *not any* at the beginning of a clause. Instead we use *no* and *none of*:
None of the runners is under 60. (not ~~Not any of the runners~~ ...)

If it is clear from the context what is meant, we can use *none* without a following noun:
I've had **none** so far. (= e.g. no injuries)

2.2 Much, many, a lot of, lots of

> **START POINT**
>
> Did you do **much** running last winter?
> There could be **many** reasons for the current interest in running.
> I get **a lot of** satisfaction out of it.
> You get to meet **lots of** interesting people.
> We use *much* (*of*) (+ uncountable noun) and *many* (*of*) (+ plural noun) particularly in negative sentences and in questions. In positive sentences we usually use *a lot* (*of*) or *lots* (*of*). However, in more formal contexts we usually prefer *much* (*of*) and *many* (*of*).

If the meaning is clear from the context, we can use *much* and *many* without a following noun:
I didn't do **much** outside school at all.

We can use *much of* and *many of* to mean 'a large part of' or 'a large number of':
I used to spend **much of** my free time sitting around.
I was in first place for **much of** the race.

We use *many* rather than *a lot of* or *lots of* with time expressions (e.g. *days, minutes, months, weeks, years*) and 'number' + *of* (e.g. *thousands of dollars*):
I spend **many hours** training.
Running clubs often have **many hundreds of members**.

6 Determiners and quantifiers

2.3 All, both, whole

> **START POINT**
>
> **All** (**of**) my friends like watching sport on TV.
> I suppose **all** exercise carries some risks.
> By the time we got to the bus stop **both of** us were completely exhausted.
> I thought **the whole** event was brilliant.
> Sometimes I go **whole** weeks without running.

We usually put *all* after the verb *be* or after the first auxiliary verb:
Next spring we**'re all** going to Madrid.
They **could all have** been Olympic athletes.
If there is no auxiliary, we usually put *all* before the verb:
We **all went** running together.
We sometimes use *all* after the noun it refers to:
My friends **all** think I'm crazy. or **All** my friends think I'm crazy.
To talk about two things or people we use *both* (*of*) in positive sentences or *neither* (*of*) in negative sentences:
We certainly **both** got a lot fitter. **Both of** us were completely exhausted.
Neither of us did any exercise. (not ~~Both of us didn't do any exercise.~~)
Before singular countable nouns we usually use *the whole* rather than *all* (*of*) *the*:
I thought **the whole** event was brilliant.
Before *day / week / night / month / summer*, etc. we prefer *all* rather than *the whole*:
After I've been sitting at my computer **all day** I can't wait to go out for a run.
I might go **all week** without a run.
We can use *all the* or *the whole* before *way* and *time*:
I was really surprised when I managed to run **all the way**. or … **the whole way**.

2.4 Every, each

> **START POINT**
>
> I go running on Wednesday and on Friday, and I try to run ten miles **each** day. or … **every** day.
> **Every** one of us will have a really good time. or **Each** one of us …
> Before a singular countable noun, we use *each* (*of*) to talk about two or more things or people, and *every* to talk about three or more. Sometimes we can use either *every* or *each* with little difference in meaning.

We use *every*:
- with *almost, nearly, practically, virtually* to emphasise we are talking about a group as a whole:
  Now I run **nearly every** day.
- to talk about events at regular intervals: *every other kilometre, every single day, every few weeks, every six months*:
  I go out running **every couple of days**.

We use *each*:
- when we talk about both people or things in a pair:
  I had to wear a bandage on **each** knee. or … on **both** knees.
- as a pronoun:
  We were **each** given a medal for completing the 5-kilometre fun run.

6 Determiners and quantifiers

2.5 (A/the) few, little; less, fewer (than)

> **START POINT**
>
> A **few of** my friends are quite good at team sports.
> I seem to have **fewer** injuries now than when I was younger.
> There is **little** evidence that running causes major problems.
> You should eat **less** protein as you prepare for a race.
> There's **not much** you can do about it. (See **2.6** for more on *much* (and *many*))
> *Few* (*of*) and *little* (*of*) are often rather formal. Less formally, we use phrases such as *not many* and *not much*.

We often use *a few* and *a little* to suggest that a small quantity or amount is enough, or more than we would expect:
He's won **a few medals**.   I've been starting to get **a little pain** in my knees.

In formal contexts, we often use *few* and *little* to suggest that a quantity or amount is not enough, or is surprisingly low:
Before I joined the club I had very **few friends** who lived nearby.

In comparisons, we use *less* with an uncountable noun, and *fewer* with a plural noun:
I should eat **less chocolate**.   You should eat **fewer biscuits**.

The opposite of both *less* and *fewer* is *more*:
I should eat **more chocolate**.   You should eat **more biscuits**.

In conversation, some people also use *less* (*than*) before a plural noun referring to a group of things or people:
There were **less than** 20 competitors.
This is grammatically incorrect and would be marked wrong in a formal written exam. *Fewer* (*than*) should be used instead:
There were **fewer than** 20 competitors.

When we talk about a period of time, a distance or a sum of money, we use *less than*:
My aim is to complete the course and do it in **less than** six hours. (not ... ~~fewer than six hours.~~)

2.6 Much, many, both, all, each, none, few, little + (of)

We usually need to put *of* after these words when they are followed by:
- a pronoun: We know that not **all of us** will finish the course.
- a determiner: **Few of the** runners were under 65.
- a possessive form: **Many of Alice's** friends are runners.

Informally after *both* and *all* we can leave out *of* before *the, these, those; this, that* (with *all*); possessive pronouns (e.g. *my, mine*) but not before *them, you, us; it* (with *all*):
I've been running regularly **all of my life**. or ... **all my life**.
Both of us decided to do more exercise. (not ~~Both us decided~~ ...)

6 Determiners and quantifiers

Grammar exercises

3.1 Fill in the gaps using the correct form of the verb in brackets. Sometimes both are possible.

1 Next week, my work colleagues are doing a bike ride across France for charity. They won't cycle the whole way – they each ___do___ (do) 30 kilometres a day and follow by car the rest of the time. That's just as well, because none of them _____ (be) terribly fit. A number of people _____ (have) already agreed to sponsor them, and they hope to raise a lot of money.

2 I think that everything _____ (be) now ready for the party. One of my sisters _____ (have) organised the drinks, and each of the people coming _____ (have) agreed to bring some food.

3 I'm having trouble selling my house. Although a lot of interest _____ (have) been shown in it – I've had lots of phone calls and visitors – the majority of potential buyers _____ (seem) surprised at how small it is. And not everybody _____ (like) the fact that there's no garden.

3.2 Choose the correct option.

1 The nuclear power station is in an earthquake zone, and it's worrying that there have been *a few* / *few* minor tremors here in the last couple of months.
2 There were four candidates in the election and *every* / *each* got about 5,000 votes.
3 The hurricane will go north of the city, so *little* / *a little* major damage is expected.
4 *We were all* / *We all were* astonished by her exam results.
5 Is there *less* / *fewer* caffeine in green tea than in coffee?
6 These old bookshelves *will all be* / *all will be* replaced by cupboards.
7 It takes me *fewer* / *less* than 30 minutes to walk to work.
8 When I was in hospital, Martha visited me *each* / *every* single day.
9 Although the management said they were going to restructure the company, in fact they made *a few* / *few* changes.
10 Nowadays, *nearly every* / *nearly each* new car is fitted with airbags.
11 When I got on, *all of the* / *the whole* bus seemed to be full of screaming schoolchildren.
12 The company has *fewer* / *less* than 20 employees.

3.3 Complete the sentences using the pairs of words or phrases in the box. Use each word or phrase once only in each pair.

many / a lot of   no / not any   ~~neither of / none of~~   much / a lot of   not any of / none of

1 a A flight from Amsterdam overshot the runway at Heathrow Airport yesterday, but ___none of___ the crew or passengers was hurt.
  b My parents came all the way to Sydney to see me, even though ___neither of___ them likes flying very much.
2 a I hope you like the present. I put _____ effort into finding it.
  b Among linguists, there is _____ debate about the origin of the word 'quiz'.

51

6 Determiners and quantifiers

3   a   The new anti-malaria drug took _____ years to develop.

    b   I've got _____ friends who live in Hong Kong.

4   a   The government has allocated two million euros to the project, but _____ the money has been spent yet.

    b   **A:** Have you been able to fix your car?

        B: No. It's _____ the usual problems, so I'll have to take it to the garage.

5   a   _____ major damage was done to the building by the earthquake.

    b   I tried to organise a tennis competition at my college, but there was _____ interest, so I gave up the idea.

3.4 Complete the newspaper article with one of these words or phrases. Use each word and phrase once.

| all | ~~all of~~ | all (of) | both | both of | each of | every | ~~few~~ | few of |
| little | little of | many | many of | much | much of | none | none of | |

'5 PORTIONS A DAY' FALLS ON DEAF EARS

Despite the government's '5 portions a day' recommendation to eat more fruit and vegetables, a recent study has found that **(1)** ___few___ British teenagers are taking its advice. A thousand teenagers were questioned in the survey, **(2)** ___all of___ them between the ages of 14 and 17. While **(3)** _____ said they knew about the campaign, **(4)** _____ the young people questioned, just 5%, said it had influenced their eating habits. In answer to the question 'How many pieces of fruit have you eaten in the last week?', an incredible 50% responded '**(5)** _____'.

Sam Brown, 15, and Sarah Goodall, 16, were among the young people who took part in the survey. **(6)** _____ them conceded that fruit and vegetables didn't figure greatly in their diets. Sam admitted: 'I don't eat **(7)** _____ fruit at all, maybe just an apple sometimes. I don't think **(8)** _____ my friends are different.' Sarah felt that the busy lifestyle of today's teenagers was partly to blame: 'I'm not into vegetables, and **(9)** _____ the time I'm too busy to eat fruit after dinner. I've got homework to do or friends to see.' **(10)** _____ agreed that the government's campaign wouldn't affect what they ate. Sam said: '**(11)** _____ the posters and adverts are hard-hitting enough. Their message is just 'Eat fruit or veg with **(12)** _____ meal.' If they want teenagers to eat more fruit and vegetables, they've got to convince us that it's really important.'

(13) _____ scientists have warned that failure to eat fruit and vegetables, particularly by young people, can lead to obesity, cancer and a host of other diseases. Professor Jess Adams from Queen's Hospital said: '**(14)** _____ the research points to a close relationship between levels of fruit and vegetable consumption and health, but surprisingly **(15)** _____ this research is reported in the press or on television. This means that the message is not getting across. The government tries to highlight the problem with its campaigns, but unfortunately there is **(16)** _____ sign that they have any long-term impact. Ultimately, however, it's up to **(17)** _____ us to think about what we eat and make healthy choices.'

Exam practice

Determiners and quantifiers **6**

Listening Part 2

▶09 You will hear a woman called Janet Naylor talking about her experience as a volunteer in Tanzania. For questions **1 – 8**, complete the sentences with a word or short phrase.

Janet can now do voluntary work because she is free of (**1**) _____.

Most of Janet's friends were (**2**) _____ by her decision to volunteer.

Janet disagrees with people who say that she is (**3**) _____ the people she is trying to help.

Janet advised on a project to improve (**4**) _____ in a farming community.

The scheme aimed to make the villagers less (**5**) _____ on outside assistance.

The villagers had relied on (**6**) _____ from charities to survive.

Janet's job was to help the villagers sell any (**7**) _____ crops.

Janet believes that the (**8**) _____ of the village have been changed dramatically by the scheme.

7 Adverbs and adjectives

Position of adverbs; *quite, rather, already, yet, still, even, only, really*; position of adjectives; gradable adjectives; patterns after adjectives

Context listening

1.1 You are going to hear an interview with an author. In the interview he mentions three countries. Look at these photos (a–c). Which countries do you think they show?

1.2 ▶10 Listen and check whether you were right. Why is each of these countries important to the author?

1.3 Read these eight extracts from the interview. Where did the words in brackets appear? Choose position a, b or c.

1 I suppose (a) I'd (b) been (c) a writer. (*always*)   ___b___
2 I left teaching and (a) I started (b) writing (c). (*professionally*)   _____
3 I go back (a) on (b) every (c) occasion. (*possible*)   _____
4 (a) I (b) know (c) how a book is going to end. (*always*)   _____
5 I'm (a) up at about (b) 7.00 in (c) the morning. (*generally*)   _____
6 (a) I (b) prefer finding (c) information from books. (*as a rule*)   _____
7 I (a) still speak (b) Swedish (c). (*quite well*)   _____
8 My mother was a (a) gentle (b) woman (c). (*rather*)   _____
9 I'm (a) sketching (b) out (c) the plot. (*still*)   _____

▶10 Listen again and check your answers.

1.4 Read these further extracts from the interview. Tick (✓) those where you can add *very* before the underlined adjective and put a cross (✗) where this is not possible.

1 Some of my close friends thought I was <u>mad</u> to give up my job.   ___✗___
2 I rarely have a <u>clear</u> idea at the beginning of how the characters will develop.   _____
3 I was <u>happy</u> to teach during the day.   _____
4 It felt <u>fantastic</u> having my first book published.   _____
5 I've just finished his <u>excellent</u> novel *Restless*.   _____
6 I felt <u>bad</u> leaving the children.   _____
7 There are a lot of <u>historical</u> links between Norway and the north of Scotland.   _____
8 My mother was a rather gentle woman and always <u>calm</u>.   _____

Adverbs and adjectives 7

Grammar

2.1 Position of adverbs

> **START POINT**
>
> There are three main positions in a clause for adverbs:
> - front position (before the subject):
>   **Normally**, I write for about six hours a day.
> - mid position (between the subject and verb, immediately after *be* as a main verb, or after the first or second auxiliary verb):
>   I **usually start** work by about 8.00. I'**m generally** up at about 7.00. I **had never** been to Norway before. If my books hadn't been successful, I would **happily have** stayed in teaching. or I would **have happily** stayed ...
> - end position (after the verb; either immediately after it or later in the clause):
>   He writes **simply**.
>
> Many adverbs can go in any of these positions, depending on the context or style of writing:
> **Gradually**, they grow into real people. or They **gradually** grow .... or They grow **gradually** ....

Some adverbs tend to appear in particular positions:
- *Always, never*; adverbs of indefinite frequency (*hardly ever, often, rarely, regularly, seldom*); and degree adverbs (*almost, hardly, nearly, quite, rather, scarcely*) are usually put in mid position:
  I **rarely have** a clear idea. I **always know** how a book is going to end.
- *Constantly, continually, regularly; absolutely, completely, entirely, greatly, perfectly* are usually put either in mid or end position, but not in front position:
  I **greatly admire** William Boyd. or I **admire** William Boyd **greatly**. (not ~~Greatly I admire~~ ...)
- Adverbs of place are usually put in end position:
  I work **upstairs**. (not ~~Upstairs I work~~. / ~~I upstairs work~~.)
- Adverbs of definite time and frequency are usually put in end position:
  I finished my previous book **last January**. (not ~~I last January finished~~ ...)
- Adverbs of time or frequency consisting of more than one word (e.g. *as a rule, from time to time, every so often*) are usually put either in front or end position, but not mid position:
  As a rule, I prefer finding information from books. (not ~~I as a rule prefer~~ ...)

We avoid putting an adverb between a main verb and a direct object, or following an *-ing* form or *to-*infinitive:
I still speak Swedish **quite well**. (not ~~I still speak quite well Swedish~~.)
I started writing **professionally**. (not ~~I started professionally writing~~.)
I'd like to go back **again**. (not ~~I'd like to go again back~~.)

In end position we usually put adverbs of place before adverbs of time:
I hadn't been to Norway **before**. (not ~~I hadn't been before to Norway~~.)

2.2 Quite, rather; already, yet, still; even, only; really

- Quite, rather

The usual position for *quite* is before *a/an* and an adjective, where it means 'moderately':
Elsa is **quite a dominant** figure.
Less often, *quite* is used between *a/an* and an adjective, where it means 'completely':
It's **a quite remarkable** story.

55

7 Adverbs and adjectives

The usual position for *rather* is between *a/an* and an adjective. Less often, but with a similar meaning, *rather* is used before *a/an* and an adjective:
*My mother was **a rather gentle** woman.* or *My mother was **rather a gentle** woman.*

- Already, yet, still

Already can go in either mid or end position:
*I'd **already decided** that I wanted to write ...* or *I'd **decided already** ...*
Yet is usually put in end position in negatives, questions and expressions of uncertainty:
*I **don't know** if I can tell you **yet**.*
Still usually goes in mid position:
*I'm **still sketching** out the plot.*

- Even, only

Even and *only* usually go in mid position:
*He **can even speak** Swedish.*
but if they refer to the subject they usually come before it:
*Sometimes **even I'm** surprised. **Only my close family** had read anything I'd written.*

- Really

The meaning of *really* can change according to its position in a sentence. Immediately before an adjective it means 'very'. In other positions it can mean 'actually' or 'in fact':
*I'd been feeling **really tired**.*
*My friends thought I was joking, but I **really** had decided to leave teaching.*

2.3 Position of adjectives

> **START POINT**
>
> *His **excellent** novel.   His novel is **excellent**.*
> Many adjectives can be used either before the noun they describe, or following the noun and a linking verb such as *be, become, feel* and *seem* that connects a subject with a word or phrase that describes the subject.

The following adjectives can be used immediately after a noun:
- many participle adjectives (i.e. adjectives that end with *-ing* or *-ed*. See **Unit 12, 2.1** for more on participle clauses):
  *There'll be a lot of **people waiting** eagerly to get hold of it.* (= a lot of people who will be waiting)
  *Some of the geographical **settings used** in A Woman Alone are based on places I visited.* (= settings which are used in A Woman Alone)
- adjectives used after indefinite pronouns (e.g. *something, nothing*):
  *I really don't think it was **anything special**.*
  *There was **nothing extraordinary** about my first novel.*

2.4 Gradable adjectives

If an adjective is gradable, we can say that a person or thing can have more or less of the quality referred to (e.g. *ambitious, busy*). Gradable adjectives can be used with adverbs such as *extremely, slightly* or *very*:
***somewhat** ambitious, **extremely** busy, **slightly** different, **very** rich, **pretty** strong*

If an adjective is non-gradable, we don't usually imagine degrees of the quality referred to (e.g. *huge, impossible*). To emphasise the extreme or absolute nature of non-gradable adjectives we can use adverbs such as *absolutely, completely* or *totally*:
***absolutely** huge, **completely** impossible, **practically** unknown, **almost** unique, **totally** useless*

Adverbs and adjectives 7

Some adjectives have both gradable and non-gradable uses:
- some (e.g. *common*) have gradable and non-gradable uses with different meanings:
  *Bardreth isn't a very **common** surname.* (gradable: common = frequent)
  *Elsa and my mother have certain **common** characteristics.* (non-gradable: common = similar)
- some (e.g. *diplomatic*) have gradable and non-gradable uses with related meanings:
  *You're being very **diplomatic**.* (gradable because it refers to the quality the person has)
  *He worked as the **diplomatic** correspondent of a national newspaper.* (non-gradable because it refers to the type of correspondent he is)

2.5 Patterns after adjectives

When an adjective comes after a linking verb, we can use a number of patterns after the adjective, including a *to*-infinitive or an *-ing* form:
*I **was unwilling to leave** teaching.*
*It **felt fantastic having** my first book published.*
*Some of my close friends thought I **was mad to give up** my job.* or *... **was mad giving up** my job.*

Many adjectives can be followed by a *that*-clause, including some that can also be followed by a *to*-infinitive or an *-ing* form:
*I **was aware that** I needed rest.*
*I **was** greatly **relieved that** my subsequent books sold quite well.* or *... **was** greatly **relieved to find** ...*
*I **felt bad that** I was leaving the children* or *I **felt bad leaving** ...*

Grammar exercises

3.1 Complete the sentences by writing the words in brackets in the correct order. Give alternatives where possible.

1 Not wanting to wake the children, I climbed ____the stairs quietly____ . (quietly – stairs – the)
2 She _____ her parents. (ever – hardly – visits)
3 When I bumped into his car, he began _____ at me. (angrily – shout – to)
4 Juan thinks we should sell our car and buy bikes instead, and _____ with him. (absolutely – agree – I)
5 Natalie is on a working holiday in New Zealand. She _____ and should be home at the end of June. (last – left – week)
6 _____ for a meal after work to catch up on news. (go – occasionally – we)
7 We _____ to see a film. (go – out – seldom)
8 As I walked out of the room, she _____ . (loudly – singing – started)

57

7 Adverbs and adjectives

3.2 Complete the sentences using the adjectives in the box. Use the same adjective in each pair of sentences. If possible, include the adverb given in brackets.

(severely) critical	(very) genuine	(rather) odd
(highly) original	~~(extremely) particular~~	(thoroughly) professional
(somewhat) technical	(pretty) wild	

1 a She's ___extremely particular___ about what she eats, and never touches processed food at all.
   b There are so many hotels in the city to choose from. Why did you go for that ___particular___ one?
2 a The launch of the space shuttle has been delayed due to a _____ fault.
   b The operating instructions were _____ and difficult to understand.
3 a The vase is a _____ antique, not a recent copy.
   b I'm sure Anya wouldn't lie to you – she's a _____ person.
4 a After protests on the streets, the government had to reconsider its _____ decision to double the tax on petrol.
   b He's admired around the world for his _____ style of guitar playing.
5 a She is a dedicated teacher, _____ and hard-working.
   b I couldn't fix my computer myself, so I had to get some _____ help.
6 a As soon as I'd eaten the oysters, I had a _____ feeling in my stomach.
   b All the houses on this side of the street have _____ numbers.
7 a The strike comes at a _____ time for the company, which has just invested in a major new factory.
   b The report was _____ of the Principal's management of the college, and she was forced to resign.
8 a The disease was passed on to chickens by _____ birds.
   b It's a _____ area of moorland, a long way from roads and settlements.

3.3 Complete the sentences with a *to*-infinitive or *-ing* form of the verb in brackets.

1 When the phone rang she was busy ___doing___ her homework. (*do*)
2 When I see pictures on TV of the flooding near the coast, I'm thankful _____ inland. (*live*)
3 My teacher's rather old and he's inclined _____ asleep during lessons. (*fall*)
4 I never felt comfortable _____ in the same office as Theresa. (*work*)
5 As soon as you're ready _____ , I'll call for a taxi. (*leave*)
6 Maria's already lent me a lot of money and I feel awkward _____ her for more. (*ask*)
7 Certain newspapers are always quick _____ the government if anything goes wrong in the country. (*blame*)
8 I felt bad _____ her to do all the clearing up after the party. (*leave*)

58

Exam practice

Adverbs and adjectives 7

Reading and Use of English Part 3

For questions **1 – 8**, read the text below. Use the word given in capitals at the end of some of the lines to form a word that fits in the gap **in the same line**. There is an example at the beginning **(0)**.

Sleep patterns

It is estimated that around one in five people have a sleep **(0)** _disorder_ of some kind, affecting their ability to get enough sleep. In particular, people who are **(1)** _____ – an increasing problem around the world – often suffer from sleeping difficulties. Most of the results of this lack of sleep are relatively minor, such as tiredness, irritability and **(2)** _____ , and the effects are not long-lasting. However, longer-term sleep deprivation can have more serious consequences and can be **(3)** _____ to physical and mental health. For example, it can result in high blood pressure and can affect a person's **(4)** _____ , reducing their ability to think and respond quickly.
Recent **(5)** _____ research has shown that people need seven to eight hours of sleep on average, although this figure is **(6)** _____ on such factors as age and health. For example, for infants the **(7)** _____ is much higher, about 16 hours a day, while older people tend to sleep less deeply and for a shorter time, often needing about the same amount of sleep as they do in late **(8)** _____ .

ORDER
WEIGH

FORGET

HARM

ALERT

SCIENCE

DEPEND
REQUIRE

CHILD

59

8 Comparison

Comparative and superlative forms of adjectives and adverbs; comparisons with *as ...*; comparisons with *so ...*, *too ...*, *enough*

Context listening

1.1 You are going to hear four friends discussing where to go on holiday. They have already decided to go to Greece, either to Athens or the island of Corfu. What do you think the advantages of going to each place are?

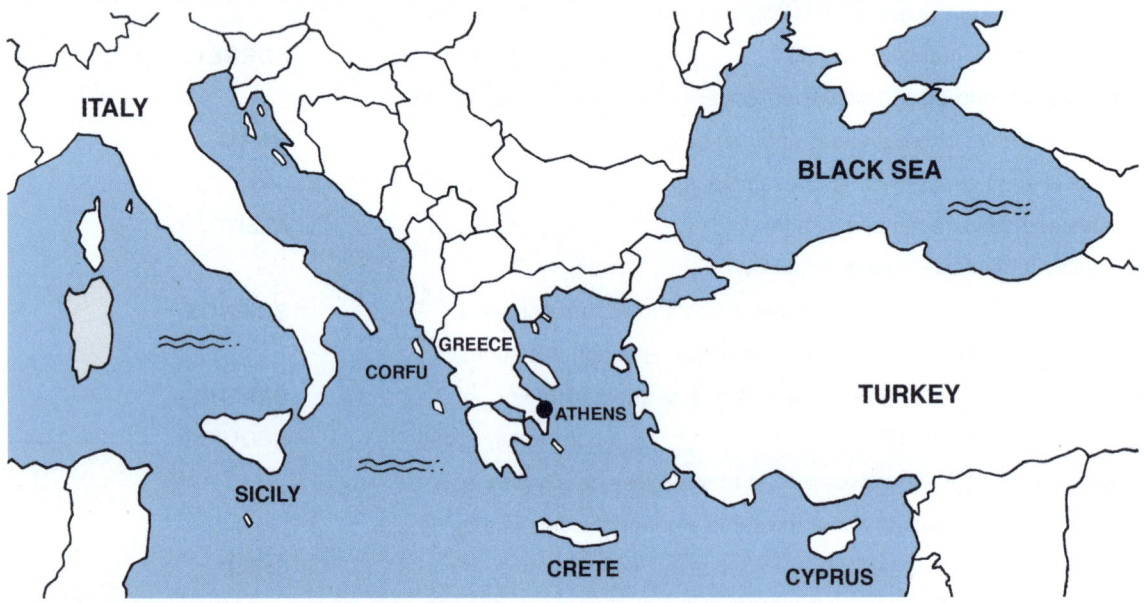

1.2 ▶11 Listen to the discussion. How many of the advantages you identified do they mention?

1.3 ▶11 Listen again and complete these extracts by writing three words in each sentence.
1 If we don't decide soon, it'll be _too late to_ get anywhere to stay.
2 They all look pretty good, and they're right next to _____ _____ beach _____ the island.
3 It says in my guidebook that there are reasonable hotel rooms for _____ _____ _____ 40 euros a night.
4 It was _____ _____ holiday I've ever had.
5 And it would be _____ _____ _____ being in a city.
6 It's still supposed to be a really beautiful place, so we'll want to see _____ _____ we can.

1.4 How are the comparative and superlative statements formed? For example:

1 _too + adjective + to-infinitive_   4 _____
2 _____   5 _____
3 _____   6 _____

Comparison 8

Grammar

2.1 Adjectives and adverbs: comparative and superlative forms

> **START POINT**
>
> Accommodation would be **cheaper** in Athens.
> It's probably the **cheapest** hotel in Athens.
> I want to come home **more relaxed** and **healthier / more healthy**.
> The walking tour in France was the **healthiest / most healthy** holiday I've had.
> It will be **more expensive** to get to Corfu than Athens.
> It's the **most expensive** flight that day.
>
> There are exceptions to the comparative and superlative forms above.

We usually add *-er/-est* to one-syllable adjectives.	However, we use *more/most*:
	• before past participle adjectives (*-ed* or *-ing* adjectives):
	  I want to come home **more relaxed**.
	• before *fun, real, right, wrong*:
	  It'd be **more fun** to go to Corfu.

We can usually add *-er/-est* or put *more/most* before two-syllable adjectives.	However, we always use *more/most* with:
	• participle adjectives:
	  It was the **most boring** holiday I've ever had.
	• adjectives ending *-ful* or *-less*:
	  It would be **more peaceful than** being in a city.
	• *afraid, alert, alike, alone, ashamed, cautious, complex, direct, exact, famous, frequent, modern, special, recent*:
	  I'm **more afraid** of flying than travelling by boat.
	  The Parthenon is one of the **most famous** buildings in the world.

We usually put *more/most* before three- or more syllable adjectives.	However, we can add *-er/-est* to *unhappy, unhealthy, unlikely, unlucky, unsteady, untidy*: I came back feeling **unhealthier** than when I went away. or I came back feeling **more unhealthy** ...

We can use a sentence with two comparatives to say that as one thing changes, another thing also changes:
The **longer** we leave it, the **more expensive** it's going to be.

We can use *less/least* as the opposite of *more/most* with all adjectives:
Hotels in Corfu are quite cheap – although **less cheap** than they used to be. It was the **least expensive** flight I could find.

In informal contexts we usually prefer *not as … as* rather than *less than*:
It's probably **not as unspoilt as** some of the other Greek islands.

The forms of comparative and superlative adverbs are similar to those of adjectives, although most adverb comparatives and superlatives take *more* and *most* rather than *-er/-est*:
We could live **more cheaply** in Athens.   **Most importantly**, we need to book our flights soon.

Common adverbs which take *-er/-est* include *hard* and *fast*.

61

8 Comparison

2.2 Superlatives: special cases

> **START POINT**
>
> That's the **most convenient of** the flights from London ...
> It's one of the **most famous** buildings **in** the world.
> They're right next to **the best beach on** the island.
> After a superlative we usually use *of* before plural words and *in* or *on* before singular words for places or groups.

For emphasis we can put an *of*-phrase at the beginning of the sentence:
Of the flights from London, that's the most convenient ...
In informal contexts we sometimes leave out *the* after a linking verb (e.g. *be, become, feel*), particularly when the superlative is at the end: *Which one's **cheapest**?*

2.3 Comparisons with *as* ...

> **START POINT**
>
> Isn't Corfu likely to be **as hot as** Athens at that time of the year? (= equally hot)
> Getting to Corfu is just **as easy as** getting to Athens. (= equally easy to get to)

Before the first *as* we use words and phrases such as *about, almost, just, just about, nearly,* and informally *not anything like, nothing like, nowhere near, not nearly* to indicate degree of similarity:
*The heat is **nowhere near as bad as** people say.* (=informal)
In negative forms we can use *not as* in informal contexts, or less commonly *not so*:
*Corfu is certainly **not as quiet as** it used to be.* or *... **not so quiet as** it used to be.*
We use *as much/many as* or *as little/few as* to say that a quantity or amount is larger or smaller than expected:
*There are reasonable hotel rooms for **as little as** 40 euros a night.*
*There are **as many as** 12 flights a day to Athens from London.*
We also use *as much/many as* with a noun phrase, a clause or the words *ever, possible* and *usual*:
*We want to see **as much as** possible.*
We can put a singular noun between an adjective and the second *as*:
*We want **as cheap a flight as** possible.*
Notice that we use *a/an* in front of the noun.
The negative form of sentences like this can use either *not as* or *not such*:
*Getting there is **not as big a problem as** you might think.*
*That's **not such a bad idea**.*
Notice that we use *not as* + adjective + *a/an* + noun but *not such a/an* + adjective + noun.

- As + clause

We can use a clause after *as* to compare two situations:
*Maybe we could hire a car, **as we did last year**.*

- As or like

When followed by a noun, *as* is used to describe the job or role of someone, or the function of something:
*My friend Mark used to work there **as an English teacher**.*

Like is used to say that one person or thing is similar to another:
*I stayed in a hotel **like** that one last year.*

Comparison 8

2.4 Comparisons with *so ..., too ..., enough*

Comparative clauses with *so*, *too* and *enough* are followed by clauses beginning *that* or *to*-infinitive.
- *so* + adjective + *that*-clause
  It gets **so hot** (comparative clause with *so*) **that** *a lot of people leave the city.* (that-clause)
  More formally we can use *so* + adjective + *as* + *to*-infinitive with a similar meaning. Compare:
  *The difference in price is **so small as to not be** worth bothering about.* (formal)
  *The difference in price is **so small that** it's not worth bothering about.* (informal)
- *too* + adjective + *to*-infinitive
  *If we don't decide soon, it'll be **too late** (**for us**) **to get** anywhere to stay.*
- adjective + *enough* + *to*-infinitive
  *It's **easy enough to get** into the centre from there.*

Grammar exercises

3.1 Complete the sentences with an appropriate comparative or superlative form of the adjective in brackets. Give alternative forms where possible.

1 Redbacks are among the <u>commonest / most common</u> spiders in this part of the country. Unfortunately, they're also the _____ . (*common, venomous*)

2 The road seemed to be getting _____ as we drove _____ into the forest. (*narrow, deep*)

3 I know coffee isn't good for me, and certainly _____ than tea, but I'm at my _____ early in the morning after a couple of cups of coffee, and I would find it difficult to give it up. (*harmful, alert*)

4 It was the _____ I had ever come to a fully grown elephant, and I was terrified. But even then I realised that I was in the presence of one of the _____ creatures on earth. (*close, magnificent*)

5 The head of Presto Stores argued that without supermarkets to provide cheap and fresh food, we would all be _____ and _____ . (*poor, unhealthy*)

6 When Emily saw Liam at the party, she thought he was the _____ man she had ever seen and went over to speak to him. But she soon realised that he was _____ with looking good than talking to her. (*handsome, concern*)

7 I couldn't have been _____ when Professor Park agreed to meet me to discuss my research. He's one of the _____ scientists in his field. But I was _____ than angry when he phoned to say that he couldn't meet me after all. I realise that he's a very busy man. (*thrilled, respected, sad*)

63

8 Comparison

3.2 Complete the sentences in this radio news report. Choose the correct or more likely option in each pair. Sometimes both are possible.

With just a few days before the general election, as (1) *many* / much as 100,000 people have demonstrated in the capital of Manistan as attacks on opposition candidates have continued. When voters were asked about their intentions in a recent opinion poll, as (2) *little* / *few* as 10% said they would be voting.

President Clarke has claimed that thanks to recent medical advances, malaria could be eradicated worldwide within as (3) *little* / *few* as ten years. In a speech to the World Health Organisation, she said that a cheap vaccine against malaria is just around the corner, (4) *as it is* / *as is* a cure for hepatitis B. She called on developed countries to invest (5) *as much* / *so much* as possible so that they can have the maximum impact on those most affected in poorer countries.

The former Formula One world champion Carl Nielsen left hospital today just six weeks after his horrific crash. Speaking to reporters outside his home, he said that damage to his back was not as (6) *serious a problem* / *a serious problem* as first thought, and he hoped to return to as (7) *normal life* / *normal a life* as possible. But there is (8) *not such a* / *not a such* positive outcome for the spectator who was hit by debris from Nielsen's car. He is said to be still in a critical condition.

A 64-year-old man who works (9) *like* / *as* a school crossing warden has become the country's biggest ever lottery winner. Mark Johns from London said that the win had come at the perfect time for him. He said: 'I'm not (10) *so* / *as* young as I was, and I can now look forward to a comfortable retirement.'

3.3 Ignoring the highlighted parts for now, complete the sentences with an adjective from the box. Use each adjective only once.

awful bright exhausted ~~good~~ loud small strong tall

1 The job offer was so ____*good*____ that I couldn't turn it down.
2 Adam is so _____ that he has to bend down to get through doorways.
3 I was so _____ that I couldn't go any further.
4 The comet is so _____ that it can be seen with the naked eye.
5 The traffic outside the theatre was so _____ that the actors couldn't make themselves heard.
6 The camera is so _____ that it can fit easily into your shirt pocket.
7 The results were so _____ that our teacher made us take the test again.
8 The earthquake was so _____ that it shook buildings across the whole country.

3.4 The shaded parts of <u>two</u> of the sentences in 3.3 can be rewritten using *too* + adjective + *to*-infinitive and <u>two others</u> can be rewritten using adjective + *enough* + *to*-infinitive. Find these sentences and rewrite the highlighted part. One is done for you.

1 The job offer was **too good to turn down**.

64

Exam practice

Comparison 8

Reading and Use of English Part 3

For questions **1 – 8**, read the text below. Use the word given in capitals at the end of some of the lines to form a word that fits in the gap **in the same line**. There is an example at the beginning **(0)**.

Cycling is good news – so what's stopping us?

The government's recent campaign, providing **(0)** _encouragement_ — **ENCOURAGE**
to leave our cars at home and get on our bikes, has been
(1) _____ to some extent, with a slight increase in — **SUCCESS**
the numbers cycling to work. We all now know that cycling is
(2) _____ ; cyclists have fewer health problems than — **BENEFIT**
non-cyclists, they have higher levels of **(3)** _____ , and — **FIT**
they don't damage the environment.

But we won't become a nation of cyclists until we **(4)** _____ — **COME**
two major barriers. First, exhaust fumes in **(5)** _____ — **HEAVY**
congested streets can be as **(6)** _____ to the lungs as — **HARM**
cigarette smoke. So there must be a greater **(7)** _____ of — **SEPARATE**
cars and bikes in towns. Perhaps more importantly, town planners must
(8) _____ that destinations for daily needs, such as schools, — **SURE**
work and shopping, are within convenient cycling distance from home.

9 Verb patterns (1)

Verbs with two objects; verb + object + adjective;
verb + reflexive pronoun; verb + *each other / one another*

Context listening

1.1 You are going to listen to part of an introductory lecture in a course on first language learning. Do you know what your first words were? Or the first words of a child you know?

1.2 ▶12 The lecturer tells the students about the first five lectures in the course. Here are the titles of these lectures. Listen and number them in the order they will take place.

Language learning problems: what and why? _____
Listening and learning: the interrelationships _____
Early communication: parents and play _____
Patterns of communication: learned behaviour? _____
Private conversations: talking to toys ___1___

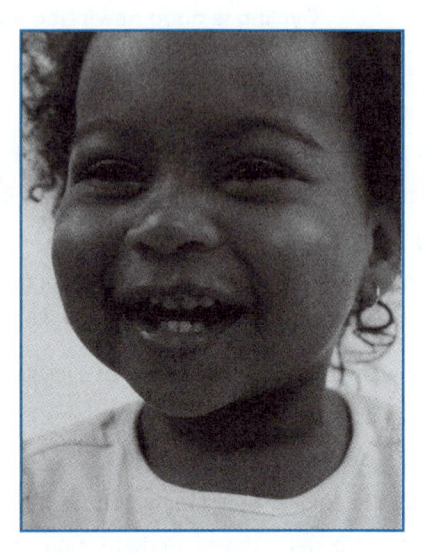

1.3 ▶12 Listen again and fill in the gaps.

- I recently (1) _bought my two-year-old daughter a cuddly elephant_, and it has become the 'person' she talks to each morning lying in bed.
- The first stage of interactive play might be a child (2) _____ or (3) _____.
- A broken toy handed to a parent with an 'Aaa' might mean (4) '_____'.
- (5) _____ is a similarly important part of this process of listening and understanding.
- Dr Jackman will be (6) _____ in detail in later talks.

1.4 Which of the following patterns do the phrases you have written have?

a   verb + person/people + thing(s)   __1__ and _____
b   verb + thing(s) + *for* + person/people   _____ and _____
c   verb + thing(s) + *to* + person/people   _____ and _____

1.5 Decide whether the phrases in 1.3 could be rewritten using the other patterns.

1   a   ✓ = bought my two-year-old daughter a cuddly elephant
    b   ✓ = bought a cuddly elephant for my two-year-old daughter
    c   ✗ = ~~bought a cuddly elephant to my two-year-old daughter~~

9 Verb patterns (1)

Grammar

> **START POINT**
>
> *Interactions between infants will often **copy** parental speech.* (transitive)
> ***Fetch** me your hat.* (transitive)
> *Infants are keen to **interact** with others.* (intransitive)
> A verb is *transitive* if it can be followed by one object (e.g. *copy **parental speech***) or two objects (e.g. *Fetch **me your hat***). If a verb has two objects, the first (the indirect object) is usually a person or group of people and the second (the direct object) is a thing. If a verb can't be followed by an object it is *intransitive* (e.g. *interact*) and it can't have a passive form.

2.1 Verbs with two objects

After many verbs with two objects, we can reverse the order of the objects if we put *for* or *to* before the indirect object:
*I recently bought **my two-year-old daughter a cuddly elephant**.* or *I recently bought **a cuddly elephant for my two-year-old daughter**.*
*A child might offer **their mother some food**.* or *A child might offer **some food to their mother**.*

We often use this pattern (with *for* or *to*) to focus particular attention on the indirect object or when the indirect object is much longer than the direct object:
*She lent the book **to one of the students who asked for some additional reading**.* (not ~~She lent one of the students who asked for some additional reading the book.~~)

We use *for* + indirect object with verbs such as *build*, *find* and *get*:
*Go to the toy box and **find the car for me**.* or *Go to the toy box and **find me the car**.*

We use *to* + indirect object with verbs such as *give*, *offer* and *show*:
*She **gave a toy to me**.* or *She **gave me a toy**.*

We can use either *for* or *to* + indirect object with verbs such as *play*, *read* and *write*. Often there is a difference in meaning:
*I couldn't find her email address, so I had to **write** a letter **to** her.*
*She was too young to write herself, so I **wrote** the letter **for** her.* (= instead of her)
Sometimes the meaning is very similar:
*Reading stories **for/to** young children is an important part of this process.*

Some verbs with two objects cannot have their objects reversed with *for/to*, including *ask*, *guarantee* and *refuse*:
*Most parents **ask themselves the question**: 'Did they copy that from us?'* (not ... ~~ask the question for/to themselves~~ ...)

If the direct object is a pronoun, we usually use direct object + *for/to* + indirect object:
*I bought **it for** my daughter.   Give **it to** me.*
While *I bought my daughter it* and *Give me it* might be heard in informal speech, this pattern is usually considered to be bad style and should be avoided in writing and in *Cambridge English: Advanced*.

Some verbs can only have two objects in the pattern direct object + *for/to* + indirect object:
- *for* (These verbs include *collect*, *fix* and *mend*.)
  *Mend this **for** me.* (not ~~Mend me this.~~)
- *to* (These verbs include *describe*, *explain* and *mention*.)
  *Dr Jackman will be describing this process **to** you in detail.* (not ~~Dr Jackman will be describing you this process in detail.~~)

9 Verb patterns (1)

2.2 Verb + object + adjective

Some verbs (e.g. *believe, consider, prove*) can be followed by an object + adjective:
*We might consider **first language learning natural** ...* (object = *first language learning*; adjective = *natural*)

2.3 Verb + reflexive pronoun

> **START POINT**
>
> *Let me introduce **myself**. I'd like to talk about what I call 'private' conversations – children talking to **themselves**.* When the subject and the object of a sentence refer to the same person or thing, we use a reflexive pronoun as the object rather than a personal pronoun. The reflexive pronouns are: *myself, yourself, herself, himself, itself, ourselves, yourselves, themselves.*

After some verbs we can use a reflexive pronoun or leave it out with little difference in meaning. These include *acclimatise to, adapt to, (un)dress, hide, move, prepare for, shave* and *wash*:
*As my three year-old daughter **dresses** (**herself**), she likes to talk.*
We include the reflexive pronoun for emphasis. In this example, we might include *herself* to emphasise that she dresses without help.

A few verbs are very often used with a reflexive pronoun followed by a particular preposition: *busy ... with, distance ... from, pride ... on*:
*When children appear to be **busying themselves with** their toys ...*

Some verbs are rarely or never used with a reflexive pronoun in English, but often are in other languages. These include: *complain, concentrate, get up, get hot, get tired, lie down, meet, relax, remember, sit down* and *wake up*:
From the moment they wake up ... (not *From the moment they wake themselves up ...*)

With verbs followed by direct object + preposition + indirect object we usually use a personal pronoun, not a reflexive pronoun, as indirect object:
*Parents sometimes **hide an object behind them**.* (not *Parents sometimes hide an object behind themselves.*)

If we need to make it clear that the subject and indirect object refer to the same person, we use a reflexive pronoun. Compare:
*Maria didn't buy the teddy bear for **her**.* (*her* = could mean either *Maria* or someone else)
*Maria didn't buy the teddy bear for **herself**.* (*herself* = *Maria*)

2.4 Verb + *each other / one another*

Compare the use of verbs with reflexive pronouns and *each other / one another*:
*Sara and Noel blamed **themselves** when their daughter broke her arm.* (= they said it was the fault of both of them)
*Sara and Noel blamed **each other** / **one another** when their daughter broke her arm.* (= Sara said it was Noel's fault and Noel said it was Sara's fault)

With some verbs (e.g. *agree, coincide, play*) we have to use the preposition *with* before *each other / one another*:
*It is wonderful to see two small children **playing with each other** peacefully.*

After the verbs *embrace, fight, hug, kiss, marry* and *meet* we can use *each other* or *(with) one another*, but this can be omitted:
*Two small children at a nursery school might **hug** (**each other** / **one another**) when they meet.*

Verb patterns (1) 9

Grammar exercises

3.1 Describe each situation using *They* + verb + (*with*) + each other. Choose from the verbs in the box.

agree blame compete disagree miss ~~resemble~~ respect trust

1 'We look alike.' _They resemble each other_ .
2 'You were right!' _____ .
3 'I always like to be better than you!' _____ .
4 'I admire your character.' _____ .
5 'I believe that you're honest.' _____ .
6 'I'm sorry you're not here.' _____ .
7 'It was your fault.' _____ .
8 'You were wrong!' _____ .

3.2 Complete the sentences using the pairs of objects in the box. Give all possible word orders, adding prepositions where necessary.

some apples / me	your car / you	some chocolate / myself
a £10 gift voucher / me	a favour / you	your glass / me
how to print out a document / me	those letters / you	a lot / you
the mistake / the manager	~~a seat / me~~	them / you
some water / you		

1 I'll be a bit late getting to the concert tonight. Can you save _a seat for me / me a seat_ ?
2 I'm on a diet, so I'm trying to cut down on sweets, although I do allow _____ after dinner.
3 I have to go past the postbox on my way home. I'll post _____ , if you like.
4 I haven't eaten any fruit all week. Can you buy _____ when you're at the supermarket? I'll pay _____ when you get back.
5 **A:** Can I ask _____ ?
   B: Of course.
   A: Can you show _____ ?
6 I'm sure they could repair _____ at Smallwood's garage. They're very good there, but it would probably cost _____ .
7 In my local supermarket I noticed a sign saying 'Two for the price of won!' I pointed out _____ and a week later she sent _____ to say 'thank you'.
8 **A:** I'm so thirsty.
   B: Give _____ and I'll pour _____ .

69

9 Verb patterns (1)

3.3 Complete the sentences by adding an appropriate personal or reflexive pronoun (e.g. *her* or *herself*), an adjective from box A and an ending from box B.

A

fit	guilty	incapable
independent	lucky	responsible
~~unable~~		

B

of the murder	for its collapse
to play again	of the Soviet Union
~~to sing~~	to be alive
of maintaining order	

1 After undergoing a minor operation on her throat, she found ___herself unable to sing___ .
2 Although the police didn't have hard evidence against Karl Stevens, they still believed _____ .
3 The police officers lacked experience in crowd control and proved _____ .
4 After all his injury troubles, Marcuson has now pronounced _____ .
5 When I looked at the damage to my car in the crash, I considered _____
6 Mary Wallis had been the company's CEO for five years and the board of directors held _____ .
7 In 1991, Estonia declared _____ .

3.4 Complete the sentences with a personal pronoun, a reflexive pronoun or a reflexive pronoun + preposition. In one sentence, no pronoun is necessary. Write the reflexive pronoun in brackets if it can be omitted.

1 When the police came to arrest him, Thomson hid ___(himself)___ under the floorboards until they had gone.
2 He had always prided _____ his physical fitness, so it surprised him when he found it so difficult to acclimatise _____ walking in the mountains.
3 Sarah came in carrying a big box of chocolates. At first I thought they were for me, but she said she'd bought them for _____ because she'd had such a bad day at work. So I had to content _____ a couple of rather boring biscuits.
4 I tried to prepare _____ the interview by looking at the company's website and familiarising _____ their range of products.
5 Thanks for taking the children to the zoo last week. They enjoyed _____ enormously. I'm looking forward to having lunch with you on Thursday. Shall I meet _____ outside the restaurant at about 12.30?
6 My father had broken his arm and couldn't shave _____ , so I had to do it for him. I found it really difficult and had to concentrate _____ hard.

Exam practice

Verb patterns (1) 9

Reading and Use of English Part 4

For questions **1 – 6**, complete the second sentence so that it has a similar meaning to the first sentence, using the word given. **Do not change the word given.** You must use between **three** and **six** words, including the word given. Here is an example **(0)**.

0 If there is a fire, you must not use the lift to leave the building.
   EVENT
   In the event of a fire , you must not use the lift to leave the building.

1 Nina was driving the car at the time of the accident, but I don't think it was her fault.
   RESPONSIBLE
   Nina was driving the car at the time of the accident, but I don't hold _____ it.

2 Jack has such a vivid imagination that it's possible that he invented the whole story.
   MADE
   Jack has such a vivid imagination that he might _____ the whole story.

3 I had only just got home when the phone rang.
   SOONER
   No _____ the phone rang.

4 She is proud of being able to write clearly.
   ABILITY
   She prides _____ to write clearly.

5 Once the lecturer had given us a clear explanation of the procedure, we were able to go ahead with the experiment.
   EXPLAINED
   Once the lecturer had _____ , we were able to go ahead with the experiment.

6 The government has banned all exports to the country except for food and medicine.
   EXCEPTION
   The government has banned all exports to the country _____ food and medicine.

71

10 Verb patterns (2)

Verb + to-infinitive / -ing; verb + (object) + bare infinitive; verb + object + to-infinitive / -ing; verb + object / possessive + -ing; other patterns after verbs

Context listening

1.1 ▶13 Listen to part of an interview from a radio travel programme. The reporter is talking about his recent visit to the island of Lombok in Indonesia. Which of these problems did the reporter encounter on his trip?

seasickness _____   shark attack _____
passport left at home _____   volcanic eruption _____
hurricane _____   missed flight _____
stung by jellyfish _____   missed boat _____

1.2 ▶13 Listen again and fill in the gaps.

1 I'd been so anxious to get into the taxi that I ___'d forgotten to pick___ it up.
2 We were _____ outside the harbour for hours.
3 A number of people _____ to the coral reefs off the northwest coast.
4 When I was younger I used to _____ in the sea.
5 As it swam past I _____ me across the stomach.
6 I really _____ me so well.
7 As we _____ the amazing sunset, it was almost possible to believe it.
8 I _____ the camera in my mobile phone, but the quality was pretty poor.

1.3 Notice that in each space in 1.2 you have written two verbs, and that the second verb has either a *to*-infinitive or an *-ing* form.

1 In three of these sentences you could use the other form of this verb and still have a correct sentence. Which three? _____ , _____ , _____
2 In only one of these three would the sentence have a similar meaning with either a *to*-infinitive or an *-ing* form. Which one? _____

72

10 Verb patterns (2)

Grammar

> **START POINT**
>
> I **managed to find** a friendly taxi driver.
> I **considered staying** for a few more days.
> I **couldn't get out** of the way.
> When two verbs are used together, the second verb is in either a *to*-infinitive, an *-ing* or a bare infinitive form (i.e. an infinitive without *to*).

2.1 Verb + *to*-infinitive / *-ing*

Some verbs can be followed by either a *to*-infinitive or an *-ing* form with little or no difference in meaning:
*I **started to scream**.* or *I **started screaming**.*
Other verbs like this include: *begin, not bother, cease, continue*. We normally avoid using two *-ing* forms together:
*I was **beginning to feel** quite at home there.* (not *I was beginning feeling* …)

After the opinion verbs *hate, like, love* and *prefer* we can use either a *to*-infinitive or an *-ing* form with little difference in meaning. However, we prefer a *to*-infinitive when we say we do something regularly. Compare:
*When I was younger, I used to **hate to swim** in the sea.* (= implies regular swimming)
*When I was younger, I used to **hate swimming** in the sea.* (= implies swimming in general)

After *would* (*'d*) with *hate, like, love* or *prefer*, we use a *to*-infinitive, not an *-ing* form:
*I**'d love to think** that it could avoid a huge expansion in visitors.*

Some verbs can be followed by either a *to*-infinitive or an *-ing* form but the meaning of the verb is different:
*I **came to realise** that the Lombok people are very kind.* (= talking about a gradual realisation)
*It **came swimming** towards me.* (= saying that something swam in your direction)

We use an *-ing* form after the preposition *to*:
*I'd really been **looking forward to staying** at the Hotel Sanar in Mataram.* (not … *looking forward to stay* …)
and after the preposition of a phrasal verb:
*I **put off going** home for as long as possible.* (not *I put off go* …)

In negative sentences, the position of *not* can influence meaning. Compare:
*I **regretted not** speaking the local language.* (= I didn't speak the language and I regretted it)
*I **didn't** regret speaking the local language.* (= I spoke it and I didn't regret it)
*I was told **not** to exercise.* (= they said I shouldn't exercise)
*I **wasn't** told to exercise.* (= they didn't say I should exercise)

2.2 Verb + (object) + bare infinitive

When *let* and *make* have an object, this is followed by a bare infinitive:
*They **made us wait** outside the harbour for hours.*
But we use a *to*-infinitive after a passive form of *make*:
*We **were made to wait** outside the harbour for hours.*

When the verbs of perception *feel, hear, notice, observe, overhear, see, watch* have an object, this is followed by an *-ing* form or a bare infinitive:
*I **felt** it **stinging** me across the stomach.* or *I **felt** it **sting** me across the stomach.*
*I sat on the beach and I **watched** the sun **setting**.* or *I **watched** the sun **set** and then went home.*

10 Verb patterns (2)

We usually prefer an *-ing* form when the action is in progress or we want to emphasise that it continued for some time, and a bare infinitive when an action is complete or we want to emphasise that it lasted for a short time.

We use a bare infinitive in certain idiomatic phrases with *dare*, *make*, *let* and *hear*:
I **dare say** you're tired after your journey. (= I think this must be true; see Unit 4, 2.7 for more on *dare*.)
I had to **make do** with a less luxurious hotel.
I had to **let go** of the rope.
He **let slip** that he hadn't got a driving licence.
I **heard tell** there were sharks around.

After *help* we can use either a bare infinitive or *to*-infinitive:
Some of the villagers **helped carry** me back to my taxi. or Some of the villagers **helped to carry** me back to my taxi.

2.3 Verb + object + *to*-infinitive / *-ing*

After some verbs we have to include an object before a *to*-infinitive in active sentences:
A number of people had **encouraged me to go** to the coral reefs off the northwest coast of the island.
Other verbs like this include: *advise, persuade, tell*.

Some verbs can't include an object before a *to*-infinitive:
I **decided to go** ahead.
Other verbs like this include: *agree, guarantee, refuse*.

With some verbs we have to include the preposition *for* before an object + *to*-infinitive:
I **arranged for the taxi to collect** me.
Other verbs like this include: *advertise, apply, campaign, pay, wait*.
(See Unit 24, 2.2 for more on prepositions after verbs.)

Some verbs are only followed by an *-ing* form when they have an object:
I **saw the jellyfish coming** towards me.
Other verbs like this include: *feel, find, hear*.

2.4 Verb + object/possessive + *-ing*

Some verbs can be followed either by an object or, more formally, a possessive form:
I really **appreciated them looking** after me so well. or I really **appreciated their looking** after me so well.
Other verbs like this include verbs of (dis)liking (e.g. *appreciate, detest, (dis)approve of, (dis)like, enjoy, hate, love, object to*) and verbs of thinking (e.g. *forget, imagine, remember, think of*).

We can only use a possessive form to talk about a person or a group of people:
I'll never **forget it swimming** towards me. (not ... ~~its swimming towards me~~)

We don't use a possessive form if the object is complex:
I really enjoyed **Arun and his sister** showing me around. (not ... ~~Arun('s) and his sister's~~ ...)

2.5 Other patterns after verbs

The *to*-infinitive can also have perfect, passive and continuous forms.

- Verb + *to have* + past participle

We use forms of the perfect infinitive to talk about an event that happened earlier or is complete:
The Sasaks **are thought to have** originally **come** to Lombok from India or Burma.

This is particularly used to talk about actions that did not happen or may not have happened:
I **was supposed to have arrived** on the 14th October.
I **was supposed to have been flying** from London to Singapore.
The mountain's **thought** by some **to have been created** by the god Batara.

10 Verb patterns (2)

- Verb + *having* + past participle

We use the perfect *-ing* form to emphasise that one action happens before another:
*I really **regret not having taken** my camera with me.*
This form is most often used with the verbs *admit, deny, forget, recall, regret* and *remember*.

- Verb + *to be* + present/past participle

Future actions can also be indicated using the continuous infinitive (verb + *to be* + present participle) and the passive infinitive (verb + *to be* + past participle):
*I **hope to be going** back again.*
*More flights to the island **are expected to be introduced** next year.*

Grammar exercises

3.1 Choose the correct answer. Sometimes more than one option is possible.

1 The President *has urged people vote / has urged to vote / has urged people to vote* 'Yes' in tomorrow's referendum on joining the European Union.
2 After Chan injured his knee last year, a number of specialists *advised him to give up / advised to give up / advised him giving up* football, but he is still playing as well as ever.
3 A video recording from a security camera at the bank was used in Thomas's trial. It clearly *showed pointing / showed him pointing / showed him to point* a gun at the cashier.
4 If you have any questions, please write to me at the above address. I can't *guarantee you to reply / guarantee to reply / guarantee you replying* immediately, but I will certainly write back before the end of the month.
5 'You can lead a horse to water but you can't *make it drink / make it to drink / make it drinking*.' (a proverb)
6 We really *appreciate you help / appreciate you helping / appreciate your helping* us move house.
7 I've decided to look for a new job as I *enjoy not sitting / don't enjoy to sit / don't enjoy sitting* in front of a computer all day.
8 Now that Lena has bought a house in Brussels, I will have to *advertise for someone to share / advertise someone sharing / advertise someone to share* my flat with me.

3.2 Complete these texts using each verb in the appropriate form. If necessary, add a preposition and/or object before the verb.

A

| ~~be~~ | have | sack | steal | talk |

'I think it's fair to say that Jim Thompson wasn't liked in our company and when he was made sales manager, many of us objected to **(1)** _his being_ promoted. Over the next few weeks, things just got worse. When we walked past his office, we often heard **(2)** _____ to his friends on the phone. Then one of my colleagues caught **(3)** _____ some money from the cash box. Eventually, a group of us went to the Managing Director of the company and demanded **(4)** _____ Thompson dismissed. But despite our objections, the MD said that he wasn't prepared **(5)** _____ his own son!'

10 Verb patterns (2)

B

capture call eat escape get

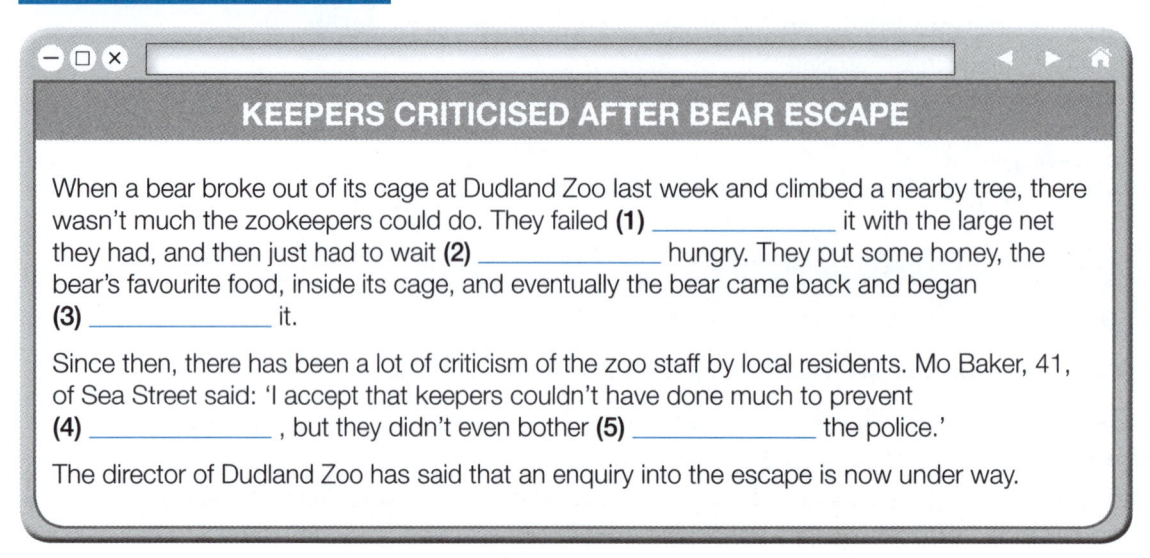

KEEPERS CRITICISED AFTER BEAR ESCAPE

When a bear broke out of its cage at Dudland Zoo last week and climbed a nearby tree, there wasn't much the zookeepers could do. They failed **(1)** _____ it with the large net they had, and then just had to wait **(2)** _____ hungry. They put some honey, the bear's favourite food, inside its cage, and eventually the bear came back and began **(3)** _____ it.

Since then, there has been a lot of criticism of the zoo staff by local residents. Mo Baker, 41, of Sea Street said: 'I accept that keepers couldn't have done much to prevent **(4)** _____ , but they didn't even bother **(5)** _____ the police.'

The director of Dudland Zoo has said that an enquiry into the escape is now under way.

C

collect do get have say see

Hi!

Do you remember **(1)** _____ that you wanted a recent photo of me? Well, here it is (please see attachment). Yes, it's not very flattering, but you know how I hate **(2)** _____ my photo taken. Can't wait **(3)** _____ you again in July. Until then, you'll have to make **(4)** _____ with this photo! Btw, let me know when your flight gets in and I'll get Laura or Daniel **(5)** _____ you from the airport.

Must go. We're off to the cinema tonight, so I have to hurry **(6)** _____ dinner ready. Will email again soon.

Love,

Luis

Verb patterns (2) 10

3.3 Complete the sentences with phrases from the box. Use a *to*-infinitive, bare infinitive or *-ing* form of the verb (including perfect and continuous forms).

argue with him	be a successful businesswoman	get more exercise
have her around	be killed in the earthquake	shout at anyone
~~take a couple of paracetamol~~	talk on my mobile	

1 If your headache doesn't go soon, try _taking a couple of paracetamol_.
2 The Department of Health has just launched a campaign to encourage people _____.
3 Around 2,000 people are believed _____.
4 I didn't want to speak to Jakub, so when he walked past I pretended _____.
5 He had such a bad temper that no one dared _____.
6 They say that Mark can be quite aggressive, but personally I've never heard him _____.
7 She started life as a teacher, but went on _____.
8 Now that Laura has gone away to college, I really miss _____.

Exam practice

Reading and Use of English Part 5

You are going to read a newspaper article about the writer's experience as a cyclist. For questions **1 – 6**, choose the answer (**A**, **B**, **C** or **D**) which you think fits best according to the text.

My life as a human speed bump

Giving up a car has not been quite the liberating experience that George Monbiot had hoped.

Seventeen years after giving up my car, I still feel like a second-class citizen. I am trying to do the right thing, but the United Kingdom just isn't run for people like me. Take our bus services. My home city, Oxford, has invested massively in a park-and-ride scheme: buses carry people into the centre from car parks on the outskirts. At first I thought this was a great idea. Now, having stood for what must amount to weeks at bus stops, watching the full double deckers go by every couple of minutes without stopping, I realise it's not just the roads which have been taken over by drivers, but also the public transport system.

Or take the bike lanes. Most consist of lines painted on the road where it is wide and safe, which disappear as soon as it becomes narrow and dangerous. One of them, in Oxford, has been surfaced with small stones, which shows that the people who designed them have never ridden a bicycle. When we asked for a bike lane on one of the city's busiest streets, the council chose instead to narrow the street and widen the pavements, in the hope that the bicycles would slow down the cars. The cyclists, reluctant to become human speed bumps, started travelling down the pavement.

Now there is almost nowhere reserved for people like me. Out of political cowardice, councils and the police have given up enforcing the law. Preventing people from parking on the pavement would mean cutting the number of parking places, as the streets are otherwise too narrow. In one part of Oxford they have solved the problem by painting parking places on the pavement. Since my daughter was born, and I have started pushing a pram, I have been forced to walk in the middle of the road. In one respect this makes sense: the pavements are so badly maintained that she will only sleep when she's being pushed down the smooth grey carpet laid out for the cars.

My problem is that by seeking to reduce my impact on the planet, I joined a political minority that is diminishing every year. As car ownership increases, its only remaining members are a handful of strange people like me, the very poor and those not qualified to drive. None of these groups have political power. Our demands run counter to the usual wish to be successful, and have a better home, job and car, and are therefore of little interest to either politicians or the media.

Now, to my horror, I find I am beginning to question even the environmental impact of my 17 years of moderation. It is true that my own carbon emissions have been reduced. It is also true that if everyone did the same thing the total saving would be enormous. The problem is that, in the absence of regulation, traffic expands to fill the available space. By refusing to own a car I have merely opened up road space for other people, who tend to drive more fuel-hungry models than I would have chosen. We can do little to reduce our impacts on the environment if the government won't support us.

There are some compensations, however. About three or four times a year I hire a car. When I stop at motorway service stations, I am struck by the staggering levels of obesity: it appears to be far more prevalent there than on trains or coaches. People who take public transport must at least walk to the bus stop. The cyclists among us keep fit without even noticing.

Being without a car in Oxford has forced me to become more engaged with my home town. It throws me into contact with far more people than I would otherwise encounter. There are a couple of routes which make cycling a real pleasure: the footpath along the River Thames, for example, takes me most of the way to the station. But overall, as far as self-interest is concerned, I would struggle to claim that giving up my car was a wholly positive decision.

Exam practice

Verb patterns (2) **10**

1. In the first paragraph, the writer says his view of the Oxford park-and-ride scheme is that
   A it has actually encouraged people to drive into town.
   B it has been an unqualified success.
   C it has had insufficient funding.
   D its popularity has become problematic.

2. The writer thinks that cyclists started travelling down the pavement in one of Oxford's busiest streets because
   A the council put in a speed restriction measure.
   B the pavement is very wide.
   C there is no bike lane.
   D in the bike lane cyclists are too close to cars.

3. In the third paragraph, the writer says he believes that Oxford city council has shown 'political cowardice' because it
   A is reluctant to stop cars being left in pedestrian areas.
   B doesn't want cyclists on the city's roads.
   C has narrowed some roads to discourage cyclists from using them.
   D is unwilling to improve the standard of pavements.

4. In the fifth paragraph, the writer suggests that the effect of his actions has been to
   A discourage the government from giving support.
   B lower maintenance standards for pavements.
   C create more room on the road for other cars.
   D encourage others to drive bigger cars.

5. The writer's observations at motorway service stations suggest to him that
   A car drivers are more overweight than public transport users.
   B people who own cars are thinner than people who hire them.
   C people who use public transport don't get enough exercise.
   D cyclists ride bikes in order to keep fit.

6. According to the writer, being without a car in Oxford
   A has been a completely positive experience.
   B has increased the number of acquaintances he has made.
   C has made him stay at home more.
   D has been a complete mistake.

11 Relative clauses (1)

Defining and non-defining relative clauses; relative pronouns; other words beginning relative clauses; prepositions in relative clauses

Context listening

1.1 You are going to hear part of a commentary from an audio-guide in a museum of science and technology. Before you listen, look at these photos. What do you think the commentary is about?

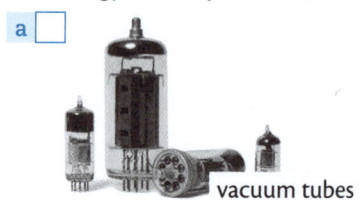

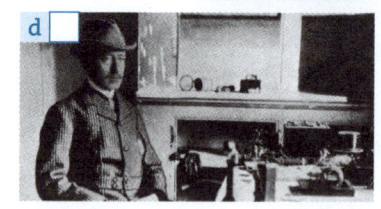

a ☐
vacuum tubes

b ☐
Hertz's experiment

c ☐

d ☐

e ☐
wireless telegraph

1.2 ▶14 Listen to the commentary. Number the photos in the order they are mentioned.

1.3 ▶14 Listen again and fill in the gaps.

1 He devised an experiment ___in which___ a spark jumped across a gap in a metal ring when a sparking coil was held a few metres away.

2 For most people, however, it is the Italian Guglielmo Marconi _____ name is mainly associated with the development of radio.

3 The first public demonstration of the power of radio came in 1901, _____ Marconi announced that he had received a transmission from across the Atlantic.

4 There are just a few of the 'wireless telegraphs' that the factory produced left in the world, an example _____ you can see in Case 2.

5 Radio waves could not carry speech until a method had been developed _____ the low-frequency waves produced in a microphone could be combined with high-frequency radio waves.

6 In Britain, the popularity of radio increased until 1952, _____ four out of five households owned one.

1.4 What do the words in the gaps in 1.3 refer to?

1 He devised <u>an experiment</u> ___in which___ a spark jumped across a gap in a metal ring when a sparking coil was held a few metres away.

80

11 Relative clauses (1)

Grammar

2.1 Defining and non-defining relative clauses

> **START POINT**
>
> The old photograph **that you can see ahead of you** shows Marconi at Signal Hill. (defining relative clause)
> The story of radio probably begins with Heinrich Hertz, **who was the first to produce radio waves in a laboratory**. (non-defining relative clause)
> *Relative clauses* give more information about someone or something referred to in the main clause.
> *Defining relative clauses* specify which (or which type of) person or thing we mean.
> *Non-defining relative clauses* simply add extra information about a noun.

We put a relative clause as close as possible to the noun it refers to:
There are just a few of the 'wireless telegraphs' *that the factory produced* left in the world. rather than *There are just a few of* the 'wireless telegraphs' *left in the world that the factory produced.*

Some relative clauses refer back to the whole idea in the previous clause, not just the previous noun. Most of these begin with *which*:
The owner of the old radio claims that it is in excellent condition – *which is obviously not the case*.

2.2 Relative pronouns

Adding information about people

- defining relative clause (subject pronoun – the relative pronoun is the subject of the relative clause):

  subject pronoun
  There were many people ← who doubted that Marconi would ever succeed.
  (Or informally: *There were many people* **that** *doubted Marconi would ever succeed.*)

- defining relative clause (object pronoun – the relative pronoun is the object of the relative clause):

  object pronoun subject
  Augusto Righi *was an Italian physicist* who Marconi *studied with in the 1890s.*
  (Or informally: *an Italian physicist* (**that**) *Marconi studied with.*)
  We can leave out the relative pronoun if it is the object of a defining relative clause.

- non-defining relative clause (subject pronoun):

  subject pronoun
  The story of radio probably begins with Heinrich Hertz, ← who *was the first to produce radio waves in a laboratory.*

- non-defining relative clause (object pronoun):

  object pronoun subject
  Augusto Righi, who Marconi *respected greatly, guided his research.* (Very formally: *Augusto Righi,* **whom** *Marconi respected greatly, guided his research.*)
  Note that *whom* is now used only in very formal styles, mostly in writing.

81

11 Relative clauses (1)

Adding information about things or animals

- defining relative clause (subject pronoun):
  *The invention **that** made this possible was the vacuum tube.* More formally: *The invention **which** made this possible ...*
- defining relative clause (object pronoun):
  *The model (**that**) you can see in Case 1 shows how this works.* More formally: *The model **which** you can see ...*
- non-defining relative clause (subject and object pronoun):
  *Marconi opened a 'wireless telegraph' factory in England, **which** employed around 50 people.*
  *Marconi's 'wireless telegraph' factory, **which** he set up in England, employed around 50 people.*
  Although some people use *that* here, it is grammatically incorrect and should be avoided in *Cambridge English: Advanced*.

In both defining and non-defining relative clauses we can often use *who, that* or *which* with collective nouns referring to groups of people (e.g. *company, government, orchestra*):
*The company **who/which/that** made the first radios was set up by Marconi.*

2.3 Other words beginning relative clauses

We often use *when* after a noun referring to a time, or words such as *day, period, time*:
The first public demonstration of the power of radio came in 1901 *, **when** Marconi announced that he had received a transmission from across the Atlantic.*
More formally, we can often use a preposition + *which*:
It was a period *during which they met very infrequently.* or *...* a period *when ...*
Less formally, we can use *that* or no relative pronoun in defining relative clauses:
I can still remember the time *(**that**) I first watched television.* or *...* the time *when ...*

We often use *why* after *reason*:
You can probably guess the reason ***why** radio began to lose some of its popularity.* or informally *...* the reason *(**that**) radio began to lose ...*

We often use *where* after a noun referring to a location, and after the words *case, condition, example, experiment, instance, point, process, situation* and *system*:
Move now to room 36 *, **where** you can find information and displays.*
Marconi's goal was to find a system ***where** telegraphic messages could be transmitted.*
More formally, we can use a preposition + *which*:
He devised an experiment *in which a spark jumped across a gap in a metal ring.*

We use *whose* + noun to talk about something belonging to or connected with a person, town, country or organisation:
For most people, however, it is the Italian Guglielmo Marconi ***whose name** is mainly associated with the development of radio.*
In formal uses, noun + *of which* can sometimes replace *whose* + noun:
Project Geneva is a computing project, the purpose *of which is to analyse very large amounts of data on environmental change.* or *Project Geneva is* a computing project ***whose purpose** is to analyse large amounts of data on environmental change.*

Relative clauses (1) 11

2.4 Prepositions in relative clauses

> **START POINT**
>
> These early radio systems could only be used for Morse code, **in which** each letter of the alphabet is represented by a combination of dots and dashes. (= These early radio systems could only be used for Morse code. In Morse code, each letter of the alphabet is represented by a combination of dots and dashes.)

A preposition usually comes before the relative pronoun in formal styles:
In 1901 Marconi made the announcement **for which** he will always be remembered.

After a preposition we usually use *whom* rather than *who* in formal styles:
Augusto Righi, **with whom** Marconi studied in the 1890s, was a physicist. or
Augusto Righi, **whom** Marconi studied **with** in the 1890s, was a physicist.

A preposition usually comes at the end of the clause in less formal styles:
In 1901, Marconi made the announcement **which** he will always be remembered **for**.
Augusto Righi, **who** Marconi studied **with** in the 1890s, was a physicist.

We can use *of which* and *of whom* (or very informally *of who*) after *all, both, each, many, most, neither, part, several, some*; a number (e.g. *one, the first, half*) and superlatives:
Radio entertainers, **many of whom** became household names, were highly paid.

We can use a preposition, usually *from*, with *where* and *when*:
Marconi set up a transmission station in Cornwall, **from where** the first transatlantic radio message was sent.

Grammar exercises

3.1 Match the sentence halves and join them with one of the words in the box.

when	~~where~~	which	whose	why

1 The new factory will be located in an area
2 The photograph reminded him of the time
3 Any complaints should be sent to the Broadcasting Regulator,
4 I couldn't see any reason
5 The university has introduced an initiative in

a job it is to maintain standards in television programmes.
b he used to live in Thailand.
c talented students can complete their degree in only two years.
d Irina should be offended by my letter.
e there are high levels of unemployment.

1 *The new factory will be located in an area where there are high levels of unemployment.*

83

11 Relative clauses (1)

3.2 Underline all the possible relative pronouns that can complete each sentence. ('–' means that the sentence is correct with no relative pronoun.) If there is more than one possible answer, decide which one(s) are less formal.

1 The new drug should be of benefit for anyone _____ suffers from severe back pain.
   A <u>who</u>   B –   C which   D <u>that</u> *'that' is less formal than 'who'*

2 Did the committee _____ took the decision on the new housing estate meet local protestors?
   A –   B which   C who   D whom

3 The wallpaper, _____ is available in a number of colours, is based on an eighteenth-century design.
   A which   B that   C –   D who

4 Howard Stevens was one of the artists _____ Carlson worked with in his youth.
   A whom   B –   C which   D who

5 Conservationists have called for a programme to eliminate the rats _____ are killing seabirds on the island.
   A that   B –   C which   D whom

6 A government spokesperson, _____ did not wish to be named, said that there had been a major disagreement between the Prime Minister and the Finance Minister.
   A which   B that   C who   D –

7 Were the coins _____ he dug up worth a lot of money?
   A who   B –   C that   D which

8 He was survived by his wife Anastasia, _____ he married in 1936.
   A whom   B that   C –   D who

3.3 Complete these sentences with an appropriate preposition.

1 There were many excellent matches in the World Cup, the best ____of____ which, in my view, was France against Brazil in the semi-final.
2 There were criticisms of the way _____ which the election was conducted.
3 We climbed to the top of the mountain, _____ where it is possible to see three countries.
4 She has recently published a collection of short stories, most _____ which first appeared in the London Literary Magazine.
5 They showed enormous kindness to me, _____ which I will always be grateful.
6 The Red Spider has spread rapidly _____ when it was spotted in the country in 2005.
7 He was married in 1253 to a woman named Purcelle, _____ whom nothing more is known.
8 We're trying to speed up the process _____ which decisions are made in the company.

84

11 Relative clauses (1)

3.4 Complete the sentences using a phrase from A, a relative word or phrase from B and a phrase from C. Write the letters in the spaces.

A
- a a Muslim doctor
- b a narrow piece of wood at the end of a swimming pool
- c ~~housing for old and ill people~~
- d women's narrow trousers
- e an early period in human history
- f a person or company

B
- g whose
- h from which
- i when
- j which
- k ~~where~~
- l who

C
- m end just below the knee.
- n people made tools and weapons only out of stone then.
- o job is to organise the sending of goods from one place to another.
- p ~~help can be given if it is needed.~~
- q uses traditional methods to treat people.
- r people can dive.

1 Sheltered accommodation: __c__ + __k__ + __p__
2 A diving board: _____ + _____ + _____
3 Capri pants: _____ + _____ + _____
4 A shipper: _____ + _____ + _____
5 A hakim: _____ + _____ + _____
6 The Stone Age: _____ + _____ + _____

1 Sheltered accommodation is housing for old and ill people where help can be given if it is needed.

Exam practice

Reading and Use of English Part 1

For questions **1 – 8**, read the text below and decide which answer (**A, B, C** or **D**) best fits each gap. There is an example at the beginning (**0**).

Origami

Origami is the art (0) __B__ paper folding, the aim of (1) _____ is to make objects using folds and creases. Although other shapes are possible, in (2) _____ , objects begin with a square sheet of paper (3) _____ sides may be different colours. This is usually folded without cutting. The origins of origami are not known for (4) _____ . Some are of the (5) _____ that it began in Japan, others that it originated in China, from where it was taken to Japan in the seventh century. It may also have developed independently in the West. What is (6) _____ is that it reached its greatest development in Japan. Probably the most famous modern origami artist was Akira Yoshizawa, who died in 2005. He pioneered origami as a creative art, as well as (7) _____ up with a symbolic method of representing paper folding. In all, he created more than 50,000 models, only a few hundred (8) _____ which were shown in his books.

0	**A** for	**B** of	**C** to	**D** with
1	**A** what	**B** which	**C** whose	**D** how
2	**A** all	**B** addition	**C** time	**D** general
3	**A** who	**B** whose	**C** who's	**D** that
4	**A** certain	**B** definitely	**C** conclusive	**D** positive
5	**A** idea	**B** viewpoint	**C** opinion	**D** theory
6	**A** admitted	**B** final	**C** clear	**D** decided
7	**A** coming	**B** turning	**C** ending	**D** keeping
8	**A** with	**B** in	**C** by	**D** of

12 Relative clauses (2)

Participle clauses; *to*-infinitive clauses; adjective phrases; prepositional phrases

Context listening

1.1 You are going to hear an interview with a food photographer. Which of these items do you think she uses in her work and what for?

1.2 🎧15 Listen and check whether you were right.

1.3 🎧15 Listen again and fill in the gaps at the end of each sentence with what the speakers actually said.

1 When I was quite young – 10 or 11 – I started using an old camera ~~which belonged~~ to my father. _belonging_
2 It was easy to find a photographer <u>who wanted</u> to take an assistant for no pay! _____
3 She was really the first person <u>who encouraged</u> me to take up food photography. _____
4 I was the youngest person in the competition <u>who won</u> any of the major categories. _____
5 The biggest problem is the heat <u>that is produced</u> by the lights. _____
6 Personally, I prefer food <u>that is not made</u> of cardboard! _____
7 I generally have with me a spray bottle <u>which contains</u> glycerine mixed with water. _____
8 We use cotton wool balls <u>that have been soaked</u> in water. _____

1.4 Look at your answers for 1.3. In which did the speakers use:

1 a present participle (*-ing* form)? __1__ , _____ , _____
2 a past participle (*-ed* form)? _____ , _____ , _____
3 a *to*-infinitive? _____ , _____

87

12 Relative clauses (2)

Grammar

2.1 Participle clauses

> **START POINT**
>
> I started using an old camera **belonging** to my father.
> The food in photographs **used** to illustrate cookbooks and magazine articles isn't always entirely authentic.
> And then we put in some material **to substitute** for the food.
> We can often reduce a defining relative clause so that it begins with a present participle (*-ing*), past participle (*-ed*), or *to*-infinitive.

-ing clauses correspond to defining relative clauses with an active verb, and *-ed* clauses correspond to defining relative clauses with a passive verb:
*The editor **working** on the cookbook or magazine is often there, too.* (= *The editor **who is working** ...*)
*A challenge **facing** food photographers is how to keep food looking fresh.* (= *A challenge **which faces** ...*)
*The big problem is the heat **produced** by the lights.* (= *... the heat **that is produced** ...*)
*Personally, I prefer food **not made** of cardboard!* (= *... food **which is not made** of cardboard!*)

Verbs which are not normally used in continuous forms may be used in reduced relative *-ing* clauses.
*This spray bottle **contains** glycerine mixed with water.* (not *... is containing ...*)
However, we can say:
*I generally have with me a spray bottle **containing** glycerine and water.*
Other verbs like this include *belong to, comprise, consist of, constitute, equal, own, possess, resemble, result from, surround*.

It is not always possible to use a reduced form of a relative clause.
- We can't use a reduced form when the first verb in the relative clause is a modal verb:
  *A technique **that might be used** in photographing meat is to use a glycerine spray.*
  *Food **that can't be frozen** is particularly difficult to photograph.*
- We can't use an *-ing* reduced form when we talk about a single, completed action. Compare:
  *Sometimes the chef **who created** the dish in their restaurant comes to the studio.*
  (not *... the chef creating the dish ...*)
  *The chef **preparing** the food today works in a well-known restaurant.*
  (= *The chef **who is preparing** the food today ...*)

Reduced relative clauses can also be used instead of non-defining relative clauses, particularly in written English:
*Her photographs, **taken** in her studio in California ...* (= *... **which were taken** in her studio in California ...*)
*My parents – **not having much money** – rarely took us to restaurants.* (= *... **who didn't have** much money ...*)
These are usually written between commas (,) or dashes (–).

2.2 *To*-infinitive clauses

We often use a *to*-infinitive clause instead of a relative clause after:
- a superlative + noun (phrase):
  *I was the youngest person in the competition **to win** any of the major categories.*
- *the first/second*, etc. + noun (phrase):
  *She was really the first person **to encourage** me to take up food photography.*
- *the only / the next / the last / another / one* + noun (phrase):
  *By the time we photograph the food, it's completely cold. The only thing **to do** in that case is to create steam from elsewhere.*

Relative clauses (2)   12

Often we can use an active or passive *to*-infinitive clause with little difference in meaning:
The **only thing to do** in that case is to create steam from elsewhere. or The **only thing to be done** ...

2.3 Adjective phrases

Adjectives and adjective phrases can be used after nouns with a meaning similar to a relative clause. Often the adjective is followed by a *to*-infinitive or preposition, or used with an adverb:
It was easy to find a photographer **willing to take** an assistant for no pay! (= ... a photographer **who was willing to take** an assistant for no pay!)
It's a job **difficult for** even a skilled photographer. (= ... a job **which is difficult for** even a skilled photographer.)
Glycerine's a liquid, **completely colourless**, that's often used to sweeten food. (= ... a liquid **which is completely colourless**, ...)

A few adjectives (e.g. *affected, available, present*) can be used alone after a noun with a meaning similar to a relative clause:
We use cardboard or any other material **available**. or ... material **which is available**.
(See **Unit 7**, **2.3** for more on the position of adjectives.)

2.4 Prepositional phrases

We can give additional information about a thing or person using a prepositional phrase. Often these have a meaning similar to a relative clause:
The vegetables **around** that succulent piece of meat could be made from plastic. (= The vegetables **which are around** ...)

Grammar exercises

3.1 Complete each pair of sentences using a verb from the box. In (a) use a relative pronoun and a form of the verb; in (b) use a reduced relative *-ing* or *-ed* form.

belong   carry   injure   play   not see   ~~want~~

1   a   People _____who want_____ tickets for the cup final can expect to pay over 100 euros.
    b   People _____wanting_____ tickets for the cup final can expect to pay over 100 euros.
2   a   The Internet is bringing about a degree of cultural change _____ for centuries.
    b   The Internet is bringing about a degree of cultural change _____ for centuries.
3   a   All the passengers _____ in the train crash have been released from hospital.
    b   All the passengers _____ in the train crash have been released from hospital.
4   a   Our teacher, _____ a huge pile of textbooks, came hurrying into the room.
    b   Our teacher, _____ a huge pile of textbooks, came hurrying into the room.
5   a   Some jewellery _____ to the Queen has been stolen from Buckingham Palace.
    b   Some jewellery _____ to the Queen has been stolen from Buckingham Palace.
6   a   The woman _____ the piano over there – is she your sister?
    b   The woman _____ the piano over there – is she your sister?

12 Relative clauses (2)

3.2 Use the information in the brackets to complete these newspaper extracts. Use reduced relative clauses beginning with an *-ing* or *-ed* form, *being* + *-ed* or *to be* + *-ed*. If a reduced relative clause is not possible, use a relative clause + relative pronoun (e.g. *which*).

1. The government has brought in new legislation _____ (*It will affect Britain's 5.4 million dog owners.*). From next year all dogs will have to be tagged with tiny electronic chips _____. (*They will hold information about the dog's owner.*)

2. The inquiry into the wreck of the oil tanker Panmax, _____ (*It sank off the southwest coast in 2014.*), has produced its final report. The report, _____ , (*It is to be published tomorrow.*) is thought to show that the captain was mainly responsible for the collision with a smaller vessel.

3. Demonstrators _____ (*They have been protesting.*) against the play *Global Strife* at the Crest Theatre, claiming it to be 'anti-religious', have succeeded in preventing it being performed. The theatre management, _____ (*They were advised by police that security could not be guaranteed.*), cancelled last night's performance. On Thursday, a number of demonstrators _____ (*They broke through police lines.*) caused damage to the theatre and terrified members of the audience.

4. Researchers in New Zealand are developing a new drug _____ (*It might prevent memory loss in older people.*). A group of 20 elderly people _____ (*They were suffering from dementia.*) were given the drug over a two-year period, and results showed a significant slowing down in memory decline. The drug, _____ (*It is derived from a plant. The plant is found only in New Zealand.*), will now be tested on a larger group before being made more widely available.

Relative clauses (2) 12

3.3 Complete the sentences with phrases from the box. Use a *to*-infinitive clause, an adjective phrase or a prepositional phrase. Make changes and additions as necessary.

ring today about the car	announce large-scale redundancies
very similar to Romanian	you should contact the human resources manager
take part in the London Marathon	the south side of the city
would be happy to help out	~~orbit the Earth~~

1 In 1962, John Glenn became the first American ___to orbit the Earth___ .
2 If you want to find out if there are any job vacancies in the company, the person _____ .
3 It was really expensive living in the centre, so we've just bought a flat _____ .
4 You won't have to organise the party yourself. I'm sure there'll be a lot of people _____ .
5 At 91, Abraham Weintraub is the oldest competitor ever _____ .
6 The state language of Moldova is Moldovan, a language _____ .
7 With fewer cars being sold around the world, Nisda has become the latest car company _____ .
8 You're the tenth person _____ . I'm sorry, but it's already been sold.

3.4 Underline the twelve relative clauses in this newspaper article (the first one has been done for you). Which ones could be rewritten as reduced relative clauses?

Monitors to cut home electricity use

Monitors <u>which show the real-time cost of electricity use</u> are to be provided free of charge to homes across the UK in an effort to slow down climate change. Under the new government proposals, from next year electricity suppliers will have to provide the devices – which have cut power use by up to 6.5% in Canada – to all customers who want them. Domestic appliances which are left on unnecessarily are estimated to waste £900 million of electricity a year.

Traditional electricity meters are usually kept out of sight in cupboards. However, the monitors, which use microchip technology and a digital display, are intended to be placed in full view as a constant reminder of the electricity that is being used in a house at any given moment.

The Environment Secretary said: 'People want to do their bit to help protect the environment as well as save money, and visual display units that are provided free of charge will help people do both.' A spokeswoman for the Electricity Consumer Council said it supported any plan that would give customers access to free monitors. The shadow environment secretary said: 'Although it is an interesting and welcome measure, there are still many details that should be considered, not least the reliability of these meters.'

However, the Energy Retail Council has criticised the proposal, saying that it did not go far enough. In a statement, their chief executive said: 'We had hoped the government would recommend the introduction of 'smart meters' – which communicate electricity consumption to both the customer and the energy supplier – rather than meters that are only able to do half the job.'

Exam practice

Reading and Use of English Part 5

You are going to read a newspaper article. For questions **1 – 6**, choose the answer (**A**, **B**, **C** or **D**) which you think fits best according to the text.

Should children be taken to art galleries?

The debate about taking young children to art galleries has a long history. On one side are traditionalists – conservators and keen gallery-goers – who disapprove of the noise and disruption caused by children and worry about damage to fragile paintings and sculptures. In opposition are the progressives – educationalists and parents – who contend that viewing art enriches the lives of children. This dispute has resurfaced in the media recently following a claim by the visual artist Jake Chapman that dragging children round galleries is "a total waste of time". Parents are "arrogant", he says, for thinking children could understand the work of such complex artists as Jackson Pollock and Mark Rothko.

Current thinking, of course, sides with the progressives. Early exposure to art widens children's horizons, develops their curiosity about the world, and boosts their creativity. Further, it significantly increases the chances that they will have a life-long interest. With this in mind, many galleries have adopted a more child-friendly approach, encouraging parents to bring their children by arranging special events and handing out quizzes and worksheets to children as they arrive. From this perspective, expecting children to conform to adult behaviour in galleries is a form of punishment, which should be subverted at every turn.

But maybe Chapman does have a point. Developmental psychology suggests that before the age of 8 or 9 children view art only for what it represents in the real world. It is only in their early teens that children begin to go beyond representation and understand that art is created to express certain meanings and values beyond the literal. Art education is necessary before the adolescent can appreciate stylistic elements and develop a critical facility, making their own judgments about the merits of a piece. Faced with abstract expressionism such as Pollock's drips and looping swirls or Rothko's rectangles of colours, it's no wonder that young children quickly lose interest. We shouldn't be surprised if most prefer the joys of running up and down the polished gallery floors as they search the paintings for answers to worksheet questions, or even, heaven forbid, run their sticky fingers over priceless masterpieces. Should children be allowed to ruin other visitors' experience by causing a din among the Pre-Raphaelites? Of course not.

Against this, I think back to my own experience of viewing art as a young child. I was taken to galleries regularly – but for short visits to see just a handful of paintings each time. My parents would talk about each of the paintings and always ask me what I liked most about it. I wouldn't say that I understood everything they said, but through this exposure, over time I came to learn something about the subject matter of art, artistic techniques and, above all, the experience of viewing: what's most important is how a piece of art makes you feel. I was lucky enough, though, to have knowledgeable and sensitive parents, and local galleries available that we could visit again and again. Access to art has undoubtedly improved my quality of life, and I only have to watch a child engaging with a painting to realize it is the same for many others.

Jake Chapman was right to reignite the debate, but his conclusion is wrong. We shouldn't be excluding children from art galleries. Instead, we should be educating parents, helping them to improve the experience of their children's gallery visits – good both for their children and other visitors. First, parents should know some simple ground rules of gallery behaviour and make sure they and their children stick to them: don't touch paintings and sculptures (it can cause damage); don't have loud phone conversations (it's annoying for everyone else); and don't take photos of the artworks (paintings are meant to be looked at, not posed next to – buy a guidebook afterwards if you want a record of what you've seen). More importantly, though, they need advice on how to encourage their children to look at and talk about artwork. The worksheets given to children could be replaced with ones for parents, including relevant information and suggested discussion topics to share with their children. Through interaction of this kind, children will grow up believing that art is for all, not just for adults or for some exclusive group of 'art appreciators' to which they do not belong. And by being involved, interest and enthusiasm will replace boredom.

Exam practice

Relative clauses (2) **12**

1. What view does the artist Jake Chapman put forward about art galleries?
   - A Parents think they are too difficult for children to understand.
   - B Parents overestimate their value.
   - C Children learn little about art by visiting them.
   - D Children tend not to enjoy visiting them.

2. According to the writer, 'progressives' believe that galleries
   - A should be organized with children in mind.
   - B should prioritize children over adults.
   - C should encourage children to paint more themselves.
   - D should not restrict how children behave.

3. In the third paragraph, the writer says that very young children
   - A can be taught to judge the quality of a painting.
   - B are not ready to appreciate abstract art.
   - C are reluctant to criticize paintings.
   - D are attracted only to paintings showing scenes of real life.

4. During the writer's visits to art galleries as a young child
   - A her parents told her which paintings were noteworthy.
   - B she accumulated knowledge of a large number of paintings.
   - C she was surprised at her parents' knowledge of art.
   - D she was encouraged to evaluate art.

5. What point does the writer make in the fifth paragraph?
   - A Parents need to learn more about art appreciation.
   - B Gallery rules need to be enforced more strictly.
   - C Not all parents can appreciate art.
   - D Adults should be more tolerant of children's behaviour in galleries.

6. An idea recurring in the text is that
   - A both adults and children behave badly in galleries.
   - B children know as much about art as their parents.
   - C it takes time for children to learn to appreciate art.
   - D galleries are not doing enough to help children understand art.

13 Adverbial clauses

Adverbial clauses including time clauses, contrast and concession clauses, reason clauses, purpose and result clauses

Context listening

1.1 Maria and Stefan are being interviewed about their eating habits. Before you listen, look at some definitions of words and phrases used in the interview. What do you think they are? Check your answers in the Key.

1. Food with substances added to it to preserve it or to give it a new colour or taste.
2. A meal cooked before you buy it so that you only have to heat it before eating.
3. A combination of the correct quantities and sorts of food eaten every day.
4. The process of getting the right sorts of food and drink in order to keep you healthy.

1.2 ▶16 Listen to the interview and fill in the gaps.

1. At the weekend I like to make something myself ____*so as not to*____ eat processed food all the time.
2. We'll usually go out to eat _____ none of us likes cooking.
3. She also talked to me about the food she made _____ I'd learn about diet and nutrition.
4. If I get hungry, I'll eat some fruit, _____ at school I'd buy a bar of chocolate.
5. I don't eat much for breakfast _____ I'm always in a rush.
6. I have to get out by 7.30 _____ catch my bus.
7. Sometimes I get up in the night and have a snack, _____ I know it's bad for me.
8. I was absolutely exhausted _____ I had to run for the bus yesterday.
9. I don't have the opportunity to go shopping _____ I'm working.
10. It's very hard to put a healthy diet into practice _____ I know all about the theory.

1.3 Look at the word or phrase you wrote in sentence 5 in 1.2. What other word or phrase you wrote in 1.2 has a similar meaning? What other words or phrases are similar to the one in sentence 7?

Adverbial clauses 13

Grammar

2.1 Adverbial clauses: general

> **START POINT**
>
> I seem to eat less healthily **as I get older**.
> **Although I'd like to eat more fresh food**, I don't have time to prepare meals in the evenings.
> An adverbial clause adds extra information to a main clause about things such as time, reason or purpose. Most adverbial clauses begin with a conjunction (e.g. *as, although*) and can come before or after the main clause.

An adverbial clause must be connected to a main clause; we can't use it as a separate sentence:
I don't eat much for breakfast **because I'm always in a rush**. (not *I don't eat much for breakfast. Because I'm always in a rush.*)
We only use one conjunction to connect an adverbial clause and a main clause: (not *Because I'm always in a rush, so I don't eat breakfast.*)

2.2 Time clauses

> **START POINT**
>
> I generally have a sandwich and a packet of crisps **as/when/while** I'm sitting at my desk.
> We can use *as*, *when* or *while* to talk about something that happens when something else takes place.
> *As* can sometimes mean either 'because' or 'during the time that':
> I opened the window **as** I was cooking. (= ... **because** I was cooking or ... **while** I was cooking)

We don't use *will* in a clause with a time conjunction (e.g. *before, until, when*) to talk about a future action or an action that is completed before another in the main clause:
I'd like to have something more substantial **before I leave** home in the morning. (not ... *before I will leave home in the morning.*)
When I've written up the research, I'll let you have a copy. (not *When I will have written up the research, ...*)
We use *when* (not *as* or *while*) at the beginning of an adverbial clause which:

- refers to a point in time:
  I remember once I was eating some sweets in my bedroom **when my mother walked in**.
- describes the circumstances in which the event in the main clause happens:
  When I get home late, I take a ready meal out of the freezer.
- refers to a past period of our lives:
  When I was younger, my mother used to keep an eye on what I ate.
- talks about 'every time' something happens:
  When/Whenever I've had one of those ready meals, I feel hungry by the time I go to bed.

We prefer *as* to show that one thing changes at the same time as another:
As I put on weight, it gets more and more difficult to exercise. (rather than *When/While I put on weight*)
We can use *as* or *when* to highlight the moment that something happens:
As/When I turned the corner, the bus was just pulling up ... (not *While I turned ...*)

13 Adverbial clauses

2.3 Contrast and concession clauses

We use *although* or, less formally, *though* to say that there is a contrast between what happens in the main clause and the adverbial clause:

*Sometimes I get up in the night and have a snack, **although I know it's bad for me**.*

or to introduce a concession clause that suggests the opposite of the main clause:

***Although I don't enjoy cooking**, I prepare a meal for myself every evening.*

We can use *though* at the end of a clause:

*In some ways, it's better now, **though**.* (not ... it's better now, although.)

We can use *despite the fact that / in spite of the fact that* or *despite / in spite of + -ing* with a similar meaning to *although*:

***Despite the fact that** I know all about the theory of a healthy diet, it's very hard to put it into practice.* or ***In spite of the fact that** I know ...*
***Despite** (**my**) **knowing** all about the theory of a healthy diet, it's very hard to put it into practice.* or ***In spite of** (**my**) **knowing** ...*

We can use *while* or *whereas* to say that there is a contrast with something in the main clause. The *while/whereas* clause may come before or after the main clause:

*If I got hungry at school, I'd buy a chocolate bar, **whereas nowadays I'll eat some fruit**.* or *... **while** nowadays ...*
***Whereas nowadays I'll eat some fruit**, at school I'd buy a chocolate bar.* or ***While** nowadays ...*

We can use *whilst* as a more formal alternative to *while*.

(See also Unit **14**, 2.3 *Even if* and *even though*.)

2.4 Reason clauses

> ### START POINT
> *I must be eating too much **because** I've been getting a bit overweight recently.*
> ***Because** it's so easy to buy ready meals from the supermarket, it makes me quite lazy.*
> *I have to get out by 7.30, **so** I really don't have time.*
>
> A very common way of giving a reason or explanation for something, particularly in speech, is to use an adverbial clause with *because*. A clause beginning *so* is also often used to express a similar meaning.
>
> *Most recipes in magazines are no use to me **because of** the time they take.*
>
> ***Because of*** can also be used before a noun or noun phrase to give a reason for something.

Formal alternatives to *because* are *as* and *since*:

*She made a particular effort **because/as/since** I was often ill as a child.*

Informal alternatives to *because* are *seeing that* and *seeing as*:

*We'll usually go out to eat **seeing that/as** none of us likes cooking.*

2.5 Purpose and result clauses

To talk about the purpose of an action we can use *in order / so as + to*-infinitive:

*I have to get out by 7.30 **in order to catch** my bus.* or *... **so as to catch** ...*

Informally, it is more common to use a *to*-infinitive to express the same meaning:

*I have to get out by 7.30 **to catch** my train.*

In negatives we prefer *in order not / so as not + to*-infinitive rather than *not + to*-infinitive:

*I like to make something myself **so as not to / in order not to** eat processed food all the time.*

We also use *in order that* and *so that* to talk about a purpose:

*She also talked to me about the food she made **in order that** I'd learn about diet and nutrition.* or less formally ...
***so** (**that**) I'd learn about ...*

Adverbial clauses 13

We often use modal verbs after *in order / so that*:
*It'll be interesting to read the results of the research **so that I can** see how typical my diet is.*
*She also talked to me about the food she made **so that I'd** learn about diet and nutrition.*

Grammar exercises

3.1 Complete the sentences with *as*, *when* or *while*. Give all correct or likely alternatives.

1 You wouldn't think it now, but _____*when*_____ I was very young I used to have curly, brown hair.
2 It's more and more important for business people to speak foreign languages _____ business becomes increasingly international.
3 How old were you _____ you got married?
4 I was so tired last night, I went to sleep _____ my head hit the pillow.
5 _____ my children get older, I find they get even fussier about food.
6 She always brings a bunch of flowers _____ she comes to visit.
7 _____ I sat down to take my maths exam, I realised I'd forgotten to bring my calculator with me.
8 _____ the level of pesticides in the potatoes is well below the legal limit, the public have been advised to avoid eating them for the time being.

3.2 Rewrite the underlined part of the sentence using a phrase with a similar meaning beginning *Despite …*

1 <u>Although she fell</u> heavily at the start of the race, she went on to finish second. _Despite falling_
2 <u>Although we got</u> lost on the way, we were eventually only a few minutes late. _____
3 <u>Although she was</u> badly hurt herself, she helped a number of passengers out of the crashed coach. _____
4 <u>Although we lived</u> in the same village, we had never spoken to each other. _____
5 <u>Although the alarm went off</u> when the house was broken into, nobody bothered to call the police. _____
6 <u>Although there were</u> plenty of warning signs, people were still swimming in the river. _____
7 <u>Although it is</u> banned in public spaces, smoking is on the increase. _____

13 Adverbial clauses

3.3 Complete the sentences using a phrase from A (use each one twice) and an ending from B. Write the letters in the spaces.

A

| a in order that | b so as not to | c in that | d seeing that |

B

e the front wheel is smaller than the back	f it's so poorly paid
g some broken tiles could be repaired	h damage its roots
i larger planes can land there	j she's so fit
k they are carnivorous	l be overheard

1 The swimming pool had to be emptied __a__ + __g__
2 People here don't put much effort into the job ____ + ____
3 My bike is unusual ____ + ____
4 You need to lift the plant carefully ____ + ____
5 Pitcher plants are unique ____ + ____
6 The runway is going to be extended ____ + ____
7 She'll probably recover from the illness quickly ____ + ____
8 We spoke very quietly ____ + ____

1 *The swimming pool had to be emptied in order that some broken tiles could be repaired.*

3.4 Choose the correct or more likely options in these texts.

A

Hello Alison,

I couldn't contact you this **(1)** *morning because* / *morning. Because* we had a power cut here. Sorry. Thanks for the invitation to lunch tomorrow. I'm not sure I'll be able to make it, **(2)** *though* / *although*. **(3)** *In spite of that* / *In spite of the fact that* we've got extra staff at work, we're struggling to meet the deadline to finish writing the software. This means I've got a huge amount of work to do **(4)** *before I go* / *before I will go* on holiday at the end of the week. I feel really guilty **(5)** *seeing* / *seeing that* this is the second time this year I've had to turn down your invitation.

Hope to see you in the near future.

Regards,

Ros

B

A: I'm sorry I'm not here to take your call. Please leave a message after the tone and I'll get back to you as soon as I can.

B: Hello, Omar, it's Martha. I'm afraid I have to cancel our meeting tomorrow. My father's just phoned to say my mother's been taken ill. **(1)** *Because of* / *Because* it sounds quite serious, **(2)** *I'll have to* / *so I'll have to* take time off to go and see her. I may be away for a few days, but I'll have my laptop with me **(3)** *while* / *whilst* I'm there **(4)** *so as I can* / *so that I can* do some work. When **(5)** *you will get* / *you get* the chance, give me a ring and we'll sort out another time to meet. Bye for now.

98

Exam practice

Adverbial clauses **13**

Reading and Use of English Part 2

For questions **1 – 8**, read the text below and think of the word which best fits each gap. Use only **one** word in each gap. There is an example at the beginning **(0)**.

Life in Spain

Spain is a vast and varied country, and its people have **(0)** _few_ things in common **(1)** _____ for their friendliness, sociability, and hospitality. Spaniards have a reputation for not letting work get in the way of enjoyment, and for spending as **(2)** _____ time and energy as possible on their social lives. Their frequent use of the word *mañana* – leave things **(3)** _____ tomorrow - is seen as being characteristic of this tendency. While this may be a stereotypical view of Spanish life, it is true that many people organise their working hours **(4)** _____ as to make the most of their free time. Spaniards are sociable **(5)** _____ that they like nothing better than spending time with friends and relatives. Eating together is an important part of social life, and large groups often **(6)** _____ up for dinner. Not **(7)** _____ , Spain is thought to have more restaurants per head of population than any **(8)** _____ European country.

14 Conditionals

Real and unreal conditionals; *if ... not* and *unless*; *even if* and *even though*; *if only* and *wish*; other conditional expressions

Context listening

1.1 Look at these photos of places where wild animals can be seen. Which places are shown here?

a   b   c

1.2 [▶17] Listen to part of a radio discussion programme where three people are being interviewed about the opening of a new zoo. Which speaker or speakers (Liam, Nadia or Mariam) make these points?

1 Most people don't have the opportunity to see wild animals in their natural environment. *Liam and Mariam*
2 Captive breeding programmes are important in preserving wild animals. _____
3 Animals may suffer when they are being taken to zoos. _____
4 Many animals now in zoos were born there. _____
5 It is unacceptable to keep animals in cages or small enclosures. _____
6 Safari parks haven't always looked after animals well. _____
7 The main purpose of zoos and safari parks is to make money. _____
8 Game reserves need to be supported by governments in developed countries. _____

1.3 [▶17] What word or phrase did the speakers use to link these ideas? Listen again if you are not sure.

1 we didn't have zoos + most people would never see wild animals in real life _____*if*_____
2 we expand captive breeding + many more animals will die out _____
3 wild animals are born in a zoo + it's still cruel to keep them in a small enclosure _____
4 I'm all in favour of safari parks + the animals are well looked after _____
5 they say they are concerned about the welfare of animals + they are still businesses mainly out to make a profit _____
6 developed countries put money into these reserves + species will be preserved _____

1 *If we didn't have zoos, most people would never see wild animals in real life.*

100

Conditionals 14

Grammar

2.1 Real and unreal conditionals

> **START POINT**
>
> Conditional sentences may suggest that an event or situation is *real* – it is true, generally happens, has happened or is likely to happen; or *unreal* – it is imaginary or untrue, did not happen or is not likely to happen.
>
> **Real conditionals**
> *If there **is** a health problem, vets **deal** with it quickly.* (*if* + present simple, + present simple)
> *Before safari parks were opened, **if** people **wanted** to see lions and giraffes, they **had** to go to a zoo.* (*if* + past simple, + past simple)
> *If we **don't provide** safe havens for animals, many **will die** out.* (*if* + present simple, + *will* + bare infinitive)
> **Unreal conditionals**
> *If they **were** in the wild, they **would have** more space to roam free.* (*if* + past simple, + *would* + bare infinitive)
> *If we **had introduced** captive breeding programmes sooner, we **would have prevented** the extinction of a number of animals.* (*if* + past perfect, + *would have* + past participle)

Real conditionals
We can use a wide variety of other patterns in the *if*-clause and the main clause:
If we're going to protect animals in Africa, we'll need to invest much more money ... (*if* + *going to*, + *will* + bare infinitive)
If we close zoos, we might deprive people of the opportunity of seeing wild animals. (*if* + present simple, + *might* + bare infinitive)
If you think closing down zoos will improve the chances of survival of endangered species, you're making a big mistake. (*if* + present simple, + present continuous)
We don't usually use *will* in the *if*-clause:
If they're not eaten by the larger animals first, they'll be killed by visitors' cars. (not *If they won't be eaten* ...)
However, we can use *will* in the *if*-clause:
- when we talk about a result of something in the main clause:
  ... we should have captive breeding programmes if it will help save species. or *... if it helps ... .*
- when we want to show that we strongly disapprove of something:
  A: *That zookeeper was really annoyed with me.*
  B: *Well, if you will throw stones at the animals, it's not surprising!*

Unreal conditionals
We can use modals other than *would* in the main clause:
If we'd introduced captive breeding earlier, animals now extinct might have survived.
We don't usually use *would* in the *if*-clause:
If we had more funding, we would be able to do even more... (not *If we would have more funding* ...)

Mixed conditionals
We can sometimes vary conditionals by mixing the tenses:
- *if* + past tense, *would have* + past participle
  If it wasn't so expensive, we would have opened many more safari parks around the country. (= it is very expensive, so we didn't open any more)

101

14 Conditionals

- *if* + past perfect, *would* + bare infinitive
  If game reserves had been set up earlier, there would now be fewer animals in danger ... (= game reserves were not set up earlier, so more animals are in danger)

In formal contexts we can use *were* instead of *was* in the *if*-clause:
If it were not for zoos, most people would never see wild animals. or less formally *If it was not for ...*
We prefer to use *were* in the expression *If I were you ...* for giving advice.
We can use *if ... were* + *to*-infinitive rather than *if* + past simple to talk about imaginary future situations:
If the government were to ban zoos, it would put captive breeding programmes at risk. or *If the government banned zoos ...*
We don't usually use this pattern with state verbs (e.g. *belong, doubt, know, understand*):
If we understood more about animal behaviour we would be in a better position to protect them. (not *If we were to understand more about ...*)

2.2 *If ... not* and *unless*

START POINT

In real conditional sentences, we can often use either *unless* or *if ... not* when the meaning is 'except if':
Unless we expand captive breeding, many more animals will die out. or *If we don't expand ...*

We usually use *if ... not* instead of *unless*:
- when we say in the main clause that an event or action in the *if*-clause is unexpected:
  I'll be surprised if we don't get permission to build the zoo.
- usually in questions:
  How will children learn about wild animals if they don't see them in zoos?
- when the meaning is similar to 'because ... not' rather than 'except if':
  If developing countries don't have the money to establish nature reserves, more developed countries must offer help.
- in unreal conditional sentences:
  If we didn't have zoos, most people would never see wild animals.

We use *unless* instead of *if ... not* when we introduce an afterthought:
We must have zoos if we want children to learn more about wild animals – unless their parents are rich enough to go on holiday to Africa, of course.

2.3 *Even if* and *even though*

We can use *even if* to mean 'whether or not' and *even though* to mean 'despite the fact that':
Even if wild animals are born in a zoo, it is still cruel to keep them in a small enclosure. (= whether or not animals are born in a zoo)
Even though they say they are concerned about the welfare of animals, they are still businesses mainly out to make a profit. (= despite the fact that they say they are concerned)

2.4 *If only* and *wish*

We can use *if only / wish* + past simple to say that we want a present situation to be different, and *if only / wish* + past perfect to say that we regret a past event:
I wish the situation was/were different. or *If only the situation was/were different.*
If only we had acted sooner. or *I wish we had acted sooner.*

Conditionals 14

We can use *if only / wish + would* to criticise someone, to say that we want someone to change their behaviour or that we want something to change:
I **wish** Nadia Muller and the people in Save the Animals **would** read the scientific research ...
We can't say *I wish I would* ...:
I **wish** I worked in a zoo. or I **wish** I could work in a zoo. (not *I wish I would work* ...)

2.5 Other conditional expressions

A number of other expressions are used at the beginning of conditional clauses:
I'm all in favour of safari parks **provided** (*that*) / **providing** (*that*) the animals are well looked after.
So long as / **As long as** developed countries put money into these reserves, species will be preserved.
I'm willing to support the proposal **on condition that** animals are kept in large enclosures.
In the event of the alarm sounding, visitors should leave the zoo by the nearest exit.
Supposing the proposal is rejected, what will you do then?
An alarm will sound **in case of** animals escaping from the safari park.
We must protect natural habitats, **otherwise** more animals will become extinct.
But for the existence of zoos, many people would never have seen wild animals.

Grammar exercises

3.1 Underline the correct answer(s) in (b) to make a second sentence with a meaning as close as possible to the sentence in (a).

1. a With a student card you can get a discount at the bookshop.
   b If you *will have* / *have* a student card you can get a discount at the bookshop.
2. a I didn't know you were a vegetarian, otherwise I wouldn't have cooked lamb.
   b If I *know* / *had known* you were a vegetarian, I wouldn't have cooked lamb for dinner.
3. a By using more efficient light bulbs, there could be a 5% reduction in electricity consumption.
   b If we *used* / *have used* more efficient light bulbs, there could be a 5% reduction in electricity consumption.
4. a You can borrow my e-reader as long as you promise to bring it back soon.
   b If you *promise* / *promised* to bring it back soon, you can borrow my e-reader.
5. a I don't have a reliable car, so I probably won't drive to France.
   b If I *had* / *have* a reliable car I *will* / *would* probably drive to France.
6. a I wasn't promoted, so I didn't have to move to our head office in Madrid.
   b If I *am promoted* / *had been promoted*, I *had to* / *would have had to* move to our head office in Madrid.
7. a You'll have to leave the house by 7.00 to catch the 8.30 train.
   b If you *leave* / *will leave* the house by 7.00, you *will be able to catch* / *are able to catch* the 8.30 train.
8. a I didn't study hard, and that's why I have such a poorly paid job now.
   b If I *studied* / *had studied* harder, I *won't have* / *wouldn't have* such a poorly paid job now.

14 Conditionals

3.2 **Complete the sentences using a word or phrase in the box and the verb in brackets.**

> even if   even though   if   unless

1. I didn't tell my parents I was coming to a night club. _If they knew_ where I was, they'd be really annoyed. (*know*)
2. It's so cold, it would be surprising _____ we _____ snow tonight. (*not get*)
3. She didn't seem at all tired _____ she _____ all day. (*drive*)
4. I haven't lost any weight _____ I _____ lots of exercise. (*do*)
5. _____ it _____ soon, there will still be water rationing in this part of the country. (*rain*)
6. I could pick you up at about eight, and we could go to the party together – _____ you _____ to go on your own, of course. (*prefer*)
7. _____ a buyer _____ be found for the company, it is likely to close by the end of the week. (*can*)
8. The latest opinion poll suggests that _____ the election _____ to be held today, the ruling party would again have a huge majority. (*be*)

3.3 **Match the sentence beginnings and endings, joining them with one of the words or phrases in the box. Sometimes more than one word or phrase is possible.**

> in the event of   on condition that   but for   ~~in case~~   providing   otherwise

1. I'll be in my office just before the exam
2. Aid must reach the refugees before the rainy season starts.
3. The demonstrators arrested were allowed to go free
4. Car airbags were designed to prevent chest injuries to the driver
5. He would have gone on working until he was 65
6. We should get to the airport by 5.00

a. they remained outside a ten-mile zone around the nuclear power station.
b. the traffic isn't too heavy on the motorway.
c. a head-on collision.
d. anyone has any last-minute questions.
e. his poor health.
f. many thousands will die.

1. _I'll be in my office just before the exam in case anyone has any last-minute questions._
2. _____
3. _____
4. _____
5. _____
6. _____

Conditionals 14

3.4 Choose the correct verb forms in these conversations. Sometimes both are possible.

A

A: I feel terrible.
B: Well, if you **(1)** <u>will stay</u> / *stay* out until three in the morning, what do you expect?
A: I don't think I'll go to school today.
B: But supposing they **(2)** *phone* / *would phone* to find out where you are? What shall I tell them?
A: Okay, I'll go – if it **(3)** *will make* / *makes* you happy.

B

A: Grandad, before you blow out the candles, you've got to make a wish.
B: Well, I wish I **(1)** *had bought* / *would have bought* a house with a smaller garden. It's a lot of hard work to look after it.
A: And what else are you going to wish for?
B: I wish I **(2)** *have* / *had* more energy to play with my grandchildren.
A: And anything else?
B: I suppose I wish I **(3)** *was* / *would be* a young man again.
A: And have you got any more wishes?
B: Yes, I wish you **(4)** *stopped* / *would stop* asking me questions and let me eat my birthday cake!

Exam practice

Listening Part 4

▶18 You will hear five short extracts in which people are talking about cooking. **While you listen you must complete both tasks.**

TASK ONE
For questions **1 – 5**, choose from the list (**A – H**) the person who is speaking.

A	a nurse	Speaker 1	1
B	a retired person	Speaker 2	2
C	a student	Speaker 3	3
D	an author	Speaker 4	4
E	a lawyer	Speaker 5	5
F	a teacher		
G	a lorry driver		
H	an unemployed person		

TASK TWO
For questions **6 – 10**, choose from the list (**A – H**) what each speaker is expressing.

A	admiration for people who can cook well	Speaker 1	6
B	a pride in their cooking ability	Speaker 2	7
C	a reluctance to cook	Speaker 3	8
D	a criticism of current trends in cooking	Speaker 4	9
E	a desire to learn to cook	Speaker 5	10
F	a wish to try food from other countries		
G	an awareness of their poor diet		
H	a dislike of unfamiliar food		

15 Participle, to-infinitive and reduced clauses

Participle clauses including present participle (-*ing*) clauses, past participle (-*ed*) clauses, participle clauses after conjunctions and prepositions, *to*-infinitive clauses, reduced clauses

Context listening

1.1 ▶19 Sam Green has taken three months off work to do a sponsored walk through Italy raising money for charity. Each week he sends an article to his company for its newsletter. Listen to two of his colleagues talking about Sam's latest article. Which of the problems does Sam talk about?

1 ☐   2 ☐   3 ☐

4 ☐   5 ☐   6 ☐

1.2 ▶19 Listen again and complete the sentences with the exact words Sam uses.

1 _Having fallen over_ a number of times, I was feeling thoroughly miserable.
2 _____ by a difficult few days, I was only interested in finding a bed for the night.
3 _____ Naples, I bought yet more walking socks.
4 _____ the sprawl of the city behind me, I walked up into the hills.
5 _____ my sleeping bag, I discovered a scorpion.
6 _____ by a scratching sound, I found a large rat trying to get into my backpack.

107

15 Participle, to-infinitive and reduced clauses

Grammar

2.1 Participle clauses: general

> **START POINT**
>
> *Walking into each village*, I was met by a pack of unfriendly dogs.
> *Found mainly in the south of the country*, scorpions in Italy can give a nasty bite but are rarely dangerous.
> *Having spent a couple of hours exploring Amalfi*, I'm now ready for an excellent Italian dinner.
> Participle clauses are more common in writing, and are often used to express ideas in an economical way.

A participle usually refers to the subject of the main clause:
Snarling aggressively, **the dogs** were pretty terrifying at first. (= the dogs were snarling and the dogs were pretty terrifying)

We avoid using a participle clause when the subjects are different: *Snarling aggressively, I kept away from the dogs.* In this example, the writer is trying to say that the dogs were snarling and he kept away from them. However, it sounds as if he was snarling! The more accurate alternative is: *The dogs were snarling aggressively, so I kept away from them.*

In formal English, a participle clause can sometimes have its own subject, which is often a pronoun or a noun phrase including a pronoun:
*Scorpions in North Africa, **some measuring** up to 20 centimetres, can kill adults.* (*Scorpions in North Africa* = subject of the main clause; *some* = subject of the participle)

When we use *not* in a participle clause it usually comes before the participle:
***Not wanting** to carry my backpack any further, I went to the first hotel I came across.*

2.2 Present participle (-ing) clauses

We can use a present participle clause to talk about something that takes place at the same time as, or just before, an action in the main clause:
***Opening** up my sleeping bag, **I discovered** a scorpion.*

A present participle clause can be used to give background information:
***Living** mainly in warm climates, scorpions have existed for over 400 million years.*
and after quoted speech, to say what someone was doing while they were talking:
*'Wait for me here,' said Frank, **running** out of the house.*

Present participle clauses can also be used to talk about a reason or result:
***Arriving** in Amalfi early in the afternoon, I had time to look around the town.* (= because I arrived in Amalfi early in the afternoon)

2.3 Past participle (-ed) clauses

We can use a past participle clause to talk about reasons and conditions:
***Made** from the softest leather imaginable, they are as comfortable as a pair of slippers.* (reason = because they are made from the softest leather imaginable)
***Sold** in Britain, the boots would have cost a lot more.* (condition = if they were sold in Britain)

Past participles combine with forms of *be* and *have* to create passives and perfect forms:
***Having fallen** over a number of times, I was feeling thoroughly miserable.* (= I was feeling thoroughly miserable because I had fallen over a number of times)

Participle, to-infinitive and reduced clauses 15

We can use either *having* + *-ed* or a present participle with a similar meaning to describe events that follow one after another. However, *having* + *-ed* emphasises that the action in the participle clause is complete before the action in the main clause begins:
Having climbed to the top of the hill, I could see all the way to the Mediterranean. or **Climbing** to the top of the hill, …
Being made so welcome at the hotel, I was reluctant to leave. (= because I was made so welcome)
Having been woken up by a scratching sound, I found a large rat trying to get into my backpack. (= after I had been woken up)

2.4 Participle clauses after conjunctions and prepositions

We can use a present participle clause after a number of conjunctions and prepositions, including: *after, before, by, in, on, since, when, while, with, without, unless, until*:
Before leaving Naples, I bought yet more walking socks. or less formally **Before I left** Naples, I bought yet more walking socks.

We can also use *with* (or informally *what with*) to introduce a reason for something in the main clause. Notice that a subject has to come between *with* and *-ing*:
With Naples **being** such a busy city, I was surprised to find a hotel room so easily.
What with sleeping badly, and some very steep hills to walk over, it was quite a relief to get to Amalfi this afternoon. (= because I had slept badly)

In formal contexts we can use a past participle after *(al)though, as, if, once, when, while, unless* and *until*:
Walking through Italy was a fantastic experience, but **if asked**, I'm not sure I'd do it again. or … but **if I was asked** …

2.5 To-infinitive clauses

We can use a clause beginning with a *to*-infinitive to talk about purpose, result or condition:
I walked up into the hills **to avoid** the long trek around the coast. (= purpose)
I got to the hotel early, only **to find** that I couldn't check in until later. (= result)
To hear him grumbling last week, you'd think he was about to get on the next flight home. (= if you had heard him grumbling)

2.6 Reduced clauses

We can sometimes use a 'reduced' clause beginning with a conjunction or adjective, but with no verb. Reduced clauses are usually fairly formal:
While in Naples, I did what all visitors do. or **While I was in Naples**, …
Exhausted by my walk, I went straight to bed. or **Because I was exhausted** …

15 Participle, to-infinitive and reduced clauses

Grammar exercises

3.1 Complete the participle clause at the start of each sentence using the information in brackets.

1. _Swimming_ strongly, she was able to cross the river in just a few minutes. (*She swam strongly.*)
2. _____ in oil, Colin got out from under the car. (*He was covered in oil.*)
3. _____ in Latin, the two letters were sent in 1406 to the French king. (*They were written in Latin.*)
4. _____ them twice this year already, Bayern Munich are favourites to win again against Real Madrid. (*They have beaten them twice this year already.*)
5. _____ how to use the software, I found it easy to design my own website. (*I was shown how to use the software.*)
6. _____ eaten anything for hours, I was starting to feel a bit faint. (*I hadn't eaten anything for hours.*)
7. _____ her glasses, she began to read her speech. (*She put on her glasses.*)
8. _____ Portuguese, I found travelling in Brazil difficult. (*I can't speak Portuguese.*)

3.2 Read this extract from a blog about a visit to London. Rewrite the underlined parts using a participle clause, *to*-infinitive or reduced clause.

(1) While I was in London I just had to go to the British Museum. There's so much to see and I only had time to spend a few hours there. First, I went to the collection of clocks and watches. (2) When I saw the pocket watches, I was reminded of the old watch my grandfather used to wear. I don't think I ever saw him without it. Then I went to the Money Gallery. They've got an incredible collection of coins, (3) and some of them are over 2,000 years old. Next stop was the Chinese collection. (4) Because I'd lived in Hong Kong for so many years, I was very interested in this. Some of the jade objects were stunning. (5) After I looked at the Chinese collection, I had hoped to see the Mexican collection. Unfortunately, (6) when I got there I found that it was closed. (7) Because I'd spent the whole morning walking around the museum, I decided that I wanted to do something very different in the afternoon. So I went to the London Eye (8) in order that I could get a bird's-eye view of the city. (9) When they are looked at from the top of the Eye, some of the biggest buildings appear quite small – even St Paul's Cathedral, across the river. After that, (10) because I was tired from all the walking, I went back to my hotel room and slept for a couple of hours (11) before I went out to have dinner.

1. While in London ...
2. _____
3. _____
4. _____
5. _____
6. _____
7. _____
8. _____
9. _____
10. _____
11. _____

Participle, to-infinitive and reduced clauses 15

3.3 In these sentences, is the subject of the participle and the main clause the same (S) or different (D)? If it is different, think about how you could rewrite the sentence correctly.

1 Painted bright yellow, I could see the signs clearly from a distance. __D__
2 Hearing a noise from one of the bedrooms, I quietly climbed upstairs. _____
3 Laughing at her new hat, Jing looked really angry with me. _____
4 Kept in the fridge, the cheese should stay fresh for weeks. _____
5 Holding her umbrella tightly, she went out into the storm. _____
6 Talking to each other in the library, I asked them to keep quiet. _____
7 Caught in traps put on the riverbed at night, many fishermen depend on crayfish for their livelihood. _____
8 Worried that Zahira hadn't arrived, I decided to phone her home. _____

1 *Because the signs were painted bright yellow I could see them clearly from a distance.*

3.4 Complete each sentence using one of the words in the box and an appropriate form of the verb in brackets. Use either an *-ing*, an *-ed* or *being + -ed* verb form.

although before if once since while with without ~~unless~~ until

1 ___Unless___ otherwise ___stated___, all software contained on the CD is for demonstration purposes only. (*state*)
2 _____ my book on the European Union, I interviewed more than a hundred members of the European Parliament. (*research*)
3 _____ no longer _____ in the day-to-day running of the business, Mr Chen retains a keen interest in its development. (*involve*)
4 _____ Defence Minister, he was head of the army for five years. (*make*)
5 _____ her parents, she took their car and drove into town. When they found out, they were furious. (*ask*)
6 Not _____ school had anyone told me to 'sit down and be quiet'. (*leave*)
7 The virus doesn't have serious effects, but _____ it remains in the body for life. (*catch*)
8 _____ the wind _____ hurricane force, ships have been advised to head for land. (*reach*)
9 I slept deeply _____ by a fire engine going past the house. (*wake*)
10 _____ guilty, she could face ten years in prison. (*find*)

111

Exam practice

Reading and Use of English Part 3

For questions **1 – 8**, read the text below. Use the word given in capitals at the end of some of the lines to form a word that fits in the gap **in the same line**. There is an example at the beginning **(0)**.

Water: a precious resource

Access to a clean, **(0)** _reliable_ water supply is essential to our survival. **(1)** _____ over 70 percent of the earth's surface, water is apparently **(2)** _____ . But in fact, less than 1 percent of all the water on earth is accessible for human use in lakes, rivers and reservoirs. **(3)** _____ by rain and snowfall, this water supply is available to us as a finite but **(4)** _____ resource. As the demand for access to this limited supply increases, it is thought that as many as 3.5 billion people could experience water **(5)** _____ by 2025. A worldwide water management plan is vital. An international campaign must be introduced both to raise public **(6)** _____ of the importance of conserving and **(7)** _____ this precious resource. Furthermore, industry and agriculture must be made to reduce their water **(8)** _____ . Only in this way can water-related international conflicts be avoided.

RELY
COVER
PLENTY

NEW
SUSTAIN

SHORT

AWARE
CYCLE

CONSUME

16 Noun clauses

That-noun clauses; *wh*-noun clauses; *whether* and *if*

Context listening

1.1 You are going to hear Joe Simpson, head of the Norton Wildlife Trust (NWT), encouraging some residents of Norton to volunteer for projects. Before you listen, look at these pictures and identify the activities.

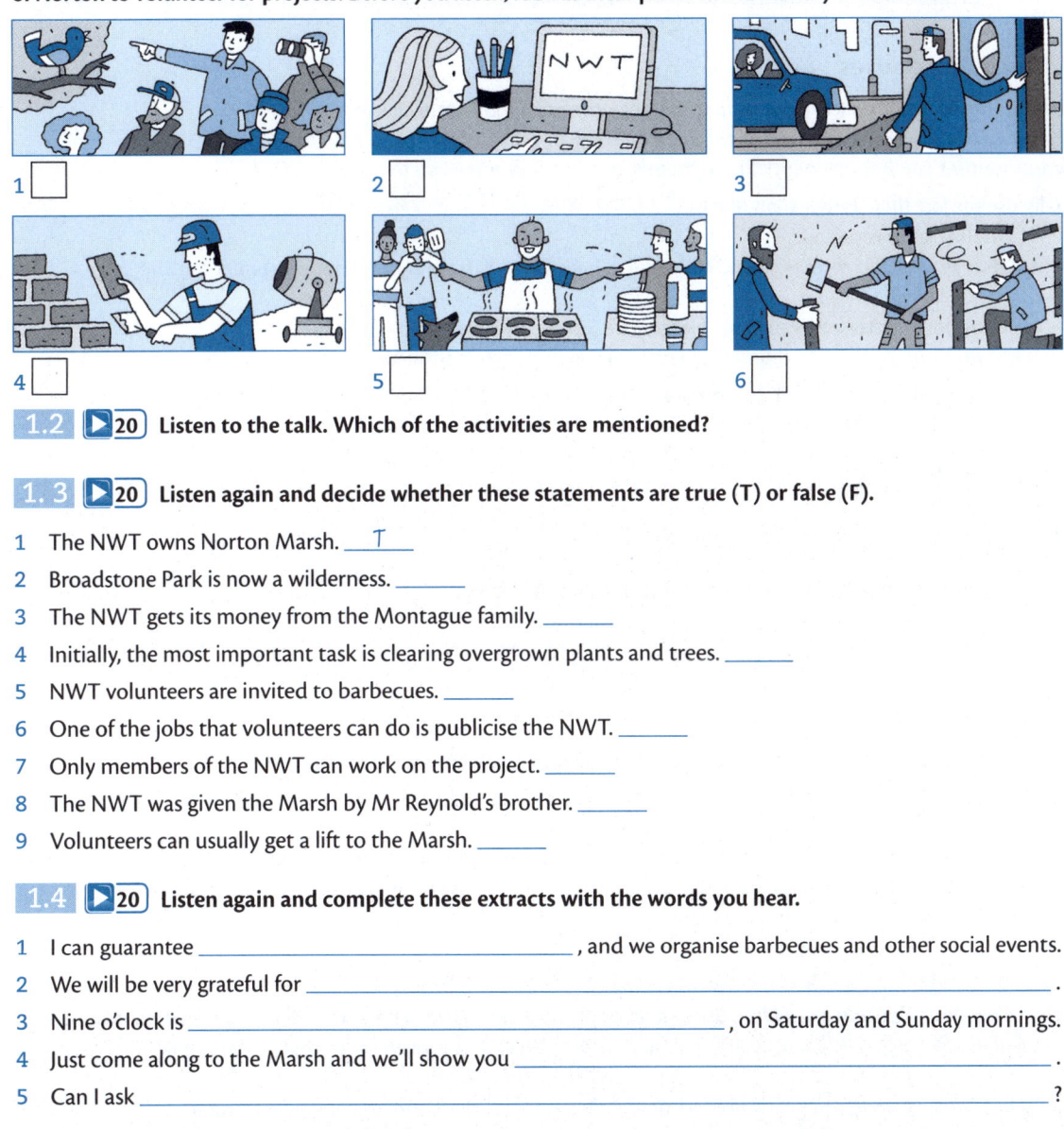

1 ☐ 2 ☐ 3 ☐

4 ☐ 5 ☐ 6 ☐

1.2 ▶20 Listen to the talk. Which of the activities are mentioned?

1.3 ▶20 Listen again and decide whether these statements are true (T) or false (F).

1 The NWT owns Norton Marsh. __T__
2 Broadstone Park is now a wilderness. _____
3 The NWT gets its money from the Montague family. _____
4 Initially, the most important task is clearing overgrown plants and trees. _____
5 NWT volunteers are invited to barbecues. _____
6 One of the jobs that volunteers can do is publicise the NWT. _____
7 Only members of the NWT can work on the project. _____
8 The NWT was given the Marsh by Mr Reynold's brother. _____
9 Volunteers can usually get a lift to the Marsh. _____

1.4 ▶20 Listen again and complete these extracts with the words you hear.

1 I can guarantee _____, and we organise barbecues and other social events.
2 We will be very grateful for _____.
3 Nine o'clock is _____, on Saturday and Sunday mornings.
4 Just come along to the Marsh and we'll show you _____.
5 Can I ask _____?

1.5 Look at your answers to 1.4. What words begin each clause you have written?

113

16 Noun clauses

Grammar

> **START POINT**
>
> *What you've told us* is very interesting. (= The *information* is very interesting.)
> You've probably also heard *that the Marsh has been given to the NWT to look after*. (= You've probably also heard this *report*.)
> Nine o'clock is *when we usually meet*. (= Nine o'clock is *our usual meeting time*.)
> A noun clause functions in a sentence in a similar way to a noun (e.g. *information*, *report*) or noun phrase (e.g. *our usual meeting time*). Noun clauses usually begin with *that* or a *wh*-word (e.g. *what, when, where, which, who, why*; also *whether, whatever, how*).

2.1 *That*-noun clauses

In informal contexts we often leave out *that* at the beginning of a *that*-noun clause:
*It's also good to know **that they're helping the environment**.* or *... to know **they're helping** ...*
*I can guarantee **that you'll make a lot of new friends**.* or *I can guarantee **you'll make** ...*

We usually use *the fact that* (rather than *that*):
- when the noun clause is subject:
  ***The fact that** you're not a member of the trust makes no difference.* (rather than *That you're not a member of the trust makes no difference.*)
- after a preposition or after verbs such as *change*, *face* (*up to*) and *overlook*:
  *We have to **face** (**up to**) **the fact that** we don't have enough resources at the moment.*

We can often use words like *argument, assumption, belief, claim, idea, notion* and *view* instead of *fact*:
***The idea that** it's all hard work is just wrong.*

2.2 *Wh*-noun clauses

When a *wh*-noun clause follows certain nouns (e.g. *example*, *problem*), we often have to include *of* before the *wh*-word:
*We'd like to follow the **example of what** they've done at Broadstone Park.*

Some verbs (e.g. *advise*, *teach*) must have an object before the *wh*-word:
*I'll be happy to **advise you when** to come.*

Noun clauses beginning *how* are commonly used after certain verbs (e.g. *decide*, *know*):
*It's entirely up to you to **decide how** much time you can give.*

We can use a *wh*-noun clause, but not a *that*-noun clause, after a preposition:
*If you've got any questions **about what I've said so far**, I'd be happy to answer them.* (not *... about that I've said so far ...*)

We can also use noun clauses beginning with *whatever* (= anything, or it doesn't matter what), *whoever* (= the person/group who, or any person/group who) or *whichever* (= one thing or person from a limited number) to talk about things, people or times that are indefinite or unknown:
*We will be very grateful for **whatever** time people can spare.*
*You can phone **whoever** is in charge of arranging lifts on the weekend you want to come.*

Rather than a *wh*-noun clause, we can often use a noun or pronoun which has a meaning related to the *wh*-word:
***Why** most people volunteer is that they want fresh air and exercise.* or ***The reason** (**why/that**) most people volunteer ...*
*Clearing the vegetation is **what** is urgently needed.* or *Clearing the vegetation is **something which/that** is urgently needed.*

16 Noun clauses

Other words used in this way include *the place* (rather than *where*), *the time* (rather than *when*), *the way* (rather than *how*) and *somebody/someone* (rather than *who*).

2.3 *Whether* and *if*

We can use *whether* as the *wh*-word in a noun clause when we talk about possible choices. *Whether* has a similar meaning to *if*:
*I can't remember **whether** it runs on Sundays.*

Notice the difference between sentences with *whether*- and *that*-noun clauses:
*I didn't know **whether/if** the bus service has been cancelled.* (= it may or may not have been cancelled)
*I didn't know **that** the bus service had been cancelled.* (= it was cancelled; now I know)

In more formal contexts, particularly in writing, we can use *as to* with a meaning similar to 'about' or 'concerning' before a *whether*-noun clause:
*There was some debate **as to whether** he could legally give us the land.*

We use *whether*, not *if*:
- before *or not*:
  *I don't know **whether or not** I'd be able to come on a regular basis.*
  However:
  *I don't know **whether/if** I'd be able to come on a regular basis or not.*
- before a *to*-infinitive:
  *I can't make up my mind **whether to help** on Saturdays or Sundays.*
- usually after a preposition, and also after the verbs *advise, choose, consider, debate, discuss, enquire, question*:
  *You can think **about whether** you'd like to be involved.*
  *You can **choose whether** you want to work indoors or outdoors.*
- in a clause acting as a subject or complement:
  ***Whether you help with the outdoor or indoor work** depends on you.* (= subject)
  *What I'm not clear about is **whether we can get a lift to the reserve**.* (= complement)

Grammar exercises

3.1 Read these comments by a resident, a fire officer and a climate change expert about a recent flood. Complete each text with *that* or *the fact that*.

Resident: Nobody really thought (1) ____that____ flooding this bad would happen again, but as the river level rose, we had to face up to (2) _____ we'd have to leave our home. Personally, I blame the fire service. (3) _____ it's been raining heavily here for five days should have meant that they were better prepared to help us.

Fire officer: I really feel (4) _____ some of the criticisms of my fire officers are unfair, although (5) _____ today is a public holiday did mean that many of our staff weren't here to help with the rescue. However, we warned residents yesterday (6) _____ they might have to evacuate their houses with little notice, and the difficulty in evacuating people from their houses wasn't helped by (7) _____ they wanted to take large amounts of personal belongings with them.

Climate change expert: We can't ignore (8) _____ climate change is going to increase the risk of flooding, and a number of studies have suggested (9) _____ winter river levels throughout the country will be much higher than in the past. Unfortunately, the situation in this area is complicated by (10) _____ so many trees have been cut down on the hills around here and rainwater flows more quickly into the rivers. So there's a real possibility (11) _____ serious flooding could now happen here every winter.

16 Noun clauses

3.2 Read this extract from the blog of an American woman living in Paris. Complete the text using a word from Box A and a phrase from Box B.

A

how	if	the way
what	when	where
whether	whichever	who
whoever	~~why~~	

B

the light shines through them	I'd make it
the cathedral was built	to take a guided tour
designed the cathedral	they managed to do that
direction you approach it	~~it was built there~~
conditions were like for the builders	wrote that
the building materials came from	

I rented a car yesterday and drove about 50 miles from Paris to Chartres. The area around Chartres is very flat. That's probably the reason **(1)** _why it was built there_ . It dominates the landscape from **(2)** _____ . At first, I wasn't sure **(3)** _____ of the cathedral. I'm pretty independent and like to wander around on my own. But this time I decided to go for it, and I'm really glad I did – the guide was excellent! She talked a lot about **(4)** _____ – it was begun before 1200 – and told us **(5)** _____ . Some of the stone was transported from hundreds of miles away – I'll never understand **(6)** _____ . **(7)** _____ isn't known. Apparently in those days architecture was a cooperative effort by the stonemasons working on the site. She also gave us some idea of **(8)** _____ . It sounds like an incredibly hard life. I thought the stained-glass windows were awesome. I was so impressed with **(9)** _____ and creates patterns on the cathedral floor. After the tour, I looked again at my guidebook and noticed that it mentioned the 'easy climb' up the north tower, so off I went. But **(10)** _____ must have been super-fit. For me it was a long, exhausting climb, and there were times when I didn't know **(11)** _____ . The magnificent view was certainly worth the effort when I got to the top, but be warned!

3.3 Match the sentence halves and join them by filling the gaps in a–h with *whatever*, *whoever* or *whichever*.

1. Mr Kato has resigned as managing director, and it will be a difficult job for
2. I must have that painting, and will pay
3. The police have said that to protect the public they will take
4. I've bought this armchair that adjusts itself to the body shape of
5. We've got lots of cakes, so just choose
6. At the first modern Olympic games in 1896, athletes could wear
7. Houses next to the river are at risk of flooding,
8. Both the number 45 and 47 buses go into town, so get on

a _____ is sitting in it.
b _____ side they are on.
c _whoever_ replaces him.
d _____ action is necessary.
e _____ it costs.
f _____ comes first.
g _____ one you like the look of.
h _____ they wanted to.

116

Noun clauses 16

3.4 Complete the sentences using the notes in brackets and *where, what, when, why* or *how*. Add any other words necessary.

1. Our Maths teacher made the exam quite easy for us. In our last lesson he gave us some
   (1) _examples of what would_ (*examples / would*) be in the paper, and he
   (2) _____ (*told / questions*) to answer.

2. **A:** There's a job advert here for a train driver. Do you think I should go for it?

   B: But (3) _____ (*know / to drive*) a train?

   A: No, but I'm sure they'll be able (4) _____ (*teach / to do*). I might send for an application form.

3. When I got to hospital, a nurse took me into a room and (5) _____ (*showed / to sit*). I was very anxious (6) _____ (*would happen / next*) and (7) _____ (*asked / the doctor*) would be coming.

4. **A:** Remember (8) _____ (*time / were*) in London and our wallets and train tickets were stolen?

   B: I certainly do. Then we had (9) _____ (*problem / to get back*) to Manchester without tickets or money.

   A: (10) _____ (*reason / mention*) now is that the man who gave us the money to get home is on the front of today's paper. He's wanted for robbing a bank!

Exam practice

Reading and Use of English Part 1

For questions **1 – 8**, read the text below and decide which answer (**A, B, C** or **D**) best fits each gap. There is an example at the beginning **(0)**.

Homework: how useful is it?

Homework is an **(0)** _B_ part of school life in most countries around the world. However, there is still considerable debate among teachers about **(1)** _____ homework has a significant educational value. On the one side are those who **(2)** _____ that it takes too much time away from other more useful activities. On the other are those who see homework as reinforcing school lessons so that concepts will not be forgotten. **(3)** _____ is often neglected in this debate is the role of parental involvement and **(4)** _____ or not the child's home provides support for effective homework. Parents in low-income families often don't have the time to make homework a priority or aren't able to afford a computer or additional books. **(5)** _____ money they have goes on the basic necessities of life – accommodation, food, clothing and heating. However, the **(6)** _____ that only middle-class parents support their children's education is quite obviously wrong. Not **(7)** _____ well-to-do parents give the support they should, and some parents living in the most impoverished circumstances **(8)** _____ find the time and energy to involve themselves in their children's homework.

0	A ingrained	B (established)	C allowed	D accustomed
1	A if	B that	C whether	D supposing
2	A tell	B describe	C claim	D inform
3	A Whatever	B Which	C That	D What
4	A whether	B why	C whatever	D if
5	A Whichever	B That	C Whatever	D Which
6	A fact	B concept	C idea	D reason
7	A each	B all	C any	D every
8	A imaginable	B imagining	C imagined	D imagine

17 Conjunctions and connectors

Before, hardly, first(ly), however, even so, on the other hand, etc.

Context listening

1.1 Which of these do you think learner drivers find most difficult?

reversing around corners	overtaking
parking	starting on a hill
getting into the correct lane	changing gear
driving at night	using the rear-view mirror

1.2 ▶21 Listen to Sahar and Claudio talking about their experiences of learning to drive. Which of the things in 1.1 were particular problems for them?

1.3 ▶21 Listen again.

1 In what order does **Sahar** mention these advantages of being taught by a professional instructor?
  a he passed on useful tips _____
  b he was always encouraging _____
  c he used a dual-control car __1__
  d he could tell when she was ready to take her test _____
2 In what order does **Claudio** mention these advantages of being taught by his mother?
  e she was calm most of the time _____
  f he got lots of time to practise _____
  g she knew a quiet place to practise _____
  h he didn't have to pay for lessons _____

1.4 What words or phrases are used to connect these ideas?

1 I stalled in the middle of a busy road + my instructor stayed completely cool
   _____even if_____
2 I had the mirror positioned + I just couldn't judge where the back of the car was _____
3 it was disappointing to have replacement instructors + the replacements were patient and helpful
   _____
4 it's expensive to have driving lessons + I would recommend it _____
5 my mum doesn't have a professional qualification + she has lots of experience _____
6 I didn't do anything stupid + she stayed calm _____
1 <u>Even if</u> I did something incredibly stupid like stalling in the middle of a busy road, he'd stay completely cool.

119

17 Conjunctions and connectors

Grammar

2.1 Sentence connectors and conjunctions: general

> **START POINT**
>
> *My mum used to come and collect me from college in the car and I'd drive home. **What's more**, she'd let me drive when we went shopping.*
> A *sentence connector* (e.g. *what's more*) links one sentence with another.
> *My mum taught me to drive **because** I couldn't afford to pay for driving lessons.*
> A *conjunction* (e.g. *because*) links clauses within a single sentence.

To link two clauses, we use only one conjunction, not two:
***Although** it's expensive having driving lessons, I'd really recommend it.* (not ~~Although it's expensive having driving lessons, but I'd really recommend it.~~)

We usually put a comma between clauses linked by a conjunction:
***As long as** I didn't do anything stupid, she stayed pretty calm.*

However, when *because* or *while* (referring to time) begin the second clause in a sentence, we don't need a comma.

Sentence connectors usually come at the beginning of a sentence and less often at the end or in another position. The only ones that can't come at the beginning are *too* and *as well*:
*You can spend a lot more time practising, **as well**.*

We usually put a comma after a sentence connector at the beginning or end of a sentence:
*My mum thought I was ready to take my driving test. **However**, I failed first time.*

When a sentence connector comes elsewhere in a sentence, punctuation is more variable.
*There are lots of advantages in having your parents teach you. There's the cost, **for instance** …*

Sentence connectors can be used to link clauses in a sentence if the clauses are joined with *and, but, or, so,* or a semi-colon (;), colon (:) or dash (–):
*My instructor was very experienced **and, as a result**, he had lots of useful tips to pass on.*
*Having a professional teach you to drive is best; **however**, it can be very expensive.*

2.2 Conjunctions: *before, until*

Sometimes we can use either *before* or *until* with little difference in meaning:
*She wouldn't let me drive on busy roads **before**/**until** I could control the car well.*

We use *until*, not *before*, when an action continues to a particular time and then stops:
*I just carried on having lessons **until** my instructor said I was ready to take the driving test.*

2.3 Conjunctions: *hardly, no sooner, scarcely*

After *hardly* and *scarcely* the second clause usually begins with *when* or *before*; after *no sooner* it begins with *than* or *when*:
*We'd **hardly** driven out of our road **before** we were shouting at each other.*
*I'd **no sooner** passed my test **than**/**when** my friends started asking me for lifts.*

We often use the past perfect in a clause with *hardly, no sooner* or *scarcely* and a past simple in the other clause. (See **Unit 21, 2.3** for word order in sentences with *hardly, no sooner* and *scarcely*.)

Conjunctions and connectors

2.4 Sentence connectors: *first(ly), at first; last(ly), at last*

We use *first* or *firstly* to label the first point in a list and *last* or *lastly* to label the final point. We use *at first* to indicate that there is a contrast between two past situations, and *at last* to show that something happened later than hoped or expected:

Firstly, cars like the one I learnt in have dual controls.
At first, I couldn't get the hang of this at all.
I passed my driving test at last, after taking it five times.

We don't use *at last* to label the last point in a list:
First, I had to practise starting on a hill … Finally/Lastly, the instructor made me reverse around a corner.
(not ~~At last, the instructor made me reverse …~~)

2.5 *However*

However is often a sentence connector, but can also be used:
- as an adverb when it is followed by an adjective, adverb or *much/many*:
  *My instructor never got annoyed, **however** badly I was driving.* (= despite how badly)
- as a conjunction when it means 'in whatever way':
  ***However** I had the mirror positioned, I just couldn't judge where the back of the car was.*

2.6 *Even so* (sentence connector), *even though* (conjunction)

Even so has a meaning similar to *however*. We use it to introduce a fact that is surprising given what has just been said:
*He was great and I didn't want to be taught by anyone else. **Even so**, I always found the replacements very patient and helpful.*

We use *even though* to say that a fact doesn't make the rest of the sentence untrue:
***Even though** she doesn't have a professional qualification, she's got lots of experience to pass on.*

2.7 Sentence connectors: *on the other hand, on the contrary*

We use *on the other hand* when we compare or contrast two statements. We sometimes introduce the first statement with *on the one hand*:
*It may be that the quality of the tuition is better with a professional driving instructor. **On the other hand**, it's cheaper if your parents teach you.* or ***On the one hand**, it may be that the quality of the tuition is better with a professional driving instructor. **On the other** (**hand**), it's cheaper if your parents teach you.*

On the contrary emphasises that we reject the first statement and accept the second:
*Some people say that it's more expensive to be taught by a driving instructor than a friend or relative. **On the contrary**, it works out cheaper.*

2.8 Prepositions commonly confused with conjunctions and connectors

These are prepositions, and can't be used as conjunctions or sentence connectors:
***As well as** being calm and patient, he was always very encouraging.* (not ~~As well as he was calm~~ …)
***Apart from** the cost of insurance, I think it's much better to be taught by your parents.* (not ~~Apart from the insurance costs were high~~ …)
*I think there's a lot of other good things about having your parents teach you, **besides** saving money.*
(not … ~~besides you can save money.~~)
*I'd recommend professional driving lessons **despite** / **in spite of** the expense.*
(not … ~~despite / in spite of they are expensive.~~)
*The lesson was cancelled **due to** the heavy rain.* (not … ~~due to it was raining heavily.~~)
*We used to stop driving at some point **during** the lesson, and he would ask me how I felt I'd improved.*
(not … ~~at some point during we were having the lesson …~~)

121

17 Conjunctions and connectors

Grammar exercises

3.1 Match the items, joining them with the conjunction or sentence connector given. Write either one or two sentences, as appropriate. There may be more than one way of joining the sentences.

1 Amy was on the phone for hours
2 she always finds time to talk to students
3 the restaurant's closed next Monday
4 he's a seismologist
5 tuition fees have been increased
6 we travelled much faster
7 the government is being urged to build more nuclear power stations
8 he was wearing the same clothes as me

a it's a public holiday
b such a move would be controversial
c we got onto the motorway
d I noticed she'd been crying
e he studies earthquakes
f the number of applications has fallen
g his shoes were black
h how busy she is

1 _d Amy was on the phone for hours. Later, I noticed she'd been crying._ (later)
2 _____ (no matter)
3 _____ (because)
4 _____ (that is to say)
5 _____ (as a result)
6 _____ (once)
7 _____ (however)
8 _____ (except that)

3.2 Choose the correct word or phrase.

1 She isn't very interested in science subjects. *On the contrary* / *On the other hand*, she really loves studying history.
2 He walked quickly down the corridor *before* / *until* he reached the last door.
3 My aunt was followed into the room by my two nieces and three nephews. *Lastly* / *At last* came my uncle, carrying all the suitcases.
4 I knew I had the right qualifications and experience for the job. *Even though* / *Even so*, I felt very nervous as I walked in to face the interview panel.
5 At college I had only two tutorials a week, but this didn't mean I wasn't busy. *On the contrary* / *On the other hand*, I studied at least six days a week.
6 Once he'd done the washing up and got the children to bed, Matt sat down in front of the fire. *Lastly* / *At last* he had some time to himself.
7 *Even though* / *Even so* the snow had stopped falling, it was still freezing cold.
8 We had *no sooner* / *hardly* started driving than the children said, 'Are we there yet?'

122

17 Conjunctions and connectors

3.3 Complete the sentences using a word from box A and a phrase from box B.

A
consequently	in case
in contrast	~~meanwhile~~
otherwise	whereas
while	unless

B
she's looking for a new flat	it isn't very heavy
there's a power cut	in Marketing they get an hour
the weather's bad	we'll have to walk miles to the bridge
I prefer Italian	
~~my parents are letting me borrow theirs~~	

1 I'm saving up to buy my own car. _____Meanwhile, my parents are letting me borrow theirs_____.
2 I always keep some candles in the house _____.
3 My husband adores Chinese food, _____.
4 The boat is made entirely of fibreglass. _____.
5 We should be able to wade across the river; _____.
6 Your sister can stay with us _____.
7 The lunch break in the Personnel Department is 30 minutes. _____.
8 We're planning on having a picnic in the park _____.

3.4 Complete these extracts from emails. Choose from the words and phrases in the boxes.

A

~~although~~ at first because because of despite during even so even though firstly while

I'm in Jamaica for a week. **(1)** _____Although_____ it's a work visit, I've had a few days free, so I decided to have a go at windsurfing **(2)** _____ I'm here. I'd never tried it before **(3)** _____ I'm not a very good swimmer. **(4)** _____ I found it really difficult to stay upright, but it wasn't long until I was going quite fast. **(5)** _____ I didn't go far from the beach.

B

as well as well as before even though hardly in addition in spite of no sooner until what's more

The weather here is terrible. **(1)** _____ heavy rain, we've had gale force winds. **(2)** _____ the bad weather, we're doing a lot of walking. Yesterday was typical. When we got up it was wet – of course – and we decided to wait **(3)** _____ the rain stopped. The sun came out by midday and we set off for Wicklow Hill. We had **(4)** _____ started to climb when it began pouring down! **(5)** _____, the wind was so strong, we were almost blown over. But we still got to the top!

123

Exam practice

Reading and Use of English Part 6

You are going to read four reviews from a website in which different writers give their views on a book about what the Earth would be like if people disappeared from it. For questions **1 – 4**, choose from the reviews **A – D**. The reviews may be chosen more than once.

The World Without Us

Four reviewers comment on author Alan Weisman's book called The World Without Us.

A

Alan Weisman imagines what the Earth would be like if humans were suddenly and completely wiped out. This starting point ignores the fact that nothing is likely to kill us off completely, at least not without taking a large part of the rest of life with us. Even if a virus appeared with a 99.99 percent kill rate, it would still leave more than enough naturally immune survivors to repopulate the Earth to current levels in 50,000 years. This said, Weisman's book is fascinating, readable and thought-provoking. The mass of scientific evidence of human impact that he compiles is mind-boggling. I did not know, for instance, that there are one billion annual bird deaths from flying into glass in the United States alone; or that graphic designers have been called in to imagine what warnings against approaching nuclear waste containers will be comprehensible 10,000 or more years from now. His solution is a mandatory one-child limit for all families worldwide. Radical, but undoubtedly necessary, as he convincingly argues.

B

Alan Weisman's 'thought experiment' in *The World Without Us* is to imagine what the world would be like if every human vanished tomorrow. But he offers no real context for the book, no rationale for exploring this fantasy other than his unsubstantiated belief that people find it fascinating. Perhaps they do, and we might guess their reasons. But none emerges in any compelling way to explain why it is important to know, for instance, that the Great Wall of China will crumble in a few centuries. Much of the book comprises revelations of this kind, but there is little information here that is all that new. If you follow environmental issues, nothing in *The World Without Us* is likely to shock or astound you. The way to avoid the apocalypse, so Weisman believes, is to limit to one child every human female on Earth. However, his draconian solution is only briefly described and comes much too late in the book to be convincing.

C

What Alan Weisman does is imagine what would happen to the world if we were all wiped out. And it is quite understandable, as we learn during the course of this book, to take this as a realistic prospect as we are very, very bad for our own environment. What starts out with promise continues disappointingly. For those well versed in the science of environmental degradation, the book provides numerous anecdotes about our appalling impact on the Earth that sound all too familiar. Personally, I found Weisman's journalistic style increasingly irritating as the book progressed. Is it really necessary to know that his interviewees include a 'curly-haired young director' or someone 'trim and youthful in their early fifties'? His most extreme solution, to limit families to one child, is unrealistic. Although readers might agree that there are too many of us, few will share Weisman's certainty that to trade a child for more birdsong is a good bargain.

Exam practice

Conjunctions and connectors — 17

D
What would the Earth be like if everyone was killed off by an astronomical event or disease? Such thought experiments are the stuff of Alan Weisman's new book *The World Without Us*. Weisman's argument would be an interesting read if it weren't for the nagging suspicion that there is something rather ludicrous about its very premise: that a world without human beings could possibly matter to us. The themes in Weisman's interviews with people from around the world are familiar. Over-harvesting, over-farming and over-industrialisation are destroying the planet. Unless we change our ways, we are doomed. But there isn't much new evidence to throw into the debate. The book is saved, however, by Weisman's writing. His engaging journalism makes for a gripping fantasy that will make most readers hope that at least some of us can stick around long enough to see how the journey of the human race on our planet turns out.

Which reviewer

has a different opinion from the others on how relevant Weisman's imagined situation is? **1**

supports reviewer A's opinion on Weisman's writing style? **2**

has a different view from the others on the originality of Weisman's evidence? **3**

takes a similar view to reviewer C on Weisman's proposed solution? **4**

18 The passive

Using the passive; active and passive verb forms; passive forms of verbs with two objects; *get* + past participle; *get/have* + object + past participle

Context listening

1.1 You are going to hear an interview with a government minister talking about crime statistics. Before you listen, look at these newspaper headlines and match them with the crimes they refer to.

1 burglary _____
2 firearm offences _____
3 street crime _____
4 car crime _____
5 vandalism _____

a **STREET ART SPRAYED IN CAPITAL**
b **More kids attacked in mobile thefts**
c **GUN CONTROLS FAILING, SAYS POLICE CHIEF**
d **Gang linked to 500 break-ins**
e **VEHICLE THEFT COST £800M**

1.2 ▶22 Listen to the interview. Which crimes are mentioned?
_____
_____

1.3 ▶22 Listen again. According to the minister, are these statements true (T) or false (F)?

1 The chance of being a victim of crime has fallen by 40% in the last ten years. __T__
2 Peter Miles appointed a new head of the police service. _____
3 The government has spent a lot of money on CCTV. _____
4 The government copied the *Make Amends* scheme from another country. _____
5 More people get mugged now than ten years ago. _____
6 More people sell drugs now than ten years ago. _____
7 The figures in the report are completely accurate. _____
8 Violent crime is on the increase. _____

1.4 ▶22 Listen again and complete these extracts with the exact words used in the recording. Are the verbs you have written in an active form or a passive form?

1 Yes, indeed, I was delighted when I _____ the figures.
2 This has meant that a much higher proportion of offenders _____ during the last ten years than ever before.
3 People _____ less graffiti in city centres, for example.
4 These _____ a particular target for street robbers.
5 Well, it's certainly true that more people _____ selling drugs.
6 If I can give a personal example, my house _____ only last week.

The passive 18

Grammar

2.1 Using the passive

> **START POINT**
>
> *The government **has published** a report today.* (active: focus on *the government*)
> *A report **has been published** by the government today.* (passive: focus on *a report*)

We often use passive verbs:
- when the agent (the person or thing that performs the action) is not known: *My house **was broken** into only last week.*
- when the agent is 'people in general': *The details **can be found** at the back of the report.* (= anyone can find these details)
- when the agent is unimportant, or is obvious: *A much higher proportion of offenders **have been arrested**.* (= the agent is clearly the police)
- when we don't want to say who the agent is: *It may be that some minor mistakes **were made** in collecting the figures.* (= she might not want to say who was responsible for the mistakes)
- to describe procedures or processes, focusing on what was done rather than who did it: *The figures **were collected** over a ten-year period.*
- to avoid repeating the agent in a description or narrative: *The police have made good use of CCTV. It's **been introduced** into many city centres.* rather than *The police have made good use of CCTV. The police have introduced it into many city centres.*

In informal contexts we often use active sentences with a subject such as *people, somebody/someone, something, we, they* or *you* even when we do not know who the agent is. In more formal contexts we often use a passive to avoid mentioning an agent:
People are seeing less graffiti in city centres. or more formally *Less graffiti **is being seen** …*

Some verbs describing states (e.g. *have, become, seem*) are not usually made passive:
Other countries have a similar policy. (not *A similar policy is had by other countries.*)
However, other verbs describing states can be passive (e.g. *intend, know, own*):
*Our latest poster campaign **is intended** to reassure people.*

2.2 Active and passive verb forms

Compare these passive forms of active verb patterns.

Active	Passive
They **started to keep** records ten years ago.	Records **started to be kept** only ten years ago.
This figure is expected to fall as **they start using** new technology to trace stolen phones.	This figure is expected to fall rapidly as **new technology starts being used** to trace stolen mobiles.
They **made** them **repair** the damage.	People found guilty of vandalism **are made to repair** the damage they've caused.
The police **caught** them **selling** drugs.	More people **were caught selling** drugs.
We **expect** the figure **to fall** rapidly. We **want** the crime rate **to fall** still further.	This figure **is expected to fall** rapidly. Some verbs in this pattern have no passive: (not *The crime rate is wanted to fall still further.*)

127

18 The passive

Perfect passive forms are also possible: *More people **claim to have been** the victims of crime. More people **have been caught selling** drugs this year than ever before. This figure **is expected to have fallen** by next year.*

Most passives with modal verbs are formed with modal + *be* + past participle or modal + *have been* + past participle:
*The reason for this **can be found** in the huge increase in the number of mobile phones.*
*Some of the fall **might have been caused** by lower rates of reporting.* (past)

2.3 Passive forms of verbs with two objects

> **START POINT**
>
> *I was delighted when our crime statistics department **gave me the figures**.* (active)
> *I was delighted when I **was given the figures** by our Crime Statistics Department.* (passive) or
> *I was delighted when the figures **were given (to) me** by our Crime Statistics Department.* (passive)
> (See **Unit 9**, **2.1** for more on verbs with two objects.)

Verbs followed by object + complement in the active have one passive form:
*Attitudes have changed significantly since Peter Miles **was appointed head of the police service**.*

2.4 *Get* + past participle; *get/have* + object + past participle

> **START POINT**
>
> *It's true that more people **get mugged** today than they did ten years ago.* or *... **are mugged** ...*
> *People think more carefully about committing a crime if they know they **might get caught**.* or *... **might be caught**.*
> Particularly in speech, we can use *get* + past participle instead of *be* + past participle.

Get + past participle is most commonly used to talk about unwelcome events (e.g. *get mugged*), but we can also use it with positive events: *When we **got elected** ten years ago ...*

We don't use *get* + past participle with verbs describing states:
*He **was known** to be a highly effective senior police officer.* (not *He got known to be ...*)

We can use either *have* + object + past participle or (more informally) *get* + object + past participle:
- to say that someone arranges for someone else to do something for them:
  *Virtually every person in my road **has had/got a burglar alarm fitted** recently.*
- to say that something unexpected, and usually unpleasant, happens to someone:
  *I **had my TV and stereo taken**.* or very informally *I **got my TV and stereo taken**.*

We use a reflexive pronoun with *get* to suggest that the subject is responsible for their actions.
*People will think more carefully if they know they're going to **get themselves arrested**.*

The passive 18

Grammar exercises

3.1 Complete these texts with the appropriate form, active or passive, of the verb.

A

Acupuncture **(1)** _has been practised_ (*practise*) in China for over 3,000 years, and today it **(2)** _____ (*widely use*) alongside conventional medicine. In traditional Chinese medicine, no symptom **(3)** _____ (*view*) in isolation. Instead, the body and the mind **(4)** _____ (*evaluate*) together. The goal of acupuncture **(5)** _____ (*be*) to create harmony in the body by restoring the flow of Qi (pronounced 'chee'). This **(6)** _____ (*consider*) to be the life force involved in all body functions. Qi **(7)** _____ (*collect*) in the organs and **(8)** _____ (*travel*) through energy channels in the body. Acupuncturists **(9)** _____ (*believe*) that diseases **(10)** _____ (*occur*) when the circulation of Qi **(11)** _____ (*prevent*), whether by injuries, heat, cold or other factors. By redirecting the flow of Qi, acupuncture can **(12)** _____ (*help*) cure disease.

B

The first mobile phones **(1)** _____ (*construct*) in Stockholm in the 1950s – but were not very mobile! They could only **(2)** _____ (*use*) in cars because the receiver and transmitter **(3)** _____ (*weigh*) over 40 kilos and had to **(4)** _____ (*carry*) in the boot. But technology **(5)** _____ (*advance*) so quickly that by the 1990s mobiles could **(6)** _____ (*hold*) in the hand and people talking on their mobiles **(7)** _____ (*become*) a familiar sight. Of course, not everyone welcomed mobiles, and in the mid-1990s their use **(8)** _____ (*ban*) in many schools. Even recent research which **(9)** _____ (*suggest*) that prolonged exposure to emissions from mobiles might be a health hazard **(10)** _____ (*not discourage*) their use, and analysts now **(11)** _____ (*predict*) that by 2025, 95% of all electronic communication **(12)** _____ (*conduct*) by mobile phone.

129

18 The passive

3.2 Write passive sentences with a similar meaning to the first. Start with the word(s) given and use the verb in italics. In some cases, the passive is not possible.

1 They paid him a million dollars to appear in the film.
   He <u>was paid a million dollars to appear in the film</u>.

2 His name is Robin, but his friends call him Bobby.
   His name is Robin, but _____.

3 Dr Davies demonstrated the procedure to us in the chemistry lab.
   We _____.

4 The managing director will announce the news to staff later today.
   The news _____.

5 They have offered me a new job in Hungary.
   I _____.

6 The medical staff have declared the surgery a complete success.
   The surgery _____.

7 My English teacher suggested the idea to me.
   I _____.

8 My uncle bought me this necklace when he was in Zimbabwe.
   This necklace _____.

3.3 Complete the conversations using the pairs of verbs in the box. Use *be* + past participle, *get* + (object) + past participle, or *have* + (object) + past participle. Add the object in brackets where this is supplied and give alternatives where possible.

own – break into   ~~rob~~ – steal   cut – clean   wake up – throw out

1 A: Did you hear about Natasha?
   B: What happened?
   A: She <u>was/got robbed</u> on her way to college.
   B: No! Is she okay?
   A: Yes, she's fine, but she _____. (her handbag)

2 A: You're looking tired.
   B: I _____ early by my neighbour's dog.
   A: Don't they keep it inside at night?
   B: Usually, yes, but I think it must _____ because it was barking so much.

3 A: Stefan looked different somehow.
   B: He'd _____. (his hair)
   A: Yes, and I think he'd _____. It looked much smarter! (his jacket)

The passive 18

4 A: What an amazing house!
   B: It _____ by Jason Norman. You know, the rock singer.
   A: I know him, yes.
   B: The problem is, he's never there, and it keeps _____ .

3.4 Rewrite the underlined part of the sentence using a passive form where possible. If it is not possible, write 'No passive'.

1 When <u>they invited Hugo to give</u> the main presentation at the conference he was delighted and wrote immediately to accept.
   Hugo was invited to give

2 During our military training <u>they made us run</u> five kilometres before breakfast.

3 Ella felt that the pay and conditions at Trimco were unsatisfactory, and <u>many of her colleagues seemed to support her</u>.

4 <u>We wanted Julia to come</u> to the party.

5 I still have only a very vague memory of the explosion. I <u>remember someone asking me</u> to leave the building because there was a gas leak, but not much after that.

6 Although at first the children were frightened by Mr Demir's strictness, after a few weeks <u>most of the children in the class came to like him</u>.

7 <u>They caught him trying</u> to break into an expensive sports car.

8 <u>Someone heard her remark</u> that Ben was too old for the job.

9 Henry performed badly in the last match, and <u>we need him to play better this week.</u>

10 <u>People expect over 100,000 demonstrators to march</u> through the capital in protest against the government's decision to go to war.

Exam practice

Reading and Use of English Part 7

You are going to read a newspaper article. Six paragraphs have been removed from the article. Choose from the paragraphs **A – G** the one which fits each gap **(1 – 6)**. There is one extra paragraph which you do not need to use.

Alexander McCall Smith: Terrible Orchestra?
Bestselling author Alexander McCall Smith explains why he started a band for useless musicians.

There are two emotions a parent can feel when watching the school orchestra perform. One is pride – the most common emotion in the circumstances – and the other is envy. Wouldn't it have been great fun to be in an orchestra and now … it's too late. Or is it?

1

These musical islands are full of amateur orchestras, but most of these are really rather good. We wanted something that would cater for those who really were very weak players, those who might have got as far as Grade 4 on their instruments and hovered around that level for years. So we formed the Really Terrible Orchestra in Edinburgh, a city known for having a number of fine amateur orchestras. The name was carefully chosen: what it said was what you would get.

2

Those who joined generally lived up to the name. Some, though, stood out for their musical weakness. One cello player some years ago even had the notes played by the open strings written in pencil on the bridge of the instrument. Another – a clarinetist – had had only three or four lessons and could not go above the middle B flat. He played only the bottom notes, and not very well.

3

Our heads turned, we decided to hold a concert at the Edinburgh Festival Fringe. The important thing about the Fringe is that anybody can perform, with the result that there are always a certain number of appalling performances which attract tiny audiences.

4

The fortunes of the orchestra continued to improve, even if its playing did not. We presumed to make two CDs, which somehow got into the hands of radio stations abroad. We have now been played more than once by the Australian Broadcasting Corporation, by the Canadian Broadcasting Corporation, and by National Public Radio in the United States.

5

Even if the orchestra never gets to New York, that will be enough. Of course New York was where the famous Florence Foster Jenkins would appear, at the Carnegie Hall, and torture her audience with her terrible singing. Perhaps it's ready for an orchestra that will live up to her.

6

Which makes one wonder: what is it that makes people want to listen to a group of extremely bad musicians torturing a piece that most of them cannot play? Is there something about failure and its cheerful acceptance? Whatever it is, there's certainly something quintessentially British about it. And the orchestra does a very fine 'Land of Hope and Glory' – a semitone flat.

Exam practice

The passive — 18

A The response was overwhelming, particularly from clarinettists. I suspect that a very high proportion of the population is exposed to the clarinet at some stage and that British attics are crammed full of forgotten clarinet cases. Many of these were dusted off for the first meeting of the Really Terrible Orchestra, as were various other instruments. We appointed a professional conductor, Richard Neville Towle, a well-known Edinburgh musician and founder of the ensemble Ludus Baroque, and we began to rehearse. The result was cacophony.

B The Really Terrible Orchestra, however, was an immediate hit. The concert sold out well in advance, as it has done every year since, attracting an audience of more than 500 people, some not actually related to the players.

C 'We are pretty awful,' admitted one of the bassoonists. There is a very wide range of playing abilities, she added, noting that she herself had only passed Grade 3, the examination normally taken by 11-year-old British schoolchildren.

D Eight years ago my wife and I decided that we would do something about never having played in the school orchestra. We are both very challenged musicians: at the time she played the flute – hesitantly – and I played the bassoon – extremely incompetently.

E Now what has become the world's most famous amateur orchestra is about to perform in London. The Cadogan Hall is the site of this imminent musical disaster, and all 800 tickets vanished in a trice.

F An orchestra needs to perform, and we decided to hold a concert. Wisely, we took the view that the audience should be given a glass of wine, or even more than a glass, before the concert. This assisted their enjoyment and understanding of our idiosyncratic performance. Virtually every piece we played was greeted with shouts of applause and a standing ovation.

G The orchestra's fame spread. Earlier this year the New York Times, for a mention in which many professional musicians would sell their souls, devoted a quarter of a page to an article about the Really Terrible Orchestra. A few days after the appearance of the article the orchestra's chairman, Peter Stevenson, received an approach from the same New York impresario who had first taken the Beatles to the US.

19 Reporting

Structures in the reported clause: *that*-clause, *to*-infinitive and -*ing*; verb tenses in reporting; modal verbs in reporting; reporting questions; *should* in *that*-clauses

Context listening

1.1 If you lived close to an airport, what problems would you be most concerned about?

_____
_____

1.2 ▶23 There are plans to expand the small airport near the village where Leyla and Magnus live. Leyla has been to a meeting to discuss the plans, and she tells Magnus about it. Listen to their conversation. Identify three advantages and three problems of the airport expansion that were mentioned at the meeting.

Advantages	Disadvantages
_____	_____
_____	_____
_____	_____

1.3 ▶23 Listen again and complete these extracts with the words you hear.

1 They _told us that_ the expansion would create around 2,000 jobs directly.
2 They _____ a growing number of people in the local area supported the expansion.
3 They _____ us informed about future developments.
4 They _____ there and look at the plans in detail.
5 She _____ the airport authorities were not telling the truth.
6 She _____ to our local politicians with our objections.
7 She also suggested inviting the Minister for Transport to hear our complaints. I _____ to her.

1.4 Put the past tense verbs you have written in one of the columns according to the pattern that follows them. Which one of the verbs can also be followed by one of the other patterns?

verb + *that*-clause	verb + *to*-infinitive	verb + object + *that*-clause	verb + object + *to*-infinitive
		told	

Reporting 19

Grammar

> **START POINT**
>
> We often report in our own words what people think or what they have said: *'There will be a public enquiry.'*
> Reporting clause with reporting verb → *Mr Kelly announced **that** there would a public enquiry.* ← Reported clause

2.1 Structures in the reported clause: *that*-clause

Reporting verbs can be followed by a number of structures in the reported clause. The most important ones with *that*-clauses are given below:
- verb + *that*
  Sue **reckoned that** the expansion would damage tourism.
- verb + object + *that*
  He **convinced me that** noise wouldn't be a problem for us. (not *He convinced that* ...)
- verb + (object) + *that*
  She **warned** (**us**) **that** the airport authorities were not telling the truth.
  Compare the use of *tell* and *say* in the reported clause:
  They **told us that** the expansion would create around 2,000 jobs. (*tell* + object + *that*)
  They **said** (**to us**) **that** it might increase tourism in the region. (*say* + (*to* + object) + *that*)
- verb + *that* + verb or verb + object + *to*-infinitive
  I **found that** his reassurances **were** quite convincing. or more formally I **found** his reassurances **to be** quite convincing.
- verb + (*to*/*with* + object) + *that*
  They **admitted** (**to us**) **that** they're not sure exactly how many people it will attract.
  I **agree** (**with the anti-expansion group**) **that** the plans will change the area.

We often leave out *that* in informal contexts, particularly with the most common reporting verbs (e.g. *reckon, say, tell, think*). However, we don't usually leave it out if the *that*-clause doesn't immediately follow the verb:
Sue **reckoned** (**that**) the expansion would actually damage tourism.
I **agree** with the anti-expansion group **that** the plans will change the area.

2.2 Structures in the reported clause: *to*-infinitive and *-ing*

These are the most important structures with a *to*-infinitive or *-ing* form in the reported clause:
- verb + *to*-infinitive
  I've **decided to wait** and see what happens next.
- verb + object + *to*-infinitive
  They **encouraged us to go** to the village hall.
- verb + (object) + *to*-infinitive
  I **expected them to be** confrontational. or I **expected to hear** more objections.
- verb + *to*-infinitive or verb + *that*
  They **promised to keep** us informed. or They **promised that** they would keep us informed.
- verb + object + *to*-infinitive or verb + object + *that*
  She **advised us to write** to our local politicians with our objections. or She **advised us that** we should write to our local politicians with our objections.
- verb + *-ing* or verb + *that*
  She **suggested inviting** the Minister for Transport to hear our complaints. or She **suggested that** we should invite the Minister for Transport (not *She suggested to invite* ...)

135

19 Reporting

2.3 Verb tenses in reporting

> **START POINT**
>
> When reporting, we often change the tense that was in the original.
> *'The airport authorities **are** not **telling** the truth.'* → *She warned that the airport authorities **were** not **telling** the truth.*
> *'We **carried out** the trial flights last month.'* → *Mr Kelly said that they **had carried out** the trial flights last month.* or *Mr Kelly said that they **carried out** ...*

We don't usually change a past perfect verb:
*'We **had hoped** for more support.'* → *He said they **had hoped** for more support.*

We can use a present tense verb for a situation that still exists when we report it:
*Magnus said he**'s worried** about the nuclear power station on the coast.* or *... said he **was worried** ...*

We usually use a past tense in the reporting clause. However, we can use the present simple to report current news or views, what is always said, or what many people say:
*I **hear** that Boeing 737s will be landing there.*
*Everyone I've spoken to **thinks** it's awful.*

2.4 Modal verbs in reporting

A modal verb in the original sometimes changes in the report.

- *will* changes to *would*, *can* to *could*, and *may* usually changes to *might*:
  *'It **may** increase tourism in the area.'* → *They said it **might** increase tourism in the region.*

  However, if the situation we are reporting still exists or is in the future, modals don't change if there is a present tense verb in the reporting clause:
  *'We**'ll** be displaying copies of the plans in the village hall.'* → *They say they**'ll** be putting copies of the plans in the village hall.*

  We can use either form if there is a past tense verb in the reporting clause:
  *'The expansion **will** create 2,000 jobs.'* → *They told us that the expansion **will**/**would** create around 2,000 jobs.*

- *shall* changes to *would* to talk about the future, and to *should* to report suggestions, recommendations and requests for advice:
  *'I **shall** decide later.'* → *He said he **would** decide later.*
  *'What **shall** we do next?'* → *He asked what they **should** do next.*

- *must* doesn't change or changes to *had to* when it is used to say it is necessary to do something:
  *'You **must** look at the plans before making any decisions.'* → *He said I **must** / **had to** look at the plans before making any decisions. (Had to is more natural in speech.)*

- *could, should, would, might, ought to* and *used to* don't usually change in the report:
  *'We **ought to** write to our local politicians.'* → *She **suggested** we ought to write ...*

2.5 Reporting questions

> **START POINT**
>
> *'What are your views on this?'* → *They **asked what** our views were.* or *They **asked** (**for**) our views.*
> *'Have you got any more questions?'* → *They wanted to know **if**/**whether** we had any more questions.*
> (See **Unit 16, 2.3** for more on the choice between *whether* and *if*.)

136

Reporting 19

The usual word order in the reported *wh-*, *if-* or *whether-*clause is the one we would use in a statement, and we don't use a question mark or the *do* auxiliary:
'How exactly **will it boost** tourism?' → I asked how exactly **it would boost** tourism.
'Where **did you get** your figures from?' → She asked where **they had got** their figures from.

We can use a negative form of *do* to report a negative question:
'Why **don't** you want the airport to expand?' → He asked why I **didn't** want the airport to expand.

If the original question begins *what*, *which* or *who*, followed by *be* + complement, we can put the complement before or after *be* in the report:
'Who's Sue Ray?' → He asked who **Sue Ray was**. or He asked who **was Sue Ray**.

To report a question with *should* asking for advice or information, we can use a *to-*infinitive:
'What **should** we do to protest?' → Someone asked Sue what **to do** to protest. or ... what we **should** do to protest.

We don't use a *to-*infinitive to report a *why* question:
'Why should we believe them?' → She wanted to know why we **should** believe them. (not ~~She wanted to know why to believe them.~~)

Grammar exercises

3.1 Complete the sentences with an appropriate form of the reporting verbs in the box. Add a preposition or pronoun if necessary.

~~check~~ claim commiserate emphasise explain grumble persuade reassure reveal whisper

1 Before I parked my car outside Diego's house, I _checked with_ him that it was okay.
2 It took ages to feed all the customers, and by the time we got around to the last ones they _____ that their food was cold. But I just ignored their complaints.
3 I know that Tomas enjoys his work as a gardener, but when he _____ to be the best job in the world, I wasn't sure whether he was being serious or not.
4 The company hadn't paid me for the work I'd done for them, but when I phoned, they _____ that my payment was on its way.
5 Carlson didn't want to speak to the police yet. He didn't want to _____ anyone that he knew who the murderer was until he had concrete evidence.
6 Teresa gave me the report but said it was only a first draft. She _____ that it should remain confidential until the statistics had been checked.
7 Just before I stood up to make my speech, my friend Jamir came up close and _____ me that my shirt was hanging out at the back.
8 Terry said that he was going to re-paint the car himself, but I managed to _____ that this was a bad idea.
9 When I heard about her disastrous job interview, I phoned Martha to _____ her.
10 At first, the security guard stopped me going in, but when I _____ him that I had an appointment he let me through the barrier.

19 Reporting

3.2 Stephen is an engineering student who has applied for a job when he leaves university. Complete these extracts from Stephen's letter of application using the notes in brackets. Use a *that-*, *to-*infinitive or *-ing* clause in your answer and give alternatives where possible.

> Dear Mr Clarke,
>
> I am writing with reference to the post of Senior Research Engineer advertised in Engineering Monthly. I assume **(1)** _that the post is / the post to be_ (the post) still vacant. My supervisor, Professor Ken Newton, has advised **(2)** _____ (apply) and has assured **(3)** _____ (my research), which is described in detail in the attached documents, will be of interest to you.
>
> I expect **(4)** _____ (complete) my PhD by the end of the year, and I propose **(5)** _____ (publish) the findings of my research soon afterwards. I believe **(6)** _____ (my qualifications and experience) appropriate for the post.
>
> I hope **(7)** _____ (hear) from you in the near future.
>
> Yours sincerely,
>
> *Stephen Finch*
>
> Stephen Finch

3.3 Stephen got an interview, but wasn't offered the job. Complete his account of the interview to his supervisor.

They asked **(1)** _me to explain_ (explain) the main purposes of my research. I **(2)** _____ (tell) I was working on a new hydrogen fuel cell. I admitted **(3)** _____ (have problems) in the early stages of the work. They were very helpful. They suggested **(4)** _____ (look at) Chris Hume's work at the University of Harford. They agreed **(5)** _____ (me / my research) has many practical applications. They even invited **(6)** _____ (visit) their laboratories if it would help in my research. Although they didn't offer me the job, they recommended **(7)** _____ (write) to them again after I've finished my PhD, and in the meantime they agreed **(8)** _____ (contact) if any other similar jobs come up. Of course, they couldn't guarantee **(9)** _____ (offer) a job in the future, but they were very encouraging.

3.4 Change the sentences into reported speech. Give alternative tenses where possible.

1 'I broke my leg when I was skiing.' → She said _(that) she broke / had broken her leg when she was skiing_.
2 'It's going to rain later today.' → He thinks _____ later today.
3 'I don't think this is my coat.' → She didn't think _____.
4 'You must set the alarm when you leave the house.' → She said _____.
5 'Where have I left my handbag?' → She couldn't remember _____.
6 'I'm playing football this afternoon.' → He said _____ yesterday afternoon.
7 'I won't be able to give you a lift after all.' → He said _____, so I'll have to take a taxi.
8 'How much do you earn?' → He wanted to know _____.
9 'We might go to Italy in the summer.' → She mentioned _____ in the summer.
10 'What shall I do with this painting?' → He wanted to know _____.

Exam practice

Reporting **19**

Listening Part 4

▶24 You will hear five short extracts in which people are talking about moving from the countryside to the city. **While you listen you must complete both tasks.**

TASK ONE
For questions **1 – 5**, choose from the list **(A – H)** the reason each speaker gives for leaving the countryside.

A	slow broadband connection	Speaker 1	1
B	close friends had left	Speaker 2	2
C	limited cultural activities	Speaker 3	3
D	lack of privacy	Speaker 4	4
E	transport problems	Speaker 5	5
F	difficult to find a job		
G	poor housing quality		
H	limited shopping opportunities		

TASK TWO
For questions **6 – 10**, choose from the list **(A – H)** what each speaker says about their experience of living in the city.

A	happy to have efficient transport	Speaker 1	6
B	relieved to make friends	Speaker 2	7
C	satisfied with accommodation	Speaker 3	8
D	glad to have a hospital nearby	Speaker 4	9
E	grateful for a reliable income	Speaker 5	10
F	enjoying a variety of places to eat		
G	pleased with sports facilities		
H	excited by diversity of cultures		

139

20 Substitution and ellipsis

One/ones; so + auxiliary verb + subject; neither, nor, not ... either; do so; leaving out words after auxiliary verbs and after to

Context listening

1.1 You are going to listen to two college friends talking about adventure holidays. What activities are shown in these pictures?

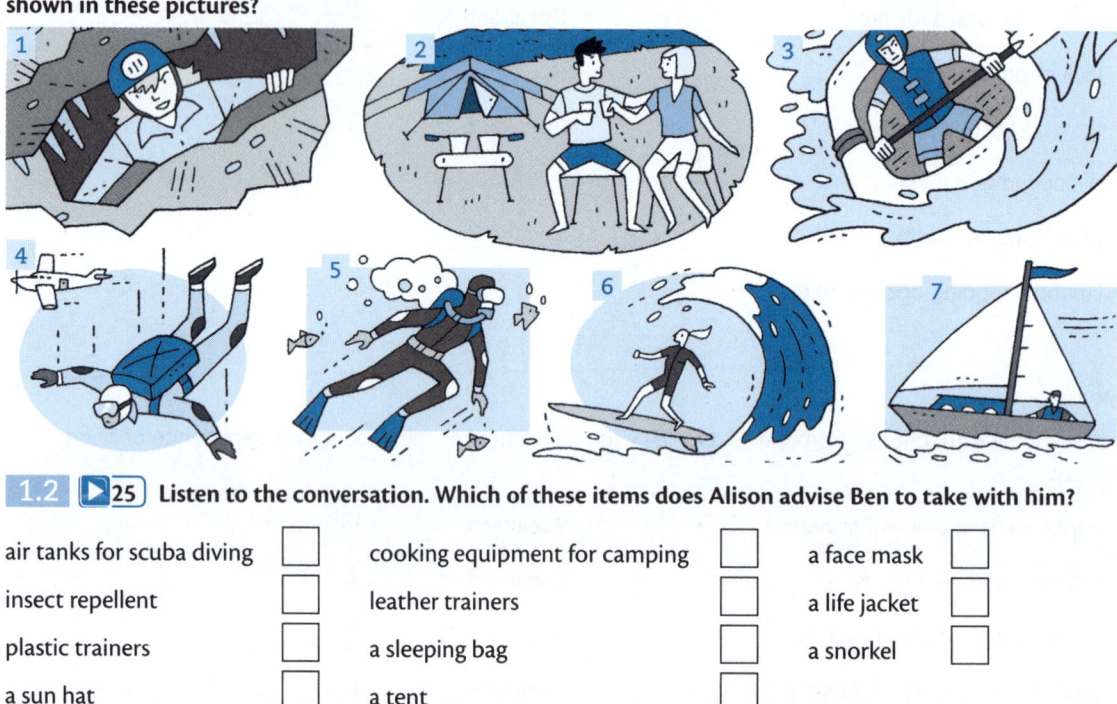

1.2 ▶25 Listen to the conversation. Which of these items does Alison advise Ben to take with him?

air tanks for scuba diving ☐	cooking equipment for camping ☐	a face mask ☐
insect repellent ☐	leather trainers ☐	a life jacket ☐
plastic trainers ☐	a sleeping bag ☐	a snorkel ☐
a sun hat ☐	a tent ☐	

1.3 ▶25 Listen again. Change these sentences to show exactly what Alison or Ben said.

                    one
1. I went for the ~~adventure holiday~~ based in Brisbane.
2. One of the local organisers met me at the airport.
3. They should provide all the equipment.
4. But you don't have to be a very good swimmer.
5. Preferably plastic trainers.
6. By the end of the holiday I was exhausted, but I was very fit!
7. You'll certainly need some insect repellent.
8. I don't imagine you'll need to take a tent and cooking things.

140

20 Substitution and ellipsis

Grammar

2.1 Substitution: *one/ones*

> **START POINT**
>
> They do diving holidays in quite a few places. I went for the **one** based in Brisbane. (*one* = *diving holiday*; *one* replaces a singular countable noun or a noun phrase)
> Take a couple of pairs of old trainers – preferably plastic **ones**. (*ones* = *trainers*; *ones* replaces a plural noun)

We don't usually use *one/ones*:
- to replace an uncountable noun. Instead we use *some*:
  Don't forget insect repellent. You'll certainly need **some**. (not ... ~~need one.~~)
- to talk about a specific item. Compare:
  Do you know anyone who's got a sleeping bag? I was hoping to borrow **one**.
  Have you still got your sleeping bag? Can I borrow **it**? (= a particular sleeping bag)
- after *the*, unless it follows an adjective:
  'Are these your trainers?' 'No, **the leather ones** are mine.'
  or unless there is a descriptive phrase after *one/ones*:
  They had a number of adventure holidays on offer, and I chose **the one that was cheapest**.
  I went for **the one based in Brisbane**.
- after a possessive adjective (e.g. *my*). Instead we prefer a possessive pronoun (e.g. *mine*) or a phrase with an adjective:
  You can borrow **mine**. or You can borrow **my old one**. rather than You can borrow my one.
  However, *one/ones* is sometimes used after a possessive adjective in informal speech.

We don't usually use *ones* on its own to replace a noun phrase. Compare:
'You'll need trainers.' 'Okay, I'll bring **some**.' or 'I'll bring some **old ones**.' (not ~~I'll bring ones.~~)

We can either include or leave out *one/ones* after *which, whichever*; superlatives; *either, neither, another, each* (but not *every*); *the first/second/last; the other; this, that, these, those*; and often after colour adjectives:
'I can't decide whether to go on the adventure holiday to Thailand or Australia.' 'I'm sure you'll enjoy **whichever** (**one**) you go on.'
Get your own face mask. Buy **the best** (**one**) you can afford.
I've had three holidays with TransWorld Adventures, but **the first** (**one**) was the best.
I've got these two sleeping bags, but **this** (**one**) is rather dirty. (*these ones* and *those ones* are only used in informal speech)
We had two small boats to practise sailing in. One was green and **the other** (**one**) was red. I used to sail in **the green** (**one**).

20 Substitution and ellipsis

2.2 Substitution: *so* + auxiliary verb + subject; *neither, nor, not ... either*

> **START POINT**
>
> *'Was diving as difficult as you expected?' 'Perhaps even more **so**.'* (so = difficult; replaces an adjective)
> *TransWorld Adventures provides all the equipment – at least I presume **so**.* (so = TransWorld Adventures provides all the equipment; replaces a clause)

We can use *so* instead of a clause after certain verbs to do with opinions (e.g. *expect, suppose, think*), but not after others (e.g. *accept, know, be sure, hear*):
*'Will I be met at the airport?' 'I **expect so**.'*
'The mozzies are really bad at that time of year.' 'I've heard that, too.' (not *I've heard so, too.*)

Some verbs are commonly used before *not* or in *not ... so* in short, negative replies:
*'You won't need a sleeping bag if it's really hot.' 'I **suppose not**.'* or *'No, I **don't suppose so**.'*
Other verbs like this include: *appear, seem; believe, expect, imagine, think*. (With the last four verbs we prefer *not ... so* in informal contexts):
*'Do you think I'll need to take a tent?' 'I **don't imagine so**.'* or formally *'I **imagine not**.'*

Before *not* we can use *be afraid* (= showing regret), *assume, guess, hope, presume, suspect*:
*'Do they offer any holidays in Africa?' 'I**'m afraid not**.'* (not *I'm not afraid so.*)

We can use *so* + auxiliary verb + subject to say that a second person does the same thing as a person already mentioned. In the negative we use *neither, nor* or *not ... either*:
*'I'd like to go to Tasmania.' '**So would I**.'*
*'I'm not really a very good swimmer.' 'No, **neither am I**.'* or *'**Nor am I**.'* or *'I'm **not either**.'* or *'I'm not a very good swimmer **either**.'*

2.3 Substitution: *do so*

We can use a form of *do so* to replace a verb and the word or phrase that follows it to complete its meaning:
*When asked whether they intended to offer holidays in Africa, TransWorld Adventures said they had no plans to **do so**.* (do so = offer holidays in Africa)
*He planned to go to Australia this year, but now that he has lost his job he has little chance of **doing so**.* (doing so = going to Australia)

We can use *do so* where the verb describes an action, but avoid it with verbs that describe states and habitual actions:
*We went down the river by boat, and saw a lot of wildlife while **doing so**.*
*Some people didn't enjoy the hard work, but I **did**.* (not *but I did so ...*)
Less formally, we use *do it* or *do that* with a similar meaning:
*We put up our tents by the side of the river. We **did that** at about four o'clock every afternoon.* or formally *We **did so** ...*

We use *do* (rather than *do so*) in informal English, especially after modals or perfect tenses (but note that we can often leave it out):
*'Do they provide all the equipment?' 'They **should** (do).'*
*'Could you have gone to Thailand instead?' 'Yes, I **could have** (done).'*

20 Substitution and ellipsis

2.4 Ellipsis: leaving out words after auxiliary verbs and after *to*

> **START POINT**
>
> 'Have you decided yet?' 'Yes, I have.' (= Yes, I have decided.)
> A lot of people go to the Great Barrier Reef when they're in Australia. Were you able to? (= Were you able to go to the Great Barrier Reef?)
> We often leave out or change verbs to avoid repeating them.

We can sometimes use *to* instead of a clause beginning with a *to*-infinitive when it is clear what we are talking about:
*I'd certainly like to go back to Australia. I **hope to** next year.* (= to go back to Australia)

We can use *to* or leave it out:
- after certain verbs (e.g. *agree, promise, start*):
  *I want to read a lot about Australia before I go. I**'ve started** (**to**) already.*
- after most nouns (e.g. *idea, opportunity*) and adjectives (e.g. *frightened, willing*) that can be followed by a *to*-infinitive clause:
  *I've always wanted to go, but I've never had the **chance** (**to**) before.*
  *I hope they don't ask us to swim if there are sharks around. I'd be **afraid** (**to**).*
- after *want* and *would like* in *if*-clauses and *wh*-clauses:
  *We must talk about it more. You can come over whenever you**'d like** (**to**).*
  We don't use *to* after *like*:
  *You can come over whenever you **like**.*

We have to use *to*:
- after verbs (e.g. *expect, mean, need*) which must have a complement:
  *You can borrow mine if you **need to**.*
- after a negative:
  *You don't have to sail on your own if you **don't want to**.*

When *have (got)* is a main verb in the first clause or sentence, we can often use either *have (got)* or *do* to avoid repetition in the following clause or sentence:
*Have you got a sleeping bag? I'm sure you **have**.* (= I'm sure you have got a sleeping bag.) or *I'm sure you **do**.*
(= I'm sure you do have a sleeping bag.)

When *have* is followed by a noun to describe an action (e.g. *have a shower, have a shave, have a good time*) we usually use *do*:
*I wasn't really expecting to **have a good time**, but I **did**.*

143

20 Substitution and ellipsis

Grammar exercises

3.1 Read the underlined parts of these dialogues. Cross out the words which can be left out.

1. **A:** What was wrong with Sue?
   B: She was frightened, or at least she appeared to be ~~frightened~~.

2. **A:** You should have asked me. I could have given you a lift into town.
   B: Thanks, but I didn't like to ask ~~you~~. I know how busy you are.

3. **A:** Has Sarah eaten anything today?
   B: No, I don't think she has ~~eaten anything today~~.

4. **A:** My grandmother would have been shocked by all the changes in the village.
   B: Yes, I'm sure she would ~~have been shocked~~.

5. **A:** Don't forget we're going out tonight. Can you leave work early?
   B: Okay, I'll try ~~to leave work early~~.

6. **A:** We could get to the island across the new bridge.
   B: But it hasn't been opened yet.
   A: I thought it had been opened.

7. **A:** I hope I get promoted this time.
   B: You certainly deserve to ~~get promoted~~. You work really hard.

8. **A:** I didn't know you were getting married.
   B: Sorry. I thought you did know ~~I was getting married~~.

3.2 Replace the underlined word(s) with *one* or *ones* where possible. If it is possible to omit *one* or *ones*, put the words in brackets.

1. **A:** Do you want one of these sweets?
   B: Are there any green sweets [ones] left?
   A: No, they've all gone.

2. **A:** It's about time we got some new curtains.
   B: Okay, well, let's go out and buy some new curtains.

3. **A:** I know it's muddy outside, but shall we go out for a walk?
   B: But I haven't got any boots.
   A: You can wear my old boots.

4. **A:** To get to your house, do I take the first or second turning?
   B: You can take either turning.

5. **A:** Why did you buy those green apples?
   B: They were the cheapest apples I could find.

144

Substitution and ellipsis 20

6 Have you seen the car keys? I can't find <u>the car keys</u> anywhere.

7 That mirror is like the <u>mirror</u> my parents have got in their sitting room.

8 This glass has got a crack in it. Have you got another <u>glass</u>?

9 I dropped my brother's mobile phone and had to buy him a new <u>mobile phone</u>.

10 We've got chocolate biscuits or these <u>biscuits</u>. Which <u>biscuits</u> would you prefer?

3.3 Complete the sentences where possible with *so*, *do*, *do so* or *so do*, using an appropriate form of *do*. If it is not possible, suggest an alternative.

1 She stood up slowly, and was obviously in pain as she ___did so___ .

2 **A:** Miller played really badly, didn't he?
   B: But _____ the rest of the team.

3 **A:** Are you going to Spain again for your holidays?
   B: I might _____ . I haven't decided yet.

4 Louise will be meeting us at the airport. At least, I hope _____ .

5 **A:** Apparently, Harun's dropped out of college.
   B: Yes, I'd heard _____ too.

6 We do more or less the same job, but he earns much more than I _____ .

7 **A:** We can take a shortcut if we wade across the stream.
   B: What's the point of _____ ? The bridge isn't far.

8 He has yet to win a tournament, but he came close to _____ in Monaco.

9 **A:** Do you really think she'll lend you the money?
   B: I'm sure _____ .

10 Megan loves horse riding, and _____ Victor.

20 Substitution and ellipsis

3.4 Improve this email by editing the underlined parts to avoid repetition.

Hi Chris,

I tried phoning you earlier, but you must have been out. But I just have to tell somebody about the terrible day I've had :-(!

It started badly and got worse! When I got up the kitchen was flooded – I'd left the freezer door open! I've never **(1)** <u>left the freezer door open</u> before. By the time I'd finished mopping up all the water it was getting late. I was going to take my big handbag to work, but I was so rushed I picked up my **(2)** <u>small handbag</u> by mistake, leaving my purse behind so I didn't have any money. Luckily, I bumped into Bob at the station and he was able to lend me **(3)** <u>some money</u>. My office key was also still at home, so when I got to work I had borrow **(4)** <u>an office key</u>.

Then I had to get to an important meeting. Our company is hoping to do some business with a Japanese firm. My boss thinks we have a good chance of signing a deal soon, but I don't think **(5)** <u>we have a good chance of signing a deal soon</u>. I thought the meeting was on the fourth floor – in fact, I was certain **(6)** <u>it was on the fourth floor</u>. But it had been rearranged and nobody had bothered to tell me. So I was 20 minutes late. I wasn't very happy, and **(7)** <u>my boss wasn't very happy either</u>. To make matters worse, I'd been hoping to run through my presentation over breakfast, but I'd had no **(8)** <u>time to run through my presentation over breakfast</u>. So my talk went really badly. Afterwards, my boss said she was disappointed with the way the meeting went. But **(9)** <u>I was disappointed with the way the meeting went, too</u>.

After such a dreadful day, I was hoping I'd have a quiet evening, but I **(10)** <u>didn't have a quiet evening</u>. When I got home I found that my cat had knocked over some glasses – you remember the beautiful old Swedish **(11)** <u>glasses</u> that my parents gave me? I wonder if I'll be able to replace them? I **(12)** <u>don't expect I'll be able to replace them</u>.

The only good thing is that it's the weekend. Come over whenever you **(13)** <u>want to come over</u>. In fact, are you able to come over tomorrow? If you **(14)** <u>'re not able to come over tomorrow</u> how about Sunday? Or are you still too busy decorating the house? I **(15)** <u>hope you're not too busy decorating the house</u>. But give me a call and let me know.

Love,
Beth x

(1) _____done that_____
(2) _____
(3) _____
(4) _____
(5) _____
(6) _____
(7) _____
(8) _____
(9) _____
(10) _____
(11) _____
(12) _____
(13) _____
(14) _____
(15) _____

Exam practice

Substitution and ellipsis **20**

Listening Part 3

▶26 You will hear part of a radio interview in which David Evans, a chef in a British school, is talking about his work. For questions **1 – 6**, choose the answer (**A**, **B**, **C** or **D**) which fits best according to what you hear.

1   What was the students' initial reaction to the food they were served?

   A They didn't like being the subjects of an experiment.
   B They would rather have eaten traditional British food.
   C They were not sure whether it was good or bad.
   D They felt that it was an adventure for them.

2   According to David, why do some students have difficulty in accepting the 'restaurant system'?

   A They are uncomfortable eating meals with adults.
   B They are not used to having meals with others.
   C They don't like talking about food.
   D They have to wait too long to be served.

3   What main role do the staff play in the school restaurant?

   A They check that students are eating their meals.
   B They find out about the students' home lives.
   C They deal with students' complaints about the food.
   D They help students find out about a balanced diet.

4   According to David, where does most of the food served in the restaurant come from?

   A anywhere that can provide fresh ingredients
   B the school grounds
   C all over the world
   D suppliers close to the school

5   In David's view, which of his previous jobs prepared him best for his work as a school chef?

   A teacher
   B manager
   C waiter
   D cook

6   Why does David think that his approach could be difficult to introduce in other schools?

   A Students tend to be resistant to change.
   B Not all students see healthy eating as important.
   C Other schools don't see healthy eating as a priority.
   D Parents would be unwilling to accept it.

21 Word order and emphasis

Fronting; cleft sentences; inversion; inversion in conditional sentences

Context listening

1.1 Which of these qualities and characteristics might people use in describing you?

| commitment | confidence | dedication | enthusiasm | loyalty | modesty |
| determined | efficient | energetic | patient | persuasive | reliable |

1.2 🔊27 Listen to this speech made in honour of Maria Adams, a music teacher. Which of the qualities and characteristics in 1.1 does the speaker use to describe her?

1.3 🔊27 Listen again and say whether these sentences are true (T) or false (F). If a sentence is false, say why.

1. Maria was a violinist before she became a conductor. __T__
2. In the *Music in Schools* project the council gives children musical instruments. _____
3. Musicians are not paid to take part in the *Music in Schools* project. _____
4. Children in city schools now have to pay for their music lessons. _____
5. Maria helps children go to other countries to play music. _____

1.4 🔊27 These ideas are expressed in a different way by the speaker. Listen again and write down exactly what he said.

1. We first met in the mid-1990s.
   It was in the mid-1990's that we first met.

2. She sees making music as a fundamental part of a child's development.
   _____

3. The way she calmly and clearly argued her case impressed us most.
   _____

4. I have rarely met anyone with such passion for their beliefs.
   _____

5. The council has tried to make changes to the *Music in Schools* project a number of times in order to save money.
   _____

6. The council backed down only after Maria threatened to withdraw her support from the project.
   _____

1.5 What difference do you notice between the sentences given and the ones you have written in 1.4?

21 Word order and emphasis

Grammar

2.1 Fronting

We can emphasise a particular part of a sentence by moving it to the front of the sentence, changing the usual word order:
She sees **making music** as a fundamental part of a child's development. → **Making music** she sees as a fundamental part of a child's development. (fronting of object)
She resisted **this**. → **This** she resisted. (fronting of object)
Maria had been writing to me **for some weeks**. → **For some weeks** Maria had been writing to me. (fronting of adverbial)

2.2 Cleft sentences

> **START POINT**
>
> It's among children from poorer backgrounds that the Music in Schools project has had most impact. (emphasising *among children from poorer backgrounds*)
> What impressed us most was the way she calmly and clearly argued her case. (emphasising *the way she calmly and clearly argued her case*)

An *it*-cleft has the structure *it* + *is/was* + emphasised part + relative clause. The relative pronoun can be *that*, *which*, *who* or no relative pronoun. *When* and *where* are used only in informal English:
It was in the mid-1990s that we first met. or informally … **when** we first met.
A sentence with a *wh*-cleft usually has the structure *what*-clause + *is/was* + emphasised part. Sometimes we use *all* instead of *what*:
What she was suggesting was that members of the YCO would volunteer their services.
All she ever wanted to do as she was growing up was play the violin. (= the only thing she ever wanted to do)
After the *what*-clause we usually use a singular form of *be* (*is* or *was*). However, informally, a plural form (*are* or *were*) is sometimes used before a plural noun:
What she hopes to see is/are children who enjoy a wide range of musical styles.
We can sometimes put a *wh*-cleft at the end of a sentence:
The way she calmly and clearly argued her case was **what impressed us most**.
The Music in Schools project is **what came out of our meeting**.
To emphasise an action we can use a *wh*-cleft with *what* + subject + form of *do* + form of *be* + (*to*) + infinitive:
What she did was (**to**) convince us of the value of a musical education.

2.3 Inversion

> **START POINT**
>
> In front of the committee **sat Maria**.   (= verb + subject)   ⎫
> Seldom **did she raise** her voice.   (= do + subject + verb)   ⎬ = inversion of normal word order
> Never **have I heard** such a persuasive speaker.   (= auxiliary + subject + verb) ⎭
> Word order is inverted after certain words and phrases when these are put at the beginning of a sentence or clause in order to emphasise them. This kind of inversion is found mainly in formal speech and writing.

149

21 Word order and emphasis

Inversion occurs after words and phrases with a 'negative' meaning:
- the negative adverbs *never (before), rarely, seldom; barely/hardly/scarcely ... when/before; no sooner ... than; nowhere; neither, nor*:
  Rarely have I met anyone with such enthusiasm.
  No sooner had Maria walked through the door than she started to talk about her proposal.
  I hadn't met Maria before, and **nor had the other members of the committee**.
  (See also **Unit 17**, **2.3** for more on *hardly, no sooner* and *scarcely*.)
- *only* + a time expression (e.g. *after, later, then*) or a prepositional phrase:
  Only after Maria threatened to withdraw her support **did the council back down**.
- the prepositional phrases *at no time, on no account, under/in no circumstances; in no way* (or *no way* in informal language):
  At no time has she ever **accepted** payment for her educational work.
  She argued that **under no circumstances should** children from poorer backgrounds **be made** to pay for music lessons.
- expressions with *not*: *not only, not until, not since, not for one moment, not once, not a* + noun:
  Not only has she persuaded YCO members to give up their time, but she has also encouraged visiting musicians to give free concerts in schools.
- *little* with a negative meaning:
  Little did she realise when she set up the project that it would be so influential.

Inversion also occurs after:
- time sequence adverbs such as *first, next, now, then* with *be* or *come*:
  And **then came an invitation** to be a special adviser to the government on music education.

  If there is a comma (,) or an intonation break in speech after the adverb, normal word order is used:
  Then, an invitation came from the government. (not ~~Then, came an invitation~~ ...)
- *so* + adjective ... *that*, emphasising the adjective:
  So successful has Music in Schools been that those involved in music education around the world have visited the city to see the project in action.
- *such + be ... that*, emphasising the extent or degree of something:
  Such was her understanding of music education that the government wanted to draw on her expertise.
  (= Her understanding of music education was such that ...)

2.4 Inversion in conditional sentences

In formal or literary English, we can use clauses beginning *were, should* and *had*, with inversion of subject and verb, instead of a hypothetical conditional:
Were she ever **to leave** the orchestra, ... (= If she left ... or If she were to leave ...)
Were he **here** tonight, ... (= If he was/were here tonight ...)
Should you **need** any more information about Music in Schools, ... (= If you need ...)
Had Maria **not been** around, ... (= If she had not been around ...)

In negative clauses with inversion, we don't use contracted forms:
Had Maria **not set up** the Music in Schools project ... (not ~~Hadn't Maria set up~~ ...)

Word order and emphasis 21

Grammar exercises

3.1 Write a new sentence with a similar meaning to the original. Emphasise the information underlined using an *it*-cleft or a *wh*-cleft at the beginning of the sentence. Sometimes both are possible.

1 I want you to <u>hold the cat tightly while I put on this collar</u>.
2 She announced she was going to join the air force <u>at her 18th birthday party</u>.
3 **A:** So how did you get the car out of the mud?
   B: We <u>asked a farmer to pull us out with his tractor</u>.
4 **A:** What do you think's wrong with the car?
   B: <u>The battery could</u> be flat.
5 This huge bunch of flowers arrived for me this morning. I don't know <u>who sent them</u>.
6 <u>My parents</u> must have given Wei my telephone number.
7 The research shows <u>a link between salt intake and rates of heart disease</u>.
8 <u>His nervous laugh</u> made me think he was lying.

1 *What I want you to do is hold the cat tightly while I put on this collar.*

3.2 Match the sentence halves. Write new sentences with a similar meaning starting *Should ...*, *Had ...* or *Were ...* .

1 If you require further details,   a she might have made a full recovery.
2 If today's match has to be postponed,   b the insurance covers a full refund.
3 If anyone had been looking at Maria when   c please contact our public information
  the police arrived,   office.
4 If taxes were to be increased further,   d there would be a huge public outcry.
5 If the doctors had operated sooner,   e we would not have begun the climb.
6 If I were president,   f it will be replayed next week.
7 If your flight is cancelled,   g they would have noticed the expression
8 If heavy snow had been forecast,   of panic on her face.
                                               h I would introduce three-day weekends.

1 + c *Should you require further details, please contact our publication information office.*
2 _____
3 _____
4 _____
5 _____
6 _____
7 _____
8 _____

151

21 Word order and emphasis

3.3 Complete the sentences with appropriate words. Use three words only in each sentence.

1 I thought the insurance policy would pay my hospital fees. At no time _was I told / was I informed_ that it did not cover skiing injuries.
2 Seldom _____ piano playing of such maturity from someone so young. I'm very impressed indeed.
3 He felt someone bump against him on the crowded bus, but only later _____ that his wallet had been stolen.
4 I found the old bracelet while I was walking along the beach. Little _____ then that I had made one of the most important archaeological discoveries of recent years.
5 Not since Philip and Gary Neville last played in 2004 _____ two brothers in the England football team.
6 I asked her to describe her attacker, but only after several minutes _____ me.
7 No sooner _____ into bed than his flatmate started playing his drums.
8 The Atlantic crossing took eight days. I was in Isabella's company on several occasions, but not a word _____ to me until near the end of the journey.

3.4 Rewrite the underlined parts of the conversation, emphasising the word(s) in italics. In each case use fronting, a cleft sentence or inversion.

A: I hear you and Anna didn't have a great holiday on the island.
B: No, not really, although (1) we liked _the island_ a lot. (2) _The hotel_ was the real problem.
A: Why? What was wrong with it?
B: Our room was just awful. The shower only had cold water and the air conditioning didn't work.
A: Didn't you complain?
B: Oh yes. Anna was pretty annoyed and went down to reception to complain. But they told her she was just being fussy and (3) she got really furious about _that_. She insisted on seeing the manager, and demanded that something should be done.
A: And was it?
B: Well, we had a steady stream of workers coming into the room after that. (4) An electrician came _first_ and then the next day a plumber. But neither of the problems got fixed. (5) It took them _three days_ to decide that we needed another room.
A: You must have been fed up with the hotel by that time.
B: I think (6) _the attitude of the staff_ annoyed me most – they really just didn't care. (7) I have _never_ seen such a total lack of interest from people who are supposed to be providing a service. (8) No one apologised _once_ the whole time we were there ...

1 _the island we liked a lot_
2 _____
3 _____
4 _____
5 _____
6 _____
7 _____
8 _____

152

Exam practice

Word order and emphasis **21**

Reading and Use of English Part 4

For questions **1 – 6**, complete the second sentence so that it has a similar meaning to the first sentence, using the word given. **Do not change the word given**. You must use between **three** and **six** words, including the word given. Here is an example **(0)**.

---

0 He always calls his house his 'castle'.
   REFERS
   He always _refers to his house as_ his 'castle'.

1 She was proud of her work, and she was also well respected by her colleagues.
   TAKE
   Not only _____ her work, she was also well respected by her colleagues.

2 She hated publicity so much that she never gave any interviews to the media.
   HER
   Such _____ of publicity, that she never gave any interviews to the media.

3 During her illness, she realised that the only choice she had was to take early retirement.
   ALTERNATIVE
   During her illness, she realised that there _____ to take early retirement.

4 I had only just complained about the new timetable when it was changed.
   MADE
   No sooner _____ about the new timetable than it was changed.

5 I'm sure she would do an excellent job if she ever became head of department.
   WERE
   I'm sure she would do an excellent job _____ head of department.

6 It is distinctly possible that I will get promoted in the near future.
   OF
   There is a _____ promoted in the near future.

153

22 Nominalisation

Nominalised forms; *do, give, have, make, take* + noun

Context listening

1.1 You are going to listen to a radio news report. Look at the photos. What do you think the report is about?

1.2 ▶28 Listen and check whether you were right. As you listen, number these events in the order the reporter mentions them.

a   Two power stations were built close to Lake Taal. _____
b   People were evacuated from around Lake Taal. _____
c   The Taal volcano erupted and around a hundred people were killed. _____
d   Scientists found that the temperature of Lake Taal was increasing. _____
e   The Taal Emergency Strategy was introduced. _____
f   A state of high alert was declared. _____
g   The Taal volcano erupted and over a thousand people were killed. __1__

1.3 ▶28 Listen again. Complete each extract from the news report with a noun in the first space and a preposition in the second.

1   The __breakdown__ __in__ communication cost at least a hundred lives.
2   There has been an _____ _____ the number of people living close to the lake.
3   The _____ _____ the power stations would leave thousands of homes and businesses without electricity.
4   There was also a dramatic _____ _____ the level of radon gas in the soil.
5   Their concerns increased with the _____ _____ thousands of dead fish.
6   Two days ago the _____ _____ around 30,000 people began.

1.4 Write new sentences with similar meanings to those in 1.3. In each case, use a verb related to the noun in the first space.

1   Communication broke down and this cost at least a hundred lives.

154

Nominalisation 22

Grammar

2.1 Nominalisation

> **START POINT**
>
> *There has been **an increase** in the number of people living close to the lake.* or *The number of people living close to the lake has **increased**.*
> *__The danger__ of the situation made it necessary to bring in the army to oversee operations.* or *The situation was so **dangerous** that it was necessary to bring in the army to oversee operations.*
> We can sometimes use a noun or noun phrase for an idea usually expressed by a verb or adjective. This process is referred to as *nominalisation*. It is especially common in formal styles of writing.

An adverb modifying a verb changes to an adjective in a nominalised form:
*Scientists noticed **a sudden rise** in the temperature of the lake.* or *Scientists noticed that the temperature of the lake had **risen suddenly**.*

The main noun in a noun phrase is often followed by one or more prepositional phrases:
*The industrial **development of the area** has increased the number of people living near the lake.*
*There was also a dramatic **rise in the level of radon gas in the soil**.*

We use nominalisation for a number of reasons:
- to avoid mentioning the agent (the person or thing that performs the action); for example, if we want to be impersonal or to make the agent less important. Compare:
  *Two days ago **the authorities began to evacuate** 30,000 people.* (agent = *the authorities*)
  *Two days ago **the evacuation** of around 30,000 people began.* (no agent mentioned)
- to express two clauses more concisely as one clause:
  ***The building of two power stations** just a few kilometres away was strongly criticised by environmentalists.* or
  ***Two power stations were built** just a few kilometres away. This was strongly criticised by environmentalists.*
- to give a different focus to the sentence. Compare:
  ***The provision** of temporary shelter in a safe location for those displaced is the army's top priority.* (New, important information is usually placed at the end of the sentence or clause. The focus here is on *the army's top priority*.)
  *Temporary shelter in a safe location for those displaced **is being provided**, and this is the army's top priority.* (No particular focus: *is being provided* and *the army's top priority* are both in 'new information' position in their clause.)

2.2 Do, give, have, make, take + noun

We can sometimes use a form with *do/give/have/make/take* + noun instead of a verb:
*The authorities **took** immediate **action**.* or *The authorities **acted** immediately.*
***The decision was made** to evacuate the area.* or ***It was decided** to evacuate the area.*

Often, the *do/give/have/make/take* + noun patterns are less formal than using a verb alone:
*When my mother was ill, I had **to cook** for the family.* (more formal)
*I had **to do** all **the cooking** last week because Mum was away.* (less formal)

155

22 Nominalisation

Grammar exercises

3.1 Rewrite the sentences to remove the agent. Use a nominalised form of the underlined verb and make any other changes needed.

1. The government <u>released</u> the prisoners unexpectedly.
2. They <u>organised</u> the conference very professionally.
3. Spectators <u>turned out</u> in huge numbers for the match.
4. The army <u>withdrew</u> the troops immediately.
5. We need to <u>shake up</u> top management for the company to be successful again.
6. The banks <u>increased</u> interest rates for the third time in two months.
7. They <u>agreed</u> on extra funding for the project.
8. They <u>decided</u> to postpone the race at the last moment.

1. *The release of the prisoners was unexpected. / There was an unexpected release of prisoners.*

3.2 Rewrite each sentence using a nominalised form at the beginning. Leave out the agent.

1. After scientists identified the HIV virus in the mid-1980s, there were enormous efforts to produce a vaccine.

   The identification of the HIV virus in the mid-1980s led to / resulted in enormous efforts to produce a vaccine.

2. Johan is obsessed with cars, and this started when he was quite young.

3. The government has expanded the nuclear power programme, but this has been criticised by opposition politicians.

4. The petrol companies have reduced the price of petrol, which is good news for drivers.

5. The council abolished parking charges in the city centre, and as a result shops have reported increased business.

6. Parent organisations are demanding healthier food in schools, and this results from growing concerns about childhood obesity.

7. The train will depart half an hour late because of engine problems.

8. A new college principal has been appointed, and staff may leave as a consequence.

Nominalisation 22

3.3 Complete the extracts from newspaper articles using the information in the box. In each sentence, use a nominalised form.

~~valuable books have disappeared~~	people have responded to its recruitment drive
the English spelling system is complex	people are strongly resisting increased taxation
the damage to property is extensive	the situation is threatening animal and plant species

1 Detectives were last night questioning a man about _the disappearance of a number of valuable books_ from the National Library over recent months.

2 'The teaching method we have developed acknowledges _____, and guides children towards a better understanding in carefully controlled stages.'

3 The Health Service is hoping to appoint 480 new nurses. Last night the Health Minister said _____ was 'excellent', with 7,000 applications in two days.

4 Chinese remedies are rooted in 4,000 years of tradition, but growing Western interest in alternative medicines has increased _____. Products confiscated by environmental officers included some using the seedpods of a rare orchid.

5 The extra public spending will need to be paid for and, with borrowing ruled out, that can only mean putting up taxes. Given _____, this could undermine the government's chances of being re-elected.

6 Residents of the south coast are beginning to return to their homes after the recent severe flooding. However, _____ means that some will be living in temporary accommodation for many months.

3.4 Make these conversations more informal where possible, replacing the underlined parts with appropriate *do/give/have/make/take* + noun forms.

1 **A:** Have you (1) <u>washed up</u> yet?
  B: I've (2) <u>started</u> on it. But there's such a lot to do, and you know how much I hate it.
  A: Well, I'm going outside to (3) <u>work in the garden</u>.
  B: (4) <u>Shout</u> if you need any help.
  A: No, thanks. You just concentrate on the washing-up!

  1 _done the washing-up_   3 _____
  2 _____   4 _____

2 **A:** Well, I've (5) <u>decided</u>. I'm going to apply for a job at Raggs.
  B: Good for you. I (6) <u>feel</u> you'd really get on there.
  A: I've (7) <u>arranged</u> to see their head of personnel next Friday.
  B: And how will you tell Terry you're thinking of leaving the company?
  A: Well, it won't be easy, but I suppose I'll just have to (8) <u>breathe deeply</u> and (9) <u>explain to him</u> why I want to go.

  5 _____   8 _____
  6 _____   9 _____
  7 _____

22 Nominalisation

3   **A:** Did you **(10)** <u>talk with</u> Natasha about the holiday?
   B: Yes, I **(11)** <u>called</u> last night and we **(12)** <u>chatted</u> about it then.
   A: And how did she react when you said we weren't going with her?
   B: She just **(13)** <u>sighed</u> and said 'That's okay'. But she was obviously upset.

   10 _____   12 _____
   11 _____   13 _____

4   **A:** I'm exhausted. I'm going to **(14)** <u>shower</u> and **(15)** <u>rest</u> before we **(16)** <u>cook</u>.
   B: I'm pretty tired, too. I'll **(17)** <u>look</u> at what's in the freezer, or maybe we could eat out?

   14 _____   16 _____
   15 _____   17 _____

Exam practice

Nominalisation **22**

Reading and Use of English Part 8

You are going to read four reviews of popular science books. For questions **1 – 10**, choose from the reviews (**A – D**). The reviews may be chosen more than once.

Which review mentions

a recent technological development that has become important for many people? — **1**

an ability to think in general terms? — **2**

the unexpected effects of scientific developments? — **3**

a scientist who began an area of scientific investigation important today? — **4**

an author's view that some people are likely to disagree with? — **5**

someone whose most influential work was done in the early part of their life? — **6**

a book aimed both at people who approve of technology and those who don't? — **7**

scientific investigations whose value was only later understood? — **8**

an author who combines practical experience with an ability to write well? — **9**

a skill that people are born with rather than learn? — **10**

Exam practice

A *A Monk and Two Peas* by Robin Marantz Henig

The work of an Augustinian monk from Brno laid the foundations of the science of genetics. Gregor Mendel was born in what is now the Czech Republic in 1822 and entered the monastery at the age of nineteen. In the mid-1840s he began to conduct a series of experiments with pea plants grown in the monastery garden and he continued these for twenty years. Over this period, by crossing pea plants which had clear differentiations in height, colour, etc and by carefully logging the results, Mendel was able to formulate the basic principles behind heredity. Mendel's work was only published in obscure journals, he was eventually led away from science by administrative duties at the monastery and it was only some years after his death that the significance of his work was appreciated. Mendel's life was a quiet one, but a very important one to the science of the twentieth century. *A Monk and Two Peas* tells the story very well, explaining clearly Mendel's experiments and drawing out their significance.

B *The Maths Gene* by Keith Devlin

For those who are mathematically challenged it's an attractive notion that everybody possesses a latent talent for maths and that it is just a question of finding the right key to access it. Devlin, despite the title of his book, is not suggesting that there is a gene for maths that the Human Genome project might identify but he is saying that we have a natural ability to do maths, that it exists in everybody and there are sound evolutionary reasons why this is the case. The ability to do maths, clearly, means an ability to handle abstract ideas and relationships and this provides advantages in evolutionary terms. As human language emerged, so also did a new capacity for abstraction and this formed the foundations on which mathematical thought has been built. Some readers might find Devlin's account of the evolution of language debatable but his ideas about the nature of our mathematical powers and his practical suggestions about how to improve them are constantly stimulating.

C *Why Things Bite Back* by Edward Tenner

Subtitled 'Technology and the Revenge of Unintended Consequences', Tenner's book is an entertaining look at the myriad ways in which advances in science and technology seem to recoil against us. What we gain on the roundabouts we lose on the swings. Antibiotics promise release from the perils of major diseases and end up encouraging microorganisms to develop resistance to them. Widespread use of air conditioning results in an increase in the temperature outdoors, thus requiring further cooling systems. American Football safety helmets become more efficient but this heralds an increase in more violent play and injuries actually rise. Tenner mounts up the evidence in a book designed to appeal to technophile and technophobe alike. And remember, the disaster at Chernobyl was triggered during a safety test. Ironies like that just aren't funny.

D *A Brief History of the Future* by John Naughton

So rapidly has the Internet become an integral part of many people's lives that it is easy to forget that only a few years ago it was known to the general public, if at all, as a playground for nerdy academics and that it is one of the most astonishing of all man's inventions. John Naughton, fellow of Churchill College, Cambridge and regular journalist on *The Observer* and other newspapers, has been on the net for many years himself and is the ideal person to write a history of what he calls this 'force of unimaginable power'. Starting with three little-known visionaries at MIT in the 1930s, Naughton traces the story through the engineers like Tim Berners-Lee who realised their vision, and on into what the future may hold. Written with the skill one might expect from a fine journalist and informed with the knowledge of an engineering professor, this is among the first histories of the net but is likely to remain among the best for some time to come.

23 *It* and *there*

Introductory *it* as subject and object; *there*; common expressions with *it's no ...* and *there's no ...*

Context listening

1.1 Liz is planning on moving out of her family home and buying her own apartment. What are the advantages and disadvantages of living in a town centre or on the edge of a town?

1.2 ▶29 Listen to the conversation. Which of the advantages and disadvantages you thought of do Liz and her parents mention?

1.3 ▶29 Listen again. Do these statements refer to the town apartment (T) or the out-of-town apartment in Canley (C)? (Ignore the letters a–m for now).

1 ªIt's been on the market for a long time. __T__
2 ᵇIt's obvious why they've been having problems selling ᶜit. _____
3 ᵈIt really shocked me to see how bad ᵉit was. _____
4 ᶠIt's about 15 kilometres from ᵍthere into the centre. _____
5 ʰThere's bound to be a regular bus service from ⁱthere. _____
6 ʲThere's that lovely little river that runs nearby. _____
7 The rooms in ᵏit are quite dark and that made ˡit feel cramped. _____
8 ᵐThere is expected to be a lot of interest in the property. _____

1.4 Look again at the sentences in 1.3. Some of the examples of *it* and *there* (a–m) refer back to a thing or a place that has been previously mentioned. Which ones are they? What do they refer back to?

1 _a – It = the town apartment_ 5 _____
2 _____   6 _____
3 _____   7 _____
4 _____   8 _____

23 It and there

Grammar

2.1 Introductory *it* as subject

> **START POINT**
>
> **Mother:** *It* struck me that the Canley apartment might be quite noisy with that busy road nearby.
> **Liz:** But *it*'s in such a lovely location. (*it* refers back to the noun phrase *the Canley apartment*)
> If *it*'s possible, I'd like to go back and look at the Canley apartment again. (*it* refers forward to going back and looking at *the Canley apartment* again)
> *It*'s going to be hard to choose between them. (introductory *it* as grammatical subject)
> Living in town would make *it* so much easier to get to work. (introductory *it* as grammatical object)

Introductory *it* as grammatical subject is commonly used:
- to talk about weather, time, distance and to describe situations:
  It's raining again.   *It*'s five o'clock.   *It*'s quiet in this part of town.
  It's about 15 kilometres from the Canley apartment into the centre.
- as an alternative to a *that-*, *wh-*, *-ing* or *to-*infinitive clause as the subject of the sentence:
  It's a pity that the town apartment is so small. rather than *That the town apartment is so small is a pity.*
  It's obvious why they've been having problems selling it. rather than *Why they've been having problems selling it is obvious.*
  It's certainly an advantage being able to walk to work. rather than *Being able to walk to work is certainly an advantage.*
  It really shocked me to see how bad it was. rather than *To see how bad it was really shocked me.*

It is more usual to use introductory *it* in these contexts, although in formal language the alternative with a *that-*, *wh-*, *-ing* or *to-*infinitive clause as subject is often used.

In writing, we don't usually use introductory *it* as an alternative to a noun as subject:
The town apartment is more expensive. (not ~~It is more expensive, the town apartment.~~)
However, this is quite common in informal speech in order to clarify what is being talked about:
It'd be good to live near work, but it's more expensive, the town apartment.

We often follow introductory *it* with *be* + adjective/noun, but other patterns are possible:
- it + verb + *to-*infinitive clause: **It might help to run** through the pros and cons.
- it + verb + object + *to-*infinitive clause: **It shocked me to see** how bad it was.
- it + verb + *that-*clause: **It appears that** they're having trouble selling the apartment.
- it + verb + object + *that-*clause: **It struck me that** the Canley apartment might be quite noisy.

In formal contexts, a common way of reporting what is said by an unspecified group of people is to use *it* + passive verb + *that-*clause or *it* + passive verb + *wh-*clause:
It is said that the cost of accommodation in the town centre will rise. or less formally *They say that the cost of accommodation in the town centre is going to go up.*
It was explained how difficult it is to prevent flooding in the area. or less formally *They explained how difficult it is to prevent flooding in the area.*

2.2 Introductory *it* as object

We can use *it* as the object of a verb in a number of patterns:
- verb + *it* + *that-*/*if-*/*wh-*clause
  I wouldn't **like it if** I had to get up at 6 o'clock.
  I couldn't **believe it when** the agent said the decoration was 'in good condition'.

23 It and there

- *would appreciate + it + if*-clause
  I **would appreciate it if** you could send me further details of the apartment.
- verb + (*it*) + *that*-clause
  We've just got to **accept that** neither of the apartments is perfect. or informally We've just got to **accept it that** neither of the apartments is perfect.
- verb + *it* + adjective + *that-/wh-/to*-infinitive clause
  The owner didn't **make it clear whether** they were included in the price.
  I think **it's** highly **unlikely** … (informal) I think **it** highly **unlikely that** the seller will reduce the price. (formal)
- *leave/owe* + *it* + *to* somebody + *to*-infinitive
  I think we should **leave it to** the estate agent **to talk** to the owner about whether curtains are included.
- verb + *it* + *as* + adjective + *that-/if-/wh*-clause
  I **see it as essential that** there should be somewhere to park.

2.3 There

> **START POINT**
>
> **There's** a bus stop just outside the apartment block.
> **There are** lots of new apartments being built in the city centre.
> *There + be* is used to introduce new information, saying that a person or thing exists, happens, or is found in a particular place.

Because we use *there* to introduce topics, the noun after *there + be* often has an indefinite meaning, so we often use *a/an*, no article, *any(one)* + noun or *some(thing)*, *no(body)*:
There's a car park behind the Canley apartment block (not ~~There's the car park~~ …)
There's something about parking in the information the estate agent gave us.

We use *there*, not *it*:
- to say or ask if people or things exist or are found in a particular place:
  There's nowhere to park. (not ~~It's nowhere to park.~~)
  Was **there** a dishwasher in the kitchen? (not ~~Was it a dishwasher in the kitchen?~~)
- to introduce information about quantities and amounts:
  There's a big grassy area at the back of the block. **There** wasn't much space in the bathroom.

There + be is often followed by:
- noun + *that-/wh-/-ing/to*-infinitive clause
  There's a chance (**that**) he might include carpets and curtains.
  There are plans **to build** new apartments not far from the one we looked at.
- *bound/certain/(un)likely/supposed/sure* + *to be*
  There's **bound to be** a regular bus service from there.

There is also often followed by *is, are, was* or *were*. However, also common are:
- *there* + auxiliary/modal verb + *be*
  There must be someone we know who would redecorate it.
- *there* + *seem/appear* + *to be*
  There seem to be good and bad aspects of each apartment.
- *there* + passive reporting verb + *to be*
  There is expected to be a lot of interest in the property.
  Other reporting verbs commonly used in this pattern are *estimate, find, reckon, report, say, think*.
- verb + *there* + *to be*
  I wouldn't **expect there to be** many people interested in buying the apartment. or I wouldn't expect many people to be interested …

163

23   It and there

If the noun after *there* is singular or uncountable, the verb is singular; if the noun is plural, the verb is usually plural (although *there's* is often used in informal speech):
There's a supermarket within walking distance.
There are so many things to think about. or informally **There's** so many things ...

If a noun phrase after *there* consists of two or more nouns in a list, we use a singular verb if the first noun is singular or uncountable, and a plural verb if the first noun is plural:
There was just a bed, a small wardrobe and some bookshelves.
There were just some bookshelves, a bed and a small wardrobe. or informally **There was** just some bookshelves ...

2.4   Common expressions with *it's no* and *there's no*

Common expressions with *it's no* include: *it's no secret that, it's no surprise that, it's no use/good + -ing, it's no coincidence/accident that, it's no longer necessary to, it's no bad thing to, it's no doubt true that, it's no doubt the case that, it's no exaggeration to say that.*
It's no wonder they've been having problems selling the apartment.

Common expressions with *there's no* include: *there's no doubt that, there's no chance/denying that, there's no choice/alternative but to, there's no chance/hope of + -ing, there's no need to, there's no point in + -ing, there's no question of + -ing, there's no reason to, there's no harm in +-ing.*
There's no hurry to decide.

Grammar exercises

3.1   Rewrite the underlined parts of the sentences where possible, beginning with *there*.

1   <u>Some tickets are left</u> for the concert. Do you want to go? *There are some tickets left ...*
2   I thought I heard voices, but when I opened the door <u>nobody was in the room</u>.
   _____
3   Omar's having a party this weekend even though <u>his birthday isn't until next month</u>.
   _____
4   You can find lots of bookshops in town. In fact, <u>one is opposite the railway station</u>.
   _____
5   <u>Only ten places are available</u> on the course, so you need to apply soon. _____
6   When I opened the fridge I found that <u>no milk was left</u>. _____
7   <u>My hands were shaking</u> as I walked into the exam room. _____
8   <u>Something was on the radio</u> this morning about using weeds in cooking.
   _____

3.2   Add the missing *it* or *there* to each sentence in an appropriate space (a, b or c).

1   When the weather (a) __–__ is dry, (b) __it__ is estimated (c) __–__ that 50,000 people cycle to work in the city.
2   Fraser has said (a) _____ he will retire from football if (b) _____ is thought to be no chance of his ankle injury healing (c) _____ in the foreseeable future.
3   Is (a) _____ a swimming pool in the hotel (b) _____ we're staying (c) _____ at?
4   I'm afraid (a) _____ worried (b) _____ me to see (c) _____ Mia looking so thin.

164

23 It and there

5 Although (a) _____ took (b) _____ hours of practice, I eventually managed (c) _____ to play a tune on the flute.

6 Most people had left (a) _____ the party and I decided (b) _____ that (c) _____ was time I went home, too.

7 Scientists say that (a) _____ is (b) _____ very little evidence that (c) _____ mobile phone use damages health.

8 How far (a) _____ is (b) _____ from (c) _____ Paris to Berlin?

3.3 Complete the sentences using an expression with *it's no* or *there's no* and one of the words from the box. Add any other words necessary.

chance good harm hurry longer need secret ~~wonder~~

1 A: The opinion polls don't look good for President Broom, do they?
   B: Well, he's raised income tax three times in the last year and over a million people are unemployed. _It's no wonder_ he's so unpopular.

2 A: If only I'd warned Rashid about the bad weather.
   B: _____ blaming yourself for the accident. He knew it was stupid to go walking in the hills when there was a risk of heavy snow.

3 A: Apparently, Lily's looking for a new job.
   B: _____ that she's thinking of leaving. She's been telling everyone about the jobs she's applied for.

4 A: Do you think your sister would lend us her car?
   B: Well, _____ asking her. She can only say 'no'.

5 A: If we run, we might just get the 9.00 train.
   B: No, _____ catching it now. Let's have a coffee and wait for the 9.30.

6 A: I'm really sorry I missed the meeting.
   B: _____ to apologise. We didn't discuss anything particularly important.

7 A: We used to spend hours playing in the river when we were children.
   B: But it's so polluted now that _____ possible to swim in it safely.

8 A: Come on, we'll be late. The film starts at 7.30, doesn't it?
   B: _____. There's always lots of adverts on before the main film starts.

3.4 Complete the conversations by reordering the words in brackets. If necessary, add *it* or *there*.

1 A: Why did you move out of the flat?
   B: My flatmates were constantly shouting at each other, and I _hate it when people argue_ all the time. (argue – hate – people – when)

2 A: Do you think you've got a chance of getting the job?
   B: Not really, but _____ put in an application, does it? (doesn't – hurt – to)

165

23 It and there

3 **A:** Hello, I've got an appointment with Dan Jackman. What room is he in?
   B: I'm sorry, but _____ the name of Dan Jackman here. (*by – is – nobody*)

4 **A:** Did you find your car keys eventually?
   B: Yes, _____ I'd left them at home. (*out – that – turned*)

5 **A:** Do you think the concert will be a sell-out?
   B: No, I _____ many people there at all. (*be – don't – expect – to*)

6 **A:** So as a classroom assistant, what do you do exactly?
   B: Well, I _____ to help the weaker pupils keep up with the rest of the class. (*as – my – role – see*)

7 **A:** Will you be able to email me from the hotel?
   B: Yes, I _____ access in every room. (*Internet – think – is*)

8 **A:** Oh, great, lemon sorbet! My favourite.
   B: I _____ you liked it. (*remember – saying – that – you*)

9 **A:** The forecast says it's going to be much cooler tomorrow. Not very good for our walk.
   B: Actually, _____ it's chilly. I don't like hot weather. (*I – if – prefer*)

10 **A:** I'm not really looking forward to going to the dentist tomorrow.
   B: You'll be fine. _____ worried about it. (*reason – get – to – no*)

166

Exam practice

It and there **23**

Reading and Use of English Part 4

For questions **1 – 6**, complete the second sentence so that it has a similar meaning to the first sentence, using the word given. **Do not change the word given**. You must use between **three** and **six** words, including the word given. Here is an example **(0)**.

---

0 People think that there are fewer than 4,000 tigers surviving in the wild in India.
THOUGHT
There _____*are thought to be*_____ fewer than 4,000 tigers surviving in the wild in India.

1 It's no secret that John moved to a part-time job so that he could spend more time playing golf.
ORDER
It's no secret that John moved to a part-time job _____ able to spend more time playing golf.

2 All the tickets have been sold, so it is impossible to rearrange the concert at this stage.
QUESTION
All the tickets have been sold, so _____ the concert at this stage.

3 I hadn't seen Mia for over 20 years, but I didn't find it difficult to recognise her at the airport.
DIFFICULTY
I hadn't seen Mia for over 20 years, but I had _____ her at the airport.

4 Although Clara and Mark have very different personalities and interests, they seem to have a good relationship.
ALONG
Although Clara and Mark have very different personalities and interests, they seem to _____ another very well.

5 They didn't mention the subject of unpaid holidays until the end of the interview.
BRING
Not until the end of the interview _____ the subject of unpaid holidays.

6 I've made my mind up, so it is useless to discuss this further.
POINT
I've made my mind up, so _____ this further.

167

24 Complex prepositions and prepositions after verbs

Complex prepositions; verb + preposition: common patterns; phrasal verbs: word order

Context listening

1.1 Osman is flying tomorrow afternoon to visit his friend Sofia in the south of France. What do you know about this part of France?

1.2 ▶30 Listen to their telephone conversation. Which of these instructions best represents the advice Sofia gives to Osman?

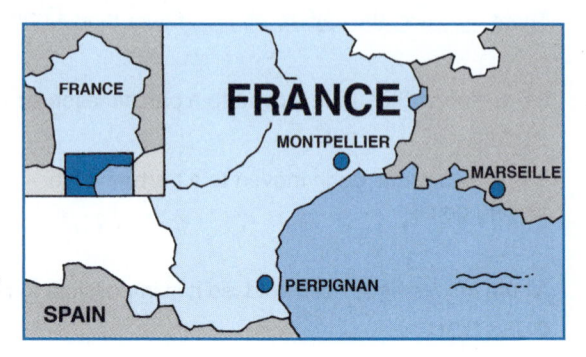

1 Take a taxi from the airport to Montpellier station. Take the bus from Montpellier to Perpignan. Take a taxi from Perpignan station to the hotel. Eat at Café Mathis on Wednesday evening. Be in the hotel foyer at two o'clock on Thursday afternoon.

2 Take the bus from the airport to Montpellier station. Take the train from Montpellier to Perpignan. Walk from Perpignan station to the hotel. Eat at Le Metropole on Wednesday evening. Be at Café Mathis at two o'clock on Thursday afternoon.

3 Take a taxi from the airport to Montpellier station. Take the train from Montpellier to Perpignan. Walk from Perpignan station to the hotel. Eat at Le Metropole on Wednesday evening. Be in the hotel foyer at two o'clock on Thursday afternoon.

4 Take a taxi from the airport to Montpellier station. Take the train from Montpellier to Perpignan. Take a taxi from Perpignan station to the hotel. Eat at Café Mathis on Wednesday evening. Be in the hotel foyer at two o'clock on Thursday afternoon.

1.3 ▶30 Listen again and write the exact words from the recording. The number of words you should write in each space is given in the square brackets.

1 I'm really sorry, but I've messed ____up____ [1] ____our plans____ [2] for tomorrow.
2 So I won't be able to pick _____ [1] _____ [1] at the airport after all.
3 I've found _____ [1] _____ [3] from the SNCF website ...
4 You'll need to buy a ticket before you get _____ [1] _____ [2].
5 ... so when you've checked _____ [1] _____ (2), I suggest you get a meal there.
6 I'll sort _____ [1] _____ [2] when I pick you up on Thursday afternoon.
7 Relax on Thursday morning and walk _____ [1] _____ [1].

1.4 In which of the extracts can you reverse the order of the words in the first space and the words in the second space?

168

24 Complex prepositions and prepositions after verbs

Grammar

2.1 Complex prepositions

Prepositions can be either simple (one word) or complex (two or more words):
*I'm really, really sorry **about** this.* (simple)
*The bus will only take you **as far as** the main square.* (complex)

Common examples of complex prepositions include: *in accordance with, as against, along with, with effect from, in the event of, in exchange for, irrespective of, on the part of, in place of, for the sake of, thanks to, by way of.*

Some complex prepositions have a meaning similar to a simple preposition:
*I wasn't able to reschedule the meeting, **in spite of** my efforts.* (= despite)
*All the people **in front of** me had been queuing for a long time.* (= before)

2.2 Verb + preposition: common patterns

> **START POINT**
>
> *Don't forget to **bring** your camera **with** you.*
> *I **insist on paying** your hotel bill.*
> After some verbs a preposition is needed to link the verb to what follows. If the preposition is followed by a second verb, the verb must be an *-ing* form.

- verb + object + prepositional phrase:
  *I tried to **reschedule the meeting for next week**, but it's just impossible.*
- verb + preposition + object + preposition + object:
  *She **complained to the company about the unreliability** of their bus service.*
- verb + preposition + *-ing*:
  *Don't **worry about getting** lost.*
- verb + object + preposition + *-ing*:
  *I'd **advise you against catching** the bus.*
- verb + preposition + object + *-ing*:
  *You can **depend on the train running** on time.*

2.3 Phrasal verbs: word order

> **START POINT**
>
> *I've **booked you into** a hotel not far from the station.* Book into is a transitive, two-word phrasal verb. The object here is *you* and the particle is *into*.
> *While you're strolling around, **look out for Café Mathis**.* Look out for is a transitive, three-word phrasal verb. The object here is *Café Mathis* and the particles are *out* and *for*.
> *Something's **come up** at work.* Come up is an intransitive phrasal verb. There is no object.

Some phrasal verbs can be used transitively or intransitively with the same meaning:
*Feel free to **call me back** if there's anything that's not clear about tomorrow.*
***Call back** later.*

169

24 Complex prepositions and prepositions after verbs

Others have different meanings when they are used transitively and intransitively:
I've **looked up** the online timetable. (transitive verb = I've found the information)
The weather seems to be **looking up** now. (intransitive verb = improving)

With most phrasal verbs, the object can go before or after the particle:
I'll **sort out the bill** when I pick you up on Thursday morning. or I'll **sort the bill out** when I pick you up on Thursday morning.

With these verbs we tend to put the object after the particle if the object is long:
You might want to **take down** some of the information I'm going to give to you. rather than You might want to **take** some of the information I'm going to give to you **down**.

and we always put the object before the particle if the object is a pronoun:
I won't be able to **pick you up** at the airport after all. (not I won't be able to pick up you at the airport after all.)

If the object consists of two or more items connected with *and*, it can occur before or after the particle even if one or both of the items is a pronoun:
When I'm next in London I'll **look you and your wife up**. or ... I'll **look up you and your wife**. (look up = go and see them)

With some phrasal verbs, the object must go after the particle(s):
When you've **checked into the hotel**, I suggest you get a meal there. (not When you've checked the hotel into ...)

With a few phrasal verbs the object must go between the verb and the particle:
Although she was the youngest in the class, she used to **order the other children about**. (not ... she used to order about the other children.)

A few three-word phrasal verbs have two objects, one after the verb and the other after the particles:
I'll **take you up on your offer** to buy me a meal. (verb = take up on; objects = you and your offer)

Grammar exercises

3.1 Complete the sentences using the notes in brackets. Use an appropriate tense for the verb. If two word orders are possible, give them both.

1 Sam sings really well. He <u>takes after his father</u> (take / his father / after).
2 I decided it was time to _____ (throw / some of my old exercise books from school / away).
3 Sofia got really angry during the meeting, and eventually she _____ (gather / her papers / up) and stormed out.
4 I _____ (bump / Lea / into) in town. She said she'll phone you later.
5 I really can't _____ (tell / the twins / apart), they look so similar.
6 I don't suppose there's any way we can _____ (talk / you / leaving college / out / of), is there?
7 Our neighbours are so inconsiderate. Last night they _____ (wake / me and my husband / up) at three o'clock in the morning playing loud music.
8 The new shop has loads of computers on show so that you can _____ (try / them / out) before buying.

Complex prepositions and prepositions after verbs — 24

3.2 Complete the sentences using a complex preposition which includes the word in brackets followed by a sentence ending from the box. Use the common complex prepositions in 2.1 in this unit to help you.

| their ability to pay | their health | ~~a cut in their salaries~~ | a strict protein-only diet |
| an apology | the 10,000 predicted | an excellent art gallery | 30th September |

1 The workers got extra paid holiday _in exchange for a cut in their salaries_. (*exchange*)
2 The concert attracted only 2,000 people _____. (*opposed*)
3 I think healthcare should be available to all people, _____. (*regardless*)
4 She's lost a lot of weight recently, _____. (*thanks*)
5 My parents want to move somewhere out of the city _____. (*sake*)
6 It may be only a small town, but it has an interesting natural history museum _____. (*along*)
7 He lost his temper with me last week, so he gave me a box of chocolates _____. (*way*)
8 The road will be closed for major repairs _____. (*effect*)

3.3 Complete these extracts from a radio news report by expanding the notes in brackets. Choose appropriate forms for the verbs and add prepositions and pronouns where necessary.

1 Police _have appealed to witnesses for information_ (*appeal / witnesses / information*) about the fire which has led to the closure of the main east coast rail line at Crewbury. A factory next to the line was burned down yesterday, causing major damage to the track. Rail passengers are currently being _____ (*advise / use*) the line.

2 In the first interview given by the Foreign Minister since newspapers reported that she personally approved illegal arms sales, she _____ (*dismiss / the reports*) 'completely untrue'. She went on to say that the accusation would not _____ (*prevent / do*) her job, and that she intended to continue in her post.

3 Ten youngsters between the ages of 12 and 16 met the Prime Minister today after they competed in the *World Youth Maths Challenge*. The Prime Minister _____ (*congratulate / achieve*) excellent results in the competition. He said that they _____ (*benefit / take part*) the *After School Maths* scheme set up by the government to encourage young people's enthusiasm for the subject.

4 The Agriculture Minister, Mariam Haddad, _____ (*quarrel / European counterparts*) the issue of fish conservation. During a discussion on the decline in fish stocks, Ms Haddad got into a heated argument, which _____ (*end / walk*) out of the meeting.

171

24 Complex prepositions and prepositions after verbs

3.4 Complete this letter by writing a preposition in each space.

Dear Jodi,

Sorry I haven't been (1) _in_ touch (2) _____ you for such a long time, but it's been a busy few months.

Earlier this year I heard that my great-aunt had died. Apart (3) _____ seeing her a couple of times at my parents' house, I didn't really know her. So you can imagine my surprise when I found (4) _____ she'd left me a cottage along (5) _____ some money in her will!

When I saw the cottage, I just fell in love with it. It's close (6) _____ a beautiful little village, and looks out (7) _____ the sea. My great-aunt used it as a holiday home, and I've decided to do the same. Unfortunately, it's been badly looked (8) _____ , so I've had to spend most weekends this year sorting the place (9) _____ .

I knew it was (10) _____ need (11) _____ some work, and at first I thought I could get away (12) _____ giving it a quick coat of paint. But I soon realised it was a much bigger job. There were holes in the roof, and the window frames were so rotten some of the panes of glass were (13) _____ danger (14) _____ falling out.

I was walking around the village one Saturday, wondering what best to do, when who should I run (15) _____ but Barney Adams. Do you remember him from school? As luck would have it, he now works in the village as a builder and decorator. We got talking, and he said he'd come (16) _____ and look (17) _____ the house.

Naturally, I took him up (18) _____ his offer! He got really enthusiastic about it. He talked me (19) _____ replacing all the windows, and he's put in a new central heating system (20) _____ place (21) _____ the old coal fires. I've had to prevent him (22) _____ extending the kitchen, which he was keen to do! He's checked the roof (23) _____ , and fortunately that doesn't need replacing. Thanks (24) _____ Barney, the house is now looking brilliant, and (25) _____ comparison (26) _____ other builders, he doesn't charge very much.

The next project for me is to clean (27) _____ the mess in the garden, as it's completely overgrown. If you want to come (28) _____ and help me (29) _____ some time, feel free! You'll always be very welcome.

Love,

Emily

Exam practice

Complex prepositions and prepositions after verbs **24**

Listening Part 1

▶ 31 You will hear three different extracts. For questions **1 – 6**, choose the answer (**A**, **B** or **C**) which fits best according to what you hear. There are two questions for each extract.

Extract One

You hear two friends talking about doing team sports in the schools they went to.

1   Which aspect of participating in team sports do the friends disagree about?
    A   that it kept them fit
    B   that they made good friends as a result
    C   that competition in team sports is positive

2   In the man's opinion, team sports at his school
    A   helped him to avoid failure in later life.
    B   distracted him from his academic studies.
    C   encouraged him to do sport as an adult.

Extract Two

You hear two friends talking about reading.

3   What is the woman doing during the conversation?
    A   persuading the man to use his e-reader
    B   complaining about paperback books
    C   encouraging the man to read more

4   What reason does the man give for preferring printed books to e-readers?
    A   They are easier to read.
    B   They display a person's interests.
    C   They can be shared with friends.

Extract Three

You hear two people talking about receiving marketing texts on mobile phones.

5   Why doesn't the man like marketing texts?
    A   They are not interesting.
    B   They are not effective.
    C   They are usually unwanted.

6   How does the woman respond to the man's criticism of marketing texts?
    A   She says people are interested in receiving them.
    B   She says she sends them to people who have agreed to receive them.
    C   She says it can be difficult to prevent companies breaking the rules.

25 Prepositions after nouns and adjectives

Noun + preposition: related verbs and adjectives; noun + preposition + -*ing* or noun + preposition + noun; noun + *of* + -*ing* or noun + *to*-infinitive; noun + *in* or noun + *of*; adjective + preposition

Context listening

1.1 Do you prefer reading the news online or in a newspaper? Why?

1.2 ▶32 Kate Pearce has set up an online newspaper called *Happening*. Recently she visited her old school to talk to students about how she set up the paper. Listen to the question and answer session and number these steps in the order Kate mentions them.

a contact advertisers _____
b learn how to design a website _____
c give more information about famous people _____
d gather feedback on the website _____
e respond to criticism _____
f borrow some money _____
g design a prototype website _____
h increase involvement of teenagers _____
i have the idea of a newspaper for teenagers __1__

1.3 ▶32 Listen again and write the exact words you hear in the spaces.

1 I'd also had the opportunity to do a course on website design, and that __influenced__ my decision.
2 I felt that there was a big _____ an online newspaper.
3 But we did _____ money to live on.
4 We took the _____ work on it for six months.
5 I think there'll always be a _____ traditional newspapers.
6 And do many people _____ *Happening*?
7 In the early days we used to get quite a lot of _____ our news coverage.
8 Young people _____ very high standards nowadays.
9 We've _____ include a section on celebrities.
10 Young people may be able to have an _____ government policies.

1.4 Underline the nouns you have written in 1.3, and find the related verb or adjective. Which nouns used the same preposition as the related verb or adjective?

1 *influenced* (verb – no preposition) + 10 *influence on*

174

Prepositions after nouns and adjectives 25

Grammar

> **START POINT**
>
> I felt that there was a big **demand for** an online newspaper.
> It was **difficult to** generate business at first.
> Many nouns and adjectives are typically followed by particular prepositions.

2.1 Noun + preposition: related verbs and adjectives

Many nouns are followed by the same prepositions as their related verb or adjective:
*We used to get quite a lot of **complaints about** our news coverage.* or *People used to **complain** a lot **about** our news coverage.*
*I wanted to increase young people's **awareness of** current affairs.* or *I wanted to make young people more **aware of** current affairs.*

A few are followed by different prepositions from their related adjective:
*We **take pride in** the design of our website.* or *We are **proud of** the design of our website.*

Some take a preposition where their related verb does not:
*Young people may be able to have an **influence on** government policies.* or *Young people may be able to **influence** government policies.*

2.2 Noun + preposition + -ing or noun + preposition + noun

Most noun + preposition combinations can be followed either by an *-ing* form or a noun:
*There have been **protests about locating** a new nuclear power station on the east coast.* or *There have been **protests about the location of** a new nuclear power station on the east coast.*

Some noun + preposition combinations are more often followed by a noun than an *-ing* form:
*I felt there was a **demand for the publication** of an online newspaper.* rather than *I felt there was a **demand for publishing** an online newspaper.*

2.3 Noun + of + -ing or noun + to-infinitive

Some nouns can be followed by either *of* + *-ing* or a *to*-infinitive with little difference in meaning:
*The **idea of setting up** some kind of newspaper for young people came from that time.* or *The **idea to set up** ...*
*I had the **opportunity to do** a course on website design.* or *I had the **opportunity of doing** a course on website design.*

Some nouns have more than one meaning and are followed by either *of* + *-ing* or *to*-infinitive depending on which meaning is used:
*Young people get the **chance to contribute** in various ways.* (*chance* = opportunity)
*The banks thought there was little **chance of making** it a commercial success.* (*chance* = likelihood)

Some nouns can be followed by *of* + *-ing*, but not a *to*-infinitive:
*The **difficulty of persuading** the banks to lend us money meant that we had to borrow money from our parents.* (not *The difficulty to persuade the banks* ...)

Some nouns can be followed by a *to*-infinitive, but not *of* + *-ing*:
*We took the **decision to work** on it for six months.* (not *We took the decision of working on it* ...)

175

25 Prepositions after nouns and adjectives

2.4 Noun + *in* or noun + *of*

We use *increase/decrease/rise/fall + in* when we talk about what is increasing or decreasing, and *increase/decrease/rise/fall + of* to talk about the amount of an increase or decrease:
The recent **increase in** hits on the website means that we can charge more for advertising space. (not *The recent increase of hits* ...)
We've had an **increase of** about 50% .... (not *We've had an increase in about 50%* ...)
Other nouns like this include: *cut, decline, downturn, drop; gain, growth, jump, leap*.

2.5 Adjective + preposition: expressing feelings

Many adjectives which refer to feelings or opinions are followed by particular prepositions:
Young people seem generally very **enthusiastic about** the site.
They were very **wary of** advertising on the site.

2.6 Adjective + preposition: different meanings

Some adjectives are followed by different prepositions, depending on meaning:
I knew they were **concerned about** what was going on. (*concerned about* = worried about)
We have a reviews section, which is **concerned with** films, CDs ... (*concerned with* = to do with)

Grammar exercises

3.1 Complete each sentence with an appropriate preposition.

1 I've been afraid ____of____ the dark ever since I was young.
2 Get Felix to do the decorating. He's particularly good _____ wallpapering.
3 We ought to get our website redesigned. I think it would be good _____ business.
4 I was really furious _____ Steve for turning up so late.
5 Local people are furious _____ the decision to build a power station.
6 The teacher kept the whole class in after school, which I thought was unfair _____ those of us who hadn't been behaving badly.
7 I'm really sorry _____ the coffee on the carpet. I didn't notice your cup there.
8 I feel really sorry _____ Azra. She lost all her work when her computer crashed.

3.2 Rewrite the underlined part of each sentence using a noun related to the shaded verb or adjective.

1 At the meeting we discussed the pros and cons of private education. ___had a discussion about / on___
2 She admitted that the salary increase influenced her decision to take the new job. _____
3 Alex has done very well at university and we are proud of his achievement. _____
4 Although I don't agree with his political beliefs, I greatly admire his writing. _____
5 The flooding seriously damaged many of the houses in the village. _____
6 To solve the problem of severe traffic congestion, drivers are to be charged £10 a day for bringing their cars into the city centre. _____

25 Prepositions after nouns and adjectives

3.3 Choose the correct option. In some sentences both are correct.

1. Researchers have developed a treatment that they claim can significantly reduce the likelihood *of getting* / *to get* skin cancer.
2. After his heart attack, Tom had the sense *of cutting* / *to cut* down on the amount of fatty foods he ate.
3. The government has withdrawn its opposition to *using* / *the use of* private hospitals in the National Health Service.
4. Has there been an increase or decrease in *visiting* / *the number of visitors to* the National Park over the last ten years?
5. It was Nur who had the idea *of organising* / *to organise* a fashion show to raise money.
6. Have you ever regretted your decision *of moving* / *to move* to Sweden?
7. There seem to be two main factors behind *closing* / *the closure of* the car factory.
8. The focus of the conference is on *protecting* / *the protection of* endangered species in the rainforests of central Africa.
9. The party still shows no sign of *recovering* / *recovery* from its election defeat last year.
10. As she was writing, I noticed she had a very strange way *of holding* / *to hold* her pen.

3.4 Choose the correct prepositions.

A *A conversation between two employees of the same company*, Trimstep.

A: I'm really fed up **(1)** *by* / *with* / *for* my job. I've been doing the same thing at *Trimstep* for ten years, and I'm tired **(2)** *of* / *in* / *to* the same old routine.
B: But I thought you were keen **(3)** *for* / *of* / *on* your job. You've always seemed so enthusiastic **(4)** *with* / *about* / *for* it.
A: Well, I used to be very impressed **(5)** *to* / *for* / *by* the managers. But now they're only interested **(6)** *in* / *to* / *with* making money and they seem indifferent **(7)** *in* / *to* / *by* how the staff feel. There are rumours that business isn't going well, so a lot of people are worried **(8)** *by* / *about* / *in* their jobs. In fact, one of the senior managers left last week. He obviously wasn't satisfied **(9)** *with* / *for* / *in* the way the company's being run. Maybe it's time I started looking around for something new, too.

B *Part of a speech made by a senior manager of* Trimstep *to employees.*

'I know that some of you have expressed anxiety **(1)** *about* / *with* / *in* Mr Madson's sudden departure **(2)** *for* / *by* / *from* the company last week. I was very disappointed **(3)** *for* / *with* / *on* his decision to resign. I must admit that the last few months have been difficult, and at times we've been very concerned ourselves **(4)** *by* / *in* / *about* the future of the company. However, we have now developed an association **(5)** *for* / *with* / *of* a firm of retailers in Southeast Asia, and we're extremely pleased **(6)** *with* / *for* / *in* this development. We did at first have a disagreement **(7)** *for* / *by* / *over* safety standards, but this has been resolved and they have now indicated their satisfaction **(8)** *for* / *to* / *with* the design changes we've made. We hope to sign a major contract with them in the next few days. To all of you I want to express my gratitude **(9)** *with* / *for* / *by* your belief **(10)** *in* / *with* / *about* the company and your continuing support **(11)** *in* / *for* / *by* the management team.'

Exam practice

Reading and Use of English Part 1

For questions **1 – 8**, read the text below and decide which answer (**A, B, C** or **D**) best fits each gap. There is an example at the beginning **(0)**.

Seasonal affective disorder

Seasonal affective disorder, or SAD, is a type of depression that follows the seasons, with most SAD sufferers **(0)** _C_ symptoms during winter months. Symptoms include disturbed sleep and difficulty staying awake during the day. For many, SAD is a **(1)** _____ condition which causes **(2)** _____ discomfort, but no severe suffering. This form of SAD is referred to as 'winter blues'. For others, however, it is a serious illness which might **(3)** _____ them living a normal life.

SAD is a response to the **(4)** _____ of daylight hours and lack of sunlight in winter. It is mainly found **(5)** _____ people living in high latitudes. However, it is rare within 30 degrees of the Equator, where daylight hours are long and constant. The relationship between reduced daylight and SAD is not **(6)** _____ understood. It is thought that it affects the brain's production of serotonin and melatonin, but precisely why depression is triggered by a fall **(7)** _____ the production of these hormones is unknown. The most common treatment **(8)** _____ SAD is light therapy in which sufferers are exposed to a very bright light for up to four hours per day.

0	A	confronting	B	addressing	C	experiencing	D	finding
1	A	mild	B	weak	C	gentle	D	slight
2	A	the	B	some	C	a	D	no
3	A	limit	B	prevent	C	obstruct	D	prohibit
4	A	weakness	B	shortage	C	failure	D	shortening
5	A	by	B	on	C	among	D	between
6	A	visibly	B	highly	C	clearly	D	extremely
7	A	from	B	to	C	in	D	of
8	A	with	B	for	C	of	D	by

178

26 Cities

Urban growth, urban living

Urban growth

1.1 Think of a city you know well. Which of these phrases do you associate with it? Put a (✓).

an important commercial centre _____
a vibrant cultural centre _____
a major tourist attraction _____
a sprawling metropolis _____
gridlocked rush-hour traffic _____
accessible open spaces _____
run-down estates _____
affluent suburbs _____
steeped in history _____
seriously polluted _____
densely populated _____
friendly and welcoming _____

1.2 Choose the best words to complete the text.

Urban sprawl is the unchecked spreading of a city or its (1) *suburbs* / *residences*. It often involves the (2) *demolition* / *construction* of residential or commercial buildings in (3) *rural* / *environmental* areas or otherwise undeveloped land on the (4) *outskirts* / *neighbourhoods* of a city. Typical (5) *residents* / *commuters* of these areas live in single-family homes and travel by car to their jobs in the city. Concerns over urban sprawl largely focus on negative (6) *costs* / *consequences* for residents and the local (7) *environment* / *space*. The tendency of people living in these neighbourhoods to commute to work means that urban sprawl is sometimes associated with increased air (8) *pollution* / *pollutant* from car exhaust fumes.

1.3 Find words in the text which match these definitions.

1 related to towns and cities _____
2 related to trade or business _____
3 particular part of a place _____
4 not previously built on _____
5 people who live in a place _____

V Vocabulary note

This book draws attention to language chunks of the following types:

COLLOCATIONS = words frequently used together: *densely populated*, *leafy suburbs*, *open spaces*, *violent crime*

COMPOUND NOUNS = nouns made up of two or more words: *tourist attraction*, *skyscraper*, *cost of living* (See **Unit 5, 2.1** for more on compound nouns.)

DEPENDENT PREPOSITIONS = some adjectives, nouns and verbs are followed by particular prepositions: *steeped in history*, *plagued by crime* (See **Unit 24, 2.1** and **Unit 25, 2.2** for more on dependent prepositions.)

PHRASAL VERBS = two- or three-part verbs with idiomatic meanings: *break down*, *get around*, *look forward to* (See **Unit 25, 2.3** for more on phrasal verbs.)

IDIOMS = phrases with special meaning that cannot be understood from the individual words: *go to town on something*, *hit the road*, *cut and dried*

26 Cities

1.4 WORD BUILDING Complete the table with words which have related meanings.

Noun	Verb	Adjective
demolition	_____	_____
_____ (place, activity)	_____	
_____ (company, person)		undeveloped
resident (person)	_____	_____
_____ (place)		
environment	x	_____
_____ (person, activist)		
pollution (problem)	_____	_____
_____ (substance)		

1.5 Complete the compound nouns in these sentences with words from the box.

area   attractions   city   fumes   jams   pollution   rush   traffic   transport

1 The Eiffel Tower is one of the most popular tourist _____ in the world.
2 Our council is doing everything it can to combat _____ congestion, including charging drivers every time they drive into the _____ centre.
3 The underground is an integral part of the public _____ system in many large cities.
4 Since the town centre became a traffic-free pedestrian _____ , shopping has been a more pleasant experience.
5 Exhaust _____ from cars, buses and lorries are the main cause of air _____ in cities.
6 There are frequent traffic _____ during the morning and evening _____ hours in many towns and cities.

1.6 Complete the following sentences using the words in bold and a suffix from the *Vocabulary note*.

1 Our neighbourhood doesn't have any **crime**. It's a _____ neighbourhood.
2 There's a zone around the school where **cars** cannot go. It's a _____ zone.
3 The council is planning to make the city centre suitable for **cyclists**. It's going to be a _____ centre.
4 I need accommodation where they allow **pets**. I need _____ accommodation.
5 The young people around here are all obsessed with their **cars**. They're all _____ .
6 Many of my colleagues are obsessive about their **work**. They're all _____ .

> **V Vocabulary note**
>
> Some adjectives have a special meaning as noun suffixes.
>
> *-free* = without an undesirable thing: *I always buy fat-free yoghurt.*
>
> *-friendly* = suitable for or welcoming of: *Child-friendly software comes pre-installed.*
>
> *-mad* = liking or doing something obsessively: *My husband is football-mad.*
>
> **Note:** The noun in these phrases is singular.

> **ERROR WARNING**
>
> In everyday speech and writing we use *people* as the plural form of *person*: *There were a lot of **people** on the station, but only one **person** got on the train.*
> The plural form *persons* is rarely used in speech, but is used in certain formal contexts: *The crime was committed by person or **persons** unknown.*

26 Cities

Urban living

2.1 ▶33 Listen to two people talking about living in a city. Complete these sentences with words used by the speakers.

1. I just love all the _____ and bustle.
2. In my work and my _____ life, I come into regular _____ with people from all over the world.
3. You just take for granted the incredible _____ of entertainment on offer.
4. The only downside is the _____ of living.
5. Her parents own a flat in the _____ of London.
6. It was really convenient, just being able to _____ on a bus or take the _____ .
7. Crime _____ are higher in cities than in _____ areas.

2.2 What do you think are the advantages and disadvantages of city life? Make two lists. Use expressions from 2.1 and add your own ideas.

ADVANTAGES	convenient public transport,
DISADVANTAGES	crime,

2.3 Match the two-part expressions in italics with their definitions.

1. I love the *hustle and bustle* of life in the city.
2. Some people move to the country for the *peace and quiet*.
3. We've been weighing up the *pros and cons* of commuting.
4. Most people have *ups and downs* at work.
5. We need some *give and take* between residents and developers.

a. good times and bad times
b. busy, noisy activity
c. compromise
d. calm atmosphere
e. advantages and disadvantages

2.4 WORD TRANSFORMATION Complete the text with the correct forms of the words in capitals at the ends of the lines.

The (0) __explosive__ growth in the number of closed-circuit television (CCTV) surveillance systems in recent years is transforming city centres in some countries. For some people, the cameras have a (1) _____ benefit, as they take comfort in the (2) _____ that they are being watched and protected. In some neighbourhoods, there are even socially (3) _____ CCTV systems, which allow local (4) _____ to tune in to community TV and watch what is happening outside their front doors. People know the cameras can be (5) _____ in solving crimes, but are they right to believe that cameras are keeping them safer? According to one crime expert, they are not. He conducted a study of 14 CCTV systems and found that, in general, the (6) _____ of cameras has (7) _____ little impact on crime. In only one of the 14 areas could a (8) _____ drop in crime levels be linked to CCTV.

EXPLODE

PSYCHOLOGY
BELIEVE

INCLUDE
RESIDE

HELP

INSTALL
SURPRISE
SIGNIFY

181

Exam practice

Reading and Use of English Part 5

You are going to read a magazine article. For questions **1 – 6**, choose the answer (**A**, **B**, **C** or **D**) which you think fits best according to the text.

> **Exam tip**
>
> There are often questions which relate to the main idea of the text as well as questions about detail. In this practice task, question 1 relates to the main idea.

Rome: ancient life in a modern city

Sigmund Freud once compared the human mind to the city of Rome. He was talking about its intriguing layers. Just as the mind has a build-up of memories, Rome has a history that goes deeper and deeper: every modern building is on top of a renaissance one, and under that you find the medieval buildings, and then ancient Rome itself. Freud might also have said that – just as with the mind – as you go deeper into the city you find the unpleasant parts like the slums as well as the clean, splendidly 'proper' parts.

Ancient Rome was home to a million people and was, in its time, the biggest city in Europe. Most of that million, from the dockworkers to the hairdressers, didn't live in spacious marble villas. They were packed into tower blocks that lined narrow streets, with hardly any public services. It must have been a tough place to survive in.

So where can you still find signs of these ordinary 'high-rise Romans'? Amazingly, the answer is 'all over the city'. You only need to know where to look, and keep your eyes open. My favourite remnant of ordinary ancient Roman life is still standing in the heart of tourist Rome. It's part of a tower block, still surviving to five storeys in a modern square – just underneath the Victor Emmanuel monument. Most of these blocks have fallen down, but this one was lucky: it survived because it was turned into a church.

It's easy to work out the basic organisation of the block. At street level, there are shops and workshops. The principle was 'the higher you went, the worse it got'. On the first floor you can see some spacious family flats; and above that, bedsits. The question is, how many people were squashed into these rooms? If they were for one person, then this was very "tight living". But if they were single rooms without bathroom or cooking facilities, designed for whole families, they must have been really dreadful conditions.

And in ancient Rome – as this particular high-rise block reminds us – rich and poor lived and worked side by side. There weren't many zones given over exclusively either to the rich or the poor. In fact, if you look hard enough, you can find traces of ordinary people inside the most luxurious and ceremonial buildings of the city.

A visit to the ancient Roman Forum can be a disappointment. This was once the centre of Roman public life, where the senate met. It is now a rather mysterious set of ruins, with just a few standing landmarks: two splendid triumphal arches and the three vast columns of the Temple of Castor. The Forum becomes far more interesting if you also look down for the evidence of the ordinary men and women who shared this space with the great and the good – and who had their own things to do there, from a bit of gambling to basic dentistry.

Running along its south side are the now decidedly unimpressive ruins of what was once the splendid Basilica Julia, home of one of Rome's law courts, plus some government offices. Not much survives beyond the floor and the steps leading up to it. A barrier now prevents visitors from walking inside; but actually you don't need to. Look over the barrier on to the steps, and you will see the clear traces cut into the stone of scores of 'gaming boards'. We haven't a clue about the exact rules of the games, but never mind. It's clear that the Basilica Julia wasn't just a place for busy lawyers; go back 2,000 years and you would find the place littered with men with time on their hands, betting on some ancient equivalent of backgammon.

Exam practice

Cities 26

Next door to the basilica is the great Temple of Castor. Here you have to take your eyes off the columns, and look more carefully at the high platform on which they stand. Built into this is a series of little shops and storage units right underneath this grand monument. One of the corner units was a primitive dentist's surgery. Among the most memorable moments for me was going to see the almost 100 teeth discovered a few years ago in its drains, each one expertly extracted and rotten to the core. Each one a witness to human agony, I thought.

1   The main point the writer is making about ancient Rome is that
    A   it is completely hidden by modern buildings.
    B   traces of it can be seen everywhere.
    C   it was very similar to modern cities.
    D   it has had a long and fascinating history.

2   One of the tall buildings of ancient Rome has been preserved because
    A   it is still inhabited by ordinary people.
    B   it is used as tourist accommodation.
    C   it has been rebuilt.
    D   it was used for a different purpose.

3   When she uses the phrase "tight living" in line 17, the writer is pointing out that
    A   people lived in very small spaces.
    B   people did not have many possessions.
    C   people tended to live alone.
    D   people did not need much living space.

4   According to the article, the citizens of ancient Rome
    A   lived with people of a similar economic status.
    B   lived on the top floor of tall buildings if they were rich.
    C   were not all housed according to how wealthy they were.
    D   tended to live in large stone houses.

5   What unofficial activities does the writer claim took place in Basilica Julia?
    A   sculpture and other visual arts
    B   athletics and other sports
    C   games that involved gambling
    D   the giving of legal advice

6   Where were the little shops in relation to the Temple of Castor?
    A   at the same height
    B   below
    C   above
    D   alongside

27 Personal history
Ancestry, autobiography

Ancestry

1.1 Where could you find out more about your ancestors? Put a (✓).

official records _____ older relatives _____ old family photo albums _____
websites _____ family diaries _____ local newspaper archives _____

1.2 Read the introduction to a talk about investigating your family history. Choose the best words to complete the text.

> There is nothing more exciting than (1) *opening* / *unlocking* the mysteries of your own past. With each additional clue, your (2) *ancestors* / *associates* will become more than just names or dates on a (3) *genealogical* / *geological* form. In this (4) *process* / *progress* you will realise that most of them were ordinary people, just like you and me.
>
> In genealogy you always start from the present and work (5) *backwards* / *forwards*. You should approach the search as if you were a detective (6) *conducting* / *concluding* an investigation; looking for clues, interviewing (7) *resources* / *sources* and carefully (8) *documenting* / *disclosing* your facts. This is important because you need to be able to prove that your line of (9) *ascent* / *descent* is correct. Anyone can claim that they are a (10) *descendant* / *successor* of George Washington, but proving it is another thing altogether.

1.3 ▶34 Listen to the talk and answer these questions.

1 Who is this advice aimed at? _____
2 What does the speaker warn listeners about?
_____
_____
_____

Error warning 👁

Information is an uncountable noun and cannot be made plural: *I'd like some information about my family.* (not ~~I'd like some informations~~ ...)

1.4 ▶34 Listen to the talk again. Find words and phrases which match these definitions. The number of words you should write in each space is given in the square brackets. Use the recording script to help you.

1 check your information is correct _____*verify your facts*_____ [3]
2 enjoy talking about memories _____ [1]
3 the most difficult problem to overcome _____ [3]
4 a small proportion of correct information _____ [4]
5 shocking personal secrets from the past _____ [4]
6 set a limit for something _____ [3]
7 separate line of your ancestry _____ [4]
8 collect a lot of data _____ [5]

Personal history 27

1.5 WORD BUILDING Complete the table with words which have related meanings.

Noun	Verb	Adjective
_____	accumulate	_____
_____ (positive) _____ (negative)	x	accurate (positive) _____ (negative)
ancestor (person) _____ (general topic)	x	_____
_____	embellish	_____
_____	reminisce	_____
_____ (process) _____ (person)	verify	verified _____ (possible to do)

1.6 Complete these sentences with words and phrases from 1.4 and 1.5.

1 Of the difficulties we faced when we moved to America, overcoming culture shock was the biggest _____ .
2 Even convincing liars usually include a few _____ of truth in their stories.
3 Researching my family tree is just a hobby and I _____ _____ _____ at spending any money on it.
4 Every time my father tells a story he adds some _____ to make them funnier or more dramatic.
5 Historians have accused a new 'biographical' film about the king's personal life of being wildly _____ .
6 There's an animal living in the woods that makes a sound strangely _____ of a crying baby.

1.7 When we talk about secrets we often use the idea that there is something unseen or hidden, e.g. *skeletons in the cupboard*. Underline the language of secrets in these sentences.

1 A recently published history of the local area exposes long-buried secrets of the family and their influence.
2 It's not fair to keep residents in the dark about development plans for the local area.
3 Journalists shouldn't spend their time digging up dirt on celebrities. It's not in the public interest.
4 The government seem to think that they can just sweep recent statistics on inner-city crime under the carpet.
5 Although he had tried hard to cover his tracks, all investigators had to do was follow the money.
6 The councillor tried to muddy the waters over the scrapped housing development when he raised the issue of anti-social behaviour.

1.8 Match the expressions you underlined in 1.7 with their definitions.

1 investigate to find unpleasant or damaging information _____
2 make evidence more difficult or impossible to find _____
3 confuse an issue under discussion _____
4 not share information with people who are interested _____
5 make information public which was unknown for many years _____
6 ignore or avoid discussion of an issue _____

185

27 Personal history

Autobiography

2.1 How is an *autobiography* different from a *biography*?

2.2 Complete the text with words from the box.

| accurate | appointments | blank | confront | ~~feelings~~ | forget |
| hoarded | myths | reports | traces |

Joan Bakewell

Autobiography is a curiously naked business. It requires intimacy with your own (1) ___feelings___ which you might have been avoiding for years. You have to (2) _____ your guilt and fears, dredging from deep down things you might rather (3) _____ . Then you must *weigh up* whether they are (4) _____ in any objective sense, or simply memories *formulated* from family (5) _____ .

Any life as long as mine has left *a multitude of* (6) _____ . The most *valuable* proved to be those nearest home. Ever since I was a child, I have (7) _____ *scraps* of paper, childish sketches, soppy poems, notes from girls in my class at school, exam papers, school (8) _____ and boxes and boxes of letters.

Then there are the diaries: the daily record of events and (9) _____ . The casual entries in numerous little pocket diaries, thrown casually into a big box at each New Year, allowed me to pinpoint, though only roughly – there are many (10) _____ pages – what I was doing in any particular year of my life.

2.3 Which of these words are possible replacements for the words in italics in 2.2?

Word in 2.2	Possible replacements
1 weigh up	consider ~~decide~~ regard think about
2 formulated	created originating put together prepared
3 a multitude of	a crowd of countless many numerous
4 valuable	expensive important precious useful
5 scraps	bits crumbs fragments small pieces

2.4 Complete these sentences with words related to the words in capital letters at the ends of the lines.

1 Many people read autobiographies out of _____ . **CURIOUS**
2 I've read the ex-president's autobiography several times. He describes the many _____ experiences of his life. **FORGET**
3 An essential _____ of any autobiography is that it should be honest. **REQUIRE**
4 It is very difficult to check the _____ of information in autobiographies. **ACCURATE**
5 Authors often write about past behaviour that still makes them feel _____ . **GUILT**
6 Authors who are _____ may not include important past events. **FORGET**

186

Exam practice

Personal history 27

Writing Part 1 An essay

You **must** answer this question. Write your answer in **220 – 260** words in an appropriate style.

> ### Exam tip
>
> Make sure that you read the question and notes carefully, so that you know exactly what you have to do. When you answer the question, remember to deal with the three methods listed. If you want to make use of any of the opinions expressed, use your own words. It is always a good idea to start by making a brief paragraph plan so that you cover all the points in the question.
>
> Look at the exam task and answer these questions.
> 1. How many of the ways listed in the notes do you have to refer to in your essay?
> 2. In what way is expressing an opinion not enough?
> 3. If you express one of the opinions listed, what should you do?

Your class has attended a panel discussion on ways in which historical information relating to your neighbourhood can be collected and recorded for future generations. You have made the notes below.

Ways in which information relating to your neighbourhood can be collected and recorded for future generations:
- consult written records
- record personal interviews
- collect old photographs

Some opinions expressed in the discussion:

"Written records can provide facts but not personal opinions or feelings."

"Old people's memories can be unreliable."

"Photographs may be in poor condition and therefore difficult to interpret."

Write an essay discussing **two** of the ways to collect and record information in your notes. You should **explain which way you think would be more effective** for collecting and recording information for future generations, **giving reasons** in support of your answer.

You may, if you wish, make use of the opinions expressed in the discussion, but you should use your own words as far as possible.

28 The arts

Arts events, reviews

Arts events

1.1 Which of these events would you enjoy? Which would you choose not to go to? Put a (✓) or a (✗).

1 an exhibition of work by a contemporary sculptor _____
2 classical music played by an orchestra and a celebrity soloist _____
3 a gig by a stand-up comic _____
4 a star-studded performance of a popular Shakespeare play _____
5 the première of the latest Hollywood blockbuster _____
6 a legendary jazz musician in concert _____
7 an exhibition of historical artefacts _____
8 a new piece by a touring ballet company _____
9 a three-day festival headlined by international rock stars _____
10 a collection of portraits by a photographer-to-the-stars _____
11 the televised auditions for a TV talent show _____
12 a collection of jewellery belonging to someone famous _____

1.2 Where would you see each of the events listed in 1.1? Write the numbers (1–12) next to the venues (a–h). Some events could be seen at more than one venue.

a an open-air stadium _____   e a prestigious museum _____
b a historic concert hall _____   f a theatre _____
c a public art gallery _____   g a comedy club _____
d a multiplex cinema _____   h a city park _____

1.3 Add your own words to these lists.

visual arts	sculpture,
styles of music	soul,
types of literature	novel,
types of dance	ballet,
genres of film	thriller,
artists	composer, dancer,

Error warning

In **1.1** there are two adjectives which are often confused with similar words.

classical/classic
classical = traditional in style or form; of the ancient civilisations of Greece and Rome: **Classical literature** usually makes heavy reading.
classic = established over time as popular, the best or most typical of its kind: The little black dress is a **classic look**.

historical/historic
historical = connected with or based on past times: It's a **historical novel** about the Tudors.
historic = very important in history: These **historic events** will shape the nation's future.

Vocabulary note

Notice that we use the definite article *the* with the names of most entertainment venues: **the** Sydney Opera House, **the** British Museum, **the** O2 Arena, **the** Odeon cinema.

(See **Unit 5, 2.4** for more on the use of the definite article.)

The arts 28

1.4 COLLOCATION Match each list of verbs with a noun.

1 play, hear, write, read
2 shoot, watch, produce, show
3 appreciate, buy, create, view
4 lead, conduct, join, hear
5 go on, take to, leave, appear on
6 book, fill, headline, choose

a art
b a venue
c a film
d music
e an orchestra
f the stage

1.5 Complete these sentences using an adjective from box A and a noun from box B.

A: academic ~~medical~~ musical scientific surgical match-winning opening third-quarter

B: instrument performance

1 A stethoscope is a ___medical instrument___.
2 A scalpel is a sharp _____.
3 The striker gave a _____.
4 The company delivered a good _____.
5 The saxophone is a _____.
6 The _____ was sold out.
7 The telescope was an early _____.
8 University entry depends upon _____.

Reviews

2.1 🎧35 Listen to three people talking about arts events. Match the speakers with the events they describe (a–d). One of the events is not described.

Speaker 1 _____
Speaker 2 _____
Speaker 3 _____

a a comedy night at an unimpressive venue
b a bizarre event at a modern art gallery
c an outdoor art installation
d a memorable concert by a new group

2.2 🎧35 Listen again and complete the sentences with words and phrases used by the speakers.

1 It was one of the best ___live music events___ I've ever been to.
2 The venue was pretty ordinary – a _____.
3 They play their rather eclectic mix of material without _____.
4 They're gaining a devoted _____.
5 I've never been _____ stand-up.
6 He had the whole audience _____.
7 I'm not even sure 'exhibition' _____.
8 The shapes are all perfectly formed, but they were made entirely _____.

189

28 The arts

2.3 Match these reviews with two of the events in 1.1.

1. Playing some of his better-known back-catalogue, the now 79-year-old free-jazz saxophonist Ornette Coleman proved to a capacity audience what a lasting genius he is. What was chaotic and painful to listen to in the 1960s sounds melodic 40 years on. The mood of the music alternates between euphoric and melancholic, but it is always exciting and often surprising.

2. Speaking an estimated forty percent of the lines in the play, Jude Law, as Hamlet, gives an exhilarating performance. He incorporates physicality throughout, and infuses a breathtaking amount of energy into the part. He also knows what he's talking about. There is no recitation or learning by rote here. It's plain that after the year he was given to prepare for this role, and after the three months of performance in London, Law has an intimate understanding of his character, the language and the play as a whole.

2.4 Find words and phrases in the reviews which match these definitions.

1. past recordings of a musician _____
2. largest crowd a venue can hold _____
3. pleasantly musical _____
4. words an actor has to say _____
5. role played by an actor _____
6. repeat in order to remember _____

2.5 Write the nouns related to these adjectives from the reviews in 2.3.

1. chaotic _____
2. melancholic _____
3. exhilarating _____
4. melodic _____
5. intimate _____
6. euphoric _____

2.6 Read these sentences. The words in italics have similar meanings. Underline the word in each pair which is more positive.

1. The portrait, which hangs in the National Gallery, is one of his more *difficult* / *challenging* works.
2. The band draws heavily on 1960s influences, giving this latest album a *classic* / *dated* sound.
3. His prose is *understated* / *bland* and his use of narrative device is *weak* / *subtle*.
4. They played in *a cramped* / *an intimate* venue to a *boisterous* / *raucous* crowd.
5. This was a typically *edgy* / *abrasive* routine from the undisputed bad boy of comedy.
6. The *sweet* / *syrupy* vocals and *repetitive* / *insistent* beat are reminiscent of disco.
7. She gives *an emotional* / *a melodramatic* performance as the late, great singer.

2.7 Complete this review of a novel with one word which best fits each gap.

The Road has a beauty which is reminiscent **(1)** _of_ classic twentieth-century novels such as *Of Mice and Men* and *The Old Man and the Sea*. The deceptively simple narrative is both gripping **(2)** _____ revealing of human nature.
The novel **(3)** _____ the story of a father and son as they travel across a desolate landscape **(4)** _____ search of food and shelter. It becomes clear **(5)** _____ a huge disaster **(6)** _____ befallen planet earth. The sun has stopped shining and, **(7)** _____ light, plants do not grow, animals have starved and humanity is **(8)** _____ the brink of extinction. Society has broken **(9)** _____ and the few people that remain have turned against **(10)** _____ another. As the father tries desperately to **(11)** _____ his son alive, he learns that the greatest human need of all is not food, **(12)** _____ hope for the future.

Exam practice

Reading and Use of English Part 1

For questions **1 – 8**, read the text below and decide which answer (**A, B, C** or **D**) best fits each gap.
There is an example at the beginning (**0**).

Exam tip

Start by reading the whole text to get a general idea of what it is about.

When choosing options, look for language clues in the text such as collocations and prepositions, as well as considering meaning.

Narrow your choice by eliminating options which are obviously incorrect.

A history of the Gotan Project

Gotan Project, (**0**) ___B___ onto the music scene in 1999 and their debut album, *La Revancha del Tango*, released two years later, helped them to achieve international (**1**) _____ .

The band members are Philippe Cohen-Solal, a former French composer, Christophe Müller, a Swiss musician and Eduardo Makaroff, an Argentinian guitarist. Their sound can be described as a fusion of electronic music and tango.

Philippe and Christophe are the founding members of the band, and first met in Paris in 1995. Philippe had already (**2**) _____ a name for himself as a composer and had also worked in the film industry as a music consultant for (**3**) _____ European film directors. Christophe, whose background was in electronica, had built up a (**4**) _____ on the Swiss electro scene.

Both Philippe and Christophe shared a (**5**) _____ for electronica and Latin American music, and (**6**) _____ it off instantly. They went on to (**7**) _____ their own record label, *YA BASTA!* and worked on a number of projects together before (**8**) _____ their two favourite musical influences to form Gotan Project with Eduardo Makaroff, an Argentinian guitarist living in Paris.

0	**A** started	**B** came	**C** set off	**D** launched
1	**A** competition	**B** gain	**C** ambition	**D** fame
2	**A** made	**B** succeeded	**C** did	**D** realised
3	**A** primary	**B** leading	**C** principal	**D** chief
4	**A** repute	**B** reputation	**C** status	**D** position
5	**A** enjoyment	**B** feeling	**C** love	**D** interest
6	**A** got	**B** did	**C** knocked	**D** hit
7	**A** begin	**B** establish	**C** create	**D** form
8	**A** combining	**B** joining	**C** sticking	**D** bridging

29 Migrations

Departures, personal stories

Departures

1.1 Complete the text with words or phrases from the box.

| asylum seekers | contract workers | expatriates |
| illegal immigrants | professionals | refugees | ~~Settlers~~ |

(1) _Settlers_ are people who intend to live permanently in a new country. Most head for just a few main countries, for example, the USA.

Some will succeed in their aims and gain status as legal residents of the country they have moved to. These people are technically called (2) _____ although this term is most commonly used by people from English-speaking nations to describe people from more developed nations living permanently abroad.

Migrants who leave their homes to escape danger or persecution may also be looking for a permanent new home. Until their claims are dealt with they are known as (3) _____, and if their claims are accepted they will be classified as (4) _____. In some cases of mass flight, when thousands of people escape across a border, they are immediately granted this status.

Looking for a job, a better income or perhaps just an experience, other migrants are admitted to countries as (5) _____. They are allowed to stay in their destination country on the understanding that it is for a specific period. Some are seasonal employees. Others will stay in the new country for a year or more. These include employees of multinational corporations who are moved around from country to country. These people are often (6) _____, with specialist knowledge in their field.

Some migrants overstay their visas or work whilst in the country on tourist visas. When this happens they become (7) _____ in the eyes of the officials. They may also try to enter an 'immigration country', often endangering their own lives, by being smuggled in by people they have paid for this service.

> **V Vocabulary note**
>
> The prefixes *en-* and *em-* add the meaning 'put into', 'cause to be' or 'provide with' to verbs.
> So *endanger* means 'to put in danger'. Other common verbs starting with *en-* include: *encase, encircle, engulf, enable, enlarge, enliven, enrich, enclose*
>
> The prefix *em-* is used before words which begin with *b* or *p*: *embed, embitter, embody, empower*

1.2 Answer these questions.

1 Which types of migrants come to your country? Which countries do they come from?
2 Which types of migrants leave your country? Which countries do they go to?

1.3 Match these words with their definitions.

1 multinational corporation   a take things or people to or from a country illegally or secretly
2 smuggle   b worker whose employment is related to a time of the year
3 seasonal employee   c company that operates in more than one country
4 overstay   d remain beyond a specific time limit
5 persecution   e cruel or unfair treatment of someone or a group of people

Migrations 29

1.4 WORD BUILDING Complete the table with words which have related meanings.

Noun	Verb	Adjective
_____	endanger	endangered _____
_____ (positive) illegality (negative) _____	_____	_____ (positive) illegal (negative)
_____ (problem) _____ (person)	persecute	_____
_____ (activity) _____ (person)	smuggle	_____
_____ (particular area) specialisation (process) _____ (person)	_____	specialist _____

Personal stories

2.1 ▶36 You will hear the first part of a radio programme about emigration. Listen and complete this summary. Write no more than two words for each gap.

Many people imagine that their life in a new country will be more exciting than the **(1)** _____ of home. But in fact, although their new **(2)** _____ are better, they often pine for aspects of their old life. Jane Foreman has experienced painful **(3)** _____ . Her husband David's job **(4)** _____ them to Kuala Lumpur in Malaysia 18 months ago. Now all she wants to do is **(5)** _____ to Northumberland.

2.2 ▶37 Now listen to the radio programme and answer these questions.

1 What positive aspects of life in Kuala Lumpur does Jane mention?
2 What has happened to make Louisa feel happier in Canada?

Error warning 👁

Many is commonly used in affirmative sentences in writing: *__Many__ people these days prefer to shop online.*
However, *many* is very formal in spoken, affirmative sentences. We prefer to use *a lot of* or *lots of* more informally: '*I know* ~~many~~ *a lot of people like her.*' '*She has* ~~many~~ *lots of good friends.*'
Many is used in questions and negative sentences whatever the level of formality. (See **Unit 6, 2.2** for more on the use of *many* and *a lot of / lots of.*)

29 Migrations

2.3 Match these definitions with words from the recordings.

1 needing or wanting something very much
2 miss something very much
3 having strong, supportive relationships
4 feel deeply sad because of a death
5 anxious, not confident
6 well known and easily recognised

a pine for
b insecure
c grieve
d familiar
e close-knit
f desperate

2.4 The adjective prefix *multi-* means 'many'. Complete the sentences with an adjective starting with *multi-*.

1 The city is home to people from many different cultures. It's a ___multicultural___ city.
2 Many different languages are spoken in our country. It's a _____ society.
3 HSBC is a bank which operates in many different nations. It's a _____ company.
4 The fabric is printed with many contrasting colours. It's _____ fabric.
5 My printer has many different functions. It's a _____ printer.

2.5 Complete these sentences with phrases from the box.

sense of belonging   sense of duty   sense of humour   sense of responsibility   ~~sense of urgency~~   sense of loss

1 We're leaving in half an hour and he hasn't finished packing yet. He has no ___sense of urgency___ .
2 I have a real _____ even though I've only lived here for six months.
3 Nothing makes you laugh. You have absolutely no _____ .
4 He didn't really want to see his parents. He only visited them out of a _____ .
5 She has looked after her brothers and sisters since they arrived in the country. She has an amazing _____ .
6 When my long-term neighbour moved house I was surprised by the _____ I felt.

2.6 Answer these questions. The idioms in italics can all be found in the recording scripts.

1 If you *dream of pastures new*, what do you want to do?
2 If you say *'my heart is'* somewhere, do you want to be in that place or not?
3 If you *find your feet*, do you feel more or less comfortable in a situation?
4 If you *do something like a shot*, do you do it slowly or quickly?
5 If you *go off the beaten track*, do you travel to popular tourist destinations or not?
6 If a *rug was pulled out from under you*, would you feel more or less confident?
7 If *things are looking up*, is your situation getting easier or more difficult?
8 If something you planned to do is *off the menu*, can you do that thing as planned?

Exam practice

Migrations 29

Listening Part 2

▶38 You will hear Lindsey Jones, a recent graduate, talking to a group of students about travelling abroad to find work. For questions **1 – 8**, complete the sentences with a word or short phrase.

According to Lindsey, Germany and Singapore are two of the more unusual **(1)** _____ for young people looking for work in other countries.

Lindsey thinks that the British jobs she could apply for are not the right level for a **(2)** _____ like her.

Lindsey believes she has a better chance of finding a job at home if she has experience of working in a healthier **(3)** _____ .

Food and **(4)** _____ are more expensive in New Zealand than in Britain.

A friend **(5)** _____ Lindsey not to expect to find work easily in New Zealand.

Some young people like to use **(6)** _____ to help them organise their visits.

Working as a waitress in Sydney made Lucy feel like a **(7)** _____ of the city and part of the community.

Lucy's **(8)** _____ has increased as a result of working in Australia.

195

30 Risking it

Extreme sports, risk-taking

Extreme sports

1.1 Match the pictures with the sports.

1. bungee jumping _c_
2. hang-gliding ___
3. ice climbing ___
4. potholing ___
5. scuba diving ___
6. skydiving ___
7. white-water rafting ___
8. windsurfing ___

1.2 Which of these sports have you done? Which would you try?

> **V   Vocabulary note**
>
> The compound nouns for these sporting activities are formed using the *-ing* form. Some are written as two separate words, some have a hyphen (-) and others are one word.
> (See **Unit 5**, **2.1** for more on compound nouns.)

1.3 Choose the best words to complete the text.

A defining feature of extreme sports for many people is their alleged capacity to **(1)** *induce / install* an adrenaline rush in **(2)** *participants / patients*. However, the medical view is that the 'rush' or 'high' **(3)** *associated / imparted* with an activity is not due to adrenaline being **(4)** *resumed / released* as a response to **(5)** *flight / fear*. Medical professionals now claim it is due to increased **(6)** *levels / channels* of dopamine, endorphins and serotonin resulting from extreme physical **(7)** *exhibition / exertion*. Furthermore, a recent study suggests that the link between adrenaline and 'true' extreme sports is **(8)** *tentative / understated*. The study defined 'true' extreme sports as leisure or **(9)** *recreational / residential* activities where the most likely outcome of a mismanaged **(10)** *adventure / accident* or mistake was death. This definition was designed to separate the marketing hype from the **(11)** *action / activity* itself. Another characteristic of these activities is that they tend to be **(12)** *individual / lonely* rather than team sports. Extreme sports can include both competitive and non-competitive activities.

1.4 Match these words and phrases from the text with their definitions. Use a dictionary to help you.

1. marketing hype
2. physical exertion
3. outcome
4. mismanaged
5. characteristic

a. result
b. exaggerated descriptions used in sales
c. poorly controlled or organised
d. movement of the body which raises the heart rate
e. typical or noticeable quality

196

30 Risking it

1.5 COLLOCATION
We *take risks* and *make mistakes*. Match the words in the box with *take* and *make*. Use a dictionary to help you.

> ~~action~~   advice   care   a chance   ~~a choice~~   a decision
> a difference   effect   an effort   exercise   part   precautions
> progress   responsibility   steps to   sure   use of

TAKE: _action_ _____
MAKE: _a choice_ _____

Error warning
The verb *take part* is followed by the preposition *in*: *He's hoping to **take part in** the next Olympic Games.* (not *He's hoping to take part ~~off/at~~ the next Olympic Games.*)

1.6 Complete these sentences with one of the collocations from 1.5.

1. I've only just started, but my ski instructor says I am __making__ good __progress__.
2. If you want to _____ _____ in any sporting activity, you should _____ _____ from those who are more experienced than yourself.
3. It's important that participants in extreme sports _____ full _____ for their own actions.
4. Some sports are extremely dangerous even if you do _____ the proper _____.
5. I think you have to _____ _____ about the level of risk you find acceptable.

Risk-taking

2.1 ▶39
You are going to hear a news report which says that certain groups of people are more likely to take risks than others. Choose the statement you think is correct (1–3). Listen and check.

1. Women are more likely to take risks than men.
2. Teenagers are more likely to take risks than children or adults.
3. People from difficult social backgrounds are most likely to take risks.

Vocabulary note
The speaker in 2.1 uses formal language in the report, e.g.
conclusion = decision
determine = find out
display = show
engage in = take part in
foresee = predict
onset = beginning
response = reaction, reply

2.2 ▶39
Listen again and complete these sentences with words or phrases used by the speaker. Write up to three words.

1. A US study ___set out to___ determine why people take risks.
2. The study sampled 500 participants, divided into _____.
3. One option in the study was safer, but would result in a _____.
4. The second option resulted in a two-thirds chance of _____ coins.
5. Gender was a _____ predictor of a preference to avoid risk.
6. Older generations tend to _____ when assessing risk.

2.3 What does the speaker mean by the *onset of adolescence*? Choose the best meaning.

197

30 Risking it

1 The difficulties experienced by teenagers as they develop into adults.
2 The beginning of the stage that turns someone into an adult.
3 The attitude and behaviour of adolescents as compared with adults.

2.4 Cross out the word in each list which has a different meaning from the word in the first column.

1	adolescent	teenager youth ~~sibling~~ teen
2	satisfied	content amused happy pleased
3	foreseeing	predicting anticipating analysing
4	thrill	excitement enthusiasm buzz kick

3.1 Choose the correct words to complete the text. Use a dictionary to help you.

> **How to assess the risks in your workplace**
>
> Don't overcomplicate the process. In many organisations, the risks are well known and the necessary control **(1)** *measures* / *ways* are easy to apply. You probably already know whether, for example, you have **(2)** *employees* / *employers* who move heavy loads and so could harm their backs, or the places where people are most likely to slip or trip. If so, check that you have taken **(3)** *rational* / *reasonable* precautions to **(4)** *prohibit* / *avoid* injury. If you run a small organisation and you are confident you understand what's involved, you can do the assessment yourself. You don't have to be a health and safety **(5)** *expert* / *leader*. If you work in a larger organisation, you could ask a safety adviser to help you. If you are not confident, get help from someone who is **(6)** *competent* / *talented*. In all cases, you should make sure that you involve your staff or their **(7)** *agents* / *representatives* in the process. But remember, you are **(8)** *responsible* / *responsive* for seeing that the assessment is carried out properly. When thinking about your risk assessment, remember: a hazard is anything that may cause harm, such as chemicals, electricity, working from ladders, etc. The risk is the **(9)** *chance* / *opportunity*, high or low, that somebody could be harmed by these and other hazards, together with an indication of how **(10)** *sensible* / *serious* the harm could be.

3.2 Answer these questions about a place you know well.

1 What are the most hazardous areas and objects?
2 What are the riskiest activites carried out on the premises?
3 Who might be harmed by these hazards?
4 What precautions could be taken to prevent people being harmed?

> **V Vocabulary note**
>
> **trip** = to lose your balance after hitting your foot on something: *I tripped while I was running for my train and fell flat on my face.*
>
> **slip** = to slide unintentionally on something wet or smooth, so that you lose your balance: *Several people slipped on the icy pavements and two were admitted to hospital with suspected fractures.*
>
> **stumble** = to put a foot down awkwardly and because of this begin to fall: *Running along the beach, she stumbled and fell on to the sand.*

Exam practice

Reading and Use of English Part 7

You are going to read an extract from a magazine article about cycling safely. Six paragraphs have been removed from the extract. Choose from the paragraphs **A – G** the one which fits each gap (**1 – 6**). There is one extra paragraph which you do not need to use.

Should cyclists be forced to wear helmets?

A recent attempt in the UK to make cycling helmets compulsory failed. Now, after a serious crash that put one rider into a brain injury unit, the idea is back on the table. But how much protection do helmets offer?

1

When I was 13, with my helmet hanging from my handlebars, I wobbled out into the road and was hit by a car. Later that day I remember being told how lucky I was to be wearing it. I said nothing.

2

So if they can help reduce injury, shouldn't they be compulsory, just like motorbike helmets? Australia tried it in the early 90s and the result was a 15 to 20 per cent drop in the number of hospital admissions for head injuries.

3

A recent study has shown that cycling has a positive health impact far greater than the potential for injury. Essentially, there's a small chance that you'll have an accident, but a very large chance that you'll reduce your chances of suffering mental illness and heart disease.

4

A British cycling organisation has long argued against compulsory helmet laws for a similar reason.

It claims they would make cycling seem more dangerous than it actually is, and put people off. The evidence for this is complex and contradictory, providing as much support for those who are deeply sceptical of helmets as for those in favour of them.

5

There's even evidence that wearing a helmet can put you at more risk. A study by Dr Ian Walker from the University of Bath found that drivers passed closer to cyclists who were wearing helmets when overtaking than they did to those without them. The driver's subconscious obviously sees them as less vulnerable. Dr Walker, an enthusiastic cyclist, says: "It would be sensible, and would genuinely save a lot of lives, if everybody wore a helmet all of the time; but to suggest they are more necessary for cycling than a range of other activities – including walking down the street and driving a car – is misguided."

6

Personally, I believe that wearing a helmet has more pros than cons, even though cycling is not as risky as many suggest. But there are those out there who would rather not ride than be made to wear a helmet, and for that reason the idea is a non-starter.

Exam practice

A It's undeniable that compulsory safety devices such as seatbelts in cars have been significant lifesavers. But neither had the same potential for harmful side-effects: dissuade motorcyclists from riding and they'll buy a car, which is actually far safer.

B Cycling should be promoted as an essentially safe, normal and enjoyable transport and leisure activity, which anyone can do in whatever clothes they prefer to wear, with or without helmets.

C In addition to this, there's the problem of enforcing new laws. In the first year after the Australian State of Victoria made helmets compulsory, nearly 20,000 fines were issued. Do we want to tie up that much police time on a crime which has no negative impact on a third party?

D Last year, however, I had a nasty fall and cut my face. If it wasn't for my helmet, I'm sure it could have been worse. So, personally, I now almost never ride without a helmet. I'd rather have it and not need it, than need it and not have it. Studies disagree on the benefits, but some suggest that most head injuries could be prevented in this way.

E Most people would rather not wear a helmet, especially in hot weather. It's a practical decision: ride long and often enough and one day all those years of unnecessary sweaty-hat hair could pay off.

F That means laws can actually be counterproductive; they may reduce cycling injuries, but only by reducing the number of cyclists, and those people then become more likely to come to some other kind of less-dramatic harm.

G That would have been great, but it also reduced the number of cyclists by around 35 per cent. The annoyance and, for teenagers, embarrassment of wearing one steered people away from bikes and towards public transport and cars.

31 Gender issues
Language, gender in sport

Language

1.1 Which of these job titles tell you the gender of the person? Write M (male), F (female) or N (neutral).

actor ___   midwife ___   teacher ___
cameraman ___   nurse ___   waitress ___
doctor ___   police officer ___   fireman ___
firefighter ___   solicitor ___   policewoman ___
headmistress ___   surgeon ___

1.2 Two of these phrases are definitions of the term *gender-neutral language*. Which ones?

1 language which does not specify gender
2 language which clarifies gender
3 language which is inclusive of both sexes

1.3 Complete the text with words from the box.

| biased   categorise   ~~connotations~~   neutral   sexes   stereotypes |

English words with sexist (1) __connotations__ lead those who speak the language to subconsciously (2) _____ people by their gender. Human language is deeply rooted in the subconscious and it is said that the language of a culture is clear evidence of the values and beliefs of that culture. Many gender-(3) _____ words exist in the English language. It follows that our choice of language has had an impact on our society and culture. Does sexist language contribute to how we think of both (4) _____ today? Is it possible to impose a gender-(5) _____ language on today's society? It is my view that our society should be concerned about perpetuating gender (6) _____ through language.

V Vocabulary note

When using a gender-neutral noun, for example *student* or *doctor*, we have a choice of pronouns.

If we know that the student or doctor is a man or a woman we can refer to them as *he* or *she*.

If we do not know, or do not want to specify the gender of the person, we can use *they, them, their, themselves*: *If a student fails their exams, they will usually get a chance to resit.*

V Vocabulary note

These relationship words refer to people of both genders: *partner, spouse, colleague, relative, cousin, parent, friend, sibling*

spouse = husband or wife (formal, legal); *sibling* = brother or sister (formal)

1.4 Replace the gender-biased words in italics with neutral words. Use a dictionary to help you.

1 Stand-up *comedienne* Sarah Millican's tour has sold out at venues across the UK.
2 The fate of many of the planet's species is now in the hands of *mankind*.
3 I think my *forefathers* were probably farmers because my surname is 'Farmer'.
4 The English-language requirements for *stewardesses* at some airlines are very high.
5 I can't wear clothes containing *man-made* fibres. They make me itch!
6 Transport will be provided to and from the venue for conference delegates and their *wives*.

31 Gender issues

1.5 Choose the correct prepositions for the word or phrase in bold in these sentences. There are similar sentences in 1.3.

1 The language we use is **deeply rooted** *in* / *with* our subconscious.
2 The words we choose are **evidence** *on* / *of* our fundamental beliefs and values.
3 Our early education has **an enormous impact** *at* / *on* our future life chances.
4 Urban sprawl can **contribute** *to* / *for* pollution levels.
5 Is it right to **impose** any **restrictions** *in* / *on* what people say?
6 Should we **be concerned** *about* / *for* people's use of sexist language?

1.6 ▶40 Listen to an American talking about the use of the word 'girl' in the UK and complete the sentences.

1 The speaker thought the way adult women were referred to as 'girls' was _____ .
2 A 'girl' is not someone who _____ for herself, she's a child.
3 In this society women are _____ in comparison to men.
4 We should _____ to the way women are addressed.

1.7 ▶40 Listen again and complete these sentences with phrases used by the speaker.

1 As a mature adult, you do not want to _____ a child.
2 Women are striving to _____ into male-dominated society.
3 We should look at whether the word 'girl' is used _____ or not.
4 Men do not have a _____ to deal with.

Gender in sport

2.1 Which of the adjectives in the box do you associate with sports people? Put a (✓).

aggressive _____
arrogant _____
attractive _____
competitive _____
driven _____
flexible _____
gifted _____
graceful _____
passive _____
powerful _____
pure _____
submissive _____

2.2 Write the nouns related to the adjectives in 2.1.

aggressive – aggression

202

Gender issues 31

2.3 WORD TRANSFORMATION Complete the text with the correct forms of the words in capitals at the ends of the lines.

The positive outcomes of sport for gender **(0)** ___equality___ and women's empowerment are constrained by gender-based **(1)** _____ in all areas and at all levels of sport and physical **(2)** _____ . This is fuelled by continuing stereotypes of women's physical **(3)** _____ and social roles. Women are frequently segregated involuntarily into types of sports, events and **(4)** _____ specifically targeted at women. Women's access to positions of **(5)** _____ and **(6)** _____ -making is constrained from the local to the international level. The value placed on women's sports is often lower, resulting in **(7)** _____ resources and **(8)** _____ wages and prizes. In the media, women's sport is not only marginalised but often also presented in a different style that reflects and reinforces gender stereotypes.	EQUAL DISCRIMINATE ACT ABLE COMPETE LEADER DECIDE ADEQUATE EQUAL

2.4 ▶41 Listen to someone talking about gymnastics. Are these statements true (T) or false (F) according to the speaker?

1. The speaker started doing competitive gymnastics in her late teens. _____
2. The speaker was physically different from the majority of other gymnasts. _____
3. She has always known that gymnastics is generally considered to be a female sport. _____
4. Gymnastics is regarded as a feminine sport because participants do not need to be openly aggressive. _____
5. The speaker doesn't believe that attitudes towards gender stereotyping will change in the near future. _____

2.5 WORD BUILDING Complete the table with words which have related meanings.

Noun	Verb	Adjective
_____	categorise	x
_____ (thing) _____ (person)	contribute	_____
_____	discriminate	_____
_____	equalise	equal
_____	involve	_____
_____	perpetuate	_____
_____	x	neutral

> **V Vocabulary note**
>
> **stand out** = be visibly different / be clearly visible: *My larger frame and muscular physique **stood out** among most other gymnasts.*
>
> Other phrasal verbs with *stand*:
>
> **stand by** = not act to prevent something: *I should not have **stood by** while she was bullied.*
>
> **not stand for** = refuse to accept: *I will not **stand for** rude behaviour.*
>
> **stand in for** = do someone else's job: *My colleague **stood in** for me when I was ill.*
>
> **stand up for** = defend and fight for: *It's important to **stand up for** what you believe in.*

2.6 Match the words in the box with less formal words which have similar meanings.

complete   deem   overt   participate   predominantly   ~~pursue~~

1. do ___pursue___
2. consider _____
3. finish _____
4. mainly _____
5. open _____
6. take part in _____

203

Exam practice

Reading and Use of English Part 4

For questions **1 – 6**, complete the second sentence so that it has a similar meaning to the first sentence, using the word given. **Do not change the word given**. You must use between **three** and **six** words, including the word given. Here is an example **(0)**.

> **Exam tip**
> The second sentence must mean the same as the first sentence, must include the key word unchanged and must be grammatically correct. Look to transform the second sentence minimally according to the word given.

0 It was the first time I had seen women playing competitive football.
   NEVER
   I _____had never seen_____ women playing competitive football before.

1 The manager accepted that he was fully responsible for the way his team performed.
   TOOK
   The manager _____ performance.

2 We should not accept sexist language and attitudes in the places where we work.
   ACCEPTABLE
   Sexist language and attitudes ought _____ our places of work.

3 I find people's use of the word 'girls' to refer to adult women objectionable.
   USING
   I _____ the word 'girls' to refer to adult women.

4 I first participated in competitive sport when I was six years old.
   PART
   I first _____ at the age of six.

5 His boss led him to believe that he would be promoted at the end of the year.
   IMPRESSION
   He _____ that he would be promoted at the end of the year.

6 They've cancelled this afternoon's match because of the bad weather.
   CALLED
   This afternoon's match _____ to the bad weather.

204

32 Education
Learning, training

Learning

1.1 Which of these kinds of education have you experienced? Put a (✓) or a (✗).

boarding school ___ fee-paying school ___ nursery ___ secondary school ___
distance learning course ___ independent school ___ pre-school ___ technical college ___
faith school ___ local state school ___ primary school ___ university ___

1.2 Complete the text with words from the box.

| capacity | child-centred | classroom | ~~educators~~ | foster | graduate |
| images | influence | method | needs | potential | whole |

Maria Montessori was one of the most important early years (1) _educators_ of the 20th century. She was the first woman to (2) _____ from the University of Rome medical school and became interested in education through her work as a doctor, treating children with special (3) _____. When she went on to establish schools for the disadvantaged children of working parents in Rome, she approached their education as a scientist. She used the (4) _____ as her laboratory for observing children and finding ways to help them to achieve their full (5) _____.

It soon became apparent that Dr Montessori had developed a highly effective teaching (6) _____ which could be used with great success with each and every child. She began to travel the world, establishing schools, lecturing about her discoveries, and writing articles right up to her death in 1952. She was a true pioneer of (7) _____ education. Her innovative classroom practices and ideas have had a profound (8) _____ on the education of young children all over the world.

Montessori saw that children learn best by doing and that happy self-motivated learners form positive (9) _____ of themselves as confident, successful people. She created specially designed resources to (10) _____ independence and a love for learning from an early age.

The Montessori approach is holistic, that is, it aims to develop the (11) _____ child. Fundamental to this approach is the belief that a child's early life, from birth to six years old, is the period when they have the greatest (12) _____ to learn.

1.3 Match these words and phrases with their definitions.

1 special needs
2 disadvantaged
3 achieve your potential
4 pioneer
5 child-centred
6 innovative
7 self-motivated

a person who is the first to develop an idea
b able to work at something without encouragement
c requirements due to physical or mental problems
d new and original
e suceed to the best of your ability
f based on the needs and interests of children
g without the necessary education, money, etc. to succeed in life

32 Education

1.4 Complete these sentences with the correct prepositions. There are similar sentences in 1.2.

1. My brother graduated _from_ Harvard University in 2009.
2. In some countries, children _____ special needs are taught in mainstream schools.
3. The professor toured the world, lecturing _____ his educational theories.
4. Successful teachers are those who have a good influence _____ their students.
5. Children often learn better _____ doing things themselves rather than listening passively.
6. Students who have a positive image _____ themselves are usually happy and successful.
7. Ever since I started school, I have had a real love _____ learning.
8. Everyone can succeed at something. This idea is fundamental _____ my beliefs about education.

1.5 WORD BUILDING Complete the table with words which have related meanings.

Noun	Verb	Adjective
_____	establish	_____
_____ (event, process) _____ (person)	graduate	x
education (general noun) _____ (person)	_____	_____ (of a person) _____ (for this purpose)
_____ (thing, idea, process) _____ (person)	_____	innovative
influence	_____	_____
_____ (general noun) motivator (person)	_____	motivated (of a person) _____ (of a thing, ideas, process) motivational (for the purpose of increasing this)

1.6 COLLOCATION Choose the correct adverbs for the adjectives in bold in these sentences. Use a dictionary to help you.

1. The *newly / firmly* **established** early years centre is already serving a large number of local families.
2. The historic university is *newly / firmly* **established** as top choice for international students hoping to study in the city.
3. We are seeking advice on how to recruit the *highly / poorly* **educated** workforce needed for these skilled roles.
4. He plays the character of a *highly / poorly* **educated** caretaker who has an innate gift for mathematics.
5. His theory was *increasingly / highly* **influential** in the development of educational practices in the latter part of the century.
6. The department will become *increasingly / highly* **influential** as the publication of its papers in top journals continues.
7. Focus groups showed that parents were *strongly / politically* **motivated** to do the best for their offspring whilst being wary of other parents' competitive behaviour.
8. The announcement today of additional grants for poorer students has been seen as a *strongly / politically* **motivated** attempt to deflect allegations of a U-turn.

Education 32

Training

2.1 ▶42 Listen to Peter describing his apprenticeship and answer these questions.

1. What happened to Peter after he left school?
2. What was the job market like when Peter's parents were younger?
3. What were the two major advantages of an apprenticeship for Peter?
4. Which industry do you think Peter works in?

> **Vocabulary note**
>
> The word *workshop* has two meanings:
> - a room or building where things are made or repaired: *an engineering workshop*
> - a meeting of people to discuss and/or perform practical work: *a drama workshop*

2.2 ▶42 Listen again and complete these sentences with words Peter uses.

1. Not being able to get a job without experience is an _____ situation.
2. You need experience and good _____ to get a job.
3. Peter's apprenticeship provided him with _____ work experience.
4. Peter received a lot of _____ in engineering theory.
5. Peter went on a number of health and safety _____ .
6. Peter has been given his own team of _____ to supervise.
7. Peter is now _____ to the company as an educator.

2.3 Choose the correct words in these sentences.

1. My sister *abandoned* / *left* school at the age of 16.
2. I'm going to *apply* / *request* for a catering course in September.
3. My experience has given me a real *insight* / *view* into how universities work.
4. Modern companies often organise *group-building* / *team-building* days to enable staff to work well together.
5. While he was working as an apprentice, Peter *learned* / *trained* a trade.

> **Vocabulary note**
>
> Most collective nouns like *team*, *staff* and *class* can be used with either singular or plural verb forms:
>
> *The company is/are keen to recognise this extra time.*
>
> *The government is/are bringing in new regulations related to apprenticeships.*
>
> (See **Unit 5, 2.2** for more on subject–verb agreement.)

2.4 WORD TRANSFORMATION Complete the text with the correct forms of the words in capital letters at the ends of the lines.

Mechanical Engineering is among the most diversified of the **(0)** _traditional_ engineering disciplines. Mechanical engineers design and build machines and devices that **(1)** _____ humans to live and work in space, in the air, on the ground, and under water. Their machines can extend our physical **(2)** _____ and improve our health and standard of living. Students acquire an **(3)** _____ of the fundamentals of mechanics and of the thermal energy sciences. They learn to perform **(4)** _____ design tasks using computers and to select appropriate materials for a specific **(5)** _____ . They also become familiar with the chemical and **(6)** _____ sciences, which are often essential to the total design and **(7)** _____ of a mechanical system. We have a small but active group of faculty **(8)** _____ , graduate students and undergraduates who share a passion for Mechanical Engineering.	TRADITION ABLE CAPABLE UNDERSTAND INTERACT APPLY ELECTRIC REALISE RESEARCH

207

Exam practice

Reading and Use of English Part 6

You are going to read four reviews of a book about bringing up children. For questions **1 – 4**, choose from the reviews **A – D**. The reviews may be chosen more than once.

How children succeed
Four reviewers comment on a book called Helping Children to Succeed

A

I expected this book to enlighten me about why some children succeed at school and find work, while others drop out of education early, fail to find employment and continue living with their parents well into adulthood. I had hoped that *Helping Children to Succeed* would provide me with well-researched answers to my concerns, and maybe suggest ways in which all children can be helped to achieve success. However, the author chose to concentrate on the future of students from poor families and gave no indication that he felt such children's chances of future success might be improved. There was an interesting focus on the significance of taking students' personality into account as well as their academic test scores when predicting future success, but this is not new information. The same case has been established before, based on wider research.

B

I found *Helping Children to Succeed* to be a fascinating and inspiring book. What was most interesting to me was the research finding that children from wealthy families are no more prepared for a successful independent future than children from poorer families. The author demonstrates convincingly that children from all backgrounds need to learn how to work hard but also how to deal with failure without falling to pieces. The book shows convincingly how poor children as well as middle class children and those from wealthier homes are capable of learning these skills necessary for future success. This has made me feel very optimistic that no child needs to fail because of their family background and that something can be done to increase the life chances of poor children.

C

For me the most interesting aspect of *Helping Children to Succeed* is the amount of evidence which shows that children's characters as well as their academic performance play a crucial part in their future success. This seems to be especially true in the case of children from disadvantaged families. The author's central argument is that, even though children from poor backgrounds are less likely to succeed, determination and hard work can overcome inherited disadvantages. This is not a novel idea, but I found it interesting to hear it restated with reference to today's situation. Where I disagree with the author is his assertion that our education system requires fundamental reorganisation if we are to help children from poor families. He seems to ignore completely the excellent work being done by dedicated teachers in today's schools.

D

I enjoyed *Helping Children to Succeed*, but in many ways I also found it disappointing. Having finished reading the book, my main criticism is that the title itself is misleading because it focuses primarily on children who fail. Most research studies quoted by the author illustrate how difficult it is for children from poor, disadvantaged homes to succeed or indeed to escape from a cycle of failure. I bought the book for the library where I work, thinking it might offer parents strategies for bringing up children to be successful. In practice, the main strategies recommended by the author are the following: avoid becoming poor and don't expect your child to succeed at everything. He also suggests that children should get used to occasional failure. In my opinion this is an unnecessarily negative outlook.

Exam practice

Education 32

Which reviewer

shares reviewer C's view that academic performance is not the only measure of a child's success? **1**

expresses a different view from the others about poor children's chances of future success? **2**

shares with reviewer A the feeling that the book did not live up to their expectations? **3**

agrees with reviewer A about the originality of the ideas in the book? **4**

> 💡 **Exam tip**
>
> Read the four texts to make sure you understand the subject. Pay particular attention to opinions and attitudes expressed by the writers. Look out for any similarities or differences of opinion.

33 Health

World health, water and health

World health

1.1 Which of these health issues are problems in your country? Put a (✓).

access to healthcare ___   dementia ___   heart disease ___   injury ___   obesity ___
cancer ___   depression ___ influenza ___   malnutrition ___ waterborne disease ___

1.2 Explain the difference between the words in each pair. Use a dictionary to help you.

1 infectious / contagious
2 starvation / malnutrition
3 treatment / medicine
4 transmit / contract
5 epidemic / pandemic
6 acute / preventable

1.3 Complete the sentences using information from the text.

> Despite incredible improvements in health since 1950, there are still a number of challenges which *should* have been easy to resolve. Consider the following:
> - One billion people lack access to healthcare systems.
> - Cardiovascular diseases (CVDs) are the biggest killer amongst diseases globally. An estimated 17.5 million people died from CVDs in 2005, that is 30% of all global deaths.
> - In 2002, almost 11 million people died from infectious diseases alone, far more than the number killed in the natural or man-made catastrophes that make headlines.
> - HIV has spread rapidly. UNAIDS, the joint United Nations programme on HIV/AIDS, estimates are roughly: 33.4 million living with HIV, 2.7 million new infections of HIV, two million deaths from AIDS.
> - There are 8.8 million new cases of tuberculosis (TB) and 1.75 million deaths from TB each year.
> - 1.6 million people still die from pneumococcal diseases every year, making it the number one vaccine-preventable cause of death worldwide. More than half of the victims are children.
> - Malaria causes more than 300 million acute illnesses and at least a million deaths annually.
> - Around 11 million children under five die from malnutrition and preventable diseases each year.
> - More than half a million people, mostly children, died from measles in 2003 even though effective immunisation costs just 0.30 US dollars per person, and has been available for over 40 years.

1 Thirty percent of all _____.
2 In 2002, more people died of _____.
3 Pneumococcal diseases are preventable, yet _____.
4 In 2003 over 500,000 people _____.
5 It costs only thirty cents to _____.

210

Health 33

1.4 WORD BUILDING Complete the table with words which have related meanings.

Noun	Verb	Adjective
immunization (process) _____ (state)	_____	_____ (state)
infection (problem)	_____	_____ (can spread) infected (problem)
_____	_____	medical (general) medicated (effect on person)
_____	_____	_____ (used to control) preventable (possible to control)
treatment	_____	_____ (possible to cure) untreated (no medical help)

2.1 ▶43 Listen to a talk about the smallpox virus. Answer the following questions:

1 How many people are estimated to have had smallpox in the twentieth century? _____
2 When did the immunization program begin? _____
3 Who was Edward Jenner? _____
4 When was the decision made to try and prevent smallpox globally? _____

2.2 ▶43 Listen again. Are these statements true (T) or false (F) according to the speaker? Correct the false statements.

1 Smallpox was spread easily from person to person. ___
2 The symptoms of smallpox included fever and skin problems. ___
3 Smallpox, although devastating, was not a fatal disease. ___
4 Factory workers provided the key to a vaccine for smallpox. ___
5 The smallpox vaccine was often given to children. ___
6 Smallpox is still a problem in some countries. ___

> **V Vocabulary note**
>
> As a verb, *spread* is both transitive and intransitive:
>
> *Mosquitoes spread diseases like malaria.* (transitive)
>
> *Spots can spread across the entire body.* (intransitive)
>
> (See **Unit 9, 2.1** for more on transitive and intransitive verbs.)

2.3 The prefix *mis-* adds the meaning 'bad' or 'wrong' to a word. Complete the sentences with the correct words from the box.

misconduct   misdiagnosis   ~~misfortune~~   misinformation   mismanagement   misrepresentation

1 While he was getting out of the taxi, he had the ___misfortune___ to fall over and break his leg.
2 The director is being accused of gross _____ of the hospital.
3 The psychiatrist was found guilty of professional _____ .
4 The doctor's _____ meant that the patient nearly died.
5 The drug company's advertising campaign was based on _____ and has now been banned.
6 The documentary on poor hospital hygiene was a _____ of the truth.

33 Health

Water and health

3.1 Read the text about water and choose the best summary (a–d).

a Drinking more water substantially reduces your metabolic rate.
b Drinking enough water allows increased carbohydrate storage.
c Water aids the consumption of excess energy.
d Drinking water is by far the best way to lose weight.

> The benefits of drinking water are numerous, and recent studies suggest that you need to drink water to lose weight.
>
> **Drink more water to re-hydrate and detoxify your body.**
> Water is not only essential for health, but increases the rate at which the body burns calories, as well as being a natural appetite suppressant.
>
> **Water also plays an important role in metabolising food.**
> While we know that water is critical to the healthy functioning of the human body, studies suggest that water promotes the lowering of an individual's total energy intake and alters metabolism. Most people who are on a diet do not drink enough water.
>
> **To metabolise food, the body needs water.**
> For every gram of carbohydrate, the body requires three grams of fluid. So, drinking sufficient water can help your body burn up carbohydrates instead of storing them. Additionally, proper hydration while you are on a diet is vital for health, because you are more prone to water retention as your body starts losing fluid along with the weight. If you are dehydrated, your body will slow down its calorie-burning processes. So drink water to lose weight.

3.2 Find words and phrases in the text which match these definitions.

1 remove poisonous substances from your body _____
2 something which prevents hunger _____
3 the overall amount of energy consumed _____
4 change eating habits to reduce body fat _____
5 liquid substance _____
6 be likely to have a particular problem _____
7 have insufficient water in your body _____

3.3 Complete these sentences using the correct prepositions. There are similar sentences in the text.

1 Regular meals are vital _____ healthy living, especially if people do physical activities.
2 Although we should not eat too much of it, fat is essential _____ our health.
3 You're more prone _____ illness when you're tired or run down.
4 Exercise plays an important role _____ keeping fit.
5 The rate _____ which you lose weight depends on the number of calories you burn.
6 To remain healthy, a balanced diet is important, along _____ regular exercise.
7 We live in an age where the public health infrastructure, its growth and its development are critical _____ our collective health.

Exam practice

Health 33

Writing Part 2 A report

You see the following notice in your local health centre.

> An International Health Development Agency is collecting information about attitudes to public health campaigns in countries around the world. Please help by writing a report on attitudes where you live.

Your report should outline some of the main current health concerns in your country, describe people's attitudes to any recent campaigns aimed at promoting healthy lifestyles and recommend ways in which you think people could be persuaded to take healthy living more seriously.

Write your **report** in **220 – 260** words in an appropriate style.

> ### Exam tip
>
> Decide who will read the report and how formal/informal your language should be.
>
> Your report should include factual information followed by suggestions or recommendations.
>
> Give your report a title and organise your ideas into sections, each with its own heading. Start by outlining the purpose of your report. Use your own words rather than repeating the words in the question. Explain the reasons for any recommendations you make.

34 Getting about

Private journeys, public transport

Private journeys

1.1 Complete the questions with *travel*, *journey*(s) or *trip*(s). Answer them about yourself.

1. How do you entertain yourself on a long train __journey__?
2. How long does your round _____ to school or work take?
3. How often do you _____ by taxi?
4. Where did you use to go on school _____?
5. What are the benefits of air _____?
6. Where would you like to go on your next _____ abroad?

1.2 COLLOCATION Match the phrases (1–8) to the type of transport (a–h).

1. board a packed, commuter
2. catch a sightseeing, tourist
3. fly in a light, twin-engine
4. book a cabin on a roll-on, roll-off
5. pedal a three-speed, folding
6. hail an empty, black
7. sail on a large, cargo
8. row a leaky, inflatable

a. dinghy
b. cab
c. ship
d. plane
e. ferry
f. train
g. bus
h. bicycle

1.3 ▶44 Listen to a talk about three bicycle-friendly cities. Match the features (1–7) with each city; A (Amsterdam), P (Portland) or C (Copenhagen).

1. Local authorities supply bicycles to workers with less money. _____
2. There is a scheme to stop bicycles from being stolen. _____
3. Almost a third of workers here travel to work by bicycle. _____
4. Cars are banned from part of this city. _____
5. Here cyclists have their own traffic signals. _____
6. Around half of all journeys here are by bicycle. _____
7. Many more people here cycle than ever before. _____

Error warning

Don't confuse *travel* as a noun with *journey* or *trip*.
Travel is an uncountable noun which refers to the general activity: *Air travel is much cheaper than it was in the past.*
Trip refers to an occasion when you go somewhere and come back: *I can't afford to take another trip abroad this year.*
Journey refers to an act of travelling from one place to another, especially in a vehicle: *It's a two-hour train journey from London to York.*
Travel is commonly used as a verb: *I travel to work by bus.*
Journey is only used as a verb in literary, descriptive writing. *Trip* has a different meaning as a verb (see page 198).

214

Getting about 34

1.4 ▶44 Listen again and complete these sentences with words and phrases used by the speaker.

1 People refer to Amsterdam as the _____ of the world.
2 There is an _____ of safe and fast cycle lanes in Amsterdam.
3 There is also an effective scheme designed to prevent the _____ of bicycles in the city.
4 It is possible for people who live in Amsterdam or visitors to _____ bicycles.
5 The creation of cycle paths in Portland has resulted in a _____ in the use of bicycles in the city.
6 Portland was the first city in America to provide adults on _____ with commuter bicycles.
7 The bicycles are all _____ everything needed to use them.
8 The world's most successful community cycling _____ can be found in Copenhagen.
9 In Copenhagen the majority of bicycle paths are separated from the main _____ .
10 There is a 20 kroner _____ when you use one of Copenhagen's public bicycles.

Public transport

2.1 Complete the text with the correct words from the box.

| eco-friendly   fossil fuels   get around   ~~carbon emissions~~ |
| private cars   self-driving vehicles |

Dubai recently opened its first Metro network in a bid to reduce the number of people using their cars and cut (1) _carbon emissions_ . The $7.42 billion project has so far been hailed as a success as thousands of people have opted to use it to (2) _____ the city, as opposed to their cars. It raises the question that, if governments are so enthusiastic about citizens relinquishing their (3) _____ to save the environment, what other alternatives are there? How else are people going to get to work conveniently, do their shopping or generally travel with ease and relative cheapness?

Currently, the majority of public transport runs on (4) _____ which creates pollution and is reliant on finite resources. However, many alternatives, such as (5) _____, are being researched. Some of them may seem like preposterous ideas drawn from science fiction, but the drive to find (6) _____ forms of transport is on.

> **V** Vocabulary note
>
> **get around** = travel to different places: *More and more people are **getting around** by bicycle, especially in big cities.*
>
> **get away with** = escape without punishment for something you have done wrong: *They attacked the old man in the park, but nobody saw them, so they **got away with** their crime.*
>
> **get by** = to cope in a difficult situation: *I couldn't speak the language, but I **got by** with gestures.*
>
> **get out of** = avoid doing something: *He tried to **get out of** going on the school trip, but in the end he had no choice.*
>
> **get round to** = do something after a long delay: *I've had her DVD for weeks, but yesterday I eventually **got round to** giving it back.*

2.2 Answer these questions using appropriate phrasal verbs from the *Vocabulary note*.

1 If you were in an unfamiliar city, how would you travel from place to place?
2 If you were abroad and couldn't speak the language, how would you cope?
3 How do you avoid doing things you don't want to do?

215

34 Getting about

2.3 Read about some possible new forms of public transport and answer these questions.

1. Which of the forms of transport would you like to use? Why?
2. Which do you think would be sensible transport solutions for your local area? Why?
3. Which ideas are unrealistic? Why?

Driverless pods
These vehicles seat four people and run along guideways like miniature trams. The service will not be timetabled, and will resemble a taxi service as a means of getting from A to B. Users will have the advantage of avoiding congested roads and will be able to travel at speeds of up to 32 km/h. Energy consumption per passenger is one quarter that of a car.

Zeppelins
A greener alternative to planes, these flying machines are finally making a comeback. Environmentalists praise the fact that they fly at lower altitudes than planes and use a fraction of the fuel. Another key advantage is that zeppelins do not need a runway to take off.

Backpack helicopter
Strap on a motor attached to a rotor and take to the skies with your very own backpack helicopter. Popular use of this personal flying machine would require individuals to undergo significant training in navigation and safety. Jet-packs, as seen in science-fiction films, seem an even less realistic prospect.

Segway
Powered by electricity, these clean-running, two-wheeled machines allow individuals to travel at speeds of up to 20 km/h. However, they cannot currently be used on most roads. Confined to pavements, users' speeds are restricted.

Slidewalks
Keep moving even while you're standing still when slidewalks replace conventional pavements. In tests, these devices allowed walkers to move at speeds of up to 9 km/h. Airports have long used similar systems in the form of travelators. However, equipping our city streets with slidewalks would be a costly business.

Maglev Trains
These trains use the force of magnetism to drive them, slashing CO_2 emissions and significantly reducing noise pollution in the process. They're even faster than conventional trains, with a potential top speed of 6,400 km/h. The only downside is that maglev trains are incompatible with the existent rail tracks and these would have to be replaced.

2.4 Complete these sentences with the correct prepositions. There are similar sentences in the texts.

1. In most countries, cars are not allowed to drive *to* / *at* speeds of over 110 km/h.
2. Cycling is a greener alternative *to* / *from* other forms of transport.
3. New drivers are not allowed to go *in* / *on* fast roads like motorways.
4. Drivers caught speeding have to have training *in* / *about* speed awareness or face a heavy fine.
5. The pedestrian zone is confined *about* / *to* a very small central area.
6. Make sure you get the right fuel! Diesel is incompatible *with* / *to* petrol engines.

Vocabulary note

means = method or way of doing something. *Means* can be both singular and plural:

*The tram is a cheap **means** of getting around.*

*There are several **means** of transport we can use.*

*We will get there by any **means** possible.*

Exam practice

Getting about 34

Listening Part 1

▶45 You will hear three different extracts. For questions **1 – 6**, choose the answer (**A**, **B** or **C**) which fits best according to what you hear. There are two questions for each extract.

Extract One

You hear a woman asking her friend about a change in his transport habits.

1   On what occasions does he say he used to travel by taxi?
    A   when he couldn't get a lift
    B   when he was on a short journey
    C   when he missed the last bus or train

2   What is the main reason he started walking more?
    A   He was spending too much money on taxis.
    B   He became tired of waiting for taxis.
    C   He realised that walking was beneficial for him.

Extract Two

You hear two people talking about flying.

3   What did the woman think when the pilot started speaking?
    A   She was determined not to lose control of herself.
    B   She was afraid that the plane was in real danger.
    C   She thought the plane was going to turn back because of bad weather.

4   Which is the worst part of flying for the woman?
    A   the last few moments of the flight
    B   the time she spends waiting to board the plane
    C   when the plane is about to leave the ground

Extract Three

You hear part of an interview with a man who is talking about travelling on the London Underground.

5   How did he feel about travelling when he first used the Underground?
    A   He was terrified.
    B   He was overexcited.
    C   He found it very funny.

6   What does he think of the Underground as an adult?
    A   It doesn't inspire any particular feelings in him.
    B   It is surrounded by unnecessary marketing hype.
    C   It is an important part of London's cultural heritage.

> **Exam tip**
>
> For each question there is only one correct answer but you will hear vocabulary related to all of the options. Don't choose your answers too soon. Make sure that what you hear fully answers the question. Remember, you will hear the recording twice.

35 Moods

Attitudes, memory

Attitudes

1.1 Choose the best words to complete these sentences. Which picture (A–E) do they relate to?

1 His eyes *twisted* / *narrowed* and he *frowned* / *wrinkled* deeply, sure signs that he was about to *jump* / *fly off* the handle.
2 As he delivered the *tragic* / *terrific* news, his voice *groaned* / *trembled* and it was clear that he was completely *devastated* / *destroyed*.
3 She just *drives* / *sails* through life without a *conscience* / *care* in the world. I've never met anyone so *laid-back* / *uptight*.
4 I can always tell when he's got something on his *mind* / *chest*, because he *grinds* / *bites* his nails and *stammers* / *stumbles*.
5 She may have her head in the *clouds* / *skies*, but we need more *dramatists* / *dreamers* to get the rest of us to *brighten* / *lighten* up.

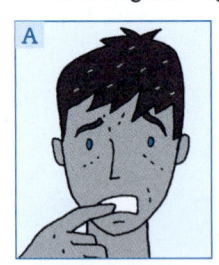

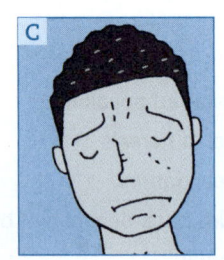

1.2 Now choose the list of adjectives which best describe the people's expressions (A–E).

1 relaxed, calm, contented __B__
2 angry, furious, confrontational _____
3 optimistic, upbeat, positive _____
4 dejected, miserable, tearful _____
5 anxious, apprehensive, nervous _____

1.3 Use an adjective from 1.2 to complete the sentences.

1 The constant rain meant we had a thoroughly __miserable__ time on holiday.
2 When it was time for us to go, she grew almost _____ and I was sorry to leave.
3 When I told him what I'd done to his car, he was obviously very _____. He was literally shaking with rage.
4 I may have looked outwardly _____ but I was actually extremely nervous.
5 Your weekly shopping budget of £20 is hopelessly _____. You'll end up spending much more than that.

Moods 35

1.4 Write the nouns related to these adjectives.

1. angry _anger_
2. anxious _____
3. apprehensive _____
4. calm _____
5. confrontational _____
6. contented _____
7. furious _____
8. miserable _____
9. optimistic _____
10. patient _____
11. positive _____
12. relaxed _____

1.5 Complete these sentences with verbs related to the adjectives in 1.4 above.

1. _Relax_ ! It'll be okay. Nothing's going to go wrong, I promise. Just try to _____ down.
2. The way to deal with bullies like that is simply to _____ them and say you're not going to put up with it any longer.
3. The arrogance of the minister's remarks _____ the opposition leader, who angrily demanded an apology.

1.6 Match an extreme adjective from the box with a gradable adjective which is similar in meaning.

| astonishing | excruciating | devastating | hideous |
| petrifying | ~~superb~~ | ravenous | ludicrous |

1. good ___superb___
2. hungry _____
3. painful _____
4. sad _____
5. scary _____
6. silly _____
7. surprising _____
8. ugly _____

> **V** Vocabulary note
>
> *Angry* is a **gradable** adjective. We can make it stronger or weaker using adverbs, e.g. *very; quite; extraordinarily; a bit; rather; mildly*.
>
> *Furious* is an example of an **extreme** adjective as it includes the idea 'very'. This means we cannot use *very* with *furious* (not ~~very furious~~). To make extreme adjectives stronger we use adverbs meaning 100%, e.g. *absolutely; completely; thoroughly; utterly; totally*:
> *I was totally furious when my brother crashed my car.*
>
> *Really* can be used to make both gradable and extreme adjectives stronger.
>
> There are many exceptions to these rules and it is useful to make a note of adverb + adjective collocations you see:
> *faintly ludicrous, thoroughly miserable, bitterly disappointing, endlessly fascinating*
>
> (See **Unit 7, 2.4** for more on gradable adjectives.)

1.7 COLLOCATION Choose the words which collocate with the words in bold to complete the sentences.

1. You're such an exaggerator! The injection wasn't **absolutely** *devastating / excruciating*. It was *mildly / completely* **painful** at worst.
2. I had a *particularly / totally* **good** meal at the sushi place in town. The only problem is I'm still **completely** *ravenous / hungry*.
3. It was **utterly** *ludicrous / funny* when the girl fled just because the man was *a bit / absolutely* **ugly**.
4. I'm *completely / rather* **petrified** of spiders. They're **totally** *hideous / ravenous*.
5. What **totally** *devastating / petrifying* news. You must both be *bitterly / absolutely* **disappointed**.

1.8 The words *mood* and *attitude* are used in many expressions. Match the sentences (1–5) with the expressions (a–e).

1. He's very up and down.
2. I wouldn't go near him just now.
3. He hates anyone with authority.
4. He's never put off by a challenge.
5. He doesn't feel like going clubbing tonight.

a. He's got a real attitude problem.
b. He's not in the mood.
c. He's in one of his moods.
d. He has terrible mood swings.
e. He's got a real can-do attitude.

35 Moods

Memory

2.1 Think about your own memory and complete these sentences.

1. I have a fantastic memory for _____.
2. I'm terrible at remembering _____.
3. A memorable event was _____.
4. I find it easy to memorise _____.
5. I always remember to _____.
6. As a child, I remember _____.

> **V Vocabulary note**
>
> *Remember* has a different meaning when followed by *to*-infinitive or the *-ing* form of a verb.
>
> *He remembered to phone work to say he was going to be late.* (= It is a fact. He definitely did phone work.)
>
> *He remembers phoning work to say he was going to be late.* (= It is a memory. He thinks he phoned work.)
>
> (See **Unit 10, 2.1** and **2.3** for more on verb + *to*-infinitive / *-ing* patterns.)

2.2 Complete the text with words from the box.

| ear | forgotten | ~~memories~~ | mind | photographic | recall | retain | short-term |

As far as our (1) __memories__ are concerned, my twin sister and I couldn't be more different. She only has to see or hear something once to remember it – it's what they call a (2) _____ memory. And she'll (3) _____ that image or that sound more or less indefinitely. As for me, I've got a (4) _____ like a sieve. If you say something to me now, I'll have (5) _____ it ten minutes later. It's a case of in one (6) _____ and out the other. I'm like an old person – I've got a terrible (7) _____ memory. By contrast, my long-term memory is fantastic. I can still (8) _____ the names of all the other children in my first class at school – that's over thirty years ago.

2.3 COLLOCATION Read the sentences about memories. Put a (✓) if the sentence is about remembering something. Put a (✗) if the sentence is about not remembering / being able to remember.

1. The visit to my old school *triggered an early memory* of my favourite teacher, Mr Bell. _____
2. Psychiatrists used to believe patients' problems were caused by *repressing traumatic childhood memories*. _____
3. A service was held to *honour the memory* of the war dead. _____
4. He refused to move on with his life, *reliving the bitter memories* of the courthouse time and time again. _____
5. My grandma loves that record. She says it *brings back treasured memories* of her youth. _____
6. It's all so *vague*! I need something to *jog my memory*. _____

2.4 Answer these questions using the words in italics from 2.3.

1. Which two adjectives are used to describe a very unpleasant memory? _____
2. Which two words describe memories from when you were young? _____
3. Which three expressions mean 'remind someone of something'? _____
4. Which word could you use to describe a memory which is not clear? _____

Exam practice

Moods 35

Reading and Use of English Part 1

For questions **1 – 8**, read the text below and decide which answer (**A, B, C** or **D**) best fits each gap. There is an example at the beginning **(0)**.

> **Exam tip**
>
> Study the spaces one by one, paying careful attention to the words before and after the gap. The four options you have to choose from will be similar in meaning but only one will fit correctly in the gap. The correct answer may also be the only word to fit grammatically.

Learning new words in a foreign language

Remembering words successfully is a chancy business, but over the last forty years psychologists have found three methods which consistently improve this important language learning **(0)** __B__ . These are: creating a visual **(1)** _____ for the word you want to remember; forming word associations; and recalling the word by **(2)** _____ of a story. **(3)** _____ into attempts to remember lists of words has shown that these methods **(4)** _____ in memory improvements of ten percent over simply reading words once.

Now, new studies have shown solid **(5)** _____ for a fourth method which can be added to the other three; it's surprisingly simple. It only **(6)** _____ saying the word you want to remember to yourself. It doesn't even seem to matter if you don't say the word aloud – it only has to be mouthed. Across eight experiments in which **(7)** _____ were asked to read and remember lists of words, researchers found memory improvements sometimes in **(8)** _____ of ten percent.

0	A capability	**B skill** (circled)	C capacity	D competence
1	A impression	B photo	C copy	D image
2	A means	B ways	C methods	D processes
3	A Enquiries	B Studies	C Research	D Questions
4	A result	B lead	C cause	D produce
5	A indication	B support	C data	D evidence
6	A includes	B needs	C involves	D implies
7	A participants	B applicants	C contestants	D contributors
8	A surplus	B excess	C addition	D extra

221

36 Fame and fortune

Celebrity culture, reality television

Celebrity culture

1.1 Write the names of people you know that fit these descriptions.

1 a national sporting legend _____
2 a television personality _____
3 a big name in showbiz _____
4 a world-famous celebrity _____
5 someone who is famous for no particular reason _____

1.2 Choose the correct words to complete the first part of this text.

Celebrities have immense social capital: they have many social perks and get jobs that are (**1**) *rarely* / *readily* available to ordinary people. Long after they are at the peak of their career, celebrities can still get (**2**) *expensive* / *lucrative* work in areas unconnected to their (**3**) *benefits* / *talents*. A former footballer, for example, might be paid to attend a public (**4**) *appearance* / *entrance* and speak on a subject totally unrelated to their accomplishments.
The mass (**5**) *medium* / *media* plays a key role in promoting the (**6**) *exposure* / *exposé* of celebrities and this has led to celebrity becoming a sought-after status. While many people aspire to achieve fame and envy celebrities, the lifestyle is not without its drawbacks. Some stars who have (**7**) *attained* / *undergone* celebrity often suffer from life in the public eye and the risk of being (**8**) *stalked* / *obsessed* by fans.

V Vocabulary note

The word *celebrity* can be a countable or uncountable noun.
Some envy **celebrities** *and many aspire to* **celebrity**.

a celebrity = a person who is famous
That magazine is full of photographs of international **celebrities**.

celebrity = the state or quality of being famous
Celebrity *has become a sought-after status.*

1.3 Find words and expressions in the text which match these definitions.

1 very large or great _____
2 wanted by many people _____
3 benefits which are not financial _____
4 skills learnt through practice _____
5 want to become in the future _____
6 feel jealous of _____
7 position in society _____
8 attention from the media _____

1.4 Which word in each group is different? Why?

1	celebrity	fame	popularity	prosperity	stardom
2	competence	benefit	gift	skill	talent
3	devotion	envy	infatuation	jealousy	obsession
4	credibility	entitlement	esteem	recognition	respect
5	compensation	fee	payment	perk	reward

1 *Prosperity is not about how much people like you.*

222

Fame and fortune 36

1.5 Complete the second part of the text from 1.2 with words from the box.

| attaining | rewards | consultancy | credibility | non-famous |
| reality | talented | royalty | ~~sectors~~ | value |

Celebrity culture has pervaded almost all **(1)** _sectors_ of society. It is no longer restricted to **(2)** _____, film stars and singers. However, only a small number of people can achieve celebrity. For those who do, the **(3)** _____ can be huge. **(4)** _____ work is often a lucrative area, as is advertising branded products.

Watch any **(5)** _____ TV show and you will find contestants who dream of **(6)** _____ celebrity. However, any fame they achieve is likely to be fleeting and with limited social or economic **(7)** _____.

In many industries, such as the arts, celebrity can be advantageous. Many **(8)** _____ people working in the arts are likely to be relatively poorly paid even though they may be as **(9)** _____ as their more famous counterparts. This results in resentment amongst colleagues, with people actually facing a loss of **(10)** _____.

> ### V Vocabulary note
>
> The prefix *non-* adds the meaning 'not' or 'the opposite of' to adjectives or nouns. Some of the more common words which begin with *non-* include:
> - adjectives: **non**-addictive, **non**-disposable, **non**-essential, **non**-judgemental, **non**-political, **non**-profit-making, **non**-specific, **non**-standard
> - nouns: **non**-believer, **non**-smoker, **non**-swimmer, **non**-fiction

1.6 COLLOCATION Complete the compound nouns in bold with a word from the box.

| attention | coverage | ~~empire~~ | endorsements | gossip | lifestyle |

1. He has a **global media** _empire_ worth billions of dollars and his wife is a supermodel.
2. She wanted to marry a footballer so that she could experience a **celebrity** _____.
3. Designers try to get **celebrity** _____ of their products as a kind of walking advertisement.
4. **Media** _____ of the royal visit largely focused on the princess's wardrobe.
5. **Celebrity** _____, true or otherwise, sells a lot of newspapers these days.
6. The persistence of **media** _____ from the likes of paparazzi can be uncomfortable and intrusive.

1.7 Find and correct the two misspelt words in each sentence.

1. ~~Paparrazi~~ who stack celebrities can earn large sums of money. _Paparazzi_ , _____
2. I dislike famos people, but think I still envie them a bit. _____ , _____
3. Celebrities who acheive fame very quickly are often forgetten just as quickly. _____ , _____
4. Many very tallented individuels never become famous. _____ , _____
5. Retired sports personnalities often earn money form speaking fees. _____ , _____
6. I highly recomend her biography. It's full of wierd celebrity anecdotes. _____ , _____

223

36 Fame and fortune

Reality television

2.1 Choose the definition of reality television which is closest to your personal opinion.

1 A TV genre featuring ordinary people in unscripted dramatic or humorous situations.
2 Live television that monitors the behaviour of real people in manufactured situations.
3 A type of programming which shows how ordinary people behave in everyday life.

2.2 ▶46 Listen to three people talking about reality television and choose the phrase from the box which represents their view. You do not need to use one of the phrases.

| complete rubbish   my kind of television   a bit of an embarrassment   relaxing entertainment |

Speaker 1 _____   Speaker 2 _____   Speaker 3 _____

2.3 ▶46 Listen again and complete these sentences with words used by the speakers.

1 Speaker 1 compares watching a reality television programme to reading a _____.
2 Speaker 1 thinks people need programmes like this to relax and _____.
3 Speaker 2 compares reality television to a _____ which you can't look away from.
4 Speaker 2 does not approve of producers manipulating the _____ of reality TV shows.
5 Speaker 3 is interested in how new acquaintances manage to find _____.
6 Speaker 3 is fascinated by the _____ of people who have never met.

2.4 WORD BUILDING Complete the table with words which have related meanings.

Noun	Verb	Adjective
_____ (person) _____ (problem)	_____	addictive _____ (problem)
drama _____ (film/TV adaptation) _____ (person)	_____	_____
fantasy _____ (person)	_____	_____
_____ _____ (person)	manipulate	_____

2.5 Answer these questions. The expressions in italics can be found in the recording script.

1 What have you read or watched that you consider *trashy*? _____
2 What are some of the things that you do to *unwind*? _____
3 What, on TV, do you consider to be *compulsive viewing*? _____
4 How do you *find common ground* with new acquaintances? _____
5 What is something that you like which *is not everyone's cup of tea*? _____

Exam practice

Fame and fortune **36**

Reading and Use of English Part 2

For questions **1 – 8**, read the text below and think of the word which best fits each gap. Use only one word in each gap. There is an example at the beginning **(0)**.

> **Exam tip**
>
> Look at the words before and after the gap in the text. This will help you to decide what type of word you need, such as a preposition, an article, a pronoun or an auxiliary verb. Missing words may be part of phrasal verbs or fixed phrases.

The Hollywood Star System

The star system was the method **(0)** __of__ creating, promoting and exploiting movie stars of early twentieth-century Hollywood cinema. In the past, studios used **(1)** _____ select promising young male and female actors, then glamorise and create new personalities for **(2)** _____, often inventing new names and even new family and social backgrounds. Legendary actors **(3)** _____ were put through the star system include Cary Grant and Joan Crawford.

The star system put an emphasis **(4)** _____ the image rather than the acting skill. **(5)** _____ was expected that women would behave like ladies at all times, and were never allowed to leave the house without stylish clothes and full make-up. Men always had to behave like gentlemen **(6)** _____ public.

Just **(7)** _____ studio executives, public relations staff and agents worked alongside the actor to create their star personality, so they would work together to cover **(8)** _____ any incidents that could damage the public image of the star. A star's personal problems, such as divorce, would be suppressed.

37 Relationships
Families, friends

Families

1.1 Quickly read the article to find the answers to these questions.

1. The writer names five roles that grandparents have in family life. The first is *adviser*. What are the other four?
2. When was it easier than it is now to teach children about beliefs and values?
3. What phenomenon is responsible for the changes in children today, according to the writer?

The role of grandparents in children's upbringing

(1) The word *grandparents* is descriptive of the unique dual parenting role that this generation assume. It emphasises the vital part they play in family life. With a wealth of old world experience behind them, and with the unique ability to metamorphose from advisers or mediators into listeners or friends, they can offer support and stability in an ever-changing world.

(2) The underlying sense of responsibility that goes with this is tremendous. Grandparents perform a balancing act between the needs of their adult children and those of their grandchildren. This role is varied. It is imperial at times, muted at others. It goes underground whenever required, but it is solid and absolutely dependable.

(3) Grandparents often bridge the gap between parents and their children. Rebellious, independent children who are trying to find their feet are almost always at loggerheads with their parents. The role of grandparents can be very important provided they act as impartial judges and are able to convey this feeling to both parties. Grandchildren prefer to listen to their grandparents rather than their parents, who often find themselves up against a brick wall.

(4) One important thing, which seems to be missing in the lives of children today, is a sense of family, values, beliefs and principles. This is where the grandparents step in. However, instilling beliefs and values is not as easy as it was fifty or sixty years ago. Then, no questions were asked and there was an implicit sense of trust. With changing times and changing outlooks, children have started to question the validity of everything around them. Globalisation has eroded their sense of belonging and weakened identification with their roots. Science and technology force them to doubt every traditional belief.

(5) Parents, who have so many demands on their time, are perhaps not in the best position to instil traditional values in their offspring. Children are very demanding and grandparents, without appearing to be pushy, have both the time and the experience to deal with tantrums. They can appease, soothe and impart values with tremendous ease. Our Indian culture is rich and varied, but how many children recognise this? Grandparents can teach them to appreciate cultural traditions and inform their moral development.

1.2 Match these expressions from paragraphs 1, 2 and 3 with their definitions.

1. have a wealth of
2. perform a balancing act
3. be at loggerheads
4. bridge a gap
5. be up against a brick wall

a. find it impossible to make progress
b. deal with different demands at the same time
c. provide a connection
d. be unable to agree
e. have a lot of

Relationships 37

1.3 Read the text again and find words which match these definitions.

1. a strong state which is unlikely to change or fail (paragraph 1) _____
2. trustworthy and reliable (paragraph 2) _____
3. not favouring one side in a disagreement (paragraph 3) _____

> **V Vocabulary note**
>
> The usual form of nouns from phrasal verbs is: *verb + particle*:
>
> Communications **broke down** between the parties.
> There was a **breakdown** in communication.
> The rocket is due to **lift off** at 5.30 this afternoon.
> **Liftoff** is at 5.30 this afternoon.
>
> Another form these nouns take is: *particle + verb*:
>
> The disease **broke out** in the poorest part of the city. The **outbreak** started in the poorest part of the city.
>
> Here are some more examples:
>
> **set out** / from the **outset**, **take in** / this year's **intake**, **cry out** / a public **outcry**

1.4 Now complete these sentences using words and phrases from 1.2 and 1.3.

1. Adults often have to perform *a balancing act* between looking after their children and caring for their ageing parents.
2. Money from parents often _____ between what students can earn and what they need to pay out.
3. My best friend is thoroughly _____. She's always there when I need her.
4. My brother and I never really got on very well. We were constantly _____.
5. Parents and grandparents provide the _____ which children need in their early years.
6. Parents should not take sides in their children's disputes. They should remain _____.

1.5 Which of these verbs from paragraphs 4 and 5 have similar meanings? Use the text to help you.

| appease   appreciate   doubt   erode   impart   inform |
| instil   question   recognise   soothe   teach   weaken |

appease – soothe

1.6 COLLOCATION Which of the adjectives in each box CANNOT replace the word in italics in the sentence below it? Why?

1. | idyllic   troubled   traumatic   turbulent |

   The siblings have some behavioural problems which are thought to result from their *difficult* childhood.
   An idyllic childhood does not cause problems.

2. | middle-class   privileged   tough   sheltered |

   My *comfortable* upbringing meant there were a lot of survival skills for me to learn when I left home.

3. | close-knit   dysfunctional   loving   supportive |

   I'm lucky to have a *strong* family, who'll always be there for me.

4. | committed   solid   stable   uneasy |

   They told me that the success of their marriage came from their *secure* relationship.

5. | concerned   distraught   pushy   worried |

   I was met at the hospital by my *anxious* parents, who suddenly seemed very old and fragile.

227

37 Relationships

Friends

2.1 Read these quotes about friendship. Put a (✓) if you agree. Put a (✗) if you disagree.

1 'A true friend is one who overlooks your failures and tolerates your successes.' (Doug Larson) _____
2 'You can make more friends in two months by becoming interested in other people than you can in two years by trying to get other people interested in you.' (Dale Carnegie) _____
3 'Few friendships would survive if each one knew what his friend says of him behind his back.' (Blaise Pascal) _____

2.2 Complete this email to a radio programme with words from the box.

advice   conflicts   contribute   ~~go into~~   partnership   ruin

My friends and I would like to (1) _go into_ business together. I think it would be an exciting opportunity, but I am reluctant because of potential (2) _____ that may (3) _____ our relationships. Does anyone have any words of (4) _____ about doing business with friends? I'd also like some suggestions on how we should structure our business (5) _____ , given that all of us will be making a different cash investment and can (6) _____ in a range of different ways.

2.3 ▶47 Four people called the radio show to give their advice. How many of them do you think will advise *against* going into business with friends? Listen and check.

2.4 ▶47 Listen again and match the speakers with the advice they give (a–d).

Speaker 1 _____
Speaker 2 _____
Speaker 3 _____
Speaker 4 _____

a warns against business partners who get upset easily.
b suggests including people who are not friends in the business.
c advises against endangering a friendship for the sake of profit.
d stresses the importance of written plans and legal documents.

2.5 Match the phrasal verbs in italics with their definitions.

1 If business partners *fall out*, the business may suffer.
2 We really don't want to *mess up* our relationship.
3 It looks like my brother and his girlfriend have *broken up*.
4 My father *fell for* my mother the first time they met.
5 Real friends will never *let* you *down*.
6 They used to be best friends, but they've *drifted apart*.

a become less close over time
b begin to feel romantic love for
c disappoint or fail someone
d end a romantic relationship
e argue and be on bad terms
f create problems, damage

2.6 Complete the sentences with a noun from the box.

break-up   falling out   letdown

1 We had such high expectations of her, so this kind of behaviour is a real _____ .
2 The news of the _____ of the star's marriage was all over the papers.
3 They had a terrible _____ . I don't think they'll be speaking to each other for a while.

Exam practice

Relationships 37

Listening Part 3

▶48 You will hear part of a radio interview in which two psychologists, Stella Burrows and Simon Peres, are giving advice to office workers. For questions **1 – 6**, choose the answer (**A**, **B**, **C** or **D**) which fits best according to what you hear.

1 Why does Stella mention 'the smooth talker' and other office types?
  A They are successful personas to adopt.
  B They are people who don't contribute much to a company.
  C They are kinds of people we should try to avoid in offices.
  D They are characters every office worker will recognise.

2 According to Simon, what should 'live-to-work' employees consider?
  A the best way to impress their boss
  B what colleagues really think of them
  C achieving a work-life balance
  D perfection is desirable

3 According to Stella, why might colleagues be irritated by 'work-to-live' types?
  A They seem to have no ambition.
  B Their excuses may be unconvincing.
  C They may not do their fair share of work.
  D Their lack of effort goes unnoticed by senior staff.

4 Simon thinks the majority of employees
  A are too conscientious.
  B are neither of the types described.
  C do not make enough effort.
  D have a healthy work-life balance.

5 According to Stella, what will happen if someone does not take their job seriously?
  A They will irritate their colleagues.
  B Their colleagues will feel obliged to work harder.
  C Their colleagues will envy them.
  D They will lose the trust of their colleagues.

6 Stella warns employees against
  A constantly seeking advice from superiors.
  B asking colleagues for their views.
  C giving advice which was not asked for.
  D openly criticising other people's contributions.

> ### Exam tip
> Before you listen, read through the questions and underline the main idea in them. This will provide a focus for your listening. While listening, wait until the speaker has finished talking before you choose your answer. Listen for the idea expressed in the four possible answers rather than for specific words.

38 Time off

Holidays, enjoying exercise

Holidays

1.1 Answer these questions from a holiday questionnaire.

1 What was your most recent holiday destination?
2 How did you travel?
3 Why did you choose this destination?
4 What kind of accommodation did you choose?

1.2 Complete the description of childhood holidays with words and phrases from the box.

| destination | entertainments | ~~international flights~~ | isolated beach | local cuisine |
| pack | self-catering | spectacular scenery | tropical resorts | two-week |

When I was a child it was fairly unusual to go on a foreign holiday. The prices of
(1) _international flights_ were exorbitant compared to those offered by today's budget airlines. Package holidays to (2) _____ were pretty much unheard-of. Instead my parents would
(3) _____ our aged car with the necessary belongings, and our family holiday would begin with a twelve-hour drive through the night. Our (4) _____ was always the same: exotic Scotland.

Each year, my parents booked a different (5) _____ cottage, usually next to an
(6) _____ and invariably with no mod cons whatsoever. The beds were always lumpy and damp. There wouldn't even be a washing machine, never mind a television.

No doubt we were surrounded by (7) _____ , but this meant little to me or my sister. Plastic buckets and spades were the basis of all our holiday (8) _____ . Armed with these and a towel, we would tear down to the beach every morning. We built extravagant castles, we buried my father alive, we saved the lives of stranded jellyfish, we collected jewels, and we dug to Australia. Summer holidays lasted at least a year back then.

I pity the kids today with their (9) _____ breaks in the sun. Who wants all-inclusive resorts boasting restaurants serving authentic (10) _____ ? Who needs artificial lagoons featuring wave machines and plastic waterfalls? Show me an eight-year-old girl on a Scottish beach with a bucket and spade and I'll show you what real holiday fun is all about.

1.3 COLLOCATION Find collocations in the Vocabulary note which match these definitions.

1 a break for parents and their children _a family holiday_
2 a holiday with outdoor activities _____
3 a holiday in another country _____
4 a day off from work for everyone _____
5 a holiday at the seaside _____
6 to arrange and pay for a holiday _____

V Vocabulary note

- verb + holiday: *go on/have a/take a/ book a/cancel a holiday*
- adjective + holiday: *public/annual/ two-week/foreign/exotic holiday*
- noun + holiday: *package/beach/ family/adventure holiday*
- holiday + noun: *holiday resort/ destination/season/insurance*

Time off 38

1.4 Write sentences of your own which include these collocations.

1 cancel a holiday   2 winter holiday   3 holiday resort   4 holiday insurance

1.5 Match each word in the box with a word in italics with a similar meaning.

artificial   authentic   exotic   extravagant   ~~isolated~~   local   spectacular   unheard-of

                          isolated

1 We wanted to honeymoon in a *remote* location with *incredible* views.
2 We searched high and low for *genuine regional* handicrafts to bring back as souvenirs.
3 I think it's *wasteful* to build a *man-made* beach when there are homeless people in this city.
4 If you want to go to a *far-flung* destination, you'll have to pay excessive amounts of money.
5 In the 1980s, Thailand was almost *unknown* as a tourist destination for Europeans, but now it's very popular.

Enjoying exercise

2.1 COLLOCATION Match the nouns in the box with the correct list of noun collocations below.

aerobics   ~~cycling~~   dance   football   martial arts   swimming   tennis   walking

1 *cycling*   accident, enthusiast, helmet
2 _____ class, routine, workout
3 _____ instructor, fighter, expert
4 _____ tour, boots, pace
5 _____ pitch, league, tournament
6 _____ lesson, coach, court
7 _____ costume, goggles, pool
8 _____ partner, move, step

2.2 Complete the following sentences with collocations from 2.1.

1 She's something of a _____*martial arts expert*_____ and is a black belt in judo and karate.
2 Our PE teacher used to make us run the length of the _____ if we misbehaved.
3 The traffic was so bad that we crept along at a _____ for most of the journey.
4 I can't come in the pool with you. I've left my _____ and my towel at home.
5 I go with some of the other girls to a regular _____ which keeps me fairly fit.
6 She needs a new _____ as David just doesn't move well enough.

231

38 Time off

2.3 Think of adjectives that express your personal opinion of each form of exercise in 2.1.

*For me aerobics is **exhausting** but **exhilarating**.*

2.4 ▶49 Listen to someone talking about exercise. Are these sentences true (T) or false (F) according to the speaker?

1 You have to be serious about getting into shape. _____
2 There is no need to drastically change your schedule to be more active. _____
3 Shopping is a healthy activity. _____
4 If you dance, you should make bigger movements. _____
5 Swimming has three major advantages as an exercise. _____
6 Gyms charge too much money. _____
7 Other people can be distracting when you're exercising. _____
8 The benefits of exercise are worth a little pain. _____

> **V Vocabulary note**
>
> *Exercise* can be uncountable or countable as a noun.
>
> The uncountable noun describes physical activity that people do to keep fit and healthy:
> *Regular **exercise** is good for you.*
> *Swimming is my favourite form of **exercise**.*
>
> The countable noun has several uses:
> - specific physical or mental activity to improve something:
>   *I do stomach **exercises** every day. I'm not keen on doing grammar **exercises**.*
> - a course of action to achieve something specific:
>   *The company statement is part of a public relations **exercise**.*

2.5 ▶49 Listen again and complete the sentences with words and phrases used by the speaker.

1 She recommends that busy people make some _____ to their daily routine.
2 She says that dancing at home is an enjoyable way of _____ .
3 She thinks that people are discouraged by the _____ at gyms.
4 She encourages listeners with a favourite sport to be more than just a _____ .
5 She reassures listeners that if they include neighbours in their plans, they'll be _____ .

2.6 Complete the phrases in bold in the questions with the correct prepositions. There are similar sentences in the recording script. Answer the questions about yourself.

1 What kind of things **put you** _____ exercising?
   _____
2 When do you **catch** _____ **with gossip**?
   _____
3 How do you **burn** _____ **calories**?
   _____
4 What do you do when you**'re low** _____ **energy**?
   _____
5 What kind of social activities do you **hang** _____ **from**?
   _____
6 How often do you **get out and** _____ in your neighbourhood?
   _____

> **V Vocabulary note**
>
> The phrasal verb particle *off* has a number of meanings:
> - departure or separation, e.g. *get off, close off*:
>   *They've **closed off** the city centre because of a bomb scare.*
> - beginning, e.g. *set off, start off, trigger off*:
>   *The incident **triggered off** a political debate.*
> - stop or cancel, e.g. *call off, cut off, switch off*:
>   *They've **called off** tomorrow's meeting.*
> - decrease or completion, e.g. *burn off, wear off, tail off*:
>   *The effect of the medicine is **wearing off** now.*

Exam practice

Reading and Use of English Part 8

You are going to read an article about travelling in China containing advice for European tourists. For questions **1 – 10**, choose from the people (**A – E**). Each person may be chosen more than once.

Which writer

advises tourists not to spend time worrying about getting the best deals?	1
gives advice to tourists considering travelling alone?	2
expresses regrets about communication with local people?	3
mentions the advantages of being with somebody who can speak the local language?	4
suggests a way to meet ordinary people on public transport?	5
suggests a region where travellers can find cheap accommodation?	6
warns against travelling by plane?	7
suggests an economical way of paying for a range of services?	8
advises people to book before they travel by rail?	9
warns travellers that one of the nighttime travel options is illegal?	10

Exam practice

China on a shoestring?

A
You can probably manage on less than 30 euros per day. To do this, you'll have to look for the lowest fares on buses or trains and stay in hostels or budget hotels, of which there are many in southwest China. Taking the train is the best way of getting from one big city to the next, but buses are more economical. There are buses you can sleep on for long journeys – but having said that, they're pretty uncomfortable. One thing I can't stress enough: you'll miss out on the real China if you fly. Getting off the beaten track is best done by other means. However, in rural areas the language barrier was a challenge for me. I'm only sorry I wasn't able to converse more effectively.

B
I'd always liked the thought of being a solo traveller, but I think I'd probably had a better time going on something organised. My travel and accommodation cost about a hundred pounds a week, then there was food and flights to China on top of that. Once I'd paid, I didn't have to worry about money or anything else and I had people to share the experience with. I'd really recommend this option if you are in the same position. Our guide was a native speaker but fluent in English. He accompanied us everywhere and made everything so easy for the group.

C
Beijing seems really expensive to start with, but you soon find out how to get by on a budget and still eat well – the restaurants near the station are a good place to start. If you're going to travel around China by train, I'd suggest that you buy your ticket in advance, especially if you want to travel on a public holiday. And if you choose the cheaper seats, you'll be sure to get acquainted with the real Chinese. I can guarantee that they'll be interested in you. I've heard that you can travel pretty cheaply by plane these days, but I don't feel like I missed out. I would not have come into contact with so many locals if I had prioritised my own comfort whilst travelling.

D
If you go all the way to China, make sure you do as much as possible, instead of constantly looking for the least expensive ways of doing things. Obviously organised trips cost a little more than doing everything yourself, but I think you have a better experience. The travel reps are very efficient and want to make sure you get a good impression of the places you visit. As everything's set up in advance, you avoid misunderstandings and difficulties which can arise if you're trying to make arrangements in an unknown language.

E
Compared with travel in Europe, the cost of public transport in Chinese cities is incredibly cheap. In the capital, Beijing, for example, it only costs the equivalent of 30 cents to travel by underground anywhere in the city. If you buy what they call a "pass", you can travel around the city, but it can also be used to pay for public phones, for taxi fares or even to buy things in supermarkets. In many cities, taxis are a real option for travellers on a tight budget. If you share with other tourists, it can be cheaper than taking the bus. If you intend to go out at night, there may be night buses, but taxis are the most likely choice of transport, although some private citizens offer a taxi service in their private cars. These are often cheaper than taxis, but if you use them, you may be in danger, and you should remember that taking a "black taxi" is actually forbidden in China.

39 Media

News and information, press freedom

News and information

1.1 Which of these sources of information are important to you? Put a (✓).

internet blogs _____   24-hour TV news _____   in-depth news analysis _____

1.2 Complete the text with words and phrases from the box.

| access to | directly | expert analyst | media channels | mobile devices |
| reported | ~~stay up-to-date~~ | subscribe to | targeted information | tuning in |

Information sources of the future

The first and most dramatic change is the advent of social news. Social news is rapidly becoming the means by which we (1) _stay up-to-date_ with what is going on in the world. News is no longer (2) _____ solely by journalists. News can now come from anyone – bypassing the traditional (3) _____ . Instead of having an edited version of what a(n) (4) _____ is saying, we hear it straight from the source. Social news is about getting information (5) _____ and unfiltered.

A new wave of entertainment has also arrived, one dominated by games, video and audio streams. Instead of (6) _____ to a TV channel, we decide what to watch and when to watch it. We no longer have to (7) _____ channels on which other people choose what we see. We control everything ourselves.

And a new concept in the form of (8) _____ is slowly emerging. We are already seeing an increasing number of services on (9) _____ which provide information for the particular area that you are in. For example, there are so-called 'geo-targeting services' which provide you with a list of restaurants within reach of your location rather than showing you establishments worldwide.

The number of these services is going to explode in years to come. In a world where we have (10) _____ more information than we can consume, selecting that which is relevant will be a very important element of delivery. And this will expand far beyond the simple geo-targeting that we see today.

1.3 Find words and phrases in the text which match these definitions.

1. ignore a normal part of procedure to progress more directly _____bypass_____
2. not edited or censored _____
3. news from websites where members decide the stories which are given priority _____
4. appear for the first time _____
5. use _____

V Vocabulary note

The original meaning of the word *channel* was a passage for water: *The English Channel lies between England and mainland Europe.*

It is now also used to mean a way to communicate information: *diplomatic channels, television channel*

Channel can also be used as a verb, meaning do something in a particular direction: *He needs to channel his energy into something more positive.*

235

39 Media

1.4 WORD BUILDING Complete the table with words which have related meanings.

Noun	Verb	Adjective
analyst (person) _____ (process)	_____	_____ _____
_____ _____	dominate	_____
_____	emerge	_____ _____
_____ (process) _____ (person)	subscribe	_____ (too much demand) _____ (not enough demand)
_____ (event) _____ (substance)	explode	_____
_____ (action) _____ (person)	consume	_____ (made to be consumed)

1.5 Complete these sentences using words from the table in 1.4.

1 I must renew my _subscription_ to *Time Magazine*, which runs out next month.
2 It has been widely reported that three civilians have been injured in a bomb _____ in the city centre.
3 A good journalist can _____ a situation quickly, process a large quantity of information and report what's happening accurately.
4 Comparison websites were one of the great successes of the dotcom boom. They allowed _____ to shop around before making their final buying decisions.
5 The _____ of online media has affected the sale of traditional newspapers and magazines.
6 Three rival companies are fighting for _____ of the information technology marketplace.

1.6 COLLOCATION All of the words below collocate with *device*, e.g. *a mobile device*. Which word is different in each list (1–3)? Why?

1	explosive	electronic	mechanical	nuclear
2	digital	handheld	mobile	portable
3	communication	navigation	labour-saving	storage

> **Error warning**
>
> The adjective *big* is often used when *great*, *large* or *wide* would be more appropriate.
> - LARGE: *a large number/a large quantity/a large amount*
> - GREAT: *great pleasure/great importance/great fun/great success*
> - WIDE: *a wide choice/a wide range/a wide variety*
> - BIG: *a big increase/a big improvement/a big problem/a big surprise/a big impact*

Press freedom

2.1 What does the term *freedom of the press* mean to you? Put a (✓) if you agree with a statement.

1 Newspapers can publish anything they like even if it is not true. _____
2 Newspapers can publish anything, but they must be able to prove that it is true. _____
3 Newspapers can publish anything as long as it is not politically sensitive. _____
4 Journalists and reporters do not have to reveal their sources of information. _____

Media 39

2.2 Complete this news story with one word which best fits each gap.

Politicians in Iceland are developing laws (1) __to__ improve freedom of speech. The 'Icelandic Modern Media Initiative' is their response to increasing pressures on the freedom of information. The laws, which are some of the most liberal in the world, are being introduced (2) _____ the aim of protecting freedom of speech in Iceland as (3) _____ as increasing the country's attractiveness to journalists.

The initiative aims to make (4) _____ possible for journalists, bloggers and publishers to publish (5) _____ fear of punishment and focuses on the need to protect sources from any investigation (6) _____ their identity. (7) _____ theory, foreign media companies operating out of Iceland could also benefit from these laws.

2.3 ▶50 Listen to four speakers reacting to Iceland's new press freedom law. Answer these questions for each speaker.

1 Are they in favour of the new law?
2 Do they think it will be completely successful?

2.4 ▶51 Listen to the first speaker again and complete the text with words she uses.

Iceland wants (1) _____ journalism to be free of unjustified interference by the rich and powerful. Although I thoroughly approve of the idea, the difficulty is that the rich and powerful also profit from freedom of (2) _____ by publishing material which is either a gross infringement of the (3) _____ of an individual, or misinforms the general public on important issues. Allowing international media organisations to say what they like, free from any (4) _____, creates a new form of totalitarian state. Iceland risks creating libel tourists – media corporations that want to profit, without fear of correction or sanction, at the (5) _____ of the individual.

> **V** Vocabulary note
>
> Notice how the speakers use adverbs to strengthen their expressions of opinion:
> I *thoroughly* approve of the idea.
> I *wholeheartedly* support Iceland's move.
> This is a fantastic proposal that will *undoubtedly* help news organisations.
> I *honestly* don't think that it's going to make much difference.

2.5 Complete these sentences with your own ideas.

1 I honestly think _____
2 I genuinely believe _____
3 I wholeheartedly approve of _____
4 I fundamentally disagree with _____

2.6 Choose the correct definitions for the words in italics used by the speakers.

1 '... by publishing *material* ...'
   a substance which objects are made from
   b information used when writing something

2 '... without fear of *sanction* ...'
   a an action taken to make people obey a law
   b official approval or permission

3 '... one European country *revises* its laws ...'
   a to study something previously learned
   b to change something in order to improve it

4 '... a fantastic and innovative *proposal* ...'
   a statement of opinion or judgement
   b formal suggestion or plan

Exam practice

Reading and Use of English Part 4

For questions **1 – 6**, complete the second sentence so that it has a similar meaning to the first sentence, using the word given. **Do not change the word given**. You must use between **three** and **six** words, including the word given. Here is an example **(0)**.

> **Exam tip**
>
> Check that you have not used too many or two few words. Remember that if you use contractions, for example *isn't*, this counts as two words, not one.
>
> Check that you have not kept any unnecessary words from the first sentence.
>
> Check that the grammar of your sentence is correct and that you have not changed the given word in any way.

0 Do you think you could buy me a newspaper when you're out?
   WONDERING
   I *was wondering whether* you could buy me a newspaper when you're out.

1 When I leave university, I hope to become a serious investigative journalist.
   AMBITION
   When I leave university, _____ to become a serious investigative journalist.

2 Individuals are not wealthy enough to take international media corporations to court.
   SUE
   Individuals cannot _____ international media corporations.

3 Traditional newspapers will probably have disappeared by the year 2020.
   LIKELY
   By the year 2020, _____ will have disappeared.

4 Regular television broadcasts began in 1937.
   SAW
   1937 _____ regular television broadcasts.

5 I don't think I could live without a daily newspaper.
   IMAGINE
   I _____ without a daily newspaper.

6 I spent all morning looking for the information I wanted.
   TOOK
   It _____ for the information I wanted.

40 The world of work
Employment patterns, economic migration

Employment patterns

1.1 Which of these industries are people employed in where you live? Put a (✓).

agriculture ___ entertainment ___ mining ___
construction ___ finance ___ public services ___
customer services ___ insurance ___ retail ___
education ___ manufacture ___ technology ___

1.2 Match each word list with one of the industries in 1.1.

1 coverage; premium; payout; policy _insurance_
2 satisfaction; expectations; bill; loyalty _____
3 contractor; labourer; site; estate _____
4 mineral; extraction; pit; drill _____
5 harvest; pesticide; tractor; produce _____
6 venue; hospitality; promotion; festival _____

V Vocabulary note

- **make an employee redundant**; **lay an employee off** (informal) = an employer no longer needs members of staff:
*My father was/has been **made redundant**.*
*They're **laying me off** next month.*
- **dismiss an employee**; **fire/sack an employee** (informal) = an employee is unsuitable:
*He was **fired** because he always came in late.*
*The management **dismissed** him for misconduct.*
- **resign** = the employee chooses to leave the employer:
*I **resigned** two weeks ago.*
- **retire** = an employee has come to the end of their career:
*My dad **retired** when he was 62.*

1.3 ▶52 Listen to three people talking about work. Are these sentences true (T) or false (F)?

Speaker 1
1 She got her first job in a local factory. ___
2 She now works in India. ___

Speaker 2
3 He has lost two jobs. ___
4 He is quite relaxed about having lost his job. ___

Speaker 3
5 His father used to run the farm. ___
6 He employs five people. ___

1.4 ▶52 Listen again and complete these sentences with words used by the speakers.

1 When Speaker 1 left school, there was very little _____ .
2 Speaker 1 was trained in _____ .
3 The work Speaker 1 did when she was younger is now done in an Indian _____ .
4 Speaker 2's father _____ at the age of sixty-five.
5 Speaker 2 has been _____ from two jobs.
6 Speaker 2 thinks it is more worrying to be _____ in middle age.
7 Speaker 3 doubts that his children will _____ him on the farm.
8 Speaker 3 finds it difficult to make enough money to _____ .

40 The world of work

1.5 Which formal words from the box can replace the words in italics in the sentences?

| acquire | compensation | dictate | dismiss | disturbs | employer | ~~enquiries~~ |

1. We always get a lot of *questions* from customers who have misplaced their bills. ____enquiries____
2. Employment laws *lay down* the warnings we have to give an employee before we *sack* them. _____
3. What *bothers* me is the significant increase in the number of unemployed graduates. _____
4. During the week you will *pick up* many of the IT skills needed in the modern workplace. _____
5. If you hurt yourself at work, your *boss* may have to give you some *money*. _____

1.6 Choose the correct word in these sentences.

1. I'll be leaving job / <u>work</u> in about ten minutes' time.
2. I came to London to improve my English and now I am planning to find a job / work here.
3. He must get to job / work by 8 o'clock, otherwise he'll lose his job / work.
4. I just need the money. I'm prepared to do job / work of any kind.
5. If you do this, you'll have more job / work and I'll have an easier job / work.

> **Error warning**
>
> *Job* is a countable noun which refers to a particular employment:
> *When she left college, she got a **job** as a magazine editor.*
> *Work* is an uncountable noun which describes the general activity in which we use effort:
> *I've got so much **work** to do.*
> *Work* is also a verb.

1.7 COLLOCATION Complete the compound nouns in these sentences with words from the table.

| JOB | ~~description~~ | market | offer | opportunities | satisfaction | security | seekers |
| WORK | clothes | colleagues | environment | experience | load | permit | space |

1. The **job** ____description____ says you need to have at least some relevant **work** _____.
2. I get absolutely no **job** _____ when my **work** _____ is so high.
3. **Job** _____ cannot be guaranteed during an economic downturn.
4. To create a healthy **work** _____, lighting, space and noise levels must be taken into consideration.
5. She's waiting for her **work** _____ to arrive and then she can accept that **job** _____.
6. The **job** _____ is particularly tough for **job** _____ fresh from school or college.
7. Many of my **work** _____ are looking for new **job** _____ outside the company.
8. When you join us next week, you'll need to bring suitable **work** _____ and please remember to keep your **work** _____ free from clutter.

1.8 Write a sentence about the country you come from for each of the issues in the box.

| child labour   equal opportunities   executive pay   ~~industrial action~~   migrant labour |
| minimum wage   redundancy   unemployment   retirement age   work-life balance |

Industrial action by airline staff disrupted flight schedules in the UK last year.

240

40 The world of work

Economic migration

2.1 Read the text and underline the parts which give you the information in these sentences.

1. Paula found Ireland depressing.
2. Paula is not sorry she moved to New York.
3. Paula expected to find a good job in Ireland.
4. Paula was determined to be promoted.

Ireland's brain drain

Complete with a degree from a top Irish University and ready to join the world of work Paula McGrath struggled to find a job at home, so she decided to try her luck in the USA and escape the *doom and gloom* of the Irish economy. Now she can be found working in a restaurant in New York.

I graduated in Media Studies and came here to the US, which for many is the land of opportunity. I haven't landed the job of my dreams yet, but the excitement of living and working in a city like New York is like a dream come true in itself.

I always thought that I would stay in Ireland after I had graduated. The days when the country had a *thriving* economy were long gone, but there were still jobs for the more educated members of the *workforce*. At university I was aware that I couldn't wait for a job opportunity to *spring up* though, as there were plenty of people to fill gaps in the labour market when jobs were created.

At the same time Ireland was continuing to *churn out* more and more highly educated and highly motivated graduates, so I needed a plan to be able to compete. I decided that I would study as hard as I could and get the grades I needed to embark on a career.

I graduated with good grades and I was lucky enough to find a job in Dublin that had really good *prospects*. From my first day there I imagined myself climbing the corporate ladder and becoming an executive in the company. It was not to be though; after six months the company went bust and, all of a sudden, I found myself without a job.

I spent about six months trying to find a permanent job, but apart from some *freelance* work I couldn't find anything. I started to feel my work *ethic* disappear. It was at this point that I decided that it was time for a change. I came to the decision that I would try my luck in America. I applied for and got my visa and I haven't looked back since.

2.2 Find words and phrases in italics from the text which match these definitions.

1. all the workers in a particular company, city, country, etc. ___workforce___
2. self-employed and working for many organisations _____
3. atmosphere of hopelessness _____
4. belief in the importance of work to life _____
5. produce something quickly and in large quantities _____
6. chances to be successful in the future _____
7. appeared suddenly _____
8. successful and profitable _____

2.3 Answer these questions which include phrases from the text. Use a dictionary to help you.

1. Why are immigrants sometimes needed to *fill gaps in the labour market*?
2. What kind of people want to *climb the corporate ladder*?

Exam practice

Reading and Use of English Part 3

For questions **1 – 8**, read the text below. Use the word given in capitals at the end of some of the lines to form a word that fits in the gap **in the same line**. There is an example at the beginning **(0)**.

> **Exam tip**
>
> Read the whole text first for a general idea of the topic, then look at the gaps and try to work out what type of word is missing, for example, a noun, adjective, etc. When deciding how to change the words given, think about whether the words need prefixes or suffixes.

My ideal work environment

I believe a work culture that matches employees' **(0)** _personalities_ | **PERSON**
is vital for workers' job **(1)** _____ as well as for a company's | **SATISFY**
business success. My ideal work environment is creative, fun and
relaxed. At work, I always feel **(2)** _____ and there is a | **APPRECIATE**
spirit of teamwork and positive energy. I respect my boss for his or her
qualities of **(3)** _____ , integrity and friendly positive nature. | **LEADER**
I know I can make a real **(4)** _____ by using my unique talents | **CONTRIBUTE**
and skills in order to make a difference in a company which is focused
on achieving clearly defined **(5)** _____ . My team and the | **OBJECT**
company work together to introduce **(6)** _____ innovations. | **TECHNOLOGY**
Within the company, each member of the **(7)** _____ is given | **WORK**
the chance to learn and develop new skills to help the company achieve
its goals. I look forward to coming to work every day because I am an
(8) _____ part of an organisation whose work I believe in. | **ESSENCE**
I face new opportunities and challenges every day.

242

41 Economics and business

Economic problems, business tips

Economic problems

1.1 Find expressions in the newspaper headlines which match the definitions. The first letters are provided.

PENSION FUND CRISIS **ECONOMIC DOWNTURN** **WORLDWIDE RECESSION**
500 firms could go bust **CRASH ON WALL STREET!** **Inflation soars**
Pound weakens against dollar **Profits fall** **INTEREST RATES CLIMB**
Stocks tumble **Slump worsens** **Credit crunch hits home**

1 money set aside to provide income for people when they are retired
   p*ension* f*und*

2 become bankrupt
   g_____ b_____

3 period of economic decline (3 different words)
   r_____ ; s_____ ; d_____

4 economic situation where banks stop lending
   c_____ c_____

5 a situation where the value of something suddenly decreases
   c_____

6 increase in prices leading to an increase in the cost of living
   i_____

7 the charge, in percent, for borrowing money
   i_____ r_____

8 go down in value (3 different words)
   t_____ ; w_____ ; f_____

1.2 🔊53 Listen to two Americans talking about their family's financial situation. What rising costs concern each speaker?

Speaker 1 _____   Speaker 2 _____

1.3 🔊53 Listen again and complete the phrases in italics with words used by the speakers.

Speaker 1
1 the whole economy's *in a* _____
2 _____ their mortgage *repayments*
3 What's _____ my family *the hardest*
4 *keep a* _____ *on* our spending

Speaker 2
5 people *finance* their college fees *through* _____
6 college fees are *going up at an* _____ *rate*.
7 Some of our friends are already *getting* _____ .
8 with the economy *in* _____ anything could happen

243

41 Economics and business

1.4 Match the definitions (a–h) with the phrases in italics from 1.3.

a become nervous _____
b continue paying off a loan _____
c worsening uncontrollably _____
d in a depressed state _____
e increase at a worrying speed _____
f control something tightly _____
g pay for something by borrowing money _____
h most seriously affected _____

1.5 Complete the news article with words from the box.

~~finances~~ income market non-essentials profits retailers spending stock

Low holiday spending due to economic worries

Americans won't be spending as much this holiday season due to continued worry about their (1) ___finances___ . New research found that 56% of Americans rated the economy as 'poor' and 46% believed the situation was getting worse.

This is bad news for (2) _____ trying to *eke out* their earnings this holiday season, especially since the survey showed that roughly 63% of respondents said they planned to spend less this holiday season. The figure is unchanged since last year, when retailers had one of the worst showings ever and had to slash prices even before Christmas to help move (3) _____ .

Even the news that household (4) _____ *inched up* is a *double-edged sword*. People surveyed indicated they'd be spending more on items like gas and groceries, but they're making up for this increase by further cutting what they spend on (5) _____ like movies or restaurant meals.

Perhaps the most troubling part of the research shows that a rising number of Americans not only have no money left over after paying their bills, but expect their (6) _____ to fall even further in the coming months. Most people have already *cut their spending to the bone*, so it's not clear what lies ahead for average Americans trying to *make ends meet*. The stock (7) _____ may be rising and some big companies may be reporting (8) _____ , but make no mistake: this data shows that we're certainly *not out of the woods* yet.

1.6 Find phrases in italics which match these definitions in the article.

1 increase slowly ___inch up___
2 survive financially _____
3 still in danger _____
4 reduce expenditure to a minimum _____
5 make something last longer _____
6 both an advantage and a disadvantage _____

> **V Vocabulary note**
>
> Notice these verbs used when reporting the findings of research:
>
> New research **found** that 56% of Americans rated the economy as poor …
>
> … the survey **showed** that roughly 63% of respondents said they planned to spend less …
>
> People **surveyed** indicated they'd be spending more on items like gas …

1.7 Add words and phrases with similar meanings from the box to the lists (1–3).

cut disconcerting disturbing lower reduce ~~rise dramatically~~ rocket soar worrying

1 shoot up ___rise dramatically___ , _____ , _____
2 slash _____ , _____ , _____
3 troubling _____ , _____ , _____

244

Economics and business 41

Business tips

2.1 Read the article and write these headings above the appropriate paragraphs.

Focus on the essentials   Play to your strengths   Get the finance you need   Take advice

---

Top tips for starting your own business

A _____
When seeking investment, make sure you put the time and effort into developing a solid business plan you can present to potential investors. The personal touch is also important, so try to *build* a good working relationship with your bank manager – it makes a big difference.

B _____
When *setting up* a business, there's often no need to spend large sums on offices, fancy logos and designer furniture. It is far more important to keep a low cost base at the start, and keep costs as variable as you can. Make sure you are not locked into long contracts, for example.

C _____
Small businesses often have advantages over their larger competitors. If you can respond quickly to customers and feedback and always maintain the personal touch, your business may *thrive* where larger competitors have to struggle to react in such a dynamic way.

D _____
Be a sponge, learn from others' mistakes, as well as your own, and proactively *seek out* mentors. The Internet and especially social networking make it easy to connect with other small business owners. It's important to be part of a buzzing business community.

2.2 Which words are possible replacements for the words in italics in the text?

Word in 2.1	Possible replacements			
1 build	develop	establish	produce	maintain
2 set up	bring on	establish	launch	start
3 thrive	accomplish	flourish	prosper	succeed
4 seek out	meet up	look for	search for	try to find

2.3 Choose the correct prepositions to complete the sentences. There are similar sentences in 2.1.

1 We are putting extra resources *into / for* training our customer service team.
2 I will be presenting this quarter's figures *to / at* the board at this afternoon's meeting.
3 It is vital that we get every member of staff to focus *about / on* what we want to achieve as an organisation.
4 As the first to enter the marketplace we will have enormous advantages *of / over* rival firms.

2.4   WORD TRANSFORMATION   Complete these sentences with the correct forms of the words in capitals.

1 Many of the _____ in the company were putting in their own money.   INVEST
2 My brother and I formed a business _____ twenty years ago.   PARTNER
3 Your business will be more _____ if you can reduce your overheads.   PRODUCE
4 The company is trying to reduce _____ on transport.   EXPEND

245

Exam practice

Writing Part 1 An essay

You **must** answer this question. Write your answer in **220 – 260** words in an appropriate style.

You have listened to a radio discussion programme about the problem of young people not being prepared for employment. You have made the notes below.

> **Solutions to the problem of young people not being prepared for employment:**
> - school training programmes
> - employers' programmes
> - work experience

> Some opinions expressed in the discussion:
>
> "Employers should not be expected to train future employees in basic skills."
>
> "It is the responsibility of schools to prepare students for the world of work."
>
> "Young people should realise that starting work requires commitment and a readiness to learn new skills."

Write an essay discussing **two** of the solutions in your notes. You should **explain which solution you think is more likely to be successful, giving reasons** to support your opinion.

You may, if you wish, make use of the opinions expressed in the discussion, but you should use your own words as far as possible.

> ### Exam tip
>
> It is important that you make sure that what you write will make sense to the reader. This means presenting clear arguments in which the sentences and paragraphs are linked in a logical way. Remember to give reasons to support your ideas.

42 The living world
Animal life, trees and plants

Animal life

1.1 Answer these questions.

1 Which animals are commonly found in your country?
2 Which animals are commonly eaten in your country?
3 Should we be worried about animal extinction?
4 How important are animal rights in your country?

1.2 Complete these sentences with the animal groups from the table below.

1 _____ use gills to breathe and can only live in water.
2 _____ are the most intelligent creatures and drink their mother's milk.
3 _____ are vertebrates and live partly on land and partly underwater.
4 _____ have dry, scaly skin and are cold-blooded.
5 _____ have six legs and their skeleton on the outside.
6 _____ have feathers, lay eggs and most are capable of flying.

Amphibians	Birds	Fish	Insects	Mammals	Reptiles
frog	owl	shark	bee	horse	snake
_____	_____	_____	_____	_____	_____
_____	_____	_____	_____	_____	_____

1.3 Complete the table with the words in the box.

ant   cricket   crocodile   lizard   mackerel   newt   salmon   swallow   toad   vulture   whale   wolf

1.4 Which animal from 1.2 and 1.3 …

1 … is nocturnal; preys on small animals; hoots; has a sharp beak; hatches fluffy chicks? _____
2 … sometimes moves in swarms; buzzes; has a sting; lives in a hive; is a source of honey? _____
3 … lives in a pack; growls, snarls and howls; has four paws; has young called cubs or pups? _____
4 … has a forked tongue; is often venomous; may hiss or rattle to warn of attack; sheds its skin? _____
5 … has scales and gills; migrates to breed; is often poached in protected waters? _____

1.5 What do the words in each list have in common?

1 calf; foal; grub; kitten _____
2 clone; rear; slaughter; vaccinate _____
3 colony; herd; pod; shoal _____
4 burrow; den; enclosure; kennel _____
5 groom; hibernate; mate; nest _____
6 antennae; claw; fang; trunk _____

247

42 The living world

1.6 Complete these sentences with your own ideas. Read the article in 1.7 to check.

1 Scientists are trying to protect bees from _____.
2 The proportion of human food production which relies on bees is _____.

1.7 Complete the article with words from the box.

declining disappear economic existence grains humans pesticides pollinate ~~population~~ vital

The bee **(1)** _population_ has been **(2)** _____ in recent years. Bees are **(3)** _____ to humans and our **(4)** _____ is linked very closely to theirs. We rely on bees to **(5)** _____ the crops we harvest and for almost every plant on Earth. Crops such as cereals, **(6)** _____ and pulses which are pollinated by bees, form a major part of global diets and approximately one quarter of all the food we eat is dependent on bees. If bees were to **(7)** _____ entirely and become extinct, the social and **(8)** _____ losses would be huge. The impact wouldn't only be disastrous for **(9)** _____ but also for many other species that rely on bees.

However, it's not all bad news. We can all do something to help maintain bee levels. We can make our environment more bee-friendly by growing plants that attract bees and avoiding the use of **(10)** _____ in our gardens.

Vocabulary note

The word *species* has the same form in the singular and the plural:
*The panda is an endangered **species**.*
*There are thousands of **species** of bees.*
The word *series* is similar:
*Have you seen the new wildlife **series** on TV?*
*There have been four **series** of these wildlife documentaries.*

1.8 WORD BUILDING Complete the table with words which have related meanings.

Noun	Verb	Adjective
_____	_____	declining
_____	disappear	_____
existence	_____	_____
		_____ (negative)
_____	x	extinct
_____ (action) _____ (substance)	pollinate	pollinated
_____ (person) _____ (concept)	theorise	_____

The living world 42

Trees and plants

2.1 Match the idioms in italics in these sentences with their definitions.

1. We didn't use to recycle things, but we've *turned over a new leaf* and we recycle everything now.
2. The government should stop *beating about the bush* and tell us the truth about climate change.
3. People had started leaving rubbish in the park, so the council introduced fines to *nip it in the bud*.
4. He doesn't look after himself any more. He's really *gone to seed* recently.

a avoid talking about something important __2__
b deal with a problem before it gets worse _____
c deteriorate in appearance or condition _____
d start behaving in a better way _____

2.2 ▶54 How do people use plants? Make a list. Listen and check your list against the uses mentioned by the speaker.

2.3 ▶55 Listen to part of the recording again. What do the following provide?

1. timber from trees
2. cotton plants
3. willow trees
4. the bark of a yew tree
5. aloe and jojoba
6. corn

> **Error warning**
>
> Plants **provide** (us) **with** the air we breathe.
> (not ~~Plants provide us the air we breathe.~~)

2.4 Explain the difference in meaning between the words in each pair.

1. gardener / farmer
2. roots / branches
3. carnivorous / omnivorous
4. shelter / habitat

2.5 WORD BUILDING Match the adjectives in the box with the nouns to make collocations. Some adjectives match with more than one noun.

| aquatic arid clean cold domestic endangered exotic flowering fresh |
| furry harsh humid marine ~~medicinal~~ mild temperate thin wild |

1. _medicinal,_ _____ + PLANT
2. _____ + ANIMAL
3. _____ + AIR
4. _____ + CLIMATE

2.6 Describe these using some of the adjectives from the box in 2.5.

1. the climate of your country
2. the air in your neighbourhood
3. your favourite animals and plants

249

Exam practice

Listening Part 4

▶56 You will hear five short extracts in which people talk about aspects of the natural world. **While you listen you must complete both tasks.**

TASK ONE
For questions **1 – 5**, choose from the list **(A – H)** the person who is speaking.

A	a farmer	Speaker 1	1
B	a vegetarian	Speaker 2	2
C	a historian	Speaker 3	3
D	an environmentalist	Speaker 4	4
E	a vet	Speaker 5	5
F	a zooworker		
G	an electrician		
H	an expert gardener		

TASK TWO
For questions **6 – 10**, choose from the list **(A – H)** the idea that each speaker is expressing.

A	to describe a typical day's routine	Speaker 1	6
B	to describe the aims of a long-term project	Speaker 2	7
C	to explain the origins of a public facility	Speaker 3	8
D	to give advice to pet owners	Speaker 4	9
E	to give useful advice to listeners	Speaker 5	10
F	to describe a scheme which will save money		
G	to recommend a place to visit		
H	to suggest a money-saving device		

Exam tip

Always listen carefully to everything the speakers say. Don't assume that one particular word or phrase which links a speaker with one of the options will provide the correct answer. Don't be misled by superficial or deliberately misleading links and clues.

43 Personal contact

Social networking, letter writing

Social networking

1.1 Which of these methods of contacting friends do you use most often? Put a (✓).

1. phone call ___
2. text message ___
3. email ___
4. social networking site ___
5. video call ___
6. letter ___
7. postcard ___

1.2 Which of the communication methods in 1.1 would you use for these purposes? Write the numbers.

a. organising a social event ___
b. sending an informal greeting ___
c. maintaining casual friendships ___
d. having a face-to-face conversation ___
e. making people take you seriously ___
f. sending a message when on the move ___
g. sending something to multiple recipients ___
h. expressing personal and private feelings ___

1.3 Complete the article with words from the box.

| business | forums | location | members | ~~networks~~ |
| profile | reconnect | relationships | share | touch |

Through social networking, people can use (1) __networks__ of online friends and group memberships to keep in (2) _____ with current friends, (3) _____ with old friends or make real-life friends through similar interests or groups. Besides establishing important social (4) _____, members can (5) _____ their interests with like-minded members by joining groups and (6) _____. Some networking sites can also help members find a job or establish (7) _____ contacts.

Most social networking sites also offer additional features like links to blogs. (8) _____ can express themselves by customising their (9) _____ page to reflect their personality. These days, much social networking is done on the move by smartphone, so users can now share their current (10) _____ as well as their photos and personal thoughts.

1.4 COLLOCATION Which word in each list does NOT form a collocation?

1	BE IN TOUCH WITH	your emotions	~~your problems~~	your relatives	reality
2	SHARE	your thoughts	a passion	a question	your view
3	ESTABLISH	your credentials	a network	a reputation	an opinion
4	CREATE	a friend	a new identity	an illusion	an impression
5	MAKE	an arrangement	a connection	an impact	an understanding

43 Personal contact

1.5 Complete each question with a suitable word from 1.4 and then answer them with your own ideas.

1 How can you establish your _____ online?
2 Have you met anyone that you share a _____ with online?
3 What problems have arisen from people creating new _____ for themselves online?
4 Is it possible to lose touch with _____ when you use social networking sites?

1.6 Match the phrases in italics to their definitions.

1 A *former friend* of the actor has revealed details of the star's personal life to the tabloid press.
2 Loads of *childhood friends* that I haven't seen for years have added me to their list of contacts.
3 The director is a *personal friend* of mine. If I recommend you, he's bound to help you out.
4 A *true friend* would have trusted me with the money without asking what it was for!
5 He hasn't called since I had the accident. He turned out to be a bit of a *fair-weather friend* really.
6 I got chatting to a woman on the train and we realised we had several *mutual friends* in the area.

a A friend you knew in your schooldays. _____
b Someone two people both have friendships with. _____
c A friend who disappears when you have problems. _____
d A friend you socialise with outside work. _____
e Someone you have ended a friendship with. _____
f A friend who is loyal, supportive and dependable. _____

> **V Vocabulary note**
>
> Some informal synonyms for *friend* are *mate*, *buddy* and *pal*.
> *befriend* = deliberately make friends with someone:
> He *befriended* me on my first day at school.

Letter writing

2.1 Answer these questions about writing letters.

1 When was the last time you wrote a letter? What kind of letter was it?
2 Have you ever sent or received these types of letter? Put a (✓).

a thank-you letter	_____	a letter of condolence	_____
a letter of resignation	_____	a handwritten letter	_____
an apology	_____	a love letter	_____
a complaint	_____	a poison-pen letter	_____

3 What is the difference between these types of written document?

letter   memo   note   card   petition   invoice   diary

> **V Vocabulary note**
>
> *pick up the phone* = answer: The phone rang, but when I *picked it up* there was no one there.
> *pick up a disease* = catch: I *picked up* a stomach bug on holiday.
> *pick up a language* = learn: I *picked up* quite a few words of Italian when I was on holiday in Rome.
> *pick someone up* = collect somebody in a motor vehicle: Would you like me to *pick you up* from the airport?

2.2 ▶57 Listen to someone talking about letter writing and answer these questions.

1 What does the speaker believe were some of the positive aspects of letter-writing?

_____

2 What other methods of communication does he mention?

_____

Personal contact 43

2.3 ▶57 **Listen again and complete these sentences with words used by the speaker.**

1 Letters were once our only m_____ of c_____ .
2 Letter writing took t_____ and c_____ .
3 You would have to r_____ if you made a mistake in a letter.
4 The telephone was much more i_____ than writing a letter.
5 Phone calls are becoming increasingly o_____ .
6 In our age of i_____ communication, the opportunities to contact people are e_____ .

2.4 **Match the words in italics with their definitions. Use a dictionary to help you.**

1	The *proliferation* of ways to communicate	a	giving attention to one thing only
2	Letter-writing took time and *concentration*	b	boring
3	The telephone *usurped* letter writing	c	causing great sadness or sympathy
4	If you had a *heartrending* message …	d	great or sudden increase
5	A *soppy* letter	e	replace or take over from
6	For many it was a *tedious* process	f	sincere
7	You could make your letter as *heartfelt* as you wanted	g	very emotional or sentimental

2.5 **Answer these questions with your own ideas.**

1 What situations require your *concentration*?
2 What housework do you find *tedious*?
3 Do you enjoy reading *soppy* books or watching *soppy* films?
4 What *heartrending* news stories have you heard about recently?

2.6 **Which words are possible replacements for the words in italics in the extracts?**

Extracts	Possible replacements
1 *means* of communicating	choice method way
2 *component* of communication	aspect feature piece
3 what the card is trying to *convey*	advise communicate express

2.7 **Decide whether the underlined words and phrases in these sentences show positive or negative feelings.**

1 <u>She couldn't be bothered</u> to speak to me in person. She just left <u>a badly written note</u> on my desk.
2 <u>It was very thoughtful of you</u> to send me a card when I was ill. <u>It really brightened up my day</u>.
3 Sending him <u>these soppy messages</u> all the time just makes <u>her sound desperate</u>.
4 Her <u>response to our ideas was scathing</u>, which I find <u>very frustrating</u> after all our hard work.
5 <u>He rambled on for hours</u> about his life, and never once asked me how I was doing.
6 <u>He's so articulate that</u>, even when <u>he dominates the conversation</u>, <u>he's a pleasure to have around</u>.

253

Exam practice

Reading and Use of English Part 2

For questions **1 – 8**, read the text below and think of the word which best fits each gap. Use only **one** word in each gap. There is an example at the beginning **(0)**.

Bathwick Historical Centre

Have any of your relatives **(0)** _____ever_____ lived or worked in Bathwick or in any of the surrounding areas? Do you have an interest **(1)** _____ finding out more about your family's past? Are you curious about your ancestors? You might want to know more about your roots, but **(2)** _____ not know where to start, or alternatively, you might want to piece together the story of a branch of your family **(3)** _____ a particular relative. If so, we can help.

We have a qualified local historian on our team who can assist you in your search for information on your ancestral roots. Additionally, we have built **(4)** _____ an extensive database, which goes back to the 1600s and contains information about local families, their genealogy, where they lived and what they did for a **(5)** _____ . We can also access data **(6)** _____ numerous other sources such as electoral registers, national censuses, parish records and historical archives, including newspaper articles. **(7)** _____ our services **(8)** _____ be of interest to you, please do not hesitate to contact us.

44 The environment
Issues, protection

Issues

1.1 Which of these issues have a negative effect on the environment where you live? Put a (✓).

coastal erosion ___   urban development ___   intensive agriculture ___   oil spills ___
overfishing ___   nuclear accidents ___   waste treatment ___
invasive species ___   deforestation ___   overgrazing ___

1.2 Read the article about environmental problems in Australia. Choose headings for paragraphs (1–6) from the expressions in 1.1.

1 _____
When large numbers of trees are cut down, the *salinity* of the soil can greatly increase. Salt water draining from such areas can affect downstream water quality.

2 _____
Pasture mismanagement is one of the main pressures on *biodiversity*. The unsustainable use of grazed pasture without giving plants time to recover has modified vast areas of grasslands. This kind of continued *defoliation* has led to desertification and *erosion*.

3 _____
Australia's fisheries are already close to collapse because of this activity, and the problem is getting worse. There are two major factors which account for the problem: slow *regeneration* of *marine populations* and depletion of fish stocks by commercial over-exploitation.

4 _____
It is estimated that Australia gains around 20 new pests each year. Examples include cane toads, willows and, more recently, red fire ants. Historically, feral cats and foxes have been a cause of local *extinctions* and reductions in range for native species through a combination of habitat modification and predation. *Weeds* are an equally significant pressure on ecosystems, with more than 2,500 species of introduced plants now thriving in the wild in Australia. They have invaded every part of the landscape.

5 _____
Bio-intensive farming is affecting Australia's coasts and oceans, particularly *estuaries* and environments near the shore. Estimates are that each year almost 19,000 tonnes of phosphorus and 141,000 tonnes of nitrogen are discharged into rivers flowing to the coast.

6 _____
Of continuing concern for Australia is population growth along the country's *coastline*. The formation of massive metropolitan centres with intensive population density on Australia's coasts could displace much valuable biodiversity and 'high-value' agricultural land.

44 The environment

1.3 Are these statements true (T) or false (F) according to the text? Explain your answers using the words in italics in the text in 1.2. Use a dictionary to help you.

1 Deforestation leads to an increase in the level of salt in the soil. __T – salinity of the soil can increase__
2 The range of organisms in the environment has not been affected by overgrazing. _____
3 Overgrazing has gradually worn away fertile soil. _____
4 Fish stocks have been able to renew themselves quickly. _____
5 In the past, new species of animals and plants wiped out some native Australian species. _____
6 Unwanted wild plants have had no effect on the environment. _____
7 Parts of rivers near to the mouth have not been affected by intensive agriculture. _____
8 Population growth is particularly worrying in inland areas of Australia. _____

Vocabulary note

The verb suffix *-ify* adds the meaning 'make' or 'become' to some adjectives:
purify (= make pure), *simplify* (= make simple), *solidify* (= become solid)
These verbs can be converted into action nouns: *purification, simplification, solidification*
Some verbs and action nouns which follow a similar pattern are: *identify/identification, modify/modification, verify/verification*

1.4 WORD BUILDING Complete the table with words which have related meanings.

Noun	Verb	Adjective
_____	x	agricultural
density	x	_____
erosion	_____	_____
_____ (action noun)	_____	intensive
modification	_____	_____
overpopulation (too much)	_____ (too much)	_____ (too much)
_____	regenerate	_____

1.5 Complete these sentences with words from the table in 1.4.

1 The stronger the wind and the heavier the rain, the more soil they can ___erode___.
2 Humans have always _____ their environment in order to survive and protect themselves.
3 Commercial _____ is responsible for a significant proportion of damage to the environment.
4 Scientists believe that we should _____ our efforts to slow the rate of climate change.
5 Some of the country's old industrial cities are undergoing a massive programme of _____.
6 The day will come when food supplies will be insufficient to meet the needs of our _____ planet.

44 The environment

Protection

2.1 Match these words with their definitions.

1. reforestation
2. biodegradable
3. conservation
4. recyclable
5. renewable

a. can be broken down by bacteria into safe substances
b. describes materials that can be processed and used again, such as glass
c. can be replaced, refreshed or restored
d. planting trees where they have been cut down
e. long-term protection and sustainable management of natural resources

2.2 Complete these sentences with words from 2.1.

1. Ideally, waste that is put in landfill sites should be _____ .
2. Wildlife _____ is becoming increasingly important as more species are threatened with extinction.
3. Many products, including packaging, have a symbol which tells consumers that they are _____ .
4. Solar power and wind power are _____ energy sources.
5. A programme of _____ in India is aimed at preventing soil erosion to reduce the risk of flooding.

2.3 ▶ 58 Listen to two *Cambridge English: Advanced* exam students discussing ways to protect the environment and complete the mindmap.

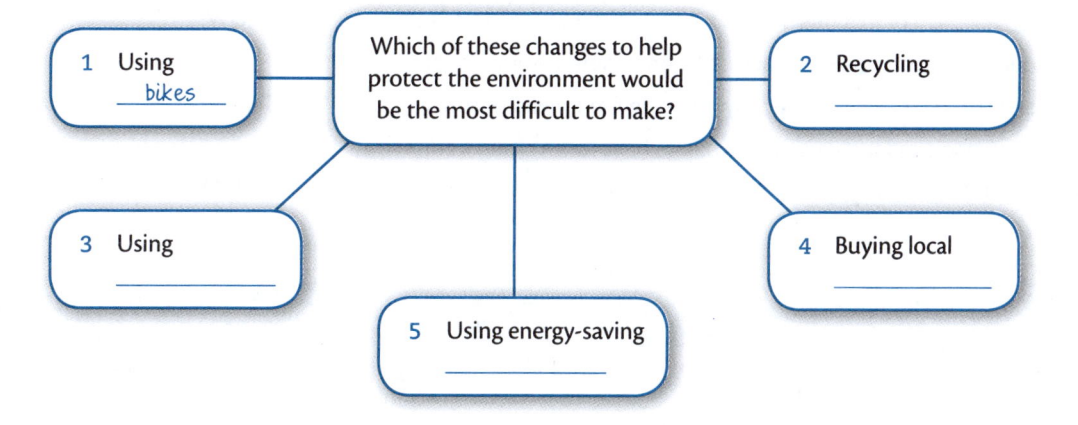

Which of these changes to help protect the environment would be the most difficult to make?

1. Using _bikes_
2. Recycling _____
3. Using _____
4. Buying local _____
5. Using energy-saving _____

2.4 ▶ 58 Listen again and complete these sentences with words used by the speakers.

1. There are quite a lot of cycling accidents in London because there aren't _____ .
2. People accepted the idea of _____ very quickly.
3. The problem with solar panels is that they're _____ .
4. Power from the sun costs nothing and doesn't _____ .
5. Some fruit and vegetables are expensive because they've been transported _____ .
6. Buying fruit and vegetables grown in your area is a good way of supporting _____ .
7. Traditional light bulbs are very _____ compared with the new type of bulbs.

257

Exam practice

Reading and Use of English Part 3

For questions **1 – 8**, read the text below. Use the word given in capitals at the end of some of the lines to form a word that fits in the gap **in the same line**. There is an example at the beginning **(0)**.

Brazil's habitats under threat

The ongoing **(0)** _expansion_ of agriculture in Brazil is seriously — **EXPAND**
threatening rare and vulnerable habitats such as the Amazon. The major
threat to some of these vast natural areas is the destructive power of
the soya bean. Soya beans are one of Brazil's main crops, with more
than 21 million hectares under **(1)** _____ . Another crop — **CULTIVATE**
which is causing concern is cocoa, which has been blamed for the
widespread **(2)** _____ of Brazilian forests. During the — **DESTROY**
(3) _____ boom of the 1970s, the growth in importance — **ECONOMY**
of this crop was a leading cause of the decline of Brazil's
(4) _____ Atlantic forest ecosystem, of which only — **DANGER**
about 10% remains. The Cerrado, an **(5)** _____ woodland — **EXTEND**
savanna ecosystem in Brazil, is threatened by cattle farming. The
(6) _____ of this business is closely linked to the increase in — **GROW**
soya production, which poses serious concerns about the impact of this
industry on **(7)** _____ ecosystems. In the forests of Brazil, — **SENSE**
some of the world's most diverse ecosystems have been converted to
fast-growing **(8)** _____ , mainly of eucalyptus, a non-native — **PLANT**
species.

> 💡 **Exam tip**
>
> For Reading and Use of English Part 3 tasks, read the whole text quickly first, thinking about what type of words are missing (for example, a noun or adjective). Then think about the exact form of each missing word. For example, if the word is a noun, should it be singular or plural? Think about whether the meaning of the word will add to the sentence as a whole. Does the word need a prefix, a suffix or both to make sense?

45 Science and technology

Discovery, solutions

Discovery

1.1 Which three of these inventions or discoveries do you think are the most important? Put a (✓).

radio ___ television ___ electricity ___ the telephone ___
the personal computer ___ the Internet ___ nuclear energy ___ the microchip ___
the aeroplane ___ penicillin ___ birth control ___ sanitation ___
the internal combustion engine ___

1.2 ▶59 Listen to three people talking about the most important discoveries and inventions. Answer these questions for each speaker.

1 What does each speaker choose?
  Speaker 1 _____
  Speaker 2 _____
  Speaker 3 _____

2 What are the reasons for these choices?
  Speaker 1 _____
  Speaker 2 _____
  Speaker 3 _____

1.3 ▶59 Listen again and complete the sentences with words used by the speakers.

1 Without electric lighting many _____ would have been more difficult.
2 Many parts of _____ depend on electricity.
3 The discovery of penicillin saved _____ .
4 Antibiotics have increased the average _____ in the developed world.
5 Microchips are the brain, heart and _____ of digital devices.
6 Since the early 1970s there have been more _____ than in any other period.

1.4 Match the branch of science (1–10) with the words lists (a–j).

1 anatomy
2 anthropology
3 archaeology
4 astronomy
5 ecology
6 genetics
7 meteorology
8 psychology
9 seismology
10 zoology

a carnivore; invertebrate; mammal; prey; venom
b biodiversity; extinction; habitat; pollution; species
c asteroid; comet; galaxy; nebula; orbit
d aftershock; earthquake; magma; tremor; volcano
e culture; custom; taboo; tribe; warfare
f joint; muscle; organ; spine; vein
g atmosphere; humidity; hurricane; pressure; temperature
h chromosome; heredity; mutation; organism; variation
i ancestor; bone; dig; remains; settlement
j behaviour; instinct; intelligence; memory; mind

259

45 Science and technology

1.5 Complete each sentence with words from two of the lists in 1.4.

ANATOMY & ZOOLOGY

1 The common characteristic of __invertebrates__ like insects is that they do not have a _____ .

ANTHROPOLOGY & SEISMOLOGY

2 Local _____ hold the belief that the _____ is a god which erupts when it is angry.

ECOLOGY & GENETICS

3 Lack of genetic _____ in the population makes a _____ vulnerable to disease.

ASTRONOMY & METEOROLOGY

4 If a _____ were to enter the earth's _____ , the results would be catastrophic.

1.6 Which of the words in each box *cannot* replace the word in italics in the sentence below it? Why?

1 | hypothesised   proved   speculated   suggested |

Researchers have *predicted* that there is a possible relationship between the two phenomena.

2 | ascertain   contradict   demonstrate   determine |

Only clinical trials can *show* whether or not the drug is truly effective.

3 | advance   breakthrough   development   drawback |

This significant *discovery* contributes more to our knowledge than any past study.

4 | carry out   conduct   experiment   undertake |

Only when we get the funding to *do* the research, can we begin to recruit our team.

5 | caused   affected   set off   triggered |

It was observed that the introduction of the compound *started* an explosive chemical reaction.

6 | conclusion   finding   outcome   prediction |

The unexpected *result* of the experiment may disprove earlier theories.

Solutions

2.1 How will science and technology be used to solve the world's problems? Make a prediction about each of the problems in the box.

| climate change   disappearance of fossil fuels   food shortages   disease   water shortages |

2.2 Read the first paragraph of an article about electric cars. According to the writer, what is the main problem associated with these cars?

> I would love electric cars to work, but they have their problems and the biggest of these is battery technology. Portable electronic gadgets like laptops, mobiles and cameras have long suffered from the limitations of the humble battery. In fact, while the performance of electronics has increased by 10,000% in the past 35 years, battery technology has lagged behind with only a sixfold increase in a century. This imbalance has important implications for the electric car. Many drivers won't consider replacing their conventional petrol-powered car with an electric model until the differences in price and performance narrow dramatically.

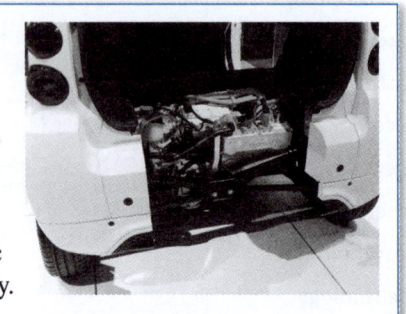

Science and technology 45

2.3 Choose the correct words to complete the rest of the article from 2.2.

Batteries have to go a lot further before they can catch up with the combustion (**1**) *engine* / *machine* and their limitations are forcing car (**2**) *creators* / *manufacturers* into designing and making electric cars with the same (**3**) *distance* / *range* as vehicles made in 1910. As an example, a typical small family car can travel over 370 miles in mixed driving (**4**) *conditions* / *circumstances* and can easily (**5**) *maintain* / *retain* a speed of 70mph. For an electric car to manage that, its batteries would weigh over 1.5 tonnes and would be similar in size to the car itself. And unlike a (**6**) *container* / *tank* of petrol, a massive battery doesn't get any lighter with each mile covered.

There are three key problems that will be difficult for manufacturers to (**7**) *overcome* / *overtake*: firstly, their range calculations may be too optimistic: to get a reasonable (**8**) *life* / *living* from batteries they should not be run from full to empty and should be kept at 20–80% of their charge.

Secondly, charging time remains a major (**9**) *obstacle* / *obstruction*. Recharging an electric vehicle battery on a domestic power supply is likely to take around 13 hours.

Finally, with the majority of our electricity likely to come from non-renewable (**10**) *resources* / *funds* in the near future, electric vehicles could actually contribute more CO_2 to the environment than one of today's high-efficiency diesel (**11**) *models* / *styles*.

I'd like to see electric cars take off but we can't assume they will. Neither can we assume they will have any impact on carbon (**12**) *discharges* / *emissions* for quite some time.

> **Error warning**
>
> *At last* and *finally* are both used with the same meaning when something happens after a long period of waiting or effort.
> *At last* I'm old enough to drive.
> I've *finally* finished my essay.
> We can use *finally* to introduce the last point in a piece of writing or a speech but we cannot use *at last*:
> *Finally*, there can be no change without governmental support ... (not ~~At last, there can be~~ ...)
> *Finally*, I'd like to thank you all for coming this evening ... (not ~~At last, I'd like to thank~~ ...)
> (See also **Unit 17, 2.4** for more on the use of *at last* and *finally*.)

2.4 Compound nouns can often be used to replace a longer phrase, which may include a preposition. For example, *power supply* is used instead of *supply of power*. Make two-word compound nouns from these phrases.

1 emissions of gas _____
2 a tank for petrol _____
3 a car suitable for a family _____
4 manufacturers of motors _____
5 resources of oil _____
6 engines using diesel _____

2.5 Choose the correct phrasal verb with *take* in these sentences.

1 The mini-disk was a wonderful invention but it never really *took off* / *took up* commercially.
2 I hear they're *taking up* / *taking on* a hundred new employees at the aircraft factory.
3 A small IT firm in our town has been *taken out* / *taken over* by a large multinational corporation.
4 When I started work in the laboratory, they *took me round* / *took me through* all the safety procedures.
5 My brother has decided to *take up* / *take to* medicine as a career.
6 The doctor has said I'm okay now, so he's *taken me away* / *taken me off* the tablets.
7 I find it difficult to *take up* / *take in* what people are saying when I'm tired.

2.6 Write sentences using each of the *take* verbs you did not use in 2.5.

1 I'd like to **take** you **up** on your offer of help.

Exam practice

Writing Part 2 A letter

Your local council is considering banning all private vehicles from the town centre between the hours of 8.00 am and 6.00 pm on working days. Outside these times and at weekends there will be no restrictions. Write a letter to the editor of your local newspaper expressing an opinion on this issue.

You may support or reject the idea. Give reasons for your position and state how this ban might affect you, the local economy and the environment.

Write your **letter** in **220 – 260** words in an appropriate style. You do not need to include postal addresses.

> **Exam tip**
>
> Before starting to write, think carefully about the purpose of the letter, who the reader will be and what this person will expect to read. Then, with this information in mind, decide how formal the language of your letter needs to be.

Answer key

1 Tenses

1.2 2 Liam 3 Karen 4 Liam 5 Luka 6 Karen 7 Sahar 8 Luka

1.3 2 'd (had) been waiting 3 'm (am) now thinking 4 'm (am) working 5 'd (had) spoken 6 've (have) enjoyed 7 've (have) been trying 8 'd (had) finished

1.4 2 past perfect continuous 3 & 4 present continuous 5 & 8 past perfect 6 present perfect 7 present perfect continuous

3.1 2 was driving 3 'm usually coming 4 was going 5 saw 6 stopped 7 was watching 8 was travelling 9 suddenly disappeared 10 didn't believe 11 is forever trying 12 exist 13 'm thinking 14 was 15 offers 16 were coming 17 suggest 18 was 19 is 20 seems 21 are getting 22 is currently researching 23 believe 24 were observing

3.2 2a expect b are … expecting 3a was measuring b measures 4a is attracting b attracts 5a Do … see b was seeing 6a imagine b is imagining

3.3 1b had played (*played* also possible) c Did … play d had been playing (*had played* also possible) 2a made b had been making c had made (*made* also possible) d have made 3a have run b had been running c had run (*ran* also possible) d ran

3.4 2 has been dropping (this is more likely as a situation is being talked about which has changed over a period of time up to now and may well continue to change.) 3 has belonged 4 has been serving (this is more likely because we are told how long it has continued.) 5 Have you considered 6 Have you been swimming 7 've (have) tried

3.5 2 started 3 remember 4 had been working 5 was doing 6 I've been working 7 had just finished 8 was feeling 9 have you been sleeping 10 hits 11 I've been having 12 I notice 13 Have you had 14 haven't had 15 I suggest 16 are working 17 doesn't solve

Exam practice: Reading and Use of English Part 2
1 have 2 that 3 far 4 some 5 is 6 If 7 neither 8 such

2 The future

1.2 The following activities are mentioned: 1 visiting the Golden Gate Bridge in San Francisco 2 camping on a beach 3 sightseeing in New York 6 visiting the Grand Canyon.

1.3 2 arrive 3 'll (will) be looking 4 's (is) going to take 5 'm (am) going to fly 6 Will 7 'll (will) have been living 8 'll (will) be staying

1.4 There are 6 different ways of referring to the future: present continuous **(1)**, present simple **(2)**, future continuous **(3 & 8)**, *be going to* + infinitive **(4 & 5)**, *will* **(6)**, future perfect continuous **(7)**

3.1 2 'm (am) having 3 is going to melt 4 will persuade 5 will rise 6 see 7 miss 8 will be enjoying

3.2 2 'm going to do 3 's going to cause 4 'll take 5 are you doing; 'll Skype 6 will commence 7 is doing; Shall 8 is; will be

3.3 2a 'm (am) going to buy b 's (is) going to have c 're (are) going to need 3a will have been working b will have been watching c will have been negotiating 4a won't be coming b will you be supporting c will be doing 5a is to create b are to be left c is / are to launch 6a will have moved b will have had c will have been analysed 7a 's (is) making b 'm (am) not going c 're (are) having

Exam practice: Reading and Use of English Part 8
1 D 2 B 3 A 4 C 5 B 6 E 7 C 8 D 9 E 10 A

3 Modals (1)

1.3 2 must accept 3 had to be 4 were able to bring 5 will be 6 ought to be 7 should give 8 will be

1.4 1 *necessity*: 2 & 3 3 *obligation*: 6 & 7 4 *possibility*: 1 5 *prediction*: 5 & 8

3.1 2 'll be able to 3 wasn't able to 4 Could 5 could 6 might 7 could 8 mightn't

3.2 2 must 3 can't 4 mightn't 5 did you have to 6 had to 7 have to 8 shouldn't 9 have to

3.3 2 b 3 a & b 4 b 5 b 6 a 7 a & b 8 b

3.4 2 g 3 e 4 a 5 i 6 h 7 b

Exam practice: Listening Part 1
1 B 2 C 3 B 4 C 5 A 6 B

4 Modals (2)

1.1 The police officers discuss pictures a, b, d, & f

1.2 2 f 3 a 4 e 5 h 6 b 7 g 8 d

1.3 1 2 f (might have been lowered) 2 3 a (must have opened); 8 d (should have finished) 3 4 e (might have been expecting); 7 g (must have been waiting) 4 5 h (might be lying); 6 b (could be hiding)

3.1 1 (must); might 2 didn't dare to admit; would have been 3 might be raining; we'd better 4 is supposed to start; couldn't 5 must have known; should have warned 6 were supposed to; might

3.2 2 have been caused 3 have changed 4 have been working 5 have found 6 be waiting 7 have been tempted 8 have been talking

3.3 2 we've (have) managed 3 there is a possibility of seeing 4 I recommend you (to) / I recommend that you (should) 5 succeeded in taking 6 are to be taken 7 you are allowed to / we will allow you to 8 it is compulsory for everyone to

3.4 2 might have been working 3 must be getting easier 4 could be facing 5 ought to have given 6 would not have been able to grow

Answer key

Exam practice: Reading and Use of English Part 4
1 would ('d) sooner watch football than play 2 must have made 3 are required to fill 4 have thought about 5 has succeeded in cutting 6 you'd (= had) better not miss

5 Nouns, agreement and articles

1.3 2 *decision*-making 3 *rainforest* 4 river *levels* 5 *energy*-saving 6 lighting *energy* 7 *recycling* scheme 8 the arms trade 9 mountain *environments*

1.4 noun + noun: 3, 4, 8, 9 -*ing* form + noun: 6, 7 noun + -*ing* form: 2, 5

1.5 1a a b the 2a the b a 3a – b the
For more details and examples see Unit 5 Grammar: 2.4 Articles

1.6 1a the first time *drought* is mentioned b it seems that *drought* has been mentioned before so the listener would know what *drought* is being talked about
2a talking generally about something that is unique – there is only one future b a particular kind of future which is then specified
3a talking about college (the institution) in general b talking about the particular college that Nazim hopes to study in

3.1 2 Adam's decision 3 an action film; a documentary about young entrepreneurs 4 the brother of someone I worked with in Malaysia 5 a moment's hesitation (*we prefer noun + 's + noun to talk about time*) 6 a children's playground 7 The construction of the new library 8 letter box; a congratulations card

3.2 2 is 3 is 4 live / lives 5 depend 6 has 7 is 8 has 9 has / have 10 is 11 is 12 are

3.3 2 fresh fruit / vegetables (both possible) 3 advertisements 4 salt* 5 advice* 6 explosives / ammunition (both possible) 7 work* 8 rubbish*
  * The other word in each pair may be used in informal context only.

3.4 2a competition b a competition 3a paper b a paper 4a a shampoo b shampoo 5a iron b an iron 6a a time b time 7a an importance (no article + *importance* also possible) b importance 8a knowledge; b a knowledge

3.5 1 My brother wasn't very good at taking exams and he left school at 16. At first he went to work in **(the)** construction industry. But he didn't enjoy it so he took **an** evening course in accounting. Eventually he started **a** company offering financial advice. He's now **the** managing director and it seems that **the** company's doing really well. ('He's now managing director' is also possible.)
2
A: Do you remember **the** summer we went to Sweden? 1995 I think it was.
B: It was **a** wonderful holiday wasn't it? And so good to see Joakim again. I'll never forget **the** picnic we had with him.
There were **a** huge number of mosquitoes.
A: Yes I remember. And then when **the** sun was going down there was **an** amazing red sky.
B: And then his car broke down on the way home and we had to go back by bus.
A: No, we got **a** taxi didn't we?
B: Oh yes, that's right.
3 Fatimah has **a** busy life as **a** lawyer but in her free time she really enjoys hiking. Most weekends she drives out into **the** countryside and walks for **a** few hours. She says she likes to forget about work and she doesn't even take **a** mobile phone with her. In **the** summer she's going hiking in **the** Philippines. She's never been there before but **the** friend she's going with knows **the** country well.

Exam practice: Reading and Use of English Part 2
1 is 2 The 3 As/Along 4 the 5 which 6 most 7 the 8 is

6 Determiners and quantifiers

1.2 **benefits:** enjoyment, (personal) satisfaction, fitness (good for heart and lungs), sleep better, social contact / friendships
problems: time commitment, running injuries (aching muscles, back pain), running in bad weather is unpleasant

1.3 1b many 2a each b every 3a a few b the few 4a less b fewer

1.4 2a & 2b: we can say *each / every day* and *every / each one of us*.

3.1 1 is/are (both possible in this informal context; however *is* would be preferred in a formal context); have 2 is; has; has/have (both possible although *have* is more likely in this informal context.) 3 has; seem; likes

3.2 2 each 3 little 4 We were all 5 less 6 will all be 7 less 8 every 9 few 10 nearly every 11 the whole 12 fewer (*fewer* is grammatically correct although *less* might be used in an informal context)

3.3 2a a lot of (more natural than *much* in this informal context) b much (more natural than *a lot of* in this formal context) 3a many b a lot of (more natural than *many* in this informal context) 4a none of b not any of (*none of* would also be possible) 5a No b not any (probably written or said *wasn't any*; *no* would also be possible)

3.4 3 all (*many* would also possible be here) 4 few of 5 None 6 Both of 7 much 8 many of 9 much of 10 Both 11 None of 12 every 13 Many 14 All (of) 15 little of 16 little 17 each of

Exam practice: Listening Part 2
1 commitments 2 impressed 3 patronising 4 irrigation 5 dependent 6 handouts 7 surplus 8 prospects

Answer key

7 Adverbs and adjectives

1.1 Photo a: Sweden, Photo b: Scotland, Photo c: Norway

1.2 The author used to live in Sweden. He was born in Scotland and he lives there now. He recently visited Norway.

1.3 2 c 3 b (c *every occasion possible* also possible.) 4 b 5 a (although not an option in the task, *Generally I'm up ... would also be possible*) 6 a (although not an option, *... finding information from books as a rule* would also be possible. *I prefer as a rule finding ...* would be possible but less likely.) 7 c 8 a (Although not an option, *was rather a gentle woman* would also be possible.) 9 a (Although not an option, *I'm sketching out the plot still* would also be possible but less likely.)

1.4 2 ✓ 3 ✓ 4 ✗ 5 ✗ 6 ✓ 7 ✗ 8 ✓

3.1 2 hardly ever visits 3 to shout angrily 4 I absolutely agree / I agree absolutely (both possible) 5 left last week 6 We occasionally go / Occasionally we go (both possible) 7 seldom go out 8 started singing loudly

3.2 2a technical b somewhat technical 3a genuine b very genuine 4a original b highly original 5a thoroughly professional b professional 6a rather odd b odd 7a critical b severely critical 8a wild b pretty wild

3.3 2 to live 3 to fall 4 working 5 to leave 6 asking 7 to blame 8 leaving

Exam practice: Reading and Use of English Part 3
1 overweight 2 forgetfulness 3 harmful 4 alertness 5 scientific 6 dependent 7 requirement 8 childhood

8 Comparison

1.3 2 the best (beach) on 3 as little as 4 the most boring 5 more peaceful than 6 as much as

1.4 2 *the best* + noun 3 *as* + adjective + *as* 4 *the most* + adjective 5 *more* + adjective + *than* 6 *as much as*

3.1 1 most venomous 2 narrower / more narrow; deeper 3 more harmful; most alert 4 closest; most magnificent 5 poorer; unhealthier / more unhealthy 6 handsomest / most handsome; more concerned 7 more thrilled; most respected; more sad

3.2 2 few 3 little 4 as is 5 as much 6 serious a problem 7 normal a life 8 not such a 9 as 10 so / as (Both are possible in informal speech but *as* is more likely.)

3.3 2 tall 3 exhausted 4 bright 5 loud 6 small 7 awful 8 strong

3.4 3 too exhausted to go 6 small enough to fit 8 strong enough to shake

Exam practice: Reading and Use of English Part 3
1 successful 2 beneficial 3 fitness 4 overcome 5 heavily 6 harmful 7 separation 8 ensure

9 Verb patterns (1)

1.2 Correct order: 2 Early communication: parents and play **3** Listening and learning: the interrelationships **4** Patterns of communication: learned behaviour? **5** Language learning problems: what and why?

1.3 2 giving a toy to their mother 3 offering her some food 4 Mend this for me 5 Reading stories for young children 6 describing this process to you

1.4 a 1 & 3 b 4 & 5 c 2 & 6

1.5 2a giving their mother a toy b ~~giving a toy for their mother~~ c giving a toy to their mother (focuses attention on *their mother*) 3a offering her some food b ~~offering some food for her~~ c offering some food to her (focuses attention on *her*) 4a ~~Mend me this~~ b Mend this for me c ~~Mend this to me~~ 5a Reading young children stories b Reading stories for young children (focuses attention on *young children* and suggests that the children themselves aren't able to read) c Reading stories to young children (focuses attention on *young children* and highlights that something is being read out loud)
6a ~~describing you this process~~ b describing this process for you c describing this process to you (*describing ... for* and *describing ... to* have a similar meaning here)

3.1 2 They agreed with each other. 3 They always compete with each other. 4 They respect each other. 5 They trust each other. 6 They miss each other. 7 They blamed each other. 8 They disagreed with each other.

3.2 2 myself some chocolate 3 those letters for you (*them for you* also possible) 4 some apples for me / me some apples; you for them 5 you a favour (*a favour of you* also possible); me how to print out a document 6 your car for you; you a lot 7 the mistake to the manager; me a £10 gift voucher / a £10 gift voucher to me 8 me your glass / your glass to me; some water for you / you some water

3.3 2 him guilty of the murder 3 (themselves) incapable of maintaining order 4 himself fit to play again 5 myself lucky to be alive 6 her responsible for its collapse 7 itself independent of the Soviet Union

3.4 2 himself on; (himself) to 3 herself (*herself* makes it clear that the chocolates were for Sarah); myself with 4 (myself) for; myself with 5 themselves; you 6 (himself); – (no reflexive or personal pronoun needed)

Exam practice: Reading and Use of English Part 4
1 her responsible for 2 have made up 3 sooner had I got home than 4 herself on her / an ability 5 clearly explained the procedure (to us) / explained the procedure clearly (to us) / explained the procedure (to us) clearly 6 with the exception of

265

Answer key

10 Verb patterns (2)

1.1 passport left at home; missed flight; seasickness; stung by jellyfish

1.2 2 made to wait 3 had encouraged me to go 4 hate swimming 5 felt it stinging 6 appreciated them looking after 7 stopped to admire 8 tried using

1.3 1 4 (When I was younger I used to hate *to swim / swimming* in the sea.), 7 (As we stopped *to admire / admiring* the amazing sunset it was almost possible to believe it.) & 8 (I tried *to use / using* the camera in my mobile phone but the quality was pretty poor.)
2 4 has a similar meaning with either a *to*-infinitive or an *-ing* form.

3.1 2 advised him to give up 3 showed him pointing 4 guarantee to reply 5 make it drink 6 appreciate you helping / appreciate your helping (*your* is more formal) 7 don't enjoy sitting 8 advertise for someone to share

3.2 A: 1 him being is also possible 2 him talking 3 him stealing 4 to have 5 to sack
B: 1 to capture 2 for the bear/it to get 3 to eat/eating (both possible) 4 it/the bear escaping 5 to call/calling (both possible)
C: 1 saying 2 having 3 to see 4 do 5 to collect 6 to get

3.3 2 to get more exercise 3 to have been killed in the earthquake 4 to be talking on my mobile 5 (to) argue with him 6 shouting/shout at anyone 7 to be a successful businesswoman 8 having her around

Exam practice: Reading and Use of English Part 5
1 D 2 C 3 A 4 C 5 A 6 B

11 Relative clauses (1)

1.1 The commentary is about the early development of radio.

1.2 The photographs and models are mentioned in the following order: b, d, e, a, c

1.3 2 whose 3 when 4 of which 5 whereby 6 by which time

1.4 2 *whose* refers to *Guglielmo Marconi*. 3 *when* refers to *1901*. 4 *of which* refers to *wireless telegraphs*. 5 *whereby* refers to *a method*. 6 *by which time* refers to *1952*.

3.1 2 when + b 3 whose + a 4 why + d 5 which + c

3.2 2 B / C (*committee* is a collective noun referring to a group of people so we can use either *which* or *who*; *that* would also be possible) 3 A 4 A (formal) / B / D 5 A / C (more formal) 6 C 7 B / C / D (more formal) 8 A (formal) / D

3.3 2 in 3 from 4 of 5 for 6 from 7 of / about 8 by

3.4 2 b, h, r – A diving board is a narrow piece of wood at the end of a swimming pool from which people can dive.
3 d, j, m – Capri pants are women's narrow trousers which end just below the knee. 4 f, g, o – A shipper is a person or company whose job is to organise the sending of goods from one place to another. 5 a, l, q – A hakim is a Muslim doctor who uses traditional methods to treat people.
6 e, i, n – The Stone Age is an early period in human history when people made tools and weapons only out of stone then.

Exam practice: Reading and Use of English Part 1
1 B 2 D 3 B 4 A 5 C 6 C 7 A 8 D

12 Relative clauses (2)

1.2 The photographer uses: studio lights for lighting the shot; glycerine to keep the food looking shiny and moist; cotton wool balls soaked in water and heated in the microwave to create steam; a blowtorch to brown or melt the food.

1.3 2 ~~who wanted~~ – wanting 3 ~~who encouraged~~ – to encourage 4 ~~who won~~ – to win 5 ~~that is produced~~ – produced 6 ~~that is not made~~ – not made 7 ~~which contains~~ – containing 8 ~~that have been soaked~~ – soaked

1.4 1 1, 2 & 7 2 5, 6 & 8 3 3 & 4

3.1 2a which/that has not been seen b not seen 3a who/that were injured b injured 4a who was carrying b carrying 5a which/that belongs b belonging 6a who is playing b playing

3.2 1 holding information about the dog's owner 2 which sank off the south-west coast in 2014; (to be) published tomorrow / being published tomorrow 3 protesting; advised by police that security could not be guaranteed; who broke through police lines 4 which might prevent memory loss in older people; suffering from dementia; derived from a plant found only in New Zealand

3.3 2 to contact is the human resources manager 3 on the south side of the city 4 happy to help out 5 to take part / to have taken part in the London Marathon 6 very similar to Romanian 7 to announce large-scale redundancies 8 to ring / to have rung today about the car

3.4 1 which show the real-time cost of electricity (*or* showing the real-time cost of electricity) 2 which have cut power use by up to 6.5% in Canada (no reduced relative clause possible) 3 who want them (*or* wanting them) 4 which are left on unnecessarily (*or* left on unnecessarily) 5 which use microchip technology and a digital display (*or* using microchip technology and a digital display) 6 that is being used in a house at any given moment (*or* being used in a house at any given moment) 7 that are provided free of charge (*or* provided free of charge) 8 that would give customers access to free monitors (*or* to give customers access to free monitors) 9 that should be considered (*or* to be considered) 10 which communicate electricity consumption to both the customer and the energy supplier (no reduced relative clause possible) 11 that are only able to do half the job (*or* only able to do half the job)

Exam practice: Reading and Use of English Part 5
1 B 2 A 3 B 4 D 5 A 6 C

Answer key

13 Adverbial clauses

1.1 **1** processed food **2** a ready meal **3** a balanced diet **4** nutrition

1.2 **2** seeing that **3** so that **4** whereas **5** because **6** in order to **7** although **8** when **9** while **10** despite the fact that

1.3 *Seeing that* (sentence 2) has a similar meaning to *because* (sentence 5). You could use *because* in sentences 8 and 9 but it would have different meanings from *when* and *while*. *whereas* (sentence 4) and *Despite the fact that* (sentence 10) have similar meanings to *although* in sentence 7.

3.1 **2** as **3** when **4** as/when* **5** As **6** when (= every time; *whenever* also possible) **7** As/When* **8** While (= Although)
*As and *when* have a similar meaning. However *when* is more common than *as* in informal contexts.

3.2 **2** Despite getting **3** Despite being **4** Despite living **5** Despite the alarm going off **6** Despite there being **7** Despite being / Despite it being

3.3 **2** d, f – People here don't put much effort into the job seeing that it's so poorly paid. **3** c, e – My bike is unusual in that the front wheel is smaller than the back. **4** b, h – You need to lift the plant carefully so as not to damage its roots. **5** c, k – Pitcher plants are unique in that they are carnivorous. **6** a, i – The runway is going to be extended in order that larger planes can land there. **7** d, j – She'll probably recover from the illness quickly seeing that she's so fit. **8** b, l – We spoke very quietly so as not to be overheard.

3.4 A: **2** though **3** In spite of the fact that **4** before I go **5** seeing that
B: **1** Because **2** I'll have to **3** while (*whilst* would be very formal in this context) **4** so that I can **5** you get

Exam practice: Reading and Use of English Part 2
1 except (*but* also possible but unlikely in a more formal text such as this) **2** much **3** until / to / till **4** so **5** in **6** meet / turn **7** surprisingly **8** other

14 Conditionals

1.1 **a** a zoo **b** a game reserve **c** a safari park.

1.2 **2** Liam & Nadia **3** Nadia **4** Liam **5** Nadia & Mariam **6** Liam **7** Nadia **8** Nadia

1.3 **2** <u>Unless</u> we expand captive breeding, many more animals will die out. **3** <u>Even if</u> wild animals are born in a zoo, it's still cruel to keep them in a small enclosure … **4** I'm all in favour of safari parks <u>provided that</u> the animals are well looked after. **5** <u>Even though</u> they say they are concerned about the welfare of animals, just like zoos, they are still businesses mainly out to make a profit. **6** <u>So long as</u> developed countries put money into these reserves, species will be preserved.

3.1 **2** had known **3** used **4** promise **5** had; would **6** had been promoted; would have had to **7** leave; will be able to catch **8** had studied; wouldn't have

3.2 **2** if (we) didn't/don't get **3** even though (she) had been driving / had driven / drove **4** even though (I) have been doing / have done / did **5** Even if (it) rains / rained **6** unless (you) prefer / would prefer **7** Even if / Unless (a buyer) can – *Even if* … means that the company is likely to close by the end of the week whether or not there is a buyer. *Unless* … means that the company is likely to close only if no buyer can be found. **8** if (the election) was / were – *were* is more formal.

3.3 **2** f otherwise **3** a on condition that **4** c in the event of **5** e but for **6** b providing

3.4 A: **2** phone **3** will make / makes (similar meaning)
B: **1** had bought **2** had **3** was **4** would stop

Exam practice: Listening Part 4
Task One: **1** F **2** G **3** A **4** C **5** D
Task Two: **6** C **7** H **8** E **9** B **10** G

15 Participle to-infinitive and reduced clauses

1.1 1, 2 & 4

1.2 **2** Exhausted **3** Before leaving **4** Having left **5** But opening up **6** Having been woken up

3.1 **2** Covered in oil **3** Written **4** Having beaten **5** Having been shown **6** Not having **7** Putting on/ Having put on **8** Not being able to speak / Not speaking

3.2 **2** Seeing the pocket watches / On seeing the pocket watches (more formal) **3** Some (of them) being / With some (of them) being **4** Living in Hong Kong / Having lived in Hong Kong **5** After looking at / After having looked at **6** I got there to find / On getting there I found (more formal) **7** Having spent **8** (In order) to get **9** (When) looked at **10** Tired **11** before going out

3.3 **1** D *Other possible improvements:* As the signs were painted bright yellow I could see them clearly from a distance. / Painted (*or* Being painted) bright yellow the signs could be clearly seen from a distance. (The alternatives with *Painted* … and *Being painted* … are more formal than those with *Because* … and *As* … and would be more appropriate in writing.) **2** S **3** D Because / When I laughed at her new hat Jing looked really angry with me. / Because I was laughing at her new hat … **4** S **5** S **6** D Because they were talking to each other in the library I asked them to keep quiet. **7** D Crayfish are caught in traps put on the riverbed at night and many fishermen depend on them for their livelihood. **8** S

3.4 **2** While researching **3** Although (no longer) involved **4** Before/Until being made **5** Without asking **6** since leaving **7** once caught **8** With (the wind) reaching **9** until / before being woken **10** If found

Answer key

Exam practice: Reading and Use of English Part 3
1 Covering 2 plentiful 3 Renewed 4 sustainable
5 shortages 6 awareness 7 recycling 8 consumption

16 Noun clauses

1.1 1 birdwatching 2 using the Internet 3 giving someone a lift 4 bricklaying / building a brick wall 5 having / organising a barbecue 6 building a fence

1.2 2, 3, 5 & 6

1.3 2 F 3 F 4 T 5 T 6 T 7 F 8 F 9 T

1.4 1 that you'll make a lot of new friends 2 whatever time people can spare 3 when we usually meet 4 what to do 5 why the marsh was given to the NWT

1.5 *that* (1) and *wh*-words (2, 3, 4 & 5)

3.1 2 the fact that 3 The fact that 4 that 5 the fact that 6 that 7 the fact that 8 the fact that 9 that 10 the fact that 11 that

3.2 2 whichever direction you approach it 3 whether to take a guided tour 4 when the cathedral was built 5 where the building materials came from 6 how they managed to do that (*the way they managed to do that* also possible) 7 Who designed the cathedral 8 what conditions were like for the builders 9 the way the light shines through them (*how the light shines through them* also possible) 10 whoever wrote that 11 if I'd make it (*whether I'd make it* also possible)

3.3 2 e whatever 3 d whatever 4 a whoever 5 g whichever / whatever 6 h whatever 7 b whichever 8 f whichever

3.4 2 told us what questions 3 do you know how to drive 4 to teach me/you what to do (*to teach me/you how to do it* also possible) 5 showed me where to sit 6 about what would happen next 7 asked (her) when the doctor 8 the time when we were (*the time we were* also possible) 9 the problem of how to get back 10 The reason why I mention it (*The reason I mention it* also possible)

Exam practice: Reading and Use of English Part 1
1 C 2 C 3 D 4 A 5 C 6 C 7 B 8 A

17 Conjunctions and connectors

1.2 reversing around corners (Sahar), overtaking (Claudio), starting on a hill (Claudio)

1.3 1 c, b, a, d 2 h, f, g, e

1.4 2 <u>However</u> I had the mirror positioned, I just couldn't judge where the back of the car was. 3 <u>Even so</u>, I always found the replacements very patient and helpful. 4 <u>Although</u> it's expensive having driving lessons, I'd really recommend it. 5 <u>Even though</u> she doesn't have a professional qualification or anything, she's got lots of experience to pass on. 6 And <u>as long as</u> I didn't do anything stupid, she stayed pretty calm.

3.1 2 h – She always finds time to talk to students no matter how busy she is. / No matter how busy she is she always finds time to talk to students. 3 a – The restaurant's closed next Monday because it's a public holiday. / Because it's a public holiday the restaurant's closed next Monday. 4 e – He's a seismologist. That is to say he studies earthquakes. / He studies earthquakes. That is to say he's a seismologist. 5 f – Tuition fees have been increased. As a result the number of applications has fallen. 6 c – We travelled much faster once we got onto the motorway. / Once we got onto the motorway we travelled much faster. 7 b – The government is being urged to build more nuclear power stations. However such a move would be controversial. 8 g – He was wearing the same clothes as me except that his shoes were black.

3.2 2 until 3 Lastly 4 Even so 5 On the contrary 6 At last 7 Even though 8 no sooner

3.3 1 Note that we can't use *while* here because it is a conjunction. A sentence connector is needed to link the two sentences. 2 in case there's a power cut 3 whereas I prefer Italian (*while* also possible) 4 Consequently it isn't very heavy 5 otherwise we'll have to walk miles to the bridge 6 while she's looking for a new flat 7 In contrast in Marketing they get an hour 8 unless the weather's bad

3.4 A: 2 while 3 because 4 At first 5 Even so
B: 1 As well as 2 In spite of 3 until 4 hardly / no sooner (similar meaning) 5 What's more

Exam practice: Reading and Use of English Part 6
1 C 2 D 3 A 4 B

18 The passive

1.1 1 d 2 c 3 b (stealing mobile phones from children) 4 e (car crime can refer to stealing cars or stealing things from cars) 5 a (spraying graffiti)

1.2 car crime, vandalism (damage to property/graffiti), street crime (stealing mobile phones), drug-related crime burglary.

1.3 2 F (Peter Miles was appointed head of the police service) 3 T 4 F (Other countries are thinking of copying the government's scheme.) 5 T (She agreed that there had been an increase in street crime.) 6 F (She said she didn't know.) 7 F (She admitted that there might be mistakes in the figures.) 8 F (There is a campaign to reassure people it is falling.)

1.4 1 was given (passive) 2 have been arrested (passive) 3 are seeing (active) 4 have become (active) 5 were caught (passive) 6 was broken into (passive)

3.1 A: 2 is widely used 3 is viewed 4 are evaluated 5 is 6 is considered 7 collects 8 travels 9 believe 10 occur 11 is prevented 12 help
B: 1 were constructed 2 be used 3 weighed 4 be carried 5 advanced 6 be held 7 became / had become 8 was banned 9 suggests / has suggested 10 has not discouraged 11 predict / are predicting 12 will be conducted

3.2 2 His name is Robin but he is called Bobby by his friends. 3 (no passive) We might instead use *We had the procedure demonstrated to us …* 4 The news will be announced to staff later today … 5 I have been offered a new job in Hungary. 6 The surgery has been declared a complete success (by the medical staff). 7 (no passive) We might instead use *I had the idea suggested to me …* 8 This necklace was bought for me by my uncle when he was in Zimbabwe.

3.3 Note that the alternatives with *get* are more informal.
1 had/got her handbag stolen 2 was/got woken up; have been/got thrown out 3 had/got his hair cut; had/got his jacket cleaned 4 's (is) owned; getting broken into

3.4 2 we were made to run 3 she seemed to be supported by many of her colleagues 4 no passive (there is no passive form of *want* + object + *to*-infinitive) 5 remember being asked 6 he came to be liked by most of the children in the class 7 He was caught trying 8 She was heard to remark 9 no passive (there is no passive form of *need* + object + *to*-infinitive) 10 Over 100,000 demonstrators are expected to march

Exam practice: Reading and Use of English Part 7
1 D 2 A 3 F 4 B 5 G 6 E (C not used)

19 Reporting

1.2 Advantages: it would create 2000 jobs at the airport; it might encourage tourism in the region; it would help local business
Problems: it would damage tourism; the noise; the danger of a plane crashing into the nuclear power station

1.3 2 said that 3 promised to keep 4 encouraged us to go 5 warned us that 6 advised us to write 7 've (have) volunteered to write

1.4

verb + *that*-clause	verb + *to*-infinitive	verb + object + *that*-clause	verb + object + *to*-infinitive
said	promised volunteered	told warned*	encouraged advised

Warn can also be followed by *that*-clause (e.g. *She **warned that** the airport authorities were not telling the truth*).

3.1 2 grumbled / were grumbling 3 claimed it 4 reassured me 5 reveal to 6 emphasised 7 whispered to 8 persuade him 9 commiserate with 10 explained to

3.2 2 me to apply / me that I should apply 3 me that my research 4 to complete / that I will complete 5 to publish / publishing / that I will publish 6 my qualifications and experience to be / that my qualifications and experience are / that my qualifications and experience will be 7 to hear / that I will hear

3.3 2 told them (that) 3 (to them) that I had (had) problems / (to) having (had) problems 4 (that) I (should) look at / looking at 5 with me that my research 6 me to visit 7 me to write / that I (should) write / writing 8 to contact me / that they would contact me 9 to offer me / that they would/could offer me

3.4 2 (that) it's going to rain 3 (that) it was her coat. (*She thought that it wasn't her coat* also possible, although less likely.) 4 (that) I had to / must set the alarm when I leave / left the house. 5 where she left / had left her handbag. 6 (that) he was playing football 7 (that) he won't / wouldn't be able to give me a lift after all 8 how much I earn / earned. 9 (that) they might go to Italy 10 what he should do with the painting. / what to do with the painting.

Exam practice: Listening Part 4
1 F 2 C 3 B 4 G 5 E 6 B 7 F 8 H 9 A 10 D

20 Substitution and ellipsis

1.1 1 caving/potholing 2 camping 3 river rafting 4 skydiving/paragliding 5 (scuba) diving 6 surfing 7 sailing

1.2 a face mask; a snorkel; a sun hat; plastic trainers & insect repellent.

1.3 2 One of the local organisers did (met me at the airport). 3 They should do provide all the equipment. 4 But you don't have to be a very good swimmer. 5 Preferably plastic ones trainers. 6 By the end of the holiday I was exhausted but I was very fit. 7 You'll certainly need some insect repellent. 8 I don't imagine so you'll need to take a tent and cooking things.

3.1 2 to ask you / to ask you 3 has eaten anything today / has eaten anything today 4 would have been shocked / would have been shocked / would have been shocked 5 to leave work early / to leave work early 6 had been opened / had been opened 7 to get promoted 8 did know I was getting married / did know I was getting married

3.2 2 No (*ones* is not used on its own to replace a noun phrase. We could say (*some*) *new ones* 3 ones 4 (one) 5 (ones) 6 No (talking about specific items; we could replace *the car keys* with *them*) 7 one 8 (one) 9 one 10 (ones) / (ones)

3.3 2 so did 3 do (*do so* would be unnaturally formal here) 4 so 5 that 6 do 7 (doing) that (*doing so* would be unnaturally formal here) 8 doing so 9 (that) she will (do) (*do so* would be unnaturally formal here particularly after a modal verb. Note that *do* is optional here.) 10 so does

3.4 2 small one 3 some 4 one 5 so 6 it was 7 neither was my boss / my boss wasn't either 8 time / time to 9 so was I / I was too 10 didn't 11 ones 12 don't expect so / expect not 13 want / want to 14 're not able to / can't 15 hope not

Exam practice: Listening Part 3
1 C 2 B 3 D 4 D 5 B 6 A

Answer key

21 Word order and emphasis

1.2 In the order they appear in the recording: enthusiasm, persuasive, determined

1.3 2 F (the council lends them musical instruments) 3 T 4 F (the council backed down from their plan to make them pay) 5 F (People come from other countries to see the project)

1.4 2 <u>Making music</u> she sees as a fundamental part of a child's development 3 <u>What impressed us most</u> was the way she calmly and clearly argued her case. 4 <u>Rarely</u> have I met anyone with such passion for their beliefs. 5 <u>A number of times</u> the council has tried to make changes to the *Music in Schools* project in order to save money. 6 <u>Only after Maria threatened to withdraw her support from the project</u> did the council back down.

1.5 The difference in the word order in the sentences you wrote emphasises the information underlined in the key to 1.4, above.

3.1 2 <u>It was at her 18th birthday party that</u> she announced she was going to join the air force. 3 <u>What we did was</u> (to) ask a farmer to pull us out with his tractor. 4 <u>It could be the battery that's</u> flat. 5 <u>What I don't know is</u> who sent them. 6 <u>It must have been my parents who/that</u> gave Wei my telephone number. 7 <u>What the research shows is</u> a link between salt intake and rates of heart disease. 8 <u>It was his nervous laugh that</u> made me think he was lying. / <u>What made me think he was lying was</u> his nervous laugh.

3.2 2 f – <u>Should/Were today's match have to be postponed</u>, it will be replayed next week. 3 g – <u>Had anyone been looking at Maria when the police arrived</u>, they would have noticed the expression of panic on her face. 4 d – <u>Should/Were taxes to be increased further</u>, there would be a huge public outcry. 5 a – <u>Had the doctors operated sooner</u>, she might have made a full recovery. 6 h – <u>Were I president</u>, I would introduce three-day weekends. 7 b – <u>Should/Were your flight to be cancelled,</u> the insurance covers a full refund. 8 e – <u>Had heavy snow been forecast</u>, we would not have begun the climb.

3.3 *Suggested answers:* 2 have I heard 3 did he discover/find/realise 4 did I know/realise 5 have there been 6 did she answer/tell 7 had he got 8 did she say

3.4 2 It was the hotel that was the real problem. / What was the real problem was the hotel. 3 that she really got furious about 4 First came an electrician 5 Three days it took them 6 What annoyed me most was the attitude of the staff / It was the attitude of the staff that annoyed me most 7 Never have I seen 8 Not once did anyone apologise

Exam practice: Reading and Use of English Part 4

1 did she take pride in 2 was her hatred / dislike 3 was no alternative (for her) but / was no alternative but for her 4 had I made a complaint 5 were she ever to become / if she were ever to become / if she ever were to become 6 distinct possibility of my / me getting

22 Nominalisation

1.2 c, e, a, d, f, b

1.3 2 increase in 3 closure of 4 rise in 5 discovery of 6 evacuation of

1.4 *Suggested answers:* 2 The number of people living close to the lake has <u>increased</u>. 3 Thousands of homes and businesses would be left without electricity if the power stations <u>closed</u>. 4 The level of radon gas in the soil <u>rose</u> dramatically. 5 Scientists discovered thousands of dead fish which <u>increased</u> their concerns. 6 30,000 people began to be <u>evacuated</u> two days ago. / The army began to <u>evacuate</u> 30,000 people two days ago.

3.1 *Suggested answers:* 2 The organisation of the conference was very professional. 3 The turnout for the match was huge. / There was a huge turnout for the match. 4 The withdrawal of the troops was immediate. / There was an immediate withdrawal of troops. 5 A shake-up in/of top management is needed for the company to be successful again. 6 The increase in interest rates was the third in two months. / There was an increase in interest rates for the third time in two months. 7 An agreement was reached on extra funding for the project. / There was an agreement reached on extra funding for the project. 8 The decision to postpone the race was taken/made/reached at the last moment.

3.2 *Suggested answers:* 2 Johan's obsession with cars started when he was quite young. 3 The expansion of the nuclear power programme has been criticised by opposition politicians. 4 The reduction in the price of petrol is good news for drivers. 5 The abolition of parking charges in the city centre has led to / has resulted in increased business for shops. 6 The demand for healthier food in school is the result of / is due to growing concerns about childhood obesity. 7 The departure of the train will be delayed for half an hour because of engine problems. 8 The appointment of a new college principal may lead to / result in staff leaving.

3.3 2 the complexity of the English spelling system 3 the response to its recruitment drive 4 the threat to animal and plant species 5 the strong resistance to increased taxation / the strength of the resistance to increased taxation 6 the extent of the damage to property

3.4 2 made a start 3 do some/the gardening 4 Give (me) a shout 5 made/taken a decision 6 I have a feeling 7 made an arrangement 8 take a deep breath 9 give him an explanation of 10 have a talk with 11 gave her a call 12 had a chat 13 gave a sigh 14 take/have a shower 15 have a rest 16 do the cooking 17 have/take a look

Exam practice: Reading and Use of English Part 8

1 D 2 B 3 C 4 A 5 B 6 A 7 C 8 A 9 D 10 B

Answer key

23 It and *there*

1.3 2 T 3 T 4 C 5 C 6 C 7 T 8 C

1.4 2 c - the town apartment 3 e – the decoration in the town apartment 4 g – Canley 5 i – Canley 6 j 7 k and l – the town apartment

3.1 2 there was nobody in the room 3 – 4 there is one opposite the railway station 5 There are only ten places available 6 there was no milk left 7 – 8 There was something on the radio

3.2 2 b there 3 a there 4 a it 5 a it 6 c it 7 a there 8 b it

3.3 2 It's no good 3 It's no secret 4 there's no harm in 5 there's no chance of 6 There's no need 7 it's no longer 8 There's no (need to) hurry

3.4 2 it doesn't hurt to 3 there is (there's) nobody by 4 it turned out that 5 don't expect there to be 6 see it as my role 7 think there is Internet 8 remember you saying that 9 I prefer it if 10 There's no reason to get

Exam practice: Reading and Use of English Part 4

1 in order to be 2 there is (there's) no question of rearranging 3 no difficulty (in) recognising 4 get along with one 5 did they bring up 6 there is (there's) no point (in) discussing

24 Complex prepositions and prepositions after verbs

1.2 Instruction 3

1.3 2 you; up 3 out; the train times 4 on; the train 5 into; the hotel 6 out; the bill 7 around; town

1.4 1 I'm afraid I've messed **our plans up** for tomorrow. 3 I've found **the train times out** from the SNCF website … 6 I'll sort **the bill out** when I pick you up on Thursday afternoon.

3.1 2 throw away some of my old exercise books from school (*more natural than* throw some of my old exercise books from school away *because the object is long*) 3 gathered her papers up / gathered up her papers 4 bumped into Lea 5 tell the twins apart 6 talk you out of leaving college 7 woke me and my husband up / woke up me and my husband 8 try them out

3.2 2 as opposed to the 10,000 predicted 3 regardless of their ability to pay 4 thanks to a strict protein-only diet 5 for the sake of their health 6 along with an excellent art gallery 7 by way of an apology 8 with effect from 30th September

3.3 1 advised against using 2 dismissed the reports as; prevent her (from) doing 3 congratulated them on achieving; had benefited from taking part in 4 has quarrelled/has been quarrelling with her European counterparts over; ended in/with her walking

3.4 2 with 3 from 4 out* 5 with 6 to 7 over/on 8 after 9 out 10 in 11 of 12 with 13 in 14 of 15 into 16 over/round* 17 (a)round/at/over 18 on 19 into 20 in 21 of 22 from* 23 over/out* 24 to 25 in 26 with/to 27 up 28 over/round* 29 out*

* No preposition also possible in these answers

Exam practice: Listening Part 1

1 C 2 B 3 A 4 B 5 C 6 B

25 Prepositions after nouns and adjectives

1.2 2 b 3 g 4 f 5 a 6 d 7 e 8 h 9 c

1.3 2 demand for 3 need 4 decision to 5 need for 6 complain about 7 complaints about 8 demand 9 decided to 10 influence on

1.4 2 <u>demand</u> for & 8 demand (verb – no preposition); 4 <u>decision</u> to & 9 decided (verb) to; 5 <u>need</u> for & 3 need (verb – no preposition); 7 <u>complaints</u> about & 6 complain (verb) about

3.1 2 at 3 for 4 with 5 about 6 on 7 about 8 for

3.2 *Suggested answers:* 2 had an influence on 3 take pride in 4 have great admiration for 5 caused serious damage to 6 As a solution to

3.3 2 to cut 3 using / the use of 4 the number of visitors to 5 of organising / to organise 6 to move 7 the closure of 8 protecting / the protection of 9 recovering / recovery 10 of holding

3.4 A: 2 of 3 on 4 about 5 by 6 in 7 to 8 about 9 with B: 1 about 2 from 3 with 4 about 5 with 6 with 7 over 8 with 9 for 10 in 11 for

Exam practice: Reading and Use of English Part 1

1 A 2 B 3 B 4 D 5 C 6 C 7 C 8 B

26 Cities

1.2 2 construction 3 rural 4 outskirts 5 residents 6 consequences 7 environment 8 pollution

1.3 1 urban 2 commercial 3 area 4 undeveloped 5 residents

1.4

Noun	Verb	Adjective
demolition	**demolish**	**demolished**
development **developer**	develop	**developed** undeveloped
resident **residence**	reside	**residential**
environment **environmentalist**	✗	**environmental**
pollution **pollutant**	pollute	polluted

271

Answer key

1.5 1 tourist *attractions* 2 *traffic* congestion; *city* centre 3 public *transport* system 4 pedestrian *area* 5 Exhaust *fumes*; air *pollution* 6 traffic *jams*; *rush* hours

1.6 1 crime-free 2 car-free 3 cyclist-friendly 4 pet-friendly 5 car-mad 6 work-mad

2.1 1 hustle 2 social; contact 3 range 4 cost 5 centre 6 hop; underground 7 rates; rural

2.3 2 d 3 e 4 a 5 c

2.4 1 psychological 2 belief 3 inclusive 4 residents 5 helpful 6 installation 7 surprisingly 8 significant

Exam practice: Reading and Use of English Part 5
1 B 2 D 3 A 4 C 5 C 6 B

27 Personal history

1.2 2 ancestors 3 genealogical 4 process 5 backwards 6 conducting 7 sources 8 documenting 9 descent 10 descendant

1.3 1 people who have Irish ancestors 2 Family legends … are rarely 100% accurate; The truth may be somewhat less attractive than … in family tales; You will find it impossible to retain (all the information) in your head; Don't be too ambitious (or you may be disappointed).

1.4 2 reminisce 3 the biggest hurdle 4 a grain of truth 5 skeletons in the cupboard 6 draw the line 7 branch of your roots 8 accumulate huge amounts of information

1.5

Noun	Verb	Adjective
accumulation	accumulate	**accumulated**
accuracy **inaccuracy**	✗	accurate **inaccurate**
ancestor **ancestry**	✗	**ancestral**
embellishment	embellish	**embellished**
reminiscence	reminisce	**reminiscent**
verification **verifier**	verify	verified **verifiable**

1.6 1 hurdle 2 grains 3 draw the line 4 embellishments 5 inaccurate 6 reminiscent

1.7 1 exposes long-buried secrets 2 keep residents in the dark 3 digging up dirt 4 sweep recent statistics on inner-city crime under the carpet 5 cover his tracks 6 muddy the waters

1.8 1 dig up dirt (on somebody) 2 cover your tracks 3 muddy the waters 4 keep (somebody) in the dark 5 expose long-buried secrets 6 sweep (something) under the carpet

2.1 An *autobiography* is the story of someone's life written by that person. A *biography* is written by another person.

2.2 2 confront 3 forget 4 accurate 5 myths 6 traces 7 hoarded 8 reports 9 appointments 10 blank

2.3 2 created; originating; put together 3 countless; many; numerous 4 expensive; important; precious 5 bits; fragments; small pieces

2.4 1 curiosity 2 unforgettable 3 requirement 4 accuracy 5 guilty 6 forgetful

Exam practice: Writing Part 1 – An essay
A model answer to this question can be found at www.cambridge.org/grammarvocabadvanced

28 The arts

1.2 a 3, 6, 9, 11 b 2, 3, 6 c 1, 10, 12 d 5 e 1, 7, 12 f 2, 3, 4, 6, 8, 11 g 3 h 1, 9

1.3 *Model answers*

visual arts	sculpture, **painting, textiles, drawing, photography, ceramics, film**
styles of music	soul, **blues, rock, pop, hip-hop, funk, jazz, classical, R&B, electronic** folk
types of literature	novel, **poetry, poem, short story, essay, play, novella**
types of dance	ballet, **jazz, modern, tap, ballroom, hip-hop, Latin, street, contemporary**
genres of film	thriller, **romantic, comedy, drama, action, fantasy, adventure, science-fiction**
artists	composer, dancer, **comedian, painter, author, director, actor, sculptor, poet**

1.4 2 c 3 a 4 e 5 f 6 b

1.5 2 surgical instrument 3 match-winning performance 4 third-quarter performance 5 musical instrument 6 opening performance 7 scientific instrument 8 academic performance

2.1 1 d 2 a 3 c

2.2 2 small provincial theatre 3 a hint of irony 4 following 5 a great fan of 6 in stitches 7 is the right word 8 by hand

2.3 1 6 2 4

2.4 1 back-catalogue 2 a capacity audience 3 melodic 4 lines/part 5 part/character 6 learn(ing) by rote

2.5 1 chaos 2 melancholy 3 exhilaration 4 melody 5 intimacy 6 euphoria

2.6 2 classic 3 understated; subtle 4 intimate; boisterous 5 edgy 6 sweet; insistent 7 emotional

2.7 2 and 3 tells/is 4 in 5 that 6 has 7 without 8 on 9 down 10 each/one 11 keep 12 but

Exam practice: Reading and Use of English Part 1
1 D 2 A 3 B 4 B 5 C 6 D 7 B 8 A

Answer key

29 Migrations

1.1 **2** expatriates **3** asylum seekers **4** refugees **5** contract workers **6** professionals **7** illegal immigrants

1.3 **2** a **3** b **4** d **5** e

1.4

Noun	Verb	Adjective
danger	endanger	endangered **dangerous**
legality illegality **legalisation**	**legalise**	**legal** illegal
persecution persecutor	persecute	**persecuted**
smuggling smuggler	smuggle	**smuggled**
specialism specialisation **specialist**	**specialise**	specialist **specialised**

2.1 **1** dreary routine **2** surroundings **3** homesickness **4** took **5** return (home)

2.2 **1** strong expat community; exciting place; multicultural; amazing places to eat and drink; one of the best cities in Asia for shopping; summer all year round **2** wedding; met Jason's friends; joined a kickboxing class; going to have a baby

2.3 **2** a **3** e **4** c **5** b **6** d

2.4 **2** multilingual **3** multinational **4** multicoloured **5** multifunctional

2.5 **2** sense of belonging **3** sense of humour **4** sense of duty **5** sense of responsibility **6** sense of loss

2.6 **1** make a life change, e.g. new job, move house, etc. **2** yes **3** more **4** quickly **5** not **6** less **7** easier **8** no

Exam practice: Listening Part 2
1 destinations **2** graduate **3** economy **4** accommodation **5** warned **6** travel companies/agencies **7** resident **8** confidence

30 Risking it

1.1 **2** g **3** f **4** b **5** h **6** a **7** e **8** d

1.3 **2** participants **3** associated **4** released **5** fear **6** levels **7** exertion **8** tentative **9** recreational **10** accident **11** activity **12** individual

1.4 **2** d **3** a **4** c **5** e

1.5 **TAKE:** advice, care, a chance, effect, exercise, part, precautions, responsibility, steps to
MAKE: a decision, a difference, an effort, progress, sure, use of

1.6 **2** take part; take advice **3** take (full) responsibility **4** take (the proper) precautions **5** make a choice (*make a decision* also possible)

2.1 **2** Teenagers enjoy the excitement that comes from taking risks.

2.2 **2** four main groups **3** worse outcome **4** losing (all) the **5** relatively minor **6** be more sensible

2.3 **2** The beginning of the stage that turns someone into an adult.

2.4 **2** amused **3** analysing **4** enthusiasm

3.1 **2** employees **3** reasonable **4** avoid **5** expert **6** competent **7** representatives **8** responsible **9** chance **10** serious

Exam practice: Reading and Use of English Part 7
1 E **2** D **3** G **4** F **5** C **6** A (B not used)

31 Gender issues

1.1 M: cameraman; fireman
N: actor; doctor; firefighter; midwife/nurse; police officer; solicitor; surgeon; teacher
F: headmistress; waitress; policewoman

1.2 1 & 3

1.3 **2** categorise **3** biased **4** sexes **5** neutral **6** stereotypes

1.4 **1** comedian/comic **2** humankind/people/humanity **3** ancestors/predecessors/forebears **4** flight attendants **5** synthetic/artificial **6** companions/partners/spouses

1.5 **2** of **3** on **4** to **5** on **6** about

1.6 **1** shocking **2** takes responsibility **3** underpaid **4** pay attention

1.7 **1** be treated as **2** make inroads **3** in a derogatory way **4** historical disadvantage

2.2 *arrogant* – arrogance; *attractive* – attraction/attractiveness; *competitive* – competition/competitiveness; *driven* – drive; *flexible* – flexibility; *gifted* – gift; *graceful* – grace; *passive* – passivity; *powerful* – power; *pure* – purity; *submissive* – submission/submissiveness

2.3 **1** discrimination **2** activity **3** abilities **4** competitions **5** leadership **6** decision **7** inadequate **8** unequal

2.4 **1** F (*She started at the age of three and finished when she was 18.*) **2** T **3** F (*She had never thought about it being a traditionally female sport.*) **4** T **5** F (*She says she can see that things are moving away from this gender-typing.*)

2.5

Noun	Verb	Adjective
category	categorise	✗
contribution contributor	contribute	**contributory**
discrimination	discriminate	**discriminatory**
equality	equalise	equal
involvement	involve	**involved**
perpetuation	perpetuate	**perpetual**
neutrality	✗	neutral

273

Answer key

2.6 2 deem 3 complete 4 predominantly 5 overt
6 participate

Exam practice: Reading and Use of English Part 4
1 took full responsibility for his/the team's 2 not to be acceptable [in/at] 3 object to people using 4 took part in competitive sport 5 was under the impression 6 has been called off due/owing

32 Education

1.2 2 graduate 3 needs 4 classroom 5 potential 6 method
7 child-centred 8 influence 9 images 10 foster 11 whole
12 capacity

1.3 2 g 3 e 4 a 5 f 6 d 7 b

1.4 2 with 3 about/on 4 on 5 by 6 of 7 for/of 8 to

1.5

Noun	Verb	Adjective
establishment	establish	**established**
graduation graduate	graduate	✗
education **educator**	**educate**	**educated** educational
innovation innovator	innovate	innovative
influence	**influence**	**influential**
motivation motivator	motivate	motivated **motivating** motivational

1.6 1 newly 2 firmly 3 highly 4 poorly 5 highly
6 increasingly 7 strongly 8 politically

2.1 1 He struggled to get a job. 2 Much better than now. (*They were able to walk into an office, talk to the manager and get a job.*) 3 You get hands-on experience and you get paid while you learn. 4 Ship/boat building (*trainee engineer, training in engineering theory and boat and ship design*).

2.2 1 impossible 2 references 3 hands-on 4 training
5 courses 6 trainees 7 giving something back

2.3 2 apply 3 insight 4 team-building 5 learned

2.4 1 enable 2 capabilities 3 understanding 4 interactive
5 application 6 electrical 7 realisation 8 researchers

Exam practice: Reading and Use of English Part 6
1 A 2 B 3 D 4 C

33 Health

1.2 1 *infectious* = spread by germs; *contagious* = spread by bodily contact 2 *starvation* = state of suffering or death caused by having no food; *malnutrition* = physical weakness and bad health caused by lack of food 3 *treatment* = includes all of the things that are done to help a sick or injured person, e.g. surgery/counselling/medication; *medicine* = substance which is drunk or swallowed as part of medical treatment 4 *transmit* = pass a disease on to another person; *contract* = get a disease from another person 5 *epidemic* = outbreak of disease that spreads through one or more communities; *pandemic* = an epidemic which spreads throughout the world 6 *acute* = suddenly very serious; *preventable* = applying current medical knowledge can stop/reduce the incidence of the disease

1.3 1 deaths globally are caused by cardiovascular diseases.
2 infectious diseases than were killed by natural or man-made catastrophes. 3 1.6 million people die from them each year. 4 (mostly children) died from measles.
5 immunise someone against measles.

1.4

Noun	Verb	Adjective
immunisation **immunity**	**immunise**	**immune**
infection	**infect**	**infectious** infected
medication	medicate	medical medicated
prevention	**prevent**	**preventative** preventable
treatment	treat	**treatable** untreated

2.1 1 300 million people. 2 In the 1700s. 3 An English doctor who developed the smallpox vaccination. 4 In 1959.

2.2 1 T 2 T 3 F (*Smallpox often led to death.*) 4 F (*Farm labourers ...*) 5 T 6 F (*The last recorded case was in 1977 and the disease was declared defeated shortly after.*)

2.3 2 mismanagement 3 misconduct 4 misdiagnosis
5 misinformation 6 misrepresentation

3.1 c

3.2 1 detoxify (your body) 2 appetite suppressant 3 total energy intake 4 be on a diet 5 fluid 6 be prone to
7 dehydrated

3.3 1 for/to 2 for 3 to 4 in 5 at 6 with 7 to

Exam practice: Writing Part 2 – A report
A model answer to this question can be found at www.cambridge.org/grammarvocabadvanced

Answer key

34 Getting about

1.1 **2** trip **3** travel **4** trips **5** travel **6** trip
1.2 **2** g **3** d **4** e **5** h **6** b **7** c **8** a
1.3 **1** P **2** A **3** C **4** C **5** C **6** A **7** P
1.4 **1** bike capital **2** extensive network **3** theft **4** rent **5** dramatic increase **6** low incomes **7** fitted with **8** programme **9** traffic lanes **10** returnable deposit
2.1 **2** get around **3** private cars **4** fossil fuels **5** self-driving vehicles **6** eco-friendly
2.2 *Model answers:* **1** I'd get around by taxi so I wouldn't get lost. **2** I'd get by with gestures and pointing. **3** I get out of doing things I don't want to by saying I'm not feeling very well.
2.4 **2** to **3** on **4** in **5** to **6** with

Exam practice: Listening Part 1
1 A **2** A **3** B **4** C **5** B **6** C

35 Moods

1.1 **1** frowned; fly off – illustration E **2** tragic; trembled; devastated – illustration C **3** sails; care; laid-back – illustration B **4** mind; bites; stammers – illustration A **5** clouds; dreamers; lighten – illustration D
1.2 **2** E **3** D **4** C **5** A
1.3 **2** tearful **3** angry **4** calm/relaxed **5** optimistic
1.4 **2** anxiety **3** apprehension **4** calm **5** confrontation **6** contentment **7** fury **8** misery **9** optimism/optimist **10** patience **11** positivity **12** relaxation
1.5 **1** calm **2** confront **3** angered/infuriated
1.6 **2** ravenous; **3** excruciating; **4** devastating **5** petrifying; **6** ludicrous; **7** astonishing; **8** hideous
1.7 **1** mildly **2** particularly; ravenous **3** ludicrous; a bit **4** completely; hideous **5** devastating; bitterly
1.8 **2** c **3** a **4** e **5** b
2.2 **2** photographic **3** retain **4** mind **5** forgotten **6** ear **7** short-term **8** recall
2.3 **1** ✓ **2** ✗ **3** ✓ **4** ✓ **5** ✓ **6** ✗
2.4 **1** traumatic; bitter **2** early, childhood **3** trigger a memory; bring back a memory; jog someone's memory **4** vague

Exam practice: Reading and Use of English Part 1
1 D **2** A **3** C **4** A **5** D **6** C **7** A **8** B

36 Fame and fortune

1.2 **2** lucrative **3** talents **4** appearance **5** media **6** exposure **7** attained **8** stalked
1.3 **1** immense **2** sought-after **3** (social) perks **4** accomplishments **5** aspire to **6** envy **7** status **8** the public eye
1.4 **2** benefit (is not an ability) **3** devotion (does not have a negative meaning) **4** entitlement (is not about people's opinions of you) **5** perk (does not consist of money)
1.5 **2** royalty **3** rewards **4** Consultancy **5** reality **6** attaining **7** value **8** non-famous **9** talented **10** credibility
1.6 **2** lifestyle **3** endorsements **4** coverage **5** gossip **6** attention
1.7 **1** stalk **2** famous; envy **3** achieve; forgotten **4** talented; individuals **5** personalities; from **6** recommend; weird
2.2 **Speaker 1:** relaxing entertainment **Speaker 2:** a bit of an embarrassment **Speaker 3:** my kind of television
2.3 **1** trashy novel **2** unwind **3** car crash **4** story lines **5** common ground **6** group dynamics
2.4

Noun	Verb	Adjective
addict **addiction**	**addict**	addictive **addicted**
drama **dramatisation dramatist**	**dramatise**	**dramatic**
fantasy **fantasist**	**fantasise**	**fantastical**
manipulation manipulator	manipulate	**manipulative**

Exam practice: Reading and Use of English Part 2
1 to **2** them **3** who / that **4** on **5** It **6** in **7** as **8** up

37 Relationships

1.1 **1** mediator; listener; friend; (impartial) judge **2** fifty or sixty years ago **3** globalisation
1.2 **2** b **3** d **4** c **5** a
1.3 **1** stability **2** dependable **3** impartial
1.4 **2** bridges the gap **3** dependable **4** at loggerheads **5** stability **6** impartial
1.5 appreciate – recognise; doubt – question; erode – weaken; impart – inform; instil – teach
1.6 **2** A *tough upbringing* teaches you survival skills. **3** People do not feel lucky to have a *dysfunctional family*. **4** An *uneasy relationship* would make marriage difficult. **5** *Pushy parents* are not fragile, they are assertive.
2.2 **2** conflicts **3** ruin **4** advice **5** partnership **6** contribute
2.3 Speaker **1** is the only speaker who advises against friends going into business together.
2.4 **Speaker 1** c **Speaker 2** b **Speaker 3** d **Speaker 4** a
2.5 **2** f **3** d **4** b **5** c **6** a
2.6 **1** letdown **2** break-up **3** falling out

Exam practice: Listening Part 3
1 D **2** B **3** C **4** B **5** A **6** C

275

Answer key

38 Time off

1.2 2 tropical resorts 3 pack 4 destination 5 self-catering 6 isolated beach 7 spectacular scenery 8 entertainments 9 two-week 10 local cuisine

1.3 2 an adventure holiday 3 a foreign holiday 4 a public holiday 5 a beach holiday 6 book a holiday

1.5 1 spectacular 2 authentic local 3 extravagant; artificial 4 exotic 5 unheard-of

2.1 2 aerobics 3 martial arts 4 walking 5 football 6 tennis 7 swimming 8 dance

2.2 2 football pitch / tennis court 3 walking pace 4 swimming costume 5 aerobics class 6 dance partner

2.4 1 F 2 T 3 T 4 F 5 T 6 T 7 F 8 F

2.5 1 minor adjustments 2 activating your muscles 3 extortionate fees 4 spectator 5 doing them a favour

2.6 1 off 2 up 3 off 4 on 5 back 6 about

Exam practice: Reading and Use of English Part 8
1 D 2 B 3 A 4 B 5 C 6 A 7 A 8 E 9 C 10 E

39 Media

1.2 2 reported 3 media channels 4 expert analyst 5 directly 6 tuning in 7 subscribe to 8 targeted information 9 mobile devices 10 access to

1.3 2 unfiltered 3 social news 4 emerge 5 consume

1.4

Noun	Verb	Adjective
analyst analysis	**analyse**	analytic analytical
domination dominance	dominate	dominant
emergence	emerge	emergent emerging
subscription subscriber	subscribe	oversubscribed undersubscribed
explosion explosive	explode	explosive
consumption consumer	consume	consumable

1.5 2 explosion 3 analyse 4 consumers 5 emergence 6 dominance/domination

1.6 1 *explosive device* – what it does not how it works 2 *digital device* – how it works not how it is used 3 *labour-saving device* – a benefit not what it does

2.2 2 with 3 well 4 it 5 without 6 into 7 In

2.3 1 All four speakers are in favour of the idea.
2 Speaker 1 does not think that the laws will be wholly successful (*media corporations that want to profit without fear of correction or sanction at the expense of the individual*). Speaker 2 thinks they will be successful. Speaker 3 does not think they will be successful (*for every move on the chessboard of free speech there is an equal and opposite move which negates openness*).
Speaker 4 does not think the laws will be successful (*I don't think from the perspective of responsible news organisations that it's going to make much difference*).

2.4 1 investigative 2 expression 3 human rights 4 accountability 5 expense

2.6 1 b 2 a 3 b 4 b

Exam practice: Reading and Use of English Part 4
1 it is my ambition / my ambition is 2 afford to sue
3 it is likely that traditional newspapers 4 first saw / saw the beginning/introduction of 5 can't imagine living / life
6 took (me) all morning to look

40 The world of work

1.2 2 customer services 3 construction 4 mining 5 agriculture 6 entertainment

1.3 1 F (Her first job was working for an insurance company.) 2 F (Her job was moved to India but she herself doesn't work there.) 3 T 4 T 5 T 6 F (Five people work on the farm including him and his wife.)

1.4 1 youth unemployment 2 general office skills 3 call centre 4 retired 5 made redundant 6 out of work 7 take over from 8 cover costs

1.5 2 dictate; dismiss 3 disturbs 4 acquire 5 employer; compensation

1.6 2 job 3 work; job 4 work 5 work; job

1.7 1 *work* experience 2 *job* satisfaction; *work*load 3 *job* security 4 *work* environment 5 *work* permit; *job* offer 6 *job* market; *job*seekers 7 *work* colleagues; *job* opportunities 8 *work* clothes; *work* space

2.1 1 She applied for a US visa to escape the doom and gloom. 2 Living and working in a city like New York is like a dream come true … 3 … there were still jobs for the more educated members of the workforce. 4 … I imagined myself climbing the corporate ladder …

2.2 2 freelance 3 doom and gloom 4 work ethic 5 churn out 6 prospects 7 spring up 8 thriving

2.3 1 Immigrants are sometimes needed to fill gaps in the labour market because there are not enough sufficiently well-qualified job seekers in a country or because there are not enough people willing to do low-level work.
2 Ambitious people want to climb the corporate ladder.

Exam practice: Reading and Use of English Part 3
1 satisfaction 2 appreciated 3 leadership 4 contribution 5 objectives 6 technological 7 workforce 8 essential

Answer key

41 Economics and business

1.1 2 go bust 3 recession; slump; downturn 4 credit crunch 5 crash 6 inflation 7 interest rate 8 tumble; weaken; fall

1.2 *Speaker 1:* fuel / gas* / heating *Speaker 2:* higher education / college fees

* In British English *gas* is used for heating houses and cooking. In American English *gas* (or *gasoline*) is fuel used in cars and other vehicles.

1.3 1 mess 2 keep up 3 hit 4 check 5 debt 6 alarming 7 jumpy 8 free fall

1.4 a 7 b 2 c 8 d 1 e 6 f 4 g 5 h 3

1.5 2 retailers 3 stock 4 spending 5 non-essentials 6 income 7 market 8 profits

1.6 2 make ends meet 3 not out of the woods 4 cut spending to the bone 5 eke out 6 a double-edged sword

1.7 1 rocket, soar 2 cut, lower, reduce 3 disconcerting, disturbing, worrying

2.1 A Get the finance you need B Focus on the essentials C Play to your strengths D Take advice

2.2 1 develop; establish; maintain 2 establish; launch; start 3 flourish; prosper; succeed 4 look for; search for; try to find

2.3 1 into 2 to 3 on 4 over

2.4 1 investors 2 partnership 3 productive 4 expenditure

Exam practice: Writing Part 1 – An essay
A model answer to this question can be found at www.cambridge.org/grammarvocabadvanced

42 The living world

1.2 1 Fish 2 Mammals 3 Amphibians 4 Reptiles 5 Insects 6 Birds

1.3

Amphibians	Birds	Fish	Insects	Mammals	Reptiles
frog	owl	shark	bee	horse	snake
newt	swallow	mackerel	ant	whale	crocodile
toad	vulture	salmon	cricket	wolf	lizard

1.4 1 owl 2 bee 3 wolf 4 snake 5 salmon

1.5 1 young animals 2 things humans do to animals 3 groups of animals 4 animal homes 5 things animals do 6 animal body parts

1.6 1 extinction / becoming extinct. 2 25%

1.7 2 declining 3 vital 4 existence 5 pollinate 6 grains 7 disappear 8 economic 9 humans 10 pesticides

1.8

Noun	Verb	Adjective
decline	**decline**	declining
disappearance	disappear	**disappearing**

existence	exist	existing existent non-existent
extinction	x	extinct
pollination **pollen**	pollinate	pollinated
theorist **theory**	theorise	**theoretical**

2.1 b 3 c 4 d 1

2.3 1 used to build homes 2 material for clothes 3 aspirin 4 taxol (cure for cancer) 5 (ingredients for) cosmetics 6 soap; glue; plastics

2.4 1 Unlike *farmers, gardeners* do not grow crops for profit. Gardeners' work is often aesthetic and they can be employed on other people's land. 2 *Roots* are parts of a tree or plant that spread underground whereas *branches* are parts of a tree that spread above ground. 3 *Carnivorous* animals eat mainly meat but *omnivorous* creatures eat vegetable foodstuffs as well. 4 *Shelter* means protection from the weather and other possible threats while *habitat* refers to a specific living environment.

2.5 1 aquatic, endangered, wild, exotic, flowering 2 wild, marine, furry, domestic, endangered, exotic, aquatic 3 clean, thin, cold, humid, fresh 4 humid, cold, mild, harsh, arid, temperate

Exam practice: Listening Part 4
Task One: 1 D 2 C 3 A 4 E 5 H
Task Two: 6 B 7 C 8 F 9 A 10 E

43 Personal contact

1.2 *Possible answers:* a 1, 2, 3, 4 b 2, 3, 4, 7 c 2, 3, 4 d 5 e 1, 3, 6
f 2, 3, 4 g 2, 3, 4 h 1, 3, 6

1.3 2 touch 3 reconnect 4 relationships 5 share 6 forums 7 business 8 Members 9 profile 10 location

1.4 2 a question 3 an opinion 4 a friend 5 an understanding

1.5 *Possible answers:* 1 credentials – using scans of official documents 2 passion – no I don't meet new people online 3 identities – fraud and other serious crimes 4 reality – yes I think people feel disconnected

1.6 1 e 2 a 3 d 4 f 5 c 6 b

2.1 3 *letter* – addressed and put in an envelope communicating messages which may be detailed; *memo* – short message about a practical subject often in work context ; *note* – short informal message; *card* – usually communicates a social greeting on a specific occasion, has an attractive design; *petition* – addressed to officials requesting a change to something with a large number of signatures; *invoice* – a bill for goods or services; *diary* – record of appointments or day-by-day account of events throughout the year

277

Answer key

2.2 1 Letters were something special and meaningful. It was a rich form of expression, you could really think about what you wanted to say. You could make your letter perfect and heartrending. 2 the telephone; the internet; email; smartphones; video conferencing; instant messaging; social networks and apps.

2.3 1 means (of) communication 2 time (and) concentration 3 rewrite 4 immediate 5 obsolete 6 instant; endless.

2.4 2 a 3 e 4 c 5 g 6 b 7 f

2.6 1 method; way 2 aspect; feature 3 communicate; express

2.7 1 *She couldn't be bothered* (negative); *a badly written note* (negative) 2 *It was very thoughtful of you* (positive); *It really brightened up my day* (positive) 3 *these soppy messages* (negative); *her sound desperate* (negative). 4 *response to our ideas was scathing* (negative); *very frustrating* (negative) 5 *He rambled on for hours* (negative) 6 *He's so articulate* (positive); *he dominates the conversation* (negative); *he's a pleasure to have around* (positive)

Exam practice: Reading and Use of English Part 2
1 in 2 do 3 or 4 up 5 living 6 from 7 If 8 would

44 The environment

1.2 1 Deforestation 2 Overgrazing 3 Overfishing 4 Invasive species 5 Intensive agriculture 6 Urban development

1.3 2 F (Overgrazing is one of the main pressures on biodiversity.) 3 T 4 F (The regeneration of marine populations happens slowly.) 5 T 6 F (Weeds are a significant pressure on ecosystems.) 7 F (Bio-intensive farming is affecting estuaries.) 8 (F Population growth on the coastline is cause for concern.)

1.4

Noun	Verb	Adjective
agriculture	x	agricultural
density	x	**dense**
erosion	**erode**	**erosive eroded**
intensity intensification	**intensify**	intensive
modification	**modify**	**modified**
population overpopulation	**populate** overpopulate	**populated** overpopulated
regeneration	regenerate	**regenerative regenerated**

1.5 2 modified 3 agriculture 4 intensify 5 regeneration 6 overpopulated

2.1 2 a 3 e 4 b 5 c

2.2 1 biodegradable 2 conservation 3 recyclable 4 renewable 5 reforestation

2.3 2 plastic 3 solar energy 4 produce/fruit and vegetables 5 lightbulbs

2.4 1 many cycle lanes 2 recycling plastic 3 expensive to install 4 pollute the environment 5 by air / so far 6 local farmers 7 wasteful of energy / bright

Exam practice: Reading and Use of English Part 3
1 cultivation 2 destruction 3 economic 4 endangered 5 extensive 6 growth 7 sensitive 8 plantations

45 Science and technology

1.2 1 **Speaker 1:** electricity **Speaker 2:** penicillin/antibiotics **Speaker 3:** the microchip
2 **Speaker 1:** Without electricity many other important modern inventions would never have happened. **Speaker 2:** Penicillin has saved many lives. These people have gone on to contribute to progress. **Speaker 3:** The microchip is central to every digital device on the planet.

1.3 1 medical advances 2 modern life 3 countless lives 4 life expectancy 5 nervous system 6 scientific breakthroughs

1.4 2 e 3 i 4 c 5 b 6 h 7 g 8 j 9 d 10 a

1.5 1 spine 2 tribes; volcano 3 variation; species 4 comet; atmosphere

1.6 1 *proved* – certain rather than possible 2 *contradict* – only a definite statement can be disproved 3 *drawback* – is negative so does not contribute anything 4 *experiment* – to experiment is to research 5 *affected* – over time rather than suddenly 6 *prediction* – happens before an experiment

2.1 *Possible answers* **climate change:** development of new clean sources of energy **disappearance of fossil fuels:** the development of new bio-fuels **food shortages:** development of new high-yield crops resistant to disease and pests **diseases:** discovery of new drugs and improved detection methods **water shortages:** rain harvesting and new efficient desalination techniques

2.2 Battery technology is primitive and has not kept up with other technological developments.

2.3 2 manufacturers 3 range 4 conditions 5 maintain 6 tank 7 overcome 8 life 9 obstacle 10 resources 11 models 12 emissions

2.4 1 gas emissions 2 petrol tank 3 family car 4 motor manufacturers 5 oil resources 6 diesel engines

2.5 2 taking on 3 taken over 4 took me through 5 take up 6 taken me off 7 take in

Exam practice: Writing Part 2 – A letter
A model answer to this question can be found at www.cambridge.org/grammarvocabadvanced